CREATIVE EXPRESSION AND PLAY IN THE EARLY CHILDHOOD CURRICULUM

Joan P. Isenberg
George Mason University

Mary Renck Jalongo
Indiana University of Pennsylvania

Merrill,
an imprint of Prentice Hall

Englewood Cliffs, New Jersey   Columbus, Ohio

Library of Congress Cataloging-in-Publication Data
Isenberg, Joan P.
 Creative expression and play in the early childhood curriculum/
Joan P. Isenberg, Mary Renck Jalongo.
  p. cm.
 Includes bibliographical references and index.
 ISBN 0-02-359945-6
 1. Play. 2. Early childhood education. 3. Creative activities
and seat work. I. Jalongo, Mary Renck. II. Title.
372.19--dc20   92-17551
                                                            CIP

Cover Art: Nenad Jakesevic/Sonja Lamut
Editor: Linda A. Sullivan
Production Editor: Christine M. Harrington
Art Coordinator: Lorraine Woost
Photo Editor: Anne Vega
Cover Designer: Robert Vega
Production Buyer: Patricia A. Tonneman
Illustrations: Steve Botts

This book was set in Palatino by Carlisle Communications, Ltd.

 © 1993 by Prentice-Hall, Inc.
A Simon & Schuster Company
Englewood Cliffs, New Jersey 07632

Printed in the United States of America

10 9 8 7 6 5 4 3

ISBN   0-02-359945-6

Prentice-Hall International (UK) Limited, *London*
Prentice-Hall of Australia Pty. Limited, *Sydney*
Prentice-Hall Canada Inc., *Toronto*
Prentice-Hall Hispanoamericana, S.A., *Mexico*
Prentice-Hall of India Private Limited, *New Delhi*
Prentice-Hall of Japan, Inc., *Tokyo*
Simon & Schuster Asia Pte. Ltd., *Singapore*
Editora Prentice-Hall do Brasil, Ltda., *Rio de Janeiro*

To Jennifer and Michelle
with love, pride, and appreciation
for showing me the importance of playful expression.

To D. T. P. and the late M. J. P.
Thanks for your support and encouragement.

—*J. P. I.*

For early childhood educators
worldwide who defend the child's
right to play and nurture creativity.

—*M. R. J.*

PREFACE

This book is an outgrowth of our combined 25 years of teaching college courses on children's creativity and play to early childhood and elementary education students. Both of us were searching for a text that would integrate creative expression and play into the total preschool–primary grades curriculum, a text that would treat both topics as fundamental to the child-centered classroom rather than as interesting additions. Our desire was to prepare teachers who not only *know about* children's play and creative expression, but who also *know how* to provide these experiences and *know why* children's creative expression and play are so important.

We are aware that many publications use the word *creative* or *play* in their titles. It distressed us that some of these "creative activities" books made minimal contributions to teachers' creative growth, much less children's. Instead, they were compilations of "cute" ideas designed to keep "little hands" busy. We respect young children's ability to build understandings about their world and to express their ideas creatively. We resent the condescending message of such materials.

In teacher preparation, as the old proverb goes, you can give a person a fish or teach that person to fish. The first condition leads to dependence, the second to self-sufficiency. Our goal was to produce a textbook that would not stop at giving teachers ideas, but rather would suggest strategies and activities to stimulate teachers' original ideas. Both of us believe that it is crucial to the future of education to prepare prospective and practicing teachers who will exercise sound professional judgment based on theory, research, and exemplary teaching practices. As a reader, you will be the judge of how close we have come to realizing these aims.

The book begins with two chapters that form the foundation for those that follow. Chapter One discusses creativity in young children: how it is defined, how it develops, and what adults can do to foster that growth. Chapter Two examines the crucial role of play in early childhood education: why it is important, how it develops, and what teachers can do to defend the child's right to play.

After establishing this base, the book covers the topics that are traditionally associated with aesthetics (art, music and movement, creative drama) and topics that are typically covered in a textbook on play. We also add chapters on three topics that are not traditional—assessment of creative expression and play, guiding children's creative behavior, and educational futures.

In addition, the book contains several features that have emerged from our understandings about how adults learn. We begin each chapter with a case study and objectives, provide a theoretical framework, suggest ways to integrate activities into all subject areas, discuss special populations, and conclude with a chapter summary. Chapters include discussion questions and a "Writing to Learn" exercise. Every chapter also includes a "Research Highlight" that examines a particular study or studies in greater depth and contains detailed suggestions on how students can apply that research to professional practice. As a continuation of this "teacher as researcher" theme, all chapters conclude with specific instructions on observing or interviewing young children, parents, or teachers. All of these materials are designed to help readers reflect upon, synthesize, apply, and solidify their knowledge.

In education, there are three common misconceptions about teaching and learning — that it is all content, that it is all process, or that there is one best curriculum for all children (Eisner, 1988, 1990). Fortunately, any course that would use this book as its text avoids these three errors. The study of creative expression and play causes us to realize that coverage is not the answer, that aimlessness is not the answer, and that there are no panaceas. Rather, the teacher must create a classroom learning community that emphasizes quality over quantity of materials, that balances freedom with control, and that respects children as individuals while integrating them into the larger society. By bringing these perspectives to teaching, we not only avoid the pervasive pitfalls of which Eisner speaks, but also become more effective, reflective, and child-centered practitioners.

References

Eisner, E. (1988). The ecology of school improvement. *Educational Leadership, 45,* 24–29.
Eisner, E. (1990). Who decides what schools teach? *Phi Delta Kappan, 71,* 523–525.

Acknowledgments

We are deeply indebted to the many people who contributed to the development of this book. We wish to acknowledge the cooperation of the students at George Mason University and Indiana University of Pennsylvania for field testing this book and for providing us with many of the rich classroom examples that appear throughout these chapters.

We are also grateful to the many teachers, parents, and children whose photographs, art material, and stories are an integral part of the text. Thanks, too, to our many colleagues who helped us clarify our thinking about creative expression and play.

We want to thank our editor, Linda Sullivan, whose strong support and encouragement have helped enormously during this project. We are also grateful to the rest of the staff at Macmillan who made the publication of this book possible. In addition, we appreciate the input from those who reviewed this book: Donna M. Bagley, Illinois State University; Audrey W. Beard, Albany State College; Jacqueline Blackwell, Indiana University; Janet E. Foster, Memphis State University; Esther M. Howard, Mississippi State University; Leanna Manna, Villa Maria College; Ruth Moffatt McBride, Colorado State University, Fort Collins; Kevin J. Swick, University of South Carolina; Phil Wishon, University of Northern Colorado; and Sue C. Wortham, University of Texas, San Antonio.

Finally, we wish to acknowledge the continuous and unwavering support of our families and close friends. We are especially grateful for their encouragement, understanding, and willingness to listen through each phase of development of this book.

Joan P. Isenberg
Mary Renck Jalongo

BRIEF CONTENTS

PART ONE
The Young Child: Thinking and
Responding Divergently   1

| Chapter One | Creativity and the Young Child | 2 |
| Chapter Two | Play in the Early Childhood Curriculum | 28 |

PART TWO
Infusing Creative Expression and Play
Into the Curriculum   59

Chapter Three	Art in the Early Childhood Curriculum	60
Chapter Four	Music and Movement in the Early Childhood Curriculum	100
Chapter Five	Creative Drama in the Early Childhood Curriculum	134

PART THREE
Contexts for Creative Expression and Play   171

| Chapter Six | Planning and Arranging the Creative Environment | 172 |
| Chapter Seven | Materials for Creative Expression and Play | 212 |

PART FOUR
Child-Centered Teaching for Today and Tomorrow   251

Chapter Eight	Guiding Young Children's Creative Growth	252
Chapter Nine	Assessing Creative Expression and Play	288
Chapter Ten	Divergent Thinking, the Integrated Personality, and the Future	328

CONTENTS

PART ONE
The Young Child: Thinking and Responding Divergently   1

Chapter One   Creativity and the Young Child   2

Case Study   4
Theoretical Framework: Defining Creativity   4
   Criteria for Creativity   5
   Creativity During Early Childhood   6
   Modes of Thinking   9
   Stages in the Creative Process   11
Identifying Creativity   11
   Children's Creative Abilities   12
   Levels of Creativity   12
Unlocking Creative Potential   13
   Psychological Safety   14
   Psychological Freedom   14
Creativity and Education   14
   Schools That Nurture Creativity   15
   Teachers' Roles and Responsibilities in Promoting
     Creative Expression   17
Special Populations   18
   Culturally Diverse Groups   18
   Children with Disabilities   19
   High-Achieving and Low-Achieving Children   19
Conclusion   20
Chapter Summary   21
Discussion Questions   21
Writing to Learn   22
Interview: The Creative Family   22
Observation: Modes of Thinking   23
*Controversy: Why Not Consider Every Child Gifted
  and Talented?   23*
*Research Highlight: Teachers' Judgments
  of Preschoolers' Creativity   23*

Chapter Two   **Play in the Early Childhood Curriculum**   **28**

Case Study   30

What Is Play?   31
  Theoretical Framework   31
  Characteristics of Play   31
  Controversies Surrounding Play   32
  The Educational Role of Play   34

Why Is Play Important?   35
  Cognitive Development   35
  Language and Literacy Development   36
  Social Development   37
  Emotional Development   37
  Creativity and Imagination   38
  Physical Development   38

How Does Play Develop?   38
  Cognitive Play   39
  Social Play   43

Why Do Children Play?   44
  Classical Theories   44
  Modern Theories   46

Teachers' Roles and Responsibilities   47
  Teachers as Observers   47
  Teachers as Extenders   47
  Teachers as Planners   47
  Teachers as Responders   48
  Teachers as Models   48

Special Populations   48
  Culturally Diverse Groups   49
  Children with Disabilities   49
  High-Achieving and Low-Achieving
    Children   50

Conclusion   51
Chapter Summary   51
Discussion Questions   52
Writing to Learn   52
*Interview: A Kindergarten Teacher's Commitment
  to Play*   52
*Observation: Theoretical Perspectives Reflected
  in Children's Play*   53
Controversy: Superhero Play in the Classroom   53
*Research Highlight: Boys and Girls: Superheroes
  in the Doll Corner*   54

PART TWO
Infusing Creative Expression and Play
Into the Curriculum   59

Chapter Three   **Art in the Early Childhood Curriculum**   60

Case Study   62

Theoretical Framework   63
    Process Over Product   63
    Originality Over Conformity   63
    Children Retain Ownership   64

Understanding Children's Art   64
    Developmental Sequence   65
    Principles of Art Education   65
    How Children Learn Through Art   70

Learning About Art   75
    Developing a Vocabulary of Art   75
    Ways of Discussing Art   76

Critical Issues in Teaching Art   76
    Selecting and Presenting Materials and Experiences   77
    Evaluating Materials and Experiences   78

Teachers' Roles and Responsibilities   79
    Establishing Rules and Limits   80
    Talking with Children About Their Art   80
    Locating Resources and Storing Materials   81
    Displaying Children's Art   84

Child-Centered Art Experiences   86
    Paper   86
    Sculpture and Pottery   87
    Fabric   88

Integrating Art Into the Subject Areas   88
    Media and Technology   88
    Mathematics and Science   89
    Language, Literacy, and Art   89
    Social Studies, Health, and Nutrition   89

Special Populations   90
    Culturally Diverse Groups   90
    Children with Disabilities   91
    High-Achieving and Low-Achieving Children   91

Conclusion   92
Chapter Summary   92
Discussion Questions   93
Writing to Learn   93

Interview: Teachers' Beliefs About
Child-Initiated Art Activities 93
Observation: Predrawing and Breaking
Stereotypes in Art 94
Controversy: How Basic Is Art? 95
Research Highlight: The Effect of Materials on Children's
Representations of the Human Form 96

Chapter Four **Music and Movement in the**
Early Childhood Curriculum **100**

Case Study 102

Theoretical Framework 102
  Children and the Musical Experience 103
  Theories of Musical Development 103
  The History of Early Childhood
  Music Education 104

The Role of Music and Movement
  in Child Development 105
  How Young Children Grow Musically 106
  The Music–Movement Connection 108

Stages in the Development of Music
  and Movement 109
Critical Issues in Teaching Music and Movement 109
  Selecting Musical Materials and Experiences 113
  Presenting Musical Materials and Experiences 113
  Evaluating Musical Materials and Experiences 118

Teachers' Roles and Responsibilities 118
  Motivator 118
  Planner 119
  Co-Participant 119
  Observer 120
  Locating Resources 120

Integrating Music and Movement Into
  the Subject Areas 121
  Mathematics, Science, and Technology 121
  Language, Literature, and Literacy 122
  Social Studies, Health, and Nutrition 123

Special Populations 124
  Culturally Diverse Groups 124
  Children with Disabilities 124
  High-Achieving and Low-Achieving Children 126

Conclusion 126
Chapter Summary 126

Discussion Questions   127
Writing to Learn   127
Interview: Children's Favorite Songs   127
Observation: Children's Responses to Music   128
Controversy: Is Musicality Natural?   128
Research Highlight: The Music Laboratory   129

Chapter Five   **Creative Drama in the Early Childhood Curriculum**   **134**

Case Study   136

Theoretical Framework   136
    The Meaning of Enactment   137
    Forms of Enactment   138

The Importance of Creative Drama
    in the Curriculum   140
Criteria for Integrating Drama into the Curriculum   142
    Selecting and Presenting Experiences
        and Materials   143
    Teachers' Roles and Responsibilities   144

Appropriate Creative Drama Activities
    and Experiences   145
    Dramatic and Sociodramatic Play   145
    Pantomime   149
    Puppets   152
    Story Drama   153
    Readers Theater   156

Integrating Creative Drama into the Subject Areas   157
    Mathematics, Science, and Technology   157
    Language, Literature, and Literacy   159
    Social Studies, Health, and Nutrition   160

Special Populations   161
    Culturally Diverse Groups   161
    Children with Disabilities   162
    High-Achieving and Low-Achieving Children   163

Conclusion   163
Chapter Summary   163
Discussion Questions   164
Writing to Learn   165
Interview: Teachers' Beliefs About Drama   165
Observation: Values of Creative Drama   165
Controversy: Is Drama Developmentally Appropriate?   166
Research Highlight: Playing About a Story:
    Its Impact on Comprehension   167

PART THREE
Contexts for Creative Expression and Play   171

Chapter Six   **Planning and Arranging the Creative Environment**   172

Case Study   174

Theoretical Framework   174
    Climate   174
    Space   176
    Time   176

Arranging the Indoor Environment   179
    Room Arrangement   179
    Centers   181
    Transitions and Routines   188

Arranging the Outdoor Environment   189
    Types of Playgrounds   192
    Characteristics of Outdoor Play Environments   194
    Outdoor Environments for Children
       of Different Ages   197

Teachers' Roles and Responsibilities   199
Special Populations   204
    Children with Disabilities   204
    High-Achieving and Low-Achieving Children   205

Conclusion   205
Chapter Summary   206
Discussion Questions   207
Writing to Learn   207
Interview: How Teachers Plan Their
   Classroom Environments   207
Observation: Evaluating a Play Space   208
Research Highlight: Preparing the Classroom Environment
   to Promote Literacy During Play   208

Chapter Seven   **Materials for Creative Expression and Play**   212

Case Study   214

Theoretical Framework   214
    History of Toys and Playthings   214
    Convergent and Divergent Play Materials   215
    Children's Responses to Materials   216

Types of Materials   217
    Skill/Concept Materials   217
    Gross Motor Materials   217
    Manipulative Materials   218

Construction Materials   218
Self-Expressive Materials   218
Natural and Everyday Objects   218

Developmentally Appropriate Materials   220
Infants and Toddlers   220
Preschoolers and Kindergartners   223
School-Age Children   226
Teachers' Roles and Responsibilities   227

Other Divergent Play Materials   229
Blocks   229
Modeling Materials   232
Sand and Water   232

Organized Games   234
What Is a Game?   235
Competition versus Cooperation   235
The Value of Games   236
Teachers' Roles and Responsibilities   236

Child-Constructed Games   237
Invented Games   238
Making Games with Children   240

Special Populations   240
Culturally Diverse Groups   241
Children with Disabilities   241
High-Achieving and Low-Achieving Children   241

Conclusion   *242*
Chapter Summary   *242*
Discussion Questions   *242*
Writing to Learn   *243*
Interview: Play Materials: A Cross-Cultural Perspective   *243*
*Observation: Organized Sports or Activities
and the Young Child*   *244*
Controversy: War Toys and War Play   *245*
*Research Highlight: Clay in the Classroom: Helping Children
Develop Cognitive and Affective Skills for Learning*   *246*

PART FOUR
Child-Centered Teaching for Today and Tomorrow 251

Chapter Eight   **Guilding Young Children's Creative Growth and
Communicating with Families**   **252**

Case Study   *254*

Theoretical Framework   255

Constructivism   255
Humanism   256
Behavioral/Social Learning   256

Teachers' Roles and Responsibilities   258
Adult–Child Interactions   259
The Creative Teacher   260

Developmentally Appropriate Guidance   263
Fostering Prosocial Behavior   263
Guidelines for Creative Growth   266

Understanding Children's Conflicts   267
Causes of Conflict   267
Guidelines for Resolving Conflicts   268

Strategies for Guiding Creative Behavior   269
Cooperative Problem Solving   269
Investigative Play   271
Project Work   272

Communicating with Families   273
Obstacles to Communication   273
Strategies for Communicating with Families   275

Special Populations   276
Culturally Diverse Groups   277
Children with Disabilities   277
High-Achieving and Low-Achieving Children   278

Conclusion   279
Chapter Summary   279
Discussion Questions   280
Writing to Learn   280
Interview: Levels of Concern About Communicating
   with Families   281
Observation: Children's Conflicts and Resolutions   281
Controversy: Home–School Partnerships:
   Why Have Them?   282
Research Highlight: Continuity and Discontinuity Between
   Home and Early Childhood Environments   283

Chapter Nine   **Assessing Creative Expression and Play**   **288**

Case Study   290

Theoretical Framework   291
Defining Assessment   291
Purposes for Assessment of Divergent
   and Lateral Thinking   291
Difficulties with Assessment   293

Criteria for Assessment   294
    Assessing Creative Processes   296
    Assessing Creative Products   296

Appropriate Assessment of Children's
    Creative Expression and Play   297
    Observing Children's Creative
        Expression and Play   299
    Types of Observation   299
    Portfolio Assessment   304

Teachers' Roles and Responsibilities   312
    Matching Observation Techniques to Purposes   312
    Providing Flexible Groups   312
    Noting Patterns   312
    Asking Good Questions   313
    Developing New Teaching Strategies   314
    Teacher and Learner Self-Evaluation   315

Special Populations   316
    Culturally Diverse Groups   316
    Children with Disabilities   317
    High-Achieving and Low-Achieving Children   317

Conclusion   318
Chapter Summary   319
Discussion Questions   319
Writing to Learn   320
Observation: Portfolio Assessment of Children's Art   320
Controversy: How Does Testing Affect Teaching?   321
Research Highlight: Analyzing Children's
    Block Structures   321

Chapter Ten   **Divergent Thinking, the Integrated Personality,
and the Future**   **328**

Case Study   330

Theoretical Framework   331
    How Basic Is Creative Expression?   331
    Yesterday's and Tomorrow's Workers   332

Teachers' Roles and Responsibilities   333
    The Realities of Teaching   334
    Redefining the Teacher's Role   335
    Teachers as Mediators of Learning   336
    Teachers' Own Creativity   337
    Creative Teaching in the Future   338

An Agenda for the Future of Creative
    Expression and Play   339

Conclusion   341
Special Populations   341
   Culturally Diverse Groups   342
   Children with Disabilities   343
   High-Achieving and Low-Achieving Children   344
Chapter Summary   345
Discussion Questions   346
Writing to Learn   346
Interview: The Ideal Educator   346
Teacher Attributes   347
*Observation: Do You Support Creative
   Expression and Play?*   347
*Controversy: Are Our Lesson Planning
   Methods Outmoded?*   350
Research Highlight: Expert and Novice Practice   352

Appendix A   **Dance Prop Box**   **357**

Appendix B   **Published Rating Scales to Evaluate
Preschool Settings**   **361**

Appendix C   **Noncompetitive Games for Children**   **363**

Appendix D   **Observations of Medical Play**   **369**

Index   **375**

PART

1

The Young Child:
Thinking and
Responding Divergently

Creativity and
the Young Child

Good judgment, originality, fluency and flexibility of thought, the ability to redefine situations or see their implications— such qualities are prized in human society. In everyday life, they reap rewards of wealth, responsibility or prestige. In times of peril, they may determine who will survive and who will not. Teaching these abilities should be a major purpose of education.

Richard de Mille, 1967, p. 6

After reading this chapter, you will be able to

- ☐ Define creativity and the criteria used to identify creative behavior.
- ☐ Recognize and appreciate the types of creativity that are especially prominent during early childhood.
- ☐ Describe creative thought processes.
- ☐ Discuss the theories that explain creative behavior.
- ☐ Identify those classroom conditions that foster creativity in young children.
- ☐ Understand and explain the influence that teachers exert on every child's creative growth.

Case Study

As 3-year-old Laura watched the movie *The Wizard of Oz* with her family, she was enthralled by Glenda the Good Witch, frightened by the Wicked Witch of the West, and charmed by the Scarecrow. This story made such an impression that it has dominated her spontaneous play for several months. Laura has been busy assembling the props necessary to play out her role as Dorothy. She located an old Easter basket, pilfered a scrap of checked gingham from the sewing basket to use as a napkin, and even renamed the family dog Toto. But Laura's preparation for her role didn't stop there. She shared her wish for "Dorfy shoes" with her grandmother, and for her birthday she received a pair of black patent leather shoes with straps and buckles. Laura's play changes from day to day, depending upon the other experiences she's had. The scarecrow knocks on her door, and they share a picnic lunch. Toto gets lost, as in *Harry the Dirty Dog* (Zion, 1956), and Glenda the Good Witch is making wedding plans, just like her aunt. Clearly, Laura's play is much more than an imitation of the movie *The Wizard of Oz*.

At age 4, Laura listens intently as her mother reads Laura Ingalls Wilder's books aloud. For months afterward, Laura plays one-room schoolhouse with her sister by wearing sunbonnets and long skirts, writing on a small slate, and plotting revenge against Nellie Olson.

When Laura is 6, her mother discovers a bag of Reese's Pieces and a small plastic flashlight under her pillow. Laura has seen the movie *ET*, identifies strongly with Elliott, and prays every night for "a real extraterrestrial to come and visit."

Today Laura is in high school, and her school career has included numerous awards for creative writing. Laura's family believes that she has always been creative; they also believe that her early childhood years contributed to her creativity as a young adult.

Theoretical Framework: Defining Creativity

The word *creativity*, as it is commonly used, is surrounded by confusion and full of contradictions. People may

- ❏ Say that creativity is an asset, but have difficulty explaining it.
- ❏ See it as an everyday thing, but limit it to the arts.
- ❏ Suppose that it is irrational, yet treat it as if it were "super-rational" or inspired.
- ❏ Believe it is impractical, yet credit it with great solutions to life's most perplexing problems (Harrison, 1984).

Creativity is a thinking and responding process that involves connecting with our previous experiences, responding to stimuli (objects, symbols, ideas, people, situations), and generating at least one unique combination (Parnes,

1963). From a psychologist's point of view, creativity is the ability to make something new out of available stored information. With young children, that "something new" may be something that is old and familiar to adults but more than a copy to the child. When 3-year-old Ruiz paints a mandala (a circle shape with sun-like rays emanating from it), it is new to him even though adults have seen it many times in other young children's drawings. When children create, they draw upon their previous experiences, respond to internal and external stimuli, and express themselves in inventive, symbolic ways. Consider, for example, the spontaneous play of two preschoolers. Arwen, a 5-year-old, is pretending to be invisible, and Jessica, a 2 ½-year-old, has wrapped a block in a blanket that she now refers to as "baby." Because they are using experience and stimuli for self-expression, we would say that they are thinking creatively. The next section examines children's creative behavior in greater detail.

Criteria for Creativity

In order for a behavior to be creative, it must meet four basic criteria (Guilford, 1957; Jackson & Messick, 1965). These criteria are described below, using four examples of young children's behavior.

Criterion 1.   Creative behavior is *original;* it has a low probability of occurrence.

Three-year-old Adam attended a college hockey game with his father and now wants to be a hockey player. When Adam asked for hockey equipment, his parents told him he was too little and that it was too expensive, so Adam invented his own. He used a wooden spoon for a hockey stick, his sister's empty lip gloss container for a puck, socks for hockey gloves, and the open door to a closet as the goal mouth. Adam's behavior is unusual and surprising rather than typical and predictable. Thus it has a low probability of occurrence.

Criterion 2.   Creative behavior is *appropriate and relevant.*

Six-year-old twins Becky and Belinda both love Hans Christian Andersen's *The Little Mermaid.* They want to look like mermaids and need to create long, flowing hair, so Becky suggests using scarves attached with bobby pins. To create a tail, Belinda uses an old sock. She cuts off the foot portion and stretches the ankle part over her ankles, then turns her feet out to represent fins. The twins' behavior is a good illustration of appropriateness. In order for behavior to be creative, it needs to be relevant to the goals of the person who produced it.

Criterion 3.   Creative behavior is *fluent;* it results in many new, meaningful forms.

Five-year-old Louie likes to invent things and does so frequently. One day he was fixing his own cereal at the breakfast table while his mother chatted on the telephone in the next room. He held up a sealed plastic sandwich bag filled with milk and cereal for his mother to see. "Look," Louie announced proudly, "I just invented portable cereal. Now I can eat breakfast without missing cartoons!" By combining several apparently unrelated elements—two foods, television viewing, convenience, and a plastic bag—Louie has created a new, meaningful form. Fluency as it relates to creativity is comparable to fluency in a language; it means that the child can generate one idea after another with apparent ease.

Criterion 4. Creative behavior is *flexible;* it explores and uses nontraditional approaches to problem solving.

Lucia is seated next to Tomas, a fellow kindergartner, who is disassembling a grease pencil. He pulls the string and unwraps the paper coiled around the lead. Lucia looks on as Tomas throws the curls of paper in the trash can; then she retrieves them. She cuts two pieces of curled paper, glues them to her drawing, and attaches a piece of string to each one. "There," she says aloud. "The windows of my house have shades just like this."

Lucia's behavior illustrates flexibility. She wanted to make her drawing three-dimensional and saw possibilities in material that others considered useless. She also used a nontraditional method when she rummaged through the trash can in order to achieve her goal.

Creativity During Early Childhood

Creative behavior in adults or older children and creative behavior in young children are somewhat different. When we talk about more mature people's creativity, we usually emphasize three things:

1. Expertise—the technical skill, artistic ability, talent, or knowledge of useful information that they bring to the task.
2. Skills having to do with creativity itself—such as work style, concentration and persistence, ability to generate new possibilities, and openness to new ideas.
3. Intrinsic task motivation—delight in doing something for its own sake rather than for an immediate, tangible reward (Amabile, 1983; Kohn, 1987).

Children obviously have less experience than adults and therefore less expertise, and their work styles are less well developed. But whatever young children may lack in terms of expertise or style, they more than compensate for in their ways of thinking about and approaching a task.

Unique Features of Children's Thought

Children excel at three things thought to be related to creative genius: (1) sensitivity to internal and external stimuli; (2) lack of inhibition; and (3) the ability to become completely absorbed in an activity (Holden, 1987).

Marina, a 3-year-old, is a good example of a child with *sensitivity to stimuli.* She is at an important gathering where the bishop of her Greek Orthodox church is visiting the congregation. All of the adults are a bit intimidated and awkward;

Marina breaks the ice by walking up to the bishop and asking, "Do you know how to color? Would you like to draw pictures with me?" Marina seems to sense that welcoming the bishop is important; she uses her knowledge of how to make friends in a way that the entire congregation still remembers fondly.

Keiko, a 4-year-old, reveals his spontaneity and *lack of inhibition* during a testing situation. When the examiner asks him if he is "very happy, happy, not very happy, a little sad, or very sad," Keiko says, "Happy!", whirls around, takes the pen from the examiner, and circles the smiling face on the test form himself.

Lauren exemplifies the young child's *complete absorption in an activity.* She has created an imaginary friend named Mousie, and before her family travels anywhere, she lifts the gas tank door and puts her hand, palm up, next to the opening so that Mousie can crawl inside. Lauren talks aloud to her imaginary pet and gives him instructions on how to behave, completely unconcerned that anyone might overhear her. She is fully absorbed in her play.

Imagination and Fantasy

In the estimation of both experts and laypersons, imagination and fantasy are the great creative assets of early childhood. *Imagination* is the ability to form rich and varied mental images or concepts of people, places, things, and situations not present. Kindergartner Mallory's drawings in Figure 1.1 illustrate this point. She has become intrigued by flowers—not just ordinary flowers, but flowers that exist only in her imagination. As she imagines an acrobatic flower and a flower with pineapple teeth, Mallory uses both objective thought (what she knows) and intuitive thought (what she feels). In addition, Mallory must think about how to communicate that knowledge, those feelings, and those possibilities to others. For this reason, "Imagination is to the young child what problem solving is to the adult"; it is an "as if" situation (Weininger, 1988, p. 142).

Fantasy is a particularly vivid use of the imagination to create mental images or concepts that have little similarity to the real world. Fantasy explores the realm of make-believe—the impossible or at least the not yet possible, the "what if" situation (Weininger, 1988, p. 144). Here is how one mother described her son's use of fantasy as he created a pretend companion:

> "My son, who just turned 4, became fascinated by deer. This happened,
> I think, because while we were visiting friends out in the country, a doe
> and her fawn came into the yard. Now Scott has created a pretend friend
> named Fawnbelly. His bedroom window faces the front porch, and that,
> according to my son, is where she sleeps. He feeds her by putting a
> plastic apple on the windowsill and, in return, she protects him at night.
> When he talks about Fawnbelly, I can picture this gentle, expectant doe
> with huge brown eyes keeping watch over our house."

This mother obviously values the vivid imagination and rich fantasy life of her child, and rightly so. It has long been the opinion of experts on creativity that for most human beings, imagination and fantasy peak during early childhood:

FIGURE 1.1   Mallory's Flowers

> . . . we have recognized that young children are active and free in imaginative play, that as they grow older they become more stereotyped in their behavior and that in adult life, only the unusual person displays the ability to put old ideas and experiences into new forms. (Meek, 1935, p. vii)

More recently, Howard Gardner (1983) has described how young children are freer in their thinking, moving easily between and among the various modes of

Imagination and fantasy are the great creative assets of early childhood.

thought: "the young child is not bothered by inconsistencies, departures from convention, nonliteralness . . . which often results in unusual and appealing juxtapositions and associations" (p. 228).

In the next section, we will see how creativity and thought are related.

Modes of Thinking

When we examine our own thinking processes—when we "think about thinking"—the process is referred to as *metacognition*. One way of thinking about thinking, which is especially useful in a discussion of creativity, is to compare/contrast different types of thought and their relationships to the creative process. Types of thinking may be broadly categorized as convergent/vertical or divergent/lateral. The creative process relies upon both (Hughes, 1991).

Convergent/Vertical Thinking

Convergent thinking, as the word *converge* implies, means that there is one acceptable answer. Convergent thinking is also referred to as *vertical thinking* because it involves moving back and forth between higher and lower levels of thought. Basically, convergent/vertical thinking "digs the same hole deeper" (de Bono, 1971, p. 5). A good example of a convergent/vertical problem-solving task involves a group of primary grade children using a balance beam to weigh various objects and arrange them from lightest to heaviest.

Divergent/Lateral Thinking

Divergent thinking has a different focus from convergent thinking. As the word *diverge* implies, divergent thinking searches for many different ways of defining or interpreting a problem. Divergent thinking is also called *lateral thinking;* it "is concerned with digging the hole in another place" (de Bono, 1971, p. 5). A good example of divergent/lateral thinking involves the teacher who encourages children to write and illustrate their own books. The teacher expects a wide variety of responses and anticipates that no two student-created books will be exactly alike. Table 1.1 summarizes the distinctions between lateral and vertical thinking.

When children create, they use both types of thinking and learn to switch from one mode to another at appropriate times in the creative process. They need appropriate experiences that allow both types of thinking to develop and flourish. They also need teachers who understand that creativity is a skillful blend of divergent/lateral and convergent/vertical modes of thought.

TABLE 1.1   Modes of Thinking

Convergent/Vertical	Divergent/Lateral
Analytical—correctness is valued; answers are deduced	Generative—information is valued for its ability to stimulate ideas; answers are inferred
Selective—one correct path; rejects the irrelevant	Explorative—many possible paths; irrelevancies are seen as potential sources of inspiration
Predictable—follows a logical sequence	Unpredictable—relies on intuition as much as on logic
Leads to good answers	Is necessary for great answers

Source: Adapted from Dacey (1989).

Stages in the Creative Process

The creative process has been traditionally conceptualized as involving four stages (Wallas, 1926). The stages are recursive, meaning that a person may move back and forth between and among them, rather than following them in an invariant sequence from first to last.

1. *Preparation or brainstorming.* During this stage, the person applies knowledge, skill, and understanding to materials, objects, problems, or combinations of them. Creative individuals "engage" with the materials, objects, or problems with a playful or experimental attitude. Engagement may be deliberate or accidental.

2. *Incubation.* During this stage, the mind continues to work on the problem, often through images and associations. Both conscious and nonconscious modes of thinking are used, and the person's critical, judgmental side is put on hold. Divergent/lateral thinking tends to dominate.

3. *Illumination.* This is an evaluative phase in which the person selects some ideas and rejects others. Ideas that are chosen during this stage are then rearranged into a satisfying form. Sometimes illumination is experienced as a flash of insight (aha!) instantly recognized as a harmonious and complete way of approaching the task.

4. *Verification/communication.* Now the person tests the product of creative thought in terms of usefulness, completeness, and correctness. The critical, judgmental side of convergent/vertical thought goes into action and the idea is fine-tuned, often through feedback from others. This is the stage at which the outcome of the creative process is shared with others.

Identifying Creativity

The creative process has been studied in three major ways: (1) as a *process* (how a task is approached); (2) as a *product* (the quality of the final result); and (3) as a personality trait (the life histories of exceptionally creative individuals). But whether we study creative processes, creative products, or the people who use them, the basic question is: Why? Why do people create? Many prominent theorists have attempted to explain what urges people to be creative. Their theories can be conceptualized as humanistic, psychoanalytic, or constructivist. From a *humanistic* perspective, people create because creativity is a feature of human thought that differentiates humans from other forms of life; creative behavior makes us more fully human. From a *psychoanalytic* perspective, people create out of a need to satisfy emotional drives. From a *constructivist* point of view, creativity is a concept-building and problem-solving strategy that depends on the child's level of intellectual functioning. Table 1.2 is an overview of these three theoretical orientations and the theorists most closely associated with each.

TABLE 1.2   Theories of Creativity

Theoretical Orientation	Theorist	Theory
Humanistic	Carl Rogers	The creative person is fully functioning
	Abraham Maslow	Creativity is a form of self-actualization
	Rollo May	Creativity is courageous; people dare to be different
Psychoanalytic	Alfred Adler	Creativity is a way of compensating for perceived physical or psychological inferiority
	Carl Jung	Creative ideas emanate from a deeper source, the *collective unconscious*
	Otto Rank	The development of creativity requires supportive parents during the first 5 years of life
Constructivist	Jean Piaget	Creativity is a form of cognition that depends upon the child's intellectual level

Children's Creative Abilities

When children are using their creative abilities, they typically

- ❑ Explore, experiment, manipulate, play, ask questions, make guesses, and discuss findings.
- ❑ Use imaginative role playing, language play, storytelling, and artwork to solve problems and make sense out of their world.
- ❑ Concentrate on a single task for a relatively long period of time.
- ❑ Try to bring order out of chaos by organizing their environment.
- ❑ Do something new with the old and familiar.
- ❑ Use repetition as an opportunity to learn more from an experience rather than becoming bored with it (Maxim, 1993).

Note that these behaviors are generally (1) active rather than passive, (2) child initiated rather than adult initiated, and (3) displayed by all children at various times or in particular situations. Does this mean that everyone is creative to some extent? Yes. While there are different levels of creativity, everyone is creative if given the chance to be.

Levels of Creativity

Every person needs the opportunity to be creative. This does not mean that all persons will invent something, perform on stage, or see their art displayed in a gallery. A teacher who invents a new activity is being creative. A mother who

Every child needs the opportunity to be creative.

provides nutritious, tasty meals on a limited food budget is being creative. A child who fashions an imaginary dinosaur out of clay is being creative. When we meet life's challenges and resolve problems, we are being creative.

Unlocking Creative Potential

There is a story about a visiting efficiency expert who reported that one of the Ford Motor Company's well-paid employees sat with his feet propped up on the desk and appeared to be daydreaming most of the time. Henry Ford reputedly replied that this was exactly how the employee looked when he had an idea that saved the company more than enough money to cover his salary in the years to come.

Valuing creativity as Ford apparently did is a prerequisite to understanding it. Warnock (1977) says that being more imaginative is analogous to being more healthy. We do not ask "Why become more healthy?" because being healthy is simply good. The same holds true for creativity, for once we understand it, we know that being creative is an end in itself, just like being healthy.

Unlocking creative potential is largely dependent upon two sets of psychological conditions: (1) psychological safety and (2) psychological freedom (Rogers, 1954).

Psychological Safety

Psychological safety is external; it is dependent upon the existence of a low-risk environment. Children feel psychologically safe when significant others accept them as having unconditional worth, avoid external evaluation, and identify and empathize with them. Consider how this mother provides psychological safety for her preschool son Lance's behavior: "Lance [age 5] loves farming, and he inherited a lot of toy farm equipment that used to belong to his dad and big brothers. One day he was playing farmer and took his toy manure spreader into the kitchen, filled it up with coffee grounds, and began spreading 'manure' on his land, which just happens to be the kitchen floor!"

Lance's mother knew that he was completely wrapped up in his farm fantasy and that his intentions were good, even if the outcome was bad from an adult perspective. She did insist that Lance help her clean up the coffee grounds, yet she did not punish him or make him feel ashamed of his desire to "test" his farm equipment. When adults respond sensitively to children's behavior, they contribute to the child's feeling of psychological safety.

Psychological Freedom

Psychological freedom is internal. It emanates from within the child. When children feel free to play with symbols and to use these symbols for self-expression, they have developed an inner state of psychological freedom. According to Rogerian theory, one person becomes more creative than the next because he or she has learned to play with elements and concepts; to be open to experience and receptive to ideas; and to rely more on self-evaluation than on the evaluations of others.

Creativity and Education

Society in general and schools in particular have been criticized for failing to provide the environmental conditions for psychological safety and helping children to acquire a sense of psychological freedom (Egan & Nadaner, 1988; Torrance, 1969). Postman (1982) puts it this way: "The child possesses . . . capacities for candor, understanding, curiosity and spontaneity that are deadened by literacy, education, reason, self-control and shame" (p. 59).

It is sad to think that education would be responsible in any way for thwarting the child's creative potential, yet there is considerable support for this point of view. In *Fundamentals of Creative Thinking,* Dacey (1989) is even more pointed in his criticism of American education:

Schools suppress creativity. How can this be stated so categorically? The reasoning goes as follows: most young children are naturally curious and highly imaginative. Then, after they have attended school for a while, something happens. They become more cautious and less innovative. Worst of all, they tend to change from being participators to being spectators. Unfortunately, it is necessary to conclude from the investigations of many researchers (most of whom have been professional educators) that our schools are the major culprit. (p. 200)

The goal of studying children's creativity and play is to change that situation; to prepare a new generation of teachers who will do a better job of meeting children on their own terms rather than trying to mold them prematurely into adults. Figure 1.2 compares and contrasts educational environments that deter and support creativity.

Schools That Nurture Creativity

When schools do respect and develop creativity in children, theory and research have shown that six conditions exist.

1. *School personnel strive to reduce stress and anxiety in children and in themselves.* Adults recognize the importance of *positive affect*—feeling good about being in school, treating one another with respect, and building self-esteem among children and colleagues (Isen, Daubman, & Nowicki, 1987).

FIGURE 1.2   Negative and Positive Environments for Creativity

Environments That Thwart Creativity

- ❏ Push children to think literally and logically rather than working to children's imaginative strengths
- ❏ Overvalue conformity and follow established traditions
- ❏ Reward children only when they follow directions, discourage them from taking risks, or make them feel ashamed of mistakes
- ❏ Control time strictly by following inflexible schedules and set time limits on every task
- ❏ Avoid children's questions and discourage exploration of ideas
- ❏ Overemphasize memorization, imitation, and rigidly planned tasks

Environments That Support Creativity

- ❏ Promote equity and reciprocal respect
- ❏ Welcome the contribution of original ideas
- ❏ Regard differing points of view as a resource for learning rather a waste of time or a threat
- ❏ Seek new approaches to problems
- ❏ Encourage the use of fantasy and imagination
- ❏ Develop research and inquiry skills
- ❏ Create learning communities that build feelings of trust and minimize risks

Source: Adapted from Burton (1989).

2. *Process is valued over product.* This means that children are encouraged to play with ideas and explore solutions rather than being pushed into making premature conclusions (Hendrick, 1986). Creativity and productivity may actually be inversely related (Amabile, 1989) because children who are dashing something off to meet someone else's schedule are not afforded the "luxury" of seeking many alternatives and refining the most promising ones; they are taught to value the quantity of work they produce rather than its quality.

3. *Time limits are removed from activities in which children are deeply involved.* Children are free to become absorbed in what they are doing. In a school committed to creative expression, children follow their interests and enjoy what they are doing along with their peers, teachers, and other school personnel. This condition of being able to pursue an idea is the "labor of love" aspect of creative processes (Amabile, 1986).

4. *A free, open atmosphere is established where self-expression is encouraged and valued.* Teachers enjoy experiences along with children, rather than singling out particular products for compliments or rewards (Amabile, 1983; Kitano, 1989). Teachers support children's creativity by providing a wide variety of interesting materials and keeping activities open-ended; they give help when needed, but they do not interfere with children's creative processes (Hendrick, 1986).

5. *The children are encouraged to share ideas, not only with the teacher but also with one another.* Creative individuals regard themselves as being creative (Katz, 1987). One of the ways children begin to regard themselves as creative is in their reflected selves, in the responses that others have to them and their ideas. This is one reason why it is important for children to give and receive supportive feedback, not only from adults but also from peers.

6. *Competition and external rewards are minimized.* When children are informed that there will be a contest, that some will win a tangible reward and others will lose, three things happen. First, they become more cautious and tend to "play it safe"; second, they feel pressured to please someone else and lose their intrinsic motivation; and third, they tend to rush to get the reward. All of these things result in less spontaneous, less complex, and less varied products—in other words, less creative responses.

Two first-grade teachers who are making puppets with their students help to illustrate how these six distinctions are put into practice. Ms. Poole shows children a paper bag puppet that she has made and demonstrates how it was assembled. She then distributes patterns that she has duplicated to the children and instructs them to work quietly, color neatly, cut out on the lines, and paste in the designated areas. She reminds them that she has just one pattern for each child and that anyone who does not follow directions will not get another copy.

When the puppets are completed, the children print their names on them, and they are posted on the bulletin board. If colleagues stop by, the teacher points out the "good" ones and ignores the "bad" ones.

In another first-grade classroom, children are getting ready to invent their own puppets. Their teacher, Mr. Lopez, uses a four-phase strategy that begins with *awareness,* moves to *exploration,* then to *inquiry,* and finally to *utilization* (National Association for the Education of Young Children, 1991). He builds the children's *awareness* by asking, "What is a robot? How are robots made? What is special about robots? What robots have you seen?" Krish says that robots are "sort of like people, only they're machines." Taro mentions R2-D2 from *Star Wars,* and Joelle expresses a wish for a toy robot. *Exploration* begins as they share and discuss a collection of robot pictures and Mr. Lopez summarizes by asking, "What have you learned about robots? What questions do you still have about robots?" Now Mr. Lopez moves the group into *inquiry* as he invites them to examine a wide array of recycled materials and invent a robot puppet. One child begins with an old sock, another with a cardboard box; one child uses Styrofoam egg carton cups for "buggy eyes," another chooses aluminum foil and cardboard tubes for arms. All of the children experiment with different fixatives such as glue, staples, tape, and sewing. The activity turns to *utilization* after the robots are completed, and the children are invited to make their puppets move to electronic music.

As you have surely surmised, the second classroom supports creativity, while the first classroom does not. As teachers we may know this intuitively, but it is also important to know why.

Teachers' Roles and Responsibilities in Promoting Creative Expression

In order to foster creative processes, each teacher must do the following:

Share Power. The teacher should function as a facilitator, allowing children to help plan (Jones, 1986). The early writing efforts of young children provide a good example of this power-sharing precept. Children have the least autonomy when they are required to trace or copy, medium autonomy when they dictate a story to an adult, and the highest autonomy when they are actively applying what they know about writing at the time. At this highest level of power sharing with teachers, some children in the same kindergarten class may make scribbles or squiggles, some may invent letter-like forms (mock letters), some may write combinations of actual and mock letters, and still others may write in more conventional ways.

Encourage Risk Taking. Children need to exert control over their own processes and have the freedom to take risks. Real learning involves a change in behavior, and making those changes is dependent upon risk taking. Children cannot simply absorb someone else's ready-made answers; they have to build their own understanding about the world, and that path to understanding is littered with errors. If we make learners self-conscious about mistakes, their progress will be slowed or even halted.

Understand Creative Activities.   After the first class meeting of a college-level creative activities course, one student said, "This isn't what I expected at all. I thought we were going to, you know, make stuff we could use when we teach." It is a common misconception that creative activities are something that teachers do *for* children, such as designing "cute" games for them to play. But whose creativity is being developed here, the child's or the teacher's? Although it is important for teachers to unlock their own creative potential, they should not do so at the expense of the children. Creative activities develop *children's* creativity by allowing them to respond in their own unique ways.

Use Praise Judiciously and Defer Judgment (Klein, 1984).   Effusive praise can actually suppress children's creativity. Suppose that a child paints an orange pumpkin with black triangle eyes and nose and a toothy grin. If adults shower the child with praise, the child may get stalled at this stage because he or she is trying to please the adult. It is best to leave much of the evaluative function to the child and to postpone evaluation until children are satisfied with their own work and are ready to "go public."

Special Populations

All children need opportunities to express their creativity in many different contexts. If teachers limit their assessment of children's potential to academic subjects and formal learning situations, they will have little idea of how truly creative the students in their classes can be.

Culturally Diverse Groups

The essence of meeting children's needs is being alert to opportunities for them to excel. Ms. Reagon's observations of her second graders on the playground offer another opportunity for a teacher to see her students in a different context. She notices that, as a group, the students from low-income homes are much more adept at inventing games and playing cooperatively than those from economically advantaged homes. Rather than allow this strength to go unnoticed, Ms. Reagon asks the children to show the class some of their games, which involve syncopated hand clapping and original jump rope chants. When the other children try to participate in these games, they gain a new appreciation for their classmates' skills. Ms. Reagon further supports and extends the children's activity by sharing several books of jump rope jingles, by inviting each child to discuss favorite childhood games with various family members, by giving children the opportunity to share what they learned from their interviews, by inviting parents to come in to demonstrate favorite childhood games, and by teaching the children new games from other eras and lands. As a result of Ms. Reagon's interest and encouragement, all of her students' outdoor play has become more cooperative and varied.

Children with Disabilities

The key to unlocking the creative potential in children with disabilities is to focus on their strengths and adapt the environment to those conditions. Visually impaired children may not be able to use crayons to produce a drawing that is pleasing to the eye, but they can use fabrics to create a fabric collage that is pleasing to the touch. Likewise, children whose physical condition prohibits the requisite fine motor skills for sculpting or painting at an easel may be able to mold large objects with clay or use hand and arm movements to fingerpaint. Rex is a 4-year-old who has been a deaf mute since birth. He sometimes gets frustrated when the other children do not understand him, but he excels as a communicator through his art and through dramatization. Rex's teacher has been doing simple enactment and pantomime activities with the children throughout the year. Often, Rex is the one who brings a particularly challenging pantomime idea to the class. Through creative drama, Rex has acquired a leadership role among his peers.

High-Achieving and Low-Achieving Children

Contrary to popular opinion, academic achievement and creativity are not the same thing. In fact, the child who has the highest scores in reading or mathematics has often learned to succeed on multiple-choice tests by relying almost exclusively on convergent/vertical thinking. Even enrollment in special programs for the gifted and talented does not guarantee that the conditions of psychological freedom and psychological safety are being met. One parent described an incident involving her daughter that helps to illustrate this point:

> When Marjorie was a first grader in the gifted and talented program, her teacher gave them the assignment of keeping a journal. Marjorie's idea was to write George Washington's diary by looking up things in books in the library and imagining the rest, but the teacher insisted that if the journal could not be historically accurate in every detail, it would be better to select a different topic. Marjorie's older sister, wise in the ways of school, advised her to "Make the teacher happy so that you get a good grade," but Marjorie was determined to pursue her original idea. She was only 6 years old, and she had such integrity! As it turned out, Marjorie proved to be right, and *she* taught the *teacher* something about respecting children's creativity.

Too often, the creativity of the low-achieving child goes unrecognized. Because these children do not perform as well as peers on academic tasks, adults sometimes lower their expectations for the children's performance in all areas. Second grader Evelyn is a good example. She was retained in both kindergarten and first grade and has been diagnosed as developmentally delayed. Yet if we observed her and her classmates fashioning things from clay, we would be impressed by Evelyn's originality. While most of the other students are making coils or baskets, Evelyn creates a mother bird and a nest filled with a combination of eggs and hatching chicks. If the teacher had limited Evelyn's play with clay to art class, she might never have glimpsed how imaginative this child is.

As teachers work with these special populations, it is essential that they provide opportunities for every child to experience success. By focusing on each child's abilities and emphasizing cooperation, teachers build understanding and acceptance among all of the children in the class.

Conclusion

Perhaps the greatest contribution of creativity to human life is that it enables us to soar (Clark & Clark, 1979). People seldom master the "art of soaring" unless

Teachers build understanding and acceptance when they focus on each child's abilities and emphasize cooperation.

their fledgling creative processes were nurtured early on, so teaching young children carries a special responsibility for fostering creativity. Early childhood educators must be fully prepared to articulate their philosophy and to defend the child's right to creative expression because:

> There seems to be a permanent war going on between reality and imagination. The battleground is childhood. On the side of imagination, we have the child, eyes great with wonder, mouth issuing fantasies, misconceptions and unreliable reports. Parents, [and] teachers . . . are on the side of reality. They keep insisting on truth, accuracy, conformity and obedience. . . . Distinctions between reality and imagination are necessary, and it is important that they be learned. But it is also important to teach the distinctions in a way that does not turn off the imagination. (de Mille, 1967, pp. 3, 4) ·

In the next chapter, we explore the foundation for children's imagination and creativity—play. Play is foundational to creativity in children and adults because "it is our playfulness that links the child within each of us to the child we teach: the feeling child, the thinking and reasoning child, the compassionate child. All of these are a whole fabric woven of the unending thread of play" (Littleton, 1989, p. xiii).

Chapter Summary

1. Creativity is a behavior characterized by originality, relevance, fluency, and flexibility.
2. Young children's thinking is different from adults' thinking because children are highly sensitive to stimuli, are uninhibited, and can become completely absorbed in imagining ("as if") and pretending ("what if").
3. If teachers value each dimension of children's creative behavior—originality, appropriateness, relevance, fluency, and flexibility—they can further develop children's creative potential.
4. Metacognitive theories suggest that creative thinking processes can be conceptualized as convergent/vertical or divergent/lateral. Creativity, imagination, and fantasy are interrelated types of thinking that are largely dependent upon the ability to use symbols in inventive ways.
5. Theories that attempt to explain the desire to create may be categorized as humanistic, psychoanalytic, and constructivist.

Discussion Questions

1. Teachers are often advised to work to children's strengths. How does an understanding of children's creativity enable you to do this more effectively?
2. Do you agree that schools sometimes actively discourage creativity? Why or why not?

3. Sometimes children's creativity is mistaken for misbehavior. Did you ever experience this yourself as a child? Did it ever happen to a child you know? How do you plan to avoid this misconception when you teach?

4. Cite several current examples of imagination and creativity at work in various fields (e.g., medical research, business, new inventions, film, music). What role did divergent/lateral thinking apparently play? What role did convergent/vertical thinking play? How would an education that fosters creativity prepare children for the workplace of the future?

5. Experts in the field of early childhood education generally advocate play in the curriculum. How does play meet the criteria for creativity and the conditions for nurturing creativity discussed in this chapter?

Writing to Learn

Using the section in this chapter on classroom conditions and teachers' roles in nurturing creativity, imagine an ideal "classroom for creativity." Make sure that your scenario incorporates all of the characteristics of teachers and environments that foster creativity (see Figure 1.2, page 15). Imagine such things as the physical arrangement of the room, some sample activities that you might observe, examples of the teachers' comments and questions, and so forth. Share your description with the group. Imagine that you are the teacher in this classroom and someone is challenging your curriculum, saying that it is not sufficiently academic. Formulate a philosophy statement that you could use to respond to this criticism.

Interview

The Creative Family

Arrange to interview parents about their young child's creativity. First, make it clear to the parents that you are seeking examples of behaviors that are original, imaginative, and creative rather than examples of their child's academic achievement on tests or grades in school subjects. Then ask the following questions and transcribe the answers:

1. Do you feel that your child is being taught creatively? Why or why not?
2. What do you do to encourage problem solving, independent thinking, and originality in your child?
3. Please describe some specific situations when your child's behavior was particularly imaginative, original, or inventive.
4. Why do you think this particular behavior illustrates creativity?
5. Do you consider yourself (or any other members of your family) to be creative in any way? If yes, how? If no, why not?
6. Do you think that creativity is important in everyday life? Why or why not?

—————————————— **Observation** ——————————————

Modes of Thinking

Arrange to observe a lesson or activity in a preschool or primary-grade class-room. Make a script tape by writing down all of the words that the teacher and the children use. (You may want to get permission to make an audiotape as well.) After you have prepared the script tape, edit the extraneous material and write down all of the important dialogue that took place. Analyze the dialogue in terms of convergent/vertical and divergent/lateral thinking processes. In other words, which parts of the activity required one right answer or delving into a single idea, and which parts encouraged children to explore many possible alternatives (divergent/lateral thinking)? Code each section of your script "CV" (for convergent/vertical) or "DL" (for divergent/lateral). Which type of thinking was reinforced more often? Compare and contrast your observations with those of the class.

—————————————— **Controversy** ——————————————

Why Not Consider Every Child Gifted and Talented?

A presenter at a conference is describing his program for gifted and talented second graders. The teacher simulates an archaeological dig in which children unearth the "artifacts" he has planted and try to discover everything they can about the society these artifacts represent. This situation raises two questions related to this chapter: (1) What does "gifted and talented" mean? and (2) How do these concepts relate to creativity? In answer to these queries, Renzulli, Reis, and Smith (1981) say: "Giftedness is an interaction among three clusters of traits: above average general abilities, high levels of task commitment, and high levels of creativity" (p. 648). Consider these questions:

How did the project described by the presenter meet the criteria for creative activities discussed in this chapter?

Why might gifted and talented programs be criticized for elitism?

How could you use the definition above to differentiate between creative behavior and giftedness?

—————————————— **Research Highlight** ——————————————

Teachers' Judgments of Preschoolers' Creativity

Summary of Research

In this research, a group of teachers was asked to identify those preschoolers in their classes who were extraordinarily creative. Nicholson and Moran (1986) then administered a battery of creativity tests to the children and compared their findings with the teachers' ratings. The correlation between these two modes of assessing creativity was much lower than one might expect, leading the researchers to conclude that teachers are not very good judges of creativity in their students. Based upon their research, Nicholson and Moran (1986) suggested three possible reasons for this conclusion:

1. *Confusing measures of intelligence with measures of creativity.* Intelligence, as measured by tests and grades, is very different from creativity. Tests and grades focus on convergent thought (right answers), while tests of creativity focus on divergent thought (many possible answers). So, the child with a record of high academic achievement and high intelligence tests scores is not necessarily the same child who does exceptionally well on tests of creativity. In the real world, apart from testing, creativity and intelligence apparently interact rather than functioning as separate entities (Runco, 1986). Creativity is a form of intelligence, but it is not the form usually assessed by tests and grades.

2. *Being overly influenced by socially desirable behavior.* Academic environments are not always accepting of children who "dare to be different." History is full of examples of people who were labeled "daydreamers," "underachievers," or even "troublemakers" during childhood, only to become highly creative or even creative geniuses in later life. When convergent thinking dominates the schools, divergent thinking can be undervalued and teachers can become intolerant.

3. *Being overly influenced by the child's rate of development.* Adults react more readily and more favorably to children's uncommon (advanced) behavior than to children's unconventional (creative) behavior (Nicholson & Moran, 1986). Compare the behavior of Aaron and Matt, both preschoolers. At age 3, Aaron could identify several words printed on flashcards. His parents think that he is creative. But even though Aaron was pushed into recognizing a few written symbols before his peers (advanced for his age), this does not make him creative. Contrast this with the experiences of Matt, another 3-year-old. His parents try to encourage independence and creative problem solving. In fact, one of Matt's favorite expressions is *"I* have an idea. We could . . ." Of the two children, Matt is getting more support in developing creativity. Aaron, on the other hand, is being conditioned to imitate adult behavior as rapidly as possible. He may be precocious, but his creativity may have been compromised in the process.

Implications for Practice

Suppose that a teacher is presenting a unit on basic shapes—circles, triangles, squares, and rectangles. When introducing a review lesson, he asks children to suggest the names of shapes that they know. Robert suggests, "There's an egg shape, only it's called an ellipse." How would you as a teacher handle this response? If a teacher is overly concerned about confusing the other children, that teacher might say, "Robert, that isn't one of the shapes we learned." If you do, what happens to Robert? He feels rejected. Over time, he will probably begin to "play the game" and tell teachers what they want to hear. He may even stop contributing in class. Situations like these, repeated day after day, not only undermine children's creativity but also prevent teachers from making accurate judgments about children's creative potential.

How will you use the information in this Research Highlight to become more skilled in identifying creative behaviors of children?

What will you do to educate other adults about these issues?

References

Amabile, T. M. (1983). *The social psychology of creativity.* New York: Springer-Verlag.

Amabile, T. M. (1986). The personality of creativity. *Creative Living, 15*(3), 12–16.

Amabile, T. M. (1989). *Growing up creative.* New York: Crown.

Bruner, J. S. (1986). *Actual minds, possible worlds.* Cambridge, MA: Harvard University Press.

Burton, L. (1989). Musical understanding through creative movement. In B. Andress (Ed.), *Promising practices: Prekindergarten music education* (pp. 97–104). Reston, VA: Music Educators National Conference.

Clark, J. W., & Clark, J. S. (1979). The art of soaring. *Journal of Creative Behavior, 13*(2), 110–118.

Dacey, J. S. (1989). *Fundamentals of creative thinking.* Lexington, MA: D. C. Heath.

de Bono, E. (1971). *New think.* New York: Avon.

de Mille, R. (1967). *Put your mother on the ceiling: Children's imagination games.* New York: Penguin.

Egan, K., & Nadaner, D. (Eds.). (1988). *Imagination and education.* New York: Teachers College Press.

Gardner, H. (1983). *Frames of mind: The theory of multiple intelligences.* New York: Basic Books.

Guilford, J. P. (1957). Creative abilities in the arts. *Psychological Review, 64*, 110–118.

Harrison, A. (1984). Creativity, class and boredom: Cognitive models for intelligent activities. *Journal of Education, 166*(2), 150–169.

Hendrick, J. (1986). *Total learning: Curriculum for the young child.* Columbus, OH: Merrill/Macmillan.

Holden, C. (1987). Creativity and the troubled mind. *Psychology Today, 21*, 9–10.

Hughes, F. P. (1991). *Play and development.* Boston: Allyn & Bacon.

Isen, A. M., Daubman, K. A., & Nowicki, G. P. (1987). Positive affect facilitates problem solving. *Journal of Personality and Social Psychology, 52*, 1121–1131.

Jackson, P. W., & Messick, S. (1965). The person, the product, and the response: Conceptual problems in the assessment of creativity. *Journal of Personality, 33*, 309–329.

Jones, E. (1986). *Teaching adults.* Washington, DC: National Association for the Education of Young Children.

Katz, A. (1987). Self-reference in the encoding of creative-relevant traits. *Journal of Personality, 55*(1), 98–120.

Kitano, M. (1989). The K-3 teacher's role in recognizing and supporting young gifted children. *Young Children, 44*(3), 57–63.

Klein, B. (1984). Power and control of praise and deferred judgment. *Journal of Creative Behavior, 17*, 9–17.

Kohn, A. (1987). Art for art's sake. *Psychology Today, 21*, 52–57.

Littleton, D. (1989). Children's play: Pathways to music learning. In B. Andress (Ed.), *Promising practices: Pre-*

kindergarten music education (pp. ix–xiii). Reston, VA: Music Educators National Conference.

Maxim, G. (1993). *The very young: Guiding children from infancy through the early years* (4th ed.). Columbus, OH: Merrill/Macmillan.

Meek, L. H. (1935). Foreword. In F. V. Markey, *The imaginative behavior of preschool children* (p. vii). New York: Teachers College Press.

National Association for the Education of Young Children and the National Association of Early Childhood Specialists in State Departments of Education (1991). Guidelines for appropriate curriculum content and assessment in programs serving children ages 3 through 8. *Young Children, March,* 21–38.

Nicholson, M. W., & Moran, J. D. (1986). Teachers' judgments of preschoolers' creativity. *Perceptual and Motor Skills, 63,*1211–1216.

Parnes, S. (1963). Development of individual creative talent. In C. W. Taylor & F. Barron (Eds.), *Scientific creativity: its recognition and development* (pp. 4–13). New York: Wiley.

Postman, N. (1982). *The disappearance of childhood.* New York: Dell.

Renzulli, J. S., Reis, S. M., & Smith, L. H. (1981). The revolving door model: A new way of identifying the gifted. *Phi Delta Kappan, 62*(9), 648–649.

Rogers, C. (1954). Towards a theory of creativity. *ETC: A Review of General Semantics, 11,* 249–260.

Runco, M. A. (1986). Predicting children's creative performance. *Psychological Reports, 59,* 1247–1252.

Torrance, E. P. (1964). *Creativity: Progress and potential.* New York: McGraw-Hill.

Torrance, E. P. (1969). *Dimensions in early learning: Creativity.* Sioux Falls, SD: Adaptation Press.

Wallas, G. (1926). *The art of thought.* New York: Harcourt Brace.

Warnock, M. (1977). *Schools of thought.* London: Faber & Faber.

Weininger, O. (1988). "What if" and "as if" imagination and pretend play in early childhood. In K. Egan & D. Nadaner (Eds.), *Imagination and education* (pp. 141–149). New York: Teachers College Press.

Children's Books

Zion, G. (1956). *Harry the dirty dog.* New York: Harper.

Play in the Early Childhood Curriculum

Play is a need of every child. Children virtually overflow with all the prerequisites for play . . . a vast reservoir of energy and curiosity, excitingly new experiences, ripe ideas, and a rich supply of imagination that pours forth freely as a constant stream of activity . . . play is an important childhood activity that helps children master all developmental needs.

George Maxim, 1989, p. 261

After reading this chapter, you will be able to

- ❏ Describe the role of play in the early childhood curriculum.
- ❏ Identify the theoretical frameworks used to study play.
- ❏ Discuss how play contributes to children's development.
- ❏ Analyze the types, functions, and purposes of play.
- ❏ Define teachers' roles and responsibilities in play.
- ❏ Identify the key elements in a play-oriented curriculum.

Case Study

Tia, Katie, and Jayson are playing in the housekeeping center in Mr. Van's kindergarten classroom. During a 10-minute play sequence, the children pretend to be the mother, big sister, bus driver, and teacher, and have an extensive dialogue in those roles.

As you read the following play episode, think about its significance. Who assumed leadership roles? What opportunities for social, emotional, language, or cognitive growth were evident?

Tia: (Tia is pushing her doll in a chair that is being used as a swing, and Jayson is writing at the table. In a singsong voice, Tia says to her doll) I get to swing for my birthday.

Katie: (Katie comes by and asks) Can I play, too?

Tia: Sure (Tia says invitingly and slides to one side so that Katie can sit next to her swing).

Katie: I'll be the big sister.

Tia: No, you be the friend.

Katie: No, I want to be the teenage sister who drives.

Tia: Okay.

Katie: (Reaching for a large, empty box and placing three dolls on it) Big sister will drive the bus. We're going to school. (She pushes the box around the outside of the housekeeping area and unloads the bus.)

Tia: (Noticing one of the dolls fall off the bus) What's happened to him?

Katie: I ran into a berry bush.

Tia: (In a concerned, motherly tone of voice, exclaims) The berry bush! Oh, poor Bobby. (Picking up Bobby, cuddling him in her arms, and wrapping him in a scarf from the dress-up box, she says) Are you hurt?

Katie: (Katie begins to push the bus, stops, looks at Tia, and asks) Where should the school be? They have to drive here. (She moves over the roadway and says) This is the school (pointing to the table and chairs in the housekeeping area where Jayson is sitting and writing on paper).

Jayson: This is the school. Good morning. How are you today? We are going to make play dough, and I need some helpers. (Tia then asks to be the cooking teacher, and they all agree.)

Throughout this play sequence, the children jointly develop and role-play a familiar family theme. When Katie announces, "I want to be the big sister who drives," she initiates the play sequence. Tia is already playing mommy. The children's words, actions, and gestures reflect their understandings of families based on their actual experiences, the media, and the context in which the play occurs.

Beyond having fun and playing out a domestic theme, Tia demonstrates what she knows about mommy and practices that role by singing to her baby and cuddling him when he is hurt. Katie reveals her knowledge about teenagers when she says: "I want to be the big sister who drives." In play, children make sense of their world by acting out meaningful themes. This chapter explores the important role of play in a play-oriented early childhood curriculum.

What Is Play?

Theoretical Framework

Over the years, theorists, researchers, and educators in different disciplines have studied children's play. Although they have proposed a variety of definitions and functions of play, definitional differences still exist. Despite these differences, most play scholars agree that certain characteristics distinguish play from other types of human behavior (Bretherton, 1984; Fromberg, 1987, 1990).

Characteristics of Play

There are at least five essential elements that characterize play. Some of them were illustrated in the opening case study.

1. *Play is voluntary and intrinsically motivated.* In play, children are free to choose the content and direction of their activity. The play is self-satisfying because it does not respond to external demands or expectations. In their roles as mommy, big sister, and teacher, Tia, Katie, and Jayson each freely chose their role and controlled how to play out the theme of riding to school.

2. *Play is symbolic and meaningful.* Play enables children to relate their past experiences to their present reality. By pretending to be others, they assume a "what if" or "as if" attitude. When Katie pretended to be the big sister, she drove the bus "as if" she were a bus driver.

3. *Play is active.* In play, children explore, experiment, investigate, and inquire about people, objects, or events. In the case study, Tia, Katie, and Jayson were actively engaged with each other and with materials as they figured out their play theme.

4. *Play is rule-bound.* In play, children are governed by either explicit or implicit rules. Young children create and change rules during play that apply to appropriate role behavior and object use. Older children accept predetermined rules that guide the play. Katie knew she had to be a teenager so that she could drive.

5. *Play is pleasurable.* In play, children pursue an activity for the pleasure it brings—not for an external reward. Play behavior can be serious or nonserious (Fromberg, 1987; Garvey, 1977; Neuman, 1971). Clearly, these three children were pursuing their play because it was meaningful to them.

Play enables children to create understandings of their world from their own experiences and exerts a strong influence on all aspects of their growth and development. Children become empowered in play to do things for themselves, to feel in control, to test and practice their skills, and to affirm confidence in themselves. Play is important for children's developing sense of competence (Wasserman, 1990). Table 2.1 lists criteria for differentiating between play and nonplay behaviors.

Controversies Surrounding Play

With agreed-upon characteristics of play, why all the controversy about its definition and purposes? First, theorists and researchers have differed in their assumptions about play and its primary purpose, yet all have attested to its significance in children's physical, social, emotional, and intellectual growth and development. Freud (1958) and Erikson (1963) emphasized the emotional significance of play, the expression and release of children's strong feelings; Piaget (1962) emphasized play's cognitive significance, the practice of known information; and Vygotsky (1967, 1978) emphasized its social significance, the rehearsal for adult roles.

Play with objects empowers children to do things for themselves, to feel in control, to test and practice skills, and to develop a sense of competence.

TABLE 2.1   When Does the Activity Cease to Be Play?

Criteria	Play	Nonplay
Control Who is in charge?	Is the child in charge of the situation? Are a variety of choices available?	Is somebody else in charge? Are limited responses available?
Motivation Why are they engaged in this behavior?	Is the child engaged for the sake of the experience or the pleasure?	Is there a reward attached to the behavior?
Reality What are the constraints of the setting on the child's behavior?	Can the child freely pretend? Can the child freely engage in creative expression and behavior?	Does the child have to conform to reality? Does the setting manipulate a child to demonstrate specific behaviors?

Source: Adapted from M. J. Ellis (1973). *Why people play.* Englewood Cliffs, NJ: Prentice-Hall.

Second, there is a distinction in our own culture between play and work (Elkind, 1988; Fromberg, 1987; Paley, 1984). Today's children are pressured more and more to participate in teacher-directed, structured, formal lessons leaving little, if any, time to learn through play. Many early childhood teachers believe that play activities should be the centerpiece of their curriculum. Yet they feel pressured to justify its use with the phrase "Play is children's work." While this statement equates play with work, it also implies that work is serious and play is trivial. This misconception equates "real" school with deskwork. Yet, if we look at the best practices in each area of the curriculum such as hands-on science, math manipulatives, music laboratories, or a writer's workshop, it is easy to see that all of these approaches are play-based.

An illustration of how teachers' orientations to play affect the early childhood classroom comes from the following two first-grade classrooms. In Ms. McGill's room, children plan their daily schedules with their teacher during their morning meeting. Then, during a 90-minute uninterrupted block of center time, the first graders complete some teacher-selected stations and then choose freely among a wide variety of accessible and well-organized materials. Some build with blocks, paint at easels, play in the family-living corner, construct with manipulatives, or investigate science ideas. The children's interactions during these diverse activities produce a quiet buzz. They also have daily opportunities for outdoor play.

Mr. Sampson's children, on the other hand, sit at desks in neat rows. He directs them to complete teacher-prepared activities, such as coloring in worksheets, tracing letters, and making an art project from a teacher model. Outdoors, children play organized ball games or practice motor skills on the climbing equipment. How do these classrooms reflect the teachers' assumptions about play?

In a classroom like Mr. Sampson's, little attention is given to the powerful relationship of play to learning and development. Historically, early childhood educators have valued the centrality of play and supported children's natural play activities in the classroom (Isenberg & Quisenberry, 1988). However, recent societal and educational developments have emphasized a more academic, structured orientation and have undermined the role of play in the curriculum. The notion of stations or centers offers one way of including play activities in today's curriculum.

The Educational Role of Play

If we could travel back in time and interview three leaders in early childhood education about the value of play, what would they say? John Dewey, Patty Smith Hill, and Susan Isaacs were all strong advocates of play in the early childhood classroom. Dewey (1938) believed that children learn about themselves and their world through play. Through meaningful firsthand experiences with concrete materials, children develop problem-solving ability and conceptual understanding. Through peer interaction, they enhance their social growth. Dewey's ideas continue to permeate today's early childhood curriculum.

Patty Smith Hill (1932), strongly influenced by Dewey's ideas, introduced a work-play period in which children freely explored the objects and materials in their environment, initiated and carried out their own ideas, and engaged in cooperative learning with their peers (Weber, 1984). Susan Isaacs (1933) believed that play contributes to all aspects of children's growth and development. She defended children's right to play and challenged parents to support play—children's natural resource for learning.

Prior to the large-scale societal and educational reforms beginning in the 1960s, most early childhood practitioners recognized the importance of play. Play reflects children's experiences, is meaningful and relevant, and is thus a rich source for learning (Spodek & Saracho, 1988). The translation of Piaget's (1962) work in the 1960s began to find support for the idea that children are active learners. At the same time, other researchers (Bloom, 1964; Bruner, 1966; Hunt, 1961) documented the importance of the early years in influencing intellectual development.

Educators soon began putting these research ideas into practice with the growing numbers of disadvantaged children but did so in inappropriate ways. Early childhood classrooms at all levels became more academic and rigorous. As curriculum designers became driven by the belief that earlier is better, academic skills replaced play as central to the curriculum, to the concern of many early childhood educators.

But the educational climate is once again changing. As educational leaders look to the skills and abilities workers will need in the twenty-first century, they are raising questions about rote learning. Schools and curricula at all levels are being refashioned to focus on children's problem-solving ability, divergent thinking, and social skills. Play provides the vehicle for young children to develop such competencies. As teachers, we must advocate strongly the restoration of play to the early childhood curriculum. As the next section details, play is what childhood is all about.

Why Is Play Important?

Guidelines from the Association for Childhood Education International and the National Association for the Education of Young Children, two respected professional associations, affirm that play

- ❑ Enables children to explore their world.
- ❑ Develops social and cultural understandings.
- ❑ Helps children express their thoughts and feelings.
- ❑ Provides opportunities to meet and solve problems.
- ❑ Develops language and literacy skills and concepts (Bredekamp, 1987; Isenberg & Quisenberry, 1988).

In the following play vignettes, consider how play contributes to children's cognitive, language and literacy, social, emotional, and creative development.

Cognitive Development

Kara, a 4-year-old, is in the housekeeping area. She dials the black toy telephone, holds the receiver to her mouth, and says:

Kara: Doctor, Speedy (the gerbil) is sick today. (She puts the receiver down, bounds over to the gerbil cage, and taps on the cage with her fingers calling) Speedy, Speedy, it's okay. I'm getting medicine. Doctor, Speedy is still sleeping, and he needs medicine. I'll go get him some. (She takes a purse and goes to the theme corner, which happens to be set up as a grocery store.)

Kara: I need some medicine for the gerbil. (A child says, "Okay", hands her a plastic jar and says, "That will be $1.00. Give it to him right away. Bye.")

Kara demonstrates three salient play characteristics that parallel cognitive development:

1. Imitating a behavior detached from the present situation when she pretends to call the doctor's office from another setting.
2. Shifting from a focus on herself to a focus on others when she says, "Speedy, Speedy, it's okay. I'm getting you some medicine."
3. Substituting objects when she uses a plastic bottle for the gerbil's medicine (Piaget, 1962; Piaget & Inhelder, 1969).

Through her pretend play, Kara safely tests her ideas about caring for sick pets and about the doctor's role. She also practices social role behavior with the telephone.

The skills children use in pretend play are essential for their success in school (Smilansky, 1968; Smilansky & Shefatya, 1990). All subjects and problems include cognitive skills children use to pretend, yet many subjects (e.g., social studies) are those with which children have limited experience. If, for example, children *imagine* a Chinese New Year celebration or solve math word problems, they use their *make-believe ability* to enhance their cognitive understanding (Smilansky & Shefatya, 1990).

Language and Literacy Development

Evan and Anna are preparing a birthday celebration for their mother in the housekeeping area of their kindergarten classroom. When they realize they need a present, Anna says, "Let's ask Mr. Bear." This is a reference to the book *Ask Mr. Bear* by Marjorie Flack (1932), in which Danny tries to find the perfect birthday present for his mother by asking the animals for suggestions. After locating the book in the library corner, they become the goose, the hen, and the sheep as they search for the perfect present.

There are at least four ways Anna and Evan's play enables them to practice language and literacy skills:

1. *Communication.* In make-believe play, children use pretend communication, role-appropriate statements, and metacommunication, language used to maintain the play episode, plan a story line, and assign roles. Pretending to be someone else enables children to use voice inflections and language in situations they may or may not have encountered. These types of communication during play give children practice with the forms and functions of language (Halliday, 1975) and help them think about ways to communicate (Garvey, 1977).

2. *Verbal interaction.* In play with others, children often use language to ask for materials, to ask a question, to express ideas, or to establish and maintain the play. Verbal give-and-take during sociodramatic play needs to be highly developed because children plan, manage, problem-solve, and maintain the play by verbal explanations, discussions, or commands (Smilansky & Shefatya, 1990).

3. *Play with language.* Young children enjoy playing with language because they feel in control. Play is their arena for experimenting with and coming to understand words, syllables, sounds, and grammatical structure (Cazden, 1976). Language play dominates the preschool years and manifests itself in the jokes, riddles, and games of elementary school children (Athey, 1984).

4. *Experiment with reading and writing.* Children's first attempts to read and write often occur during dramatic play as they read environmental print, make shopping lists, or play school. Evan and Anna demonstrated an interest in stories and displayed a knowledge of story structure (e.g., character, plot, setting, goal, and conflict), as evidenced in their pretend dramatization of preparing for a birthday. Dramatic play improves story comprehension (Pellegrini & Galda, 1982; Williamson & Silvern, 1984) and increases the understanding of story structure (Pellegrini, 1980; Roskos, 1988).

Social Development

During play, children also increase their social competence. Smilansky and She-fatya (1990) contend that children's school success largely depends on their ability to interact positively with their peers and adults. Through play, children:

❑ Practice both verbal and nonverbal communication skills by negotiating roles, trying to gain access to ongoing play, or appreciating the feelings of others (Spodek & Saracho, 1988).

❑ Respond to their peers' feelings while waiting their turn and sharing materials and experiences (Spodek & Saracho, 1988).

❑ Experiment with the roles of the people in their home, school, and community by coming into contact with the needs and wishes of others (Garvey, 1977; Rubin, 1980; Seefeldt & Barbour, 1990).

❑ Experience others' points of view. As children work through conflicts about space, materials, or rules, they build positive conflict resolution strategies (Smilansky & Shefatya, 1990).

Emotional Development

Play supports emotional development by providing a way to *express* feelings and a context to *cope* with them. Pretend play helps children to express feelings in the following four ways (Piaget, 1962):

1. *Simplifying events* by creating an imaginary character, plot, or setting to match their emotional state. A child afraid of the dark, for example, might eliminate darkness or night from the play episode.

2. *Compensating for situations* by adding forbidden acts to pretend play. A child may, for example, eat cookies and ice cream for breakfast in play, whereas in reality, this could not happen.

3. *Liquidating experiences* when children repeatedly enact unpleasant or frightening experiences to gain control over the resulting emotions. For example, when children have unpleasant feelings resulting from an accident, they often reenact the scene in order to gain mastery over it.

4. *Anticipating behaviors and events* by pretending that another character, real or imaginary, commits the act and suffers the consequences when children are concerned with the consequences of disobeying an adult often. Children who normally can watch only certain television programs can pretend to allow the doll to watch and be reprimanded for watching inappropriate programs.

In addition to expressing feelings, children learn to *cope* with their feelings as they act out being angry, sad, or worried in a situation they control (Erikson, 1963). Pretend play allows them to think out loud about experiences charged with both pleasant and unpleasant feelings (Fein, 1985). A good example is Alexander, a 4-year-old whose dog was recently hit by a car. In his dramatic play in the pet hospital, his teacher heard him say to another child, "I'm sad because my dog was hurt by the car." Here he was trying to cope with unpleasant feelings from an unpleasant situation. Play enabled Alexander to express his feelings so that he could cope with his worry about his dog (Rubin & Howe, 1986).

Creativity and Imagination

Play enables children to invent ideas and use their imaginations in risk-free environments. Research supports the notion that play and creativity are related because they both rely upon children's ability to use symbols (Johnson, Christie, & Yawkey, 1987; Spodek & Saracho, 1988). Creativity can be viewed as an aspect of problem solving that has its roots in play. When young children use their imaginations in play, they are more creative, perform better at school tasks, and develop a problem-solving approach to learning (Dansky, 1980; Dansky & Silverman, 1973; Pepler & Ross, 1981; Singer, 1973; Sutton-Smith, 1986).

Physical Development

Play contributes to children's fine and gross motor development and body awareness as they actively use their bodies. A good example of fine motor development through play is a young child's learning to use a writing tool, like a marker. The natural progression in small motor development is from scribbles to shapes and forms to representational pictures. Playing with writing tools contributes to children's refinement of small motor skills. Gross motor development, such as hopping and skipping, develop in a similar fashion. When children first learn to skip, they practice hopping on different feet or just for the pure joy of hopping. As school-aged children, their hopping skill is integrated into many games they create and play. Using their bodies during play enables them to develop and refine skills, and "to feel physically confident, secure and self-assured" (Isenberg & Quisenberry, 1988, p. 139).

The importance of play is well documented. It is the essence of how children learn and follows a developmental sequence that we examine in the following section.

How Does Play Develop?

Ten-month-old Jessie plays pat-a-cake with her Grandma Marji.

Two-year-olds Ramey and Cassie pour sand back and forth into different-sized plastic containers.

Four-year-olds Lara and Michelle are pretending to make pizzas and are taking delivery orders over the telephone.

Using their bodies during play enables children to feel competent and confident.

Six-year-olds Louise, Mark, and Kelley are pretending to eat space food in a spaceship they constructed.

Eight-year-olds Rachel and Melissa play a card game, "I Doubt It," after just finishing a game of "Rummy."

All of these children are engaged in different yet age-appropriate activities. Children's play at all ages has been studied from two major perspectives—as aspects of either cognitive or social development. Both are needed to understand its sequential nature that parallels and strengthens children's emerging cognitive and social development. Think about the following questions as you read the next section: What types of play do children demonstrate at different ages? Do these types of play reappear at later ages? How does play reflect and promote children's cognitive and social development?

Cognitive Play

Cognitive play reflects children's ages, conceptual understandings, and experiential backgrounds. The ideas of Piaget (1962), Smilansky (1968) and Smilansky and Shefatya (1990) describe the following cognitive stages of play: functional play, symbolic and constructive play, and games with rules. Although each of these types of play peaks at a particular age, it continues in some form throughout life, has unique characteristics, and contributes to children's growing understanding of themselves, others, and their world. Table 2.2 is an overview of the four categories of cognitive play and describes typical behaviors of each one.

Functional Play

Functional play (birth to age 2) is characterized by simple, pleasurable, repeated movements with objects, people, and language. It is also referred to as *sensorimotor, practice,* or *exercise play* (Piaget, 1962; Smilansky & Shefatya, 1990). Functional play dominates the first 2 years of development and parallels Piaget's sensorimotor stage of development but continues in some form through adulthood.

Through functional or practice play, children begin to feel confident and competent with their bodies, like the

One-year-old who stacks and unstacks rings on a pole.

Four-year-old who incessantly repeats "I'm the king of the castle."

Five-year-old who deliberately places pegs in a pegboard.

Seven-year-old who practices bicycling skills at every available minute.

Dramatic Play

Dramatic play (2 to 7 years), also called *pretend, fantasy, make-believe,* or *symbolic play,* emerges during the second year and continues in different forms throughout adulthood. It reflects children's growing mental ability to make objects, actions, gestures, or words stand for something or someone else (Isenberg & Jacob, 1983; Piaget, 1962) and focuses on social roles and interactions (Smilansky

TABLE 2.2   Types and Characteristics of Cognitive Play

Type	Characteristics of the Child
Functional play (practice play)	Uses repetitive muscle movement, with or without objects (e.g., running, filling, hammering).
Constructive play	Manipulates objects or materials (e.g., blocks, wood, collage) to make something.
Dramatic play (pretend play)	Uses imagination and role play to transform the self and objects and to satisfy needs. Pretends to care for a sick animal (role play). Pretends to take a shower (arm movements). Note: Unless there is role taking or pretend behavior, it is not called dramatic play.
Games with rules	Recognizes, accepts, and adapts to predetermined rules that are goal-oriented (e.g., Rummy, Candyland, Jacks).

Source: Adapted from Piaget (1962), Smilansky (1968), and Smilansky & Shefatya (1990).

& Shefatya, 1990). In dramatic play, children make mental and verbal plans of action, assume roles, and transform objects or actions to express their feelings and ideas (Garvey, 1977).

Infants and toddlers imitate actions associated with a particular prop in dramatic play, learn to substitute one thing for another, and act as if they were someone else who is familiar to them. As a young toddler, Naomi picks up her toy cup and pretends to drink from it. As an older toddler, she may offer her doll a drink from the cup. Her dramatic play shifts from pretense about herself to pretense about others.

Preschool and kindergarten children's dramatic play is more complex. They engage in both solitary and group pretend play, use nonrealistic objects, assume roles, and use objects as symbols in addition to what they stand for (Bergen, 1988). Three-year-old Miriam uses her hand as a pretend hairbrush for the baby's hair. Five-year-olds Jimbo and Celeste become firefighters as they collaborate to rescue people from a burning building. These transformations are essential for dramatic play to occur (Weininger, 1988). Dramatic play peaks during the preschool years, the golden age of make-believe play.

Elementary children's dramatic play is different from the play of children at other ages because now their thinking is less public. They can integrate their symbols into age-appropriate, socially acceptable mental games and language play. Riddles, number games, secret codes, and daydreaming form the structure of symbolic play for elementary school children (Bergen, 1988; Sutton-Smith, 1980). It is not uncommon to find 7-year-olds, such as Angie and Bud, talking in secret code, a form of dramatic play, near their lockers.

Sociodramatic Play

When dramatic play involves two or more children who communicate verbally about the play episode, it is called *sociodramatic play*. Because sociodramatic play is person-oriented rather than object-oriented, it is a higher level of play behavior. During sociodramatic play, children exchange information and ideas during a jointly elaborated play sequence or theme; they can simultaneously be actors, interactors, and observers (Smilansky & Shefatya, 1990). Repeated opportunities to engage in this type of play offer children a rich arena for developing and refining concepts, solving problems, and enhancing peer relationships. Sociodramatic play correlates highly with children's intellectual and social abilities (Smilansky & Shefatya, 1990). Table 2.3 describes Smilansky and Shefatya's six criteria for determining dramatic and sociodramatic play.

It is the last two characteristics (interaction and verbal communication) that define play as sociodramatic. A discussion of the Smilansky scale for evaluating sociodramatic play elements is presented in Chapter Nine.

Constructive Play

In *constructive play*, children create something according to a preconceived plan. Constructive play predominates during the preschool years (Rubin, Fein, & Vandenberg, 1983). Let's look at the following example, which occurred during center time in Ms. Mitsoff's combined kindergarten and first-grade classroom.

In sociodramatic play, children imitate familiar roles and develop social skills.

Emily, Porsche, and Elizabeth chose to play in the block center. They had just visited the Washington, D.C. memorials, and decided to build the Jefferson Memorial. To do this, they discussed which blocks would be appropriate for the entrances, where to build them, how to make the river, and who would be the statue. After they built their structure, which closely resembled the real Jefferson Memorial, they engaged in dramatic play. In this play episode, the girls combined constructive play (building a memorial) with symbolic play (visiting the memorial) by representing their ideas with the materials (blocks) and elaborating on them in symbolic play (playing house inside the memorial). In constructive play, the child focuses on a lasting end product (Smilansky & Shefatya, 1990).

Elementary school children engage in some constructive play in school because it is easily accommodated in work-oriented settings (Bergen, 1988). Typical constructive activities include making scenery for a play or making a mobile

TABLE 2.3　Characteristics of Dramatic and Sociodramatic Play

Play Behavior	Characteristics
Imitative role play	Child assumes a make-believe role and expresses it in imitative action and/or verbalization.
Make-believe with regard to objects	Child substitutes movements, verbal declarations, and/or materials or toys that are not replicas of the object itself for real objects.
Verbal make-believe with regard to actions and situations	Child substitutes verbal descriptions or declarations for actions and situations.
Persistence in role play	Child stays within a role or play theme for at least 10 minutes.
Interaction	At least two players interact within the context of a play episode.
Verbal communication	There is some verbal interaction related to the play episode.

Source: Adapted from Smilansky (1968).

out of recycled materials. In order to qualify as play, however, children must freely *choose* to do the activity and find it pleasurable.

Games with Rules

Games with rules rely upon prearranged rules that guide acceptable play behavior. Games with rules such as board games (e.g., Clue), card games (e.g., Rummy), or outdoor games (e.g., kickball) are the most prominent form of play among school-aged children. School-aged children's more logical ways of thinking and advanced social skills make it possible for them to follow a set of rules and negotiate with peers. Games with rules (described in Chapter Seven) enhance children's physical coordination, refine their social and language skills, and build concepts of cooperation and competition (Elkind, 1988).

Social Play

Social play, the ability of children to interact with their peers, also develops in age-related stages. The now classic ideas of Mildred Parten (1932) have focused attention on the social aspects of play during early childhood. Parten identified six types of play, beginning with the least socially mature (solitary play) and moving toward the most socially mature (cooperative play). Today, most researchers consider Parten's "levels" as descriptive of *styles* of play rather than social maturity because as children grow older, they cycle back and forth between the types of social play (Monighan-Nourot et al., 1987). Table 2.4 describes the characteristics of Parten's six levels of social play.

TABLE 2.4   Levels of Social Play

Type of Play	Characteristics of the Child
Unoccupied behavior	Watches activity of others. Plays with body, gets on and off chairs, walks about aimlessly, glances around room.
Onlooker behavior	Observes, asks questions, and talks to other children but does not enter play itself. Stands within speaking distance to see and hear. More active involvement than onlooking behavior.
Solitary play	Plays independently and is not involved with other children. Playing with own toys is the primary goal.
Parallel play	Plays alongside or nearby another. Uses like toys but plays independently. Does not share toys. Plays beside, not with, others.
Associative play	Plays with others in similar, loosely organized activity. Conversation involves asking questions, using each other's toys. Some attempts made to control who may join the group.
Cooperative play	Involves complex social organizations with shared common goals. Reciprocal role taking (e.g., turn taking) and a strong sense of belonging or not belonging to the group. Organizes group for the purpose of making a product, dramatizing a situation, or playing a formal game. Goal involves division of labor, differential role taking, and organization of activity.

Source: Adapted from Parten (1932).

Knowledge of the stages of play helps teachers provide developmentally appropriate environments that support children's development. It also enables them to enjoy, encourage, and appreciate age-appropriate play behavior. Play is children's natural resource for developing social and cognitive skills that affect their present and future interactions.

Why Do Children Play?

For over 150 years, theories of play have been proposed, yet none adequately describes the phenomenon of play. Collectively, however, these theories have influenced teachers' thinking about its importance. These theories can be categorized as *classical* (e.g., those that were prominent from the nineteenth century through World War I) and *modern* (e.g., those that were prominent after World War I) (Johnson et al., 1987; Seefeldt & Barbour, 1990). Table 2.5 summarizes the theoretical perspectives reflected in children's play.

Classical Theories

Classical theorists sought to explain the causes and purposes of play through surplus energy, recreation/relaxation, instinct, and recapitulation (Singer, 1973).

TABLE 2.5   Theoretical Perspectives Reflected in Children's Play

Theories	Theorists	Purpose of Play
Classical		
Surplus energy	Spencer	Expend excess energy
Recreation/relaxation	Lazarus	Restore energy used in work
Instinct	Groos	Practice future survival skills
Recapitulation	Hall	Revisit ancient activities
Modern		
Psychoanalytic	Freud	Master unpleasant experiences
	Erikson	Master physical and social skills to build self-esteem
Cognitive-developmental	Piaget	Practice and consolidate known information and skills through different types of play
		Functional play (repeated motions)
		Symbolic play (make believe play)
		Games with rules (predetermined rules)
	Vygotsky	Symbolic play separates meaning from objects and actions and leads to abstract thought
	Bruner	Promotes flexibility and creative problem solving
Cultural	Bateson	Play is paradoxical. On one level, children are engrossed in pretending; on another level, they are aware of their true identities.

Surplus energy theory suggests that human beings have a certain amount of energy to be used for survival. Energy not used for survival is spent on play and becomes surplus energy. When children have limited opportunities to move around, they seem to have bursts of energy that relieve stress and tension so that they can settle down again. Teachers' views about "getting rid of excess energy on the playground" support this theoretical perspective.

Recreation/relaxation theory, in contrast to surplus energy theory, suggests that play *replenishes* energy used in work. The influence of this theory is evident in early childhood classrooms, where children alternate between quiet and active activities.

Instinct theory, also known as *preexercise theory,* proposes that play prepares children for the future roles and responsibilities needed to survive in their culture. When young children pretend to be a mother, father, or teacher and invent ways to use materials to represent adult tools, they are practicing the behaviors and characteristics of significant adults in their lives. Even in war-torn countries with no materials at hand, children will use available objects to create play episodes.

Recapitulation theory, in contrast, posits that play enables children to *revisit* activities of their ancestors and shed any negative behaviors. This play prepares them for living in today's world. Popular games of chase and pursuit can be categorized within recapitulation theory.

Modern Theories

The major difference between classical and modern theories of play is that modern theories emphasize the consequences of play *for the child.* These three major theoretical orientations are psychoanalytic, supporting emotional development; cognitive-developmental, supporting intellectual growth; and cultural, focusing on social development.

Psychoanalytic theory views play as an important vehicle for emotional release (Freud 1958) and for developing self-esteem as children gain mastery of their bodies, of objects, and of social skills (Erikson, 1963). It enables children to play out feelings, without pressure, by actively reliving experiences and mastering them in reality. Moreover, it provides the teacher with clues to children's individual needs (Weber, 1984). After the birth of a new baby, it is not uncommon to hear young children say, "I'm taking you back to the hospital." Expressing resentment through play enables children to gain control of it in real situations.

Cognitive-developmental theory examines play in the context of intellectual development (Bruner, 1972; Piaget, 1962; Sutton-Smith, 1986; Vygotsky, 1967, 1978). Piaget proposes that children *individually* create their own knowledge about the world through their interactions. They practice using known information while consolidating new information and skills; test new ideas against their experiences; and construct knowledge about people, objects, and situations.

Vygotsky (1967), on the other hand, emphasizes the centrality of the *social context* as primarily influencing cognitive development. Because children first encounter knowledge in their social world that *later* becomes part of their cognitive development, play is children's way of thinking through and solving problems. Vygotsky (1978) observes: "In play a child behaves beyond his average, above his daily behavior; in play it is as though he were a head taller than himself" (p. 102).

Bruner (1972) and Sutton-Smith (1986) interpret play as flexible thinking and creative problem solving in action. Because children focus on the *process* of play, they engage in multiple combinations of ideas and solutions that they use to solve relevant life problems.

Consider Angelo, a 4-year-old, who is playing with the figures from the manger scene beneath the Christmas tree. He picks up one, inspects it closely, then says, "Here's Baby Jesus in his car seat." Angelo has looked at the mounds of hay surrounding the infant and has related them to the cushion that protects and surrounds his baby sister while she rides in the family car. Clearly, he is constructing knowledge (Piaget, 1962), affected by his social context (Vygotsky, 1967), and using his creative problem-solving skills (Bruner, 1972; Sutton-Smith, 1980).

Each theory supports the essential role of play in children's developing social, emotional, and cognitive development. Understanding its importance is necessary for incorporating play as a curricular tool and for assuming appropriate roles and responsibilities in the classroom.

Teachers' Roles and Responsibilities

Whether and how teachers intervene determines if play is enriched or disrupted. As you read each of the different roles teachers assume, think about when to use each role.

Teachers as Observers

Teachers must be good observers of children's play so that they can determine whether or not children need help with a problem; if toys or materials are adequately stimulating; and how play situations are contributing to children's developing social, motor, and cognitive skills. Skilled observers note which child plays what role, the common themes a particular child chooses, how children enter and exit a play setting, and children's developing ability to participate in group activity. (See Chapter Nine for an extended discussion of informal observation measures to study play.)

Teachers as Extenders

Sometimes children continuously repeat actions and cannot move forward with a role, theme, or idea. Teachers can extend their play by adding a new toy or prop or by asking a question that elaborates on but does not change the theme. One kindergarten teacher had a fast food restaurant in her theme corner. After a week of play, she added a "Drive Thru" sign and a cardboard window that the children used to add a new dimension to their play. In doing so, she extended children's thought processes and imagination with minimal interruption (Weininger, 1988).

Teachers as Planners

Teachers must also plan for children's play. An environment conducive to play provides enough *time* to develop and carry out a play theme; enough *space* for children to enact a theme or to construct something; a variety of *materials* that encourage all forms of play; and *common and familiar experiences* so that children can enact roles they understand (Johnson et al., 1987).

Teachers as Responders

When teachers verbally describe children's actions and words or ask questions about the role or theme, they provide feedback on what they are doing and saying. Making statements like "I see you have bought a large bag of groceries" or "I noticed you wrapped your baby up in a warm blanket before you left for the doctor's office" gives children an opportunity to elaborate on that behavior if they choose. Asking questions, making suggestions, and helping children make contact with others are all ways in which teachers can respond to children's play (Smilansky & Shefatya, 1990). These interventions, however, must address the *role* of the child and not the *child*. In this way, the intervention maintains children's dramatic or sociodramatic play and validates that playing is a valued activity.

Teachers as Models

Sometimes it is appropriate for teachers to actively join the play and model a particular behavior or role relevant to the ongoing play theme. In this way, teachers can teach individuals or groups of children a needed play skill or behavior. Consider the following example. In Mr. Blum's noncategorical preschool handicapped class, two 4-year-old girls are playing house in the housekeeping area. Mr. Blum notices that one child rocks with a doll, while the other repeatedly opens and closes the oven door. He enters the play, sits at the table, and announces: "It is time for lunch." He asks, "What smells so good in the oven?" and later asks, "Could I help set the table?" Mr. Blum's modeling of family roles and behaviors encourages the children to practice some of those skills.

Adopting roles and expecting children to play enables teachers to regain control over the early childhood curriculum and wean themselves from a skills-based curriculum. As so aptly stated by Fromberg (1990), "The teacher's most useful direct intervention is maintaining a playful attitude and accepting and encouraging children's independent problem-solving and connection-making" (p. 238).

Special Populations

With greater frequency, children with special needs are being mainstreamed back into the early childhood classroom. Play can help them cope more easily with their added burdens and stress. Hence, play for all children is necessary and integral to the early childhood curriculum. It connects children and ideas and provides a rich resource for children and teachers.

Culturally Diverse Groups

Young children's play provides information about who they are and enables them to "grow out of their egocentric and ethnocentric picture of the world" (Kendall, 1983, p. 10). Jalongo (1991) offers the following suggestions to help teachers realize play's potential for multicultural education:

1. *Accept children's cultural differences.* Teachers need to ask themselves some difficult questions to discover their basic attitudes toward others. Questions that help reveal those attitudes may include the following: Am I aware of my own biases toward different populations? For example, do I know that each subgroup of Asian-Americans is unique, or do I make the mistake of believing that there is an "Oriental" culture? Do I recognize that different child-rearing practices affect children's play? Do I give enough respect to families with different configurations or from different economic levels?

2. *Help children explore their cultural backgrounds through appropriate play centers and materials.* Teachers need to have enough background information about children to make informed curriculum decisions. Learning the background and culture of the children helps bridge the gap between school and home. Teachers need to know how long families have been in this country, what toys children use at home, what experiences children have had outside the home (e.g., in a restaurant or gas station), if the child imitates parental activities, and how the parents feel about play. Inviting children and their families to supply cultural materials for thematic centers is one way of helping children explore different cultural backgrounds. This information is critical to providing relevant play experiences.

3. *Be particularly sensitive to gender and racial issues as children enact familiar roles.* Play is a powerful vehicle for understanding gender and racial issues. How teachers communicate messages about what girls, boys, and people of color can do affects how children view themselves and their competencies. In preparing children for today's and tomorrow's world, teachers need to ensure that there are culturally diverse materials such as puppets, dolls, puzzles, music, and books in the room; that they provide enough novelty and challenge for all; and that children are free to enact different roles.

Children with Disabilities

The following suggestions support the developmental needs of children with disabilities through play (Kaplan-Sanoff, Brewster, Stillwell, & Bergen, 1988):

1. *Provide opportunities for children to practice specific skills.* Aaron, a first-grade child with spina bifida, was thrilled by the discovery that he could use his walker and participate as a goalie in the class game of kickball.

As a kindergartner, Aaron was equally excited when his teacher rearranged the housekeeping area with a wide entry so that he could gain access to the dramatic play area in his wheelchair.

2. *Enhance language development.* Often, hearing-impaired children are reluctant to use language in large group settings. In pretend play settings, however, a hearing-impaired child has the opportunity to use language during interactions with both peers and adults. Kendra, a 5-year-old child in an after-school-care program, was particularly intrigued by puppetry because she could use the puppet as her alter ego.

3. *Reduce the effects of stress in children's environments.* After a repeated hospitalization or a family disruption, play provides a powerful vehicle for helping children to regain a sense of control over their lives. After Bernice was diagnosed as a diabetic, she became fascinated by the plastic syringe in the doctor's kit and wanted to administer insulin shots to everyone else. In this way, she used play to help her cope with her need for daily shots.

High-Achieving and Low-Achieving Children

High-achieving children often exhibit divergent thinking that clearly needs to be challenged. Equally important is their need to feel part of the group, to experience a range of feelings, and to become comfortable with their bodies (Deiner, 1983). Low-achieving children often demonstrate developmental lags in several areas. We suggest the following guidelines:

1. *Provide for peer interaction.* All children need opportunities to develop social competence through peer interaction. Teachers need to encourage children's active involvement in dramatic play (e.g., a fast food theme corner), constructive play (e.g., building roads for a city), and games with rules (e.g., card games like Go Fish) that provide opportunities to develop and practice social skills. In these play contexts, all children can and do play together. There is no place or need for ability grouping.

2. *Balance small and large motor activities.* Many low-achieving children play with small and large motor materials to develop coordination and to release feelings of frustration and tension. In movement activities, for example, help them develop lateral muscles by crawling and climbing. On the other hand, if children are feeling particularly tense or frustrated, avoid excessive small motor play, which often adds to their frustration.

3. *Allow children to enact roles and work through frightening experiences.* During thematic units, be certain to discuss and model appropriate social behaviors. Knowing what behaviors are expected and practicing those behaviors in dramatic play settings help children understand them.

4. *Adjust to the children's ability levels.* Suppose that a class is creating a Big Book in small groups. High-achieving children may invent new uses for

the materials, such as creating a lift-the-flap book. They may also demonstrate skill in evaluation. If the action is kept open-ended, low-achieving children can also participate fully, yet rise to new levels of performance.

Conclusion

Play is children's most powerful learning process. It helps them make sense of their world, develop new concepts and refine others, take risks, increase social skills, obtain emotional support, and take responsibility for their own learning. Early childhood classrooms that are play-oriented are child-centered. Indeed, they provide "opportunities for developing the flexibility and creativity that may share the importance of present day 'basic skills' as we enter the 21st century" (Almy et al., 1984, p. 21).

Chapter Summary

1. Play has been studied from different perspectives, yet there is no consensus about its definition or primary purpose. There are, however, accepted identifiable characteristics.
2. Both classical and modern theories have influenced how play is viewed in the early childhood curriculum. These theories are essential to understanding why children play and must be used as a basis of curriculum planning.
3. Play contributes to all areas of children's development. It is the primary vehicle through which their cognitive, language and literacy, social, emotional, and creative development occurs. Play has been studied primarily as an aspect of social and cognitive development.
4. Teachers have five clear roles and responsibilities in children's play—observer, extender, planner, responder, and role model. Each of these roles and responsibilities must be fulfilled in order to support children's learning and development through play.
5. Teachers must utilize play to enhance the multicultural aspects of their classrooms; to challenge high-achieving children's imagination; to encourage low-achieving children; and to integrate children with disabling conditions into the mainstream.

Discussion Questions

1. This chapter has described the difficulty surrounding the study of play. Explain to your colleagues how the assumptions about play and the play–work distinction have contributed to this confusion.
2. Your role as a teacher is crucial in supporting play. Review the five roles of the teacher discussed in this chapter. What is the significance of assuming these different roles?

3. In the Research Highlight, Vivian Paley describes how she expanded her kindergarten play time as a way to cope with children's segregated play patterns. What does her major curriculum shift indicate about her views on play? About children? About herself as a teacher? Of what importance was her study?

4. An appropriate play environment is essential for children to grow through play. What principles and practices would you adopt to ensure children's healthy development?

5. In the twenty-first century, many educators believe play will be considered as fundamental as basic skills are today. What do you believe about the importance of play? Why do you believe this?

─────────────── **Writing to Learn** ───────────────

An essential aspect of your professional responsibility in support of play is to assume different teacher roles. Select three of the five teacher roles described in this chapter and write about your feelings and experiences with them. Think about where you experienced/observed these roles, under what conditions, how you (the teacher) assumed these roles and why this helped or disrupted the children's play. Share your writing with the group. Which roles seem to occur most often? Least often? In what form of play? Summarize this information in a chart. Have you identified other roles that recur and that were not mentioned in the chapter? If so, describe them.

─────────────── **Interview** ───────────────

A Kindergarten Teacher's Commitment to Play

Early childhood educators expect play to be an integral part of the curriculum. This demands a teacher's commitment for its effective and appropriate implementation. "Teachers must take the lead in articulating the need for play in children's lives, including the curriculum" (Isenberg & Quisenberry, 1988, p. 139).

To determine teachers' level of commitment to play in the curriculum, interview a kindergarten teacher and record her or his responses to each of the following questions. Ask any additional questions that emerge from your interview. As a class activity, compare your responses with those of your classmates and identify the common elements.

1. How would you define and describe children's play?
2. What kinds of practices do you believe enrich or disrupt children's ability to play?
3. How do you relate play to developmentally appropriate practice?

4. On a scale ranging from "Extremely Important" to "Unimportant," how would you rate play for children's overall development?
5. Describe how you structure your day for children's learning. How do you think play relates to learning?
6. How do you inform parents of the role of play in your kindergarten?

Observation

Theoretical Perspectives Reflected in Children's Play

The purpose of this assignment is to use what you know about theoretical positions on play to observe children's play. Using the following steps, you will gather, analyze, and code several play episodes in terms of the theories presented in the chapter.

1. Observe a single child or a group of children (infant through age 8) at play on several different occasions. Record the play session by (a) taking notes or (b) using an audio or video recorder.
2. Transcribe the children's actual words.
3. Reread the theory section at the beginning of this chapter. Using Table 2.5 (p. 45) as a guide, try to cite examples of children's behavior that could be explained by each theory.

Bring your transcripts to class so that we can generate relevant examples of theoretical foundations.

Controversy

Superhero Play in the Classroom

In Ms. Zemsky's class of 3-year-olds, Jonathan and Jordan, pretending to be Ninja Turtles, run to one corner of the room, turn around, charge at each other, jump, and scream "Cowabunga!" They then run to another corner, exchange karate chops, and repeat the sequence. Ms. Zemsky intervenes and redirects the play by suggesting that they use a boat and a fishing pole to catch more turtles. The boys change course temporarily but quickly return to boisterous pursuit and aggressive confrontation.

Superhero play is typical of 3- and 4-year-old children, yet it evokes strong, conflicting views among parents and teachers. Adults' views usually fall into one of two camps: permitting or forbidding superhero play in the classroom.

Supporters of superhero play believe that it meets children's developmental needs by directly exploring the ideas in their social and cultural world (Kostelnik, Whirren, & Stein, 1986; Wolf, 1984). Opponents of superhero play believe that it validates forms of violence and aggression (Schneiderman & Sousa, 1986; Simpson, 1985) that will surface in later life.

There are at least four main issues fueling the superhero controversy (Carlsson-Paige & Levin, 1987; Wolfe, 1984):

1. *Power and control.* Supporters of superhero play acknowledge that it lets children safely play at being in control of their lives and gain mastery over their feelings (Wolf, 1984). Opponents believe that it undermines the values we teach them.

2. *Reality and fantasy.* When children assume a superhero role, they alternate between being themselves and being the superhero. Enacting a superhero role increases familiarity with their own attributes and identities. Opponents argue that it increases the gap between reality and make-believe and will have lasting, negative effects on our society (Simpson, 1985).

3. *Sex-role stereotyping.* Because superhero figures provide graphic information about male roles, boys seem particularly attracted to them (Carlsson-Paige & Levin, 1987). "Super males and super females help children to grasp the clear differences that go into making someone a male or a female" (Wolf, 1984, p. 31). Adults who object to stereotypical figures disapprove of the representation of undesirable macho, aggressive qualities and subservient female roles (Carlsson-Paige & Levin, 1987; Wolf, 1984).

4. *Violence and aggression.* Superhero themes on television glamorize fighting and portray humans as powerless without technology. Dialogue between opposing sides and acceptance of other viewpoints are absent; characters are all good or all bad (Carlsson-Paige & Levin, 1987). Opponents of superhero play suggest that the violent content contaminates children's play.

Supporters of superhero play do not condone these models either, but they argue that violence is an inescapable part of children's world. Asking children to ignore these feelings and images only confuses them. Rather than forbidding superhero play in school, children can better understand violence by talking about it in the context in which it occurs (Wolf, 1984).

The controversy over superhero play continues. Teachers must wrestle with their beliefs, develop consistent school policies rooted in knowledge of child development, and establish guidelines for the appropriate intervention into children's superhero play. Where do you stand on this controversial issue? Why? How will you answer parents' questions about superhero play?

--- **Research Highlight** ---

Boys and Girls: Superheroes in the Doll Corner

Summary of Research

Vivian Paley is a kindergarten teacher-researcher who studied the play behavior of her kindergarten children because she wanted to be more objective about her kindergarten boys' play. She watched her children's play patterns in the doll corner to observe segregated play patterns. Based upon her observations, she concluded that children's domestic play patterns have the following age- and sex-related characteristics.

❑ Three-year-olds play peacefully in the doll corner and easily change roles, with little need to inform others.

❑ Four-year-old girls prefer to play traditional family roles (e.g., mother, father, baby), while boys prefer to be superheroes. Such divergent preferences hinder the ability of boys and girls to carry out domestic themes in the doll corner.

❑ In kindergarten, boys clearly prefer superhero play, while girls enact the roles of princess and sister. These differences virtually eliminate boys from doll corner play. The continued need for power that seems to drive boys to play superheroes widens the gap between boys and girls.

Paley recounts the strategies she employed to combat the segregated boy–girl play patterns she observed. First, she doubled the time allotted for free play to 90 minutes in the morning and 60 minutes in the afternoon. As a result, she found that girls spent the extra time in the doll corner and building with blocks, while the boys went to table games after "playing out" their need for superhero play. This increased time resulted in a less frantic pace, and the block area became "homebase rather than a walled fortress" (1984, p. 105). If one of these expanded periods was eliminated or shortened, however, she found boys and girls reverting to their earlier segregated play patterns, with the girls in the art area and the boys wanting to play.

Second, Paley decreased the amount of direct instruction. As she noticed boys rejecting structured table activities (e.g., weaving mats) in lieu of pretend play opportunities, she realized that boys want things "to happen fast" (p. 104) and are easily frustrated because their coordination does not allow this to happen. Girls' small motor coordination is improving rapidly and they, consequently, respond positively to these activities.

Implications for Practice

Paley's research yielded crucial information on the developmental play differences and needs of boys and girls. Understanding why particular types of play appeal to boys or girls influences how teachers prepare environments, the materials they provide, the time and space they allow, and their roles and responsibilities. It also emphasizes the importance of teachers' attitudes and beliefs in recognizing and admitting needed curricular changes.

References

Almy, M., Monighan, P., Scales, B., & Van Hoorn, J. (1984). Recent research on play. The perspective of the teacher. In L. G. Katz (Ed.), *Current topics in early education*, Vol. 5 (pp. 1–25). Norwood, NJ: Ablex.

Athey, I. (1984). Contributions of play to development. In T. D. Yawkey & A. D. Pellegrini (Eds.), *Child's play: Developmental and applied* (pp. 9–29). Hillsdale, NJ: Lawrence Erlbaum.

Bergen, D. (1988). Using a schema for play and learning. In D. Bergen (Ed.), *Play as a medium for learning and development: A handbook of theory and practice* (pp. 169–180). Portsmouth, NH: Heinemann.

Bloom, B. (1964). *Stability and change in human characteristics.* New York: Wiley.

Bredekamp, S. (Ed.). (1987). *Developmentally appropriate practice in early childhood programs serving children from birth through age eight.* Washington, DC: National Association for the Education of Young Children.

Bretherton, I. (Ed.). (1984). *Symbolic play: The development of social understanding.* New York: Academic Press.

Bruner, J. S. (1966). *Toward a theory of instruction.* Cambridge, MA: Harvard University Press.

Bruner, J. S. (1972). The nature and uses of immaturity. *American Psychologist, 27,* 687–708.

Carlsson-Paige, N., & Levin, D. E. (1987). *The war play dilemma: Balancing needs and values in the early childhood classroom.* New York: Teachers College Press.

Cazden, C. (1976). Play with language and metalinguistic awareness: One dimension of language experience. In J. S. Bruner, A. Jolly, & K. Sylva (Eds.), *Play—its role in development and evolution* (pp. 603–608). New York: Basic Books.

Dansky, J. L. (1980). Make-believe: A mediator of the relationship between play and associative fluency. *Child Development, 51,* 576–579.

Dansky, J. L., & Silverman, I. W. (1973). Effects of play on associative fluency in preschool children. *Developmental Psychology, 9,* 38–43.

Deiner, P. L. (1983). *Resources for teaching young children with special needs.* New York: Harcourt Brace Jovanovich.

Dewey, J. (1938). *Experience and education.* New York: Macmillan.

Elkind, D. (1988). Play. *Young Children, 43*(5), 2.

Ellis, M. J. (1973). *Why people play.* Englewood Cliffs, NJ: Prentice-Hall.

Erikson. E. H. (1963). *Childhood and society.* New York: Norton.

Fein, G. G. (1985). Learning in play: Surfaces of thinking and feeling. In J. L. Frost & S. Sunderlin (Eds.), *When children play* (pp. 19–28). Wheaton, MD: Association for Childhood Education International.

Freud, S. (1958). *On creativity and the unconscious* (I. F. Grant Doff, trans.). New York: Harper & Row. (Original work published in 1928.)

Fromberg, D. P. (1987). Play. In C. Seefeldt (Ed.), *The early childhood curriculum: A review of current research* (pp. 35–74). New York: Teachers College Press.

Fromberg, D. P. (1990). Play issues in early childhood education. In C. Seefeldt (Ed.), *Continuing issues in early childhood education* (pp. 223–243). Columbus, OH: Merrill/Macmillan.

Garvey, C. (1977). *Play.* Cambridge, MA: Harvard University Press.

Halliday, M. A. K. (1975). *Explorations in the function of language.* London: Edward Arnold.

Hill, P. S. (1932). *A conduct curriculum for the kindergarten and first grade.* New York: Scribners.

Hunt, J. M. (1961). *Intelligence and experience.* New York: Ronald Press.

Isaacs, S. (1933). *Social development in young children.* London: Routledge & Kegan Paul.

Isenberg, J., & Jacob, E. (1983). Literacy and symbolic play: A review of the literature. *Childhood Education, 59*(4), 272–274.

Isenberg, J., & Quisenberry, N. (1988). Play: A necessity for all children. *Childhood Education, 64*(3), 138–145.

Jalongo, M. R. (1990). The child's right to the expressive arts: Nurturing the imagination as well as the intellect. *Childhood Education, 66*(4), 195–201.

Jalongo, M. R. (1991). Children's play: A resource for multi-cultural education. In E. B. Vold (Ed.), *Multicultural education in the early childhood classroom* (pp. 55–63). Washington, DC: National Education Association.

Johnson, J. E., Christie, J. F., & Yawkey, T. D. (1987). *Play and early childhood development.* Glenview, IL: Scott, Foresman.

Kaplan-Sanoff, M., Brewster, A., Stillwell, J., & Bergen, D. (1988). The relationship of play to physical/motor development and children with special needs. In D. Bergen (Ed.), *Play as a medium for learning and development: A handbook of theory and practice* (pp. 137–162). Portsmouth, NH: Heinemann.

Kendall, F. E. (1983). *Diversity in the classroom: A multicultural approach to the education of young children.* New York: Teachers College Press.

Kostelnik, M. J., Whirren, A. P., & Stein, L. C. (1986). Living with He-Man: Managing superhero fantasy play. *Young Children, 41*(4), 3–9.

Maxim, G. (1993). *The very young: Guiding children from infancy through the early years.* (4th ed.). Columbus, OH: Merrill/Macmillan.

Monighan-Nourot, P., Scales, B., & Van Hoorn, J., with Almy, M. (1987). *Looking at children's play: A bridge between theory and practice.* New York: Teachers College Press.

Neumann, E. (1971). *The elements of play.* New York: MSS Information Corp.

Paley, V. G. (1984). *Boys and girls: Superheroes in the doll corner.* Chicago: University of Chicago Press.

Parten, M. (1932). Social participation among preschool children. *Journal of Abnormal and Social Psychology, 27*(2), 243–269.

Pellegrini, A. D. (1980). The relationship between kindergartners' play and achievement in pre-reading, language, and writing. *Psychology in the schools, 17*(4), 530–535.

Pellegrini, A. D., & Galda, L. (1982). Playing about a story: Its impact on comprehension. *The Reading Teacher, 35*, 52–55.

Pepler, D., & Ross, H. S. (1981). The effects of play on convergent and divergent problem-solving. *Child Development, 52*, 1202–1210.

Piaget, J. (1962). *Play, dreams and imitation in childhood.* New York: Norton.

Piaget, J., & Inhelder, B. (1969). *The psychology of the child.* New York: Basic Books.

Roskos, K. (1988). Literacy at work in play. *The Reading Teacher, 41*, 562–66.

Rubin, K. H. (1980). Fantasy play: Its role in the development of social skills and social cognition. In K. H. Rubin (Ed.), *New directions for child development: Children's play.* (No. 9, pp. 69–84). San Francisco: Jossey-Bass.

Rubin, K. H., Fein, G. S., & Vandenberg, B. (1983). Play. In E. M. Hetherington (Ed.) and P. H. Mussen (Series Ed.), *Handbook of child psychology,* Vol. 4, *Socialization, personality and development* (pp. 698–774). New York: Wiley.

Rubin, K. H., & Howe, N. (1986). Social play and perspective taking. In G. Fein & M. Rivkin (Eds.), *The young child at play. Reviews of research,* Vol. 4 (pp. 113–125). Washington, DC: National Association for the Education of Young Children.

Schneiderman, J., & Sousa, C. (1986). Superheroes in the preschool classroom. *Child Care News, 12*(9), 1, 4, 5.

Seefeldt, C., & Barbour, N. (1990). *Early childhood education: An introduction.* (2nd ed.). Columbus, OH: Merrill/Macmillan.

Simpson, C. (1985). The violence of war toys: He-Man, Voltron, Transformers, and Gobots. *The Nonviolent, 2*(8), 3–4, 6.

Singer, J. L. (1973). *The child's world of make-believe.* New York: Wiley.

Smilansky, S. (1968). *The effects of sociodramatic play on disadvantaged preschool children.* New York: Wiley.

Smilansky, S., & Shefatya, L. (1990). *Facilitating play: A medium for promoting cognitive, socio-emotional and academic development in young children*. Gaithersburg, MD: Psychosocial and Educational Publications.

Spodek, B., & Saracho, O. N. (1988). The challenge of educational play. In D. Bergen (Ed.), *Play as a medium for learning and development: A handbook of theory and practice* (pp. 9–22). Portsmouth, NH: Heinemann.

Sutton-Smith, B. (1980). Children's play: Some sources of play theorizing. In K. H. Rubin (Ed.), *New directions for child development: Children's play* (No. 9, pp. 1–16). San Francisco: Jossey-Bass.

Sutton-Smith, B. (1986). The spirit of Play. In G. Fein & M. Rivkin (Eds.), *The young child at play. Reviews of research, Vol. 4* (pp. 3–16). Washington, DC: National Association for the Education of Young Children.

Vygotsky, L. S. (1967). Play and its role in the mental development of the child. *Soviet Psychology, 12*, 62–76.

Vygotsky, L. S. (1978). Mind in society. Cambridge, MA: Harvard University Press.

Wasserman, S. (1990). *Serious players in the primary classroom*. New York: Teachers College Press.

Weber, E. (1984). *Early childhood education: Perspectives on change*. Worthington, OH: Chas. A. Jones.

Weininger, O. (1988). "What if" and "As if": Imagination and pretend play in early childhood. In K. Egan & D. Nadaner (Eds.), *Imagination and education* (pp. 141–149). New York: Teachers College Press.

Williamson, P., & Silvern, S. (1984). Creative dramatic play and language comprehension. In T. D. Yawkey & A. D. Pellegrini (Eds.), *Child's play: Developmental and applied* (pp. 347–358). Hillsdale, NJ: Lawrence Erlbaum.

Wolf, D. P. (1984). Superheroes: Yes or no? An interview with Carolee Fucigna and Michelle Heist. *Beginnings, 1*(1), 29–32.

Children's Books

Flack, M. (1932). *Ask Mr. Bear*. New York: Macmillan.

Infusing Creative Expression and Play Into the Curriculum

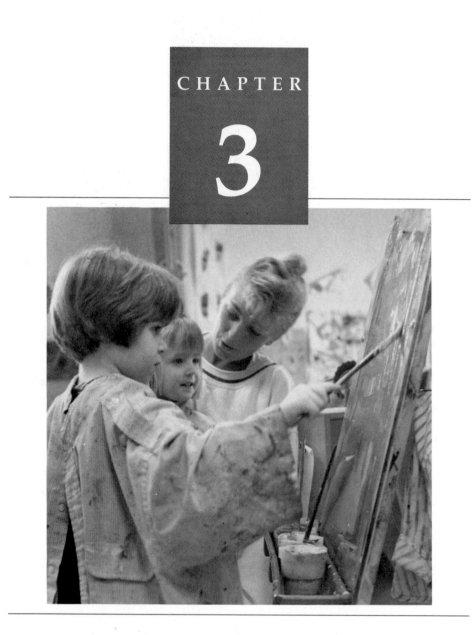

Art in the Early
Childhood Curriculum

Once I drew like Raphael, but it has taken me a whole lifetime to learn to draw like children.

Pablo Picasso

It has been proved beyond any doubt that such imitative procedures as found in coloring books and workbooks make the child dependent in his thinking; they make the child inflexible because he has to follow what he has been given. They do not provide emotional relief because they give the child no opportunity to express his own emotions; they do not even promote skills and discipline, because the child's urge for perfection grows out of his desire for expression; and finally, they condition the child to adult concepts which he cannot produce alone, and which therefore frustrate his own creative ambitions.

Viktor Lowenfeld, 1947, p. 18

After reading this chapter, you will be able to

❑ Define art and list the criteria that are used to distinguish art activities from other types of classroom activities.
❑ Understand how art contributes to every child's overall development.
❑ List and explain the components of quality art experiences and programs for young children.
❑ Describe a general sequence of children's artistic development.

❑ Examine the early childhood teacher's roles and responsibilities in providing child-centered art experiences.

❑ Develop strategies for integrating art throughout the school day and across the curriculum.

Case Study

In a large metropolitan area, four teachers are engaged in doing what each of them defines as art.

Mr. Evanko has been teaching a lesson on safety in his public school kindergarten. Each child will make a traffic signal from a rectangle of black construction paper and red, yellow, and green paper circles. When the activity is completed, each child's traffic signal looks nearly identical to the ones cut and pasted by the other children. Is this art?

In Ms. Carr's private nursery school, children can choose painting, clay, drawing with crayons, or construction paper and glue every day. She describes her philosophy as creative because she gives the children no guidance in the use and care of materials, nor does she discuss their work. Is this art?

In Ms. Lenninger's parochial school second-grade classroom, children are busily preparing for spring parent-teacher conferences. Ms. Lenninger has the idea of placing large tree branches in a flower pot filled with plaster of paris and involving her students in making paper dogwood flowers. She directs the children to trace carefully around the patterns she has provided, and even with 20 students, it takes quite some time before the branches are covered with paper blossoms. Is this art?

Mr. Ortiz's first graders have been collecting what he calls "beautiful junk" for several weeks. These materials include: bits of fabric, yarn, buttons, lace, felt, boxes, and plastic bottles of various sizes and shapes. The children have been listening to stories about amiable monsters, including *Where the Wild Things Are* (Sendak, 1963), *The Very Worst Monster* (Hutchins, 1985), *There's a Nightmare in My Closet* (Mayer, 1968), and *Harry and the Terrible Whatzit* (Gackenbach, 1977). Mr. Ortiz's challenge to his students is simply this: "Using any of the materials we have collected here or others you may have at home, create your own monster. Think about questions like these: What is special about your monster? What does it eat? Are people afraid of it? Why? Where does it live now? What makes it happy? What makes it sad? What does it like to do? After you have created your monster, you will tell the class all about it. Then you will make up a story about your monster." Is this art?

Each of these teachers is operating on a set of assumptions about art. The first three teachers (the one who was making paper traffic signals, the one who believed in complete nonintervention, and the one who was making "dogwood trees") have committed the three most common errors in teaching art: advocating formulas and requiring conformity, mistaking lack of guidance for freedom, and unduly emphasizing copying and neatness (Gaitskell, Hurwitz, & Day, 1982). Of the four examples given, only the last, Mr. Ortiz's "monster-inventing activity," could be categorized as art. Why? What characteristics differentiate an art activity from other possible types of activities?

Theoretical Framework

There are three basic criteria that must be met for an activity to qualify as art: emphasizing the process, valuing originality, and allowing children to retain ownership of their artwork.

Process Over Product

The Greek philosopher Aristotle once said that "The aim of art is to represent not the outward appearance of things, but their inward significance; for this . . . is true reality." When children are pushed to make their work represent the superficial aspects of an object or experience, product is being emphasized. The most common type of product requires children to color cute pictures neatly in designated areas, cut out predetermined shapes on the lines, paste them on paper in some preordained way, and take the result home to decorate a refrigerator door. Activities like these communicate the message that children's original artwork is not valued and that their art processes are inferior to adults'.

Originality Over Conformity

Stan overheard his second-grade teacher saying that she needed an art activity that would combine Flag Day and Valentine's Day. Stan invented a new kind of

Authentic art experiences emphasize the process, value, originality, and allow children to retain ownership of their artwork.

flag. Instead of using stars to represent the states, Stan used red hearts on a white background. For this 8-year-old, the flag was an original activity. But if the teacher requires every child in the class to copy Stan's idea, she is demanding conformity rather than encouraging originality. As stated so clearly by Alfred North Whitehead (1954): "Art flourishes where there is a sense of adventure, a sense of nothing having been done before, of complete freedom to experiment; but when caution comes in you get repetition, and repetition is the death of art" (p. 55).

Authentic art activities encourage different responses from each child; they celebrate uniqueness. The goal of art is to break stereotypes rather than to perpetuate them. Art is not coloring pages and following the dots; art is not a hand-traced turkey for Thanksgiving, a tree that looks like a lollipop, or a square-plus-triangle house. If it isn't original, it isn't art.

Children Retain Ownership

Children retain ownership of their artwork when they (1) choose their own ideas or subject matter, (2) have the freedom to express their ideas in their own way, and (3) have the right to organize their art in their own way (Jefferson, 1963). In child-centered classrooms, children are given the latitude to use many different art media. The goal is not to compete and make comparisons between and among children by singling out one child's work (or the teacher's model) as the standard for all to follow.

Ms. Romick decided to make fairy tale character puppets with her first-grade class. She used plastic eggs, cotton, yarn, fabric, and stick-on plastic eyes. First, she cut out the fabric and arranged all of the materials. Next, she showed the class pictures of puppets to copy. When it was time for the children to assemble the puppets, she spent most of her time wiping up glue and finishing the puppets for them. If teachers plan activities that depend more on their work than on the children's, it is a sign that children are being robbed of ownership. It is also an indication that the experience is developmentally inappropriate for the children. The child artist, no less than the adult artist, must have autonomy.

Understanding Children's Art

When we speak about art, we are talking about something that is perceptual, cognitive, developmental, and graphic. Consider Figure 3.1, an original picture book by Vickie, a first grader, whose mother is expecting a baby. Vickie's original picture book reveals her understandings and feelings about this important event.

Artistic responses are *perceptual* because artists of any age must be keenly aware of sensory input. It is clear from Vickie's story that she is aware of the changes in her mother's body. This leads to the second characteristic of art, its *cognitive* or intellectual aspect. When Vickie forms symbols, she must know the material (in this case, the media of paper and crayons), know the referent (in this case, the mother and baby), and use that material/medium to express something about that referent (in this case, original drawing and writing).

Vickie's art is also *developmental*, meaning that as she matures and gains experience, her art changes along with her. Drawings created by 6-year-olds are distinctively different from the scribbles produced by toddlers, for example. A drawing by a primary grade child typically resembles what it represents and includes many details—a reflection of an emerging sense of realism.

Vickie's art is also *graphic*, meaning that it is a representation and an interpretation of her reality. Her depiction of the hospital, her pregnant mother, and the new baby shows that she is learning the techniques necessary to give form to her feelings, ideas, and experiences. Those techniques include color, line, arrangement, proportion, and placement.

Developmental Sequence

Several researchers have described the sequence of children's artistic development in considerable detail (Kellogg 1979; Lowenfeld & Brittain, 1947). In more general terms, children's art may be categorized as *nonrepresentational*, meaning that it does not look like the item being represented, or *representational*, meaning that it does resemble the item being depicted. These stages correspond roughly to two stages in writing: prealphabetic (scribbles, shapes, mock letters) and alphabetic (writing that looks like letters of the alphabet). Figure 3.2 summarizes the sequence of artistic development.

Children also progress through three distinct roles in artistic growth (Gardner, 1982)

❑ *Child as direct communicator* (birth–2). The child communicates directly through body movements, such as enjoying the medium of fingerpaint and observing the effects of different hand movements on the patterns on the paper.

❑ *Child as symbol user* (2–7). The child learns to communicate through symbols, using one thing to represent another. A scribble might represent all of the child's sensory impressions of an experience with a cat— sandpapery tongue, beautiful fur, the sound of its purr, and its playfulness.

❑ *Youth as craftsman* (7–11). This stage corresponds to the industry vs. inferiority stage of Erikson's psychosocial theory. The child seeks to build competence by undertaking a wide variety of more complex art activities. Crafts such as toymaking, woodworking, painting with acrylics or oils, and making ceramic items or holiday decorative items are all common during this stage.

Principles of Art Education

In addition to these understandings about children's artistic development, there are contemporary theories about art education. One such curriculum model is

FIGURE 3.1   Vickie's Book

a.

b.

c.

d.

discipline-based art education (Getty Center for Education in the Arts, 1985). Basically, this approach contends that there are three goals of art education: (1) creating, (2) understanding, and (3) appreciating. Achieving these purposes is based upon the following four bodies of knowledge (Brutger, 1987):

1. *Art production* goals include making original works of art, learning to use different materials to express an idea or concept, learning art processes and techniques, and identifying with the role of artist. Some examples of art production activities suitable for young children are visiting a potter's studio to see what pottery looks like at various stages in its production, watching a Native American crafting jewelry, observing a weaver spinning yarn into cloth, and interviewing a craftsperson who makes musical instruments.

2. *Art history* goals involve classifying and extending works of art as they exist in time. For young children, art history is the story behind a work

FIGURE 3.1 *continued*

now it's ready
to be born

We went to the
hospital to wate for it to
be born

e.

f.

and it was born

it was so tiny

g.

h.

of art and discussions about art. When a primary grade teacher gives-children who have enjoyed many picture books by particular artists the opportunity to learn about their lives and work through the Weston Woods film series profiling them, the teacher is supporting the art history goal.

3. *Art criticism* goals encourage children to search out the meaning of the work, relate meaning to artistic style, and make judgments about works of art. A classroom example of art criticism is selecting the best ways to display art (e.g., with or without a frame, on a bulletin board, suspended from the ceiling).

4. *Aesthetic* goals refer to the appreciation and interpretation of art objects and awareness of art elements in the environment. The teacher who shares picture books about colors like *Mouse Paint* (Walsh, 1989), *Colors and Things* (Hoban, 1989) or *Color Zoo* (Ehlert, 1989) and then invites

FIGURE 3.2   Development of Art Skills

NONREPRESENTATIONAL/SCRIBBLING STAGE

Approximate Age: 2–3 years
Art Skills: Explores media through all the senses
Makes random marks on paper
Begins scribbling

FIGURE 3.2 *continued*

NONREPRESENTATIONAL/SCRIBBLING STAGE

Approximate Age: 3 years

Art Skills: Explores and manipulates materials

Makes scribbles on top of each other

Scribbles are more controlled

May cover paper with layers of color

Process, not product, is important to child

FIGURE 3.2 *continued*

NONREPRESENTATIONAL/SCRIBBLING STAGE

Approximate Age: 3–4 years
Art Skills: Scribbling stage continues
Perceives shapes in work
Attempts to make shapes
Often names scribbles

---

children to go in search of these colors on a "color walk" is supporting the goal of aesthetics.

How Children Learn Through Art

The National Art Education Association (1973) has identified nine types of learning that can be promoted through quality art programs:

1. *Examining intensively both natural and artificial objects from many sources.* Mr. Petit, a kindergarten teacher, has a collection of ceramic, wood,

FIGURE 3.2 *continued*

EMERGING REPRESENTATIONAL

Approximate Age: 4–5 years

Art Skills: Combines two shapes, often a circle and a cross, to make mandalas
Draws "suns"
Represents humans as a circle with arms and legs, a "tadpole" person
Figures appear to float on the page
Art is used to represent feelings and ideas

FIGURE 3.2 *continued*

REPRESENTATIONAL

Approximate Age: 6−8 years
Art Skills: Child's art clearly resembles whatever it represents
Baseline begins to appear in drawings
More preplanning and inclusion of details
Child strives to master various art skills and begins to evaluate own work
Work tends to be more realistic in terms of proportion and arrangement

---

metal, plastic, and fabric elephants. When he brought the collection to school, the children had an opportunity to see a carved wooden elephant from India, a stuffed toy of the storybook character Babar, and a ceramic elephant bank, to name a few. In this way, the children were able to examine these objects closely and to compare and contrast the various depictions of elephants with photographs of the actual animals.

2. *Expressing individual ideas and feelings through the use of various art media suited to the developmental level and expressive needs of children.* When a teacher provides large sheets of moistened paper and fingerpaints for young children, that teacher is providing materials that are well suited to their developmental level. Most preschoolers do nonrepresentational art, meaning that they are interested in the feel of the materials (e.g., swirling the paint with a brush), in expressing their emotions (e.g., pounding clay when they are angry), and in expressing real and imaginary images (e.g., using color, line, and shape to represent "monsterness" rather than drawing a monster). If the teacher invites children to try some different hand movements (i.e., with palms, fingertips, fists, and forearms), they have many opportunities to express themselves through an artistic medium. Older children may plan a design and become very deliberate and controlled in their use of color, form, and line to develop a particular composition.

3. *Experimenting in depth with art materials and processes to determine their effectiveness in creating new forms.* When a second-grade teacher invites his students to make a gift collage, it results in extensive experimentation with materials. Cellina makes a collage that characterizes her mother's personality. She begins with a scrap of fabric in "country" colors over a piece of cardboard, then adds lace, dried flowers, an old snapshot, and ribbon. As Cellina searches for other materials and figures out how to arrange and fasten them, she is creating a new form.

4. *Working with tools appropriate to the child's abilities and developing skills needed for satisfying aesthetic expression.* Beginning teachers are sometimes surprised to encounter preschoolers who do not know how to cut with scissors. Rather than insisting that all children begin using scissors immediately, skillful teachers give children options such as tearing paper, cutting pieces of modeling dough rolled thin, tearing at the paper with scissors, resting the scissors on the desk while cutting, and making simple cuts (e.g., a paper fringe) (Schirrmacher, 1988). A skilled teacher also knows that it is too difficult for young children to cut out small interior spaces (such as the eye holes for a mask), partly because they need pointed scissors to do the job and partly because their efforts to puncture the paper can result in injury. Teachers also wait until children have gained experience with scissors before expecting them to cut on lines or to use special equipment such as pinking shears, which must be kept at a right angle to the fabric in order to function properly.

5. *Organizing, evaluating, and reorganizing works-in-process to gain an understanding of line, form, color, and texture in space.* One way of glimpsing young children's thinking about art is to encourage them to talk as they work with materials and listen to what they say. Listen to Lynn, a 4-year-old who is drawing a picture for her sister. She explains her selection of materials as follows: "Crayons make fat lines I do not want; pencils with colors are 'thins' that make pretty pictures." By listening to Lynn, we can better understand how she is thinking about her work-

in-process, and how she will go about selecting art materials and art elements that will best enable her to express her ideas.

6. *Looking at, reading about, and discussing a variety of works of art;* as well as

7. *Seeing artists produce art in a studio, workshop, or film studio.* Every community offers examples of sculpture, constructions, architecture, industrial products, and handcrafted products. Four residents of the senior center (which meets in the same building as the county-supported after-school care program) are making a quilt for the church bazaar. When Mr. Donlevy learns of this, he invites the women to talk with the children. On the first visit, the ladies develop the concept that a quilt can tell a story. They show the children several actual quilts, as well as examples in quilt pattern books. Next, the ladies share their plans and pattern for the quilt and give each child a small scrap of fabric to keep. Mr. Donlevy uses educational media to extend and enrich the project, including several picture books about quilts—*The Quilt* (Jonas, 1989), *Quilt Story* (Johnston, 1984), and *The Patchwork Quilt* (Flournoy, 1985)—and excerpts from a movie about quilting borrowed from the library. On the second visit, the ladies demonstrate how a quilt is put together. The children learn about stitching, appliques, polyester fiberfill, and a quilting frame. On the third visit, a portion of the quilt is done and a piece is added while the children observe closely. On the fourth and final visit, the ladies show the children a completed quilt and donate a tiny quilt for the baby's crib in the housekeeping corner. Through this simple project, children have looked at, discussed, and directly experienced folk art using educational media and community resources.

8. *Evaluating art of both students and mature artists, as well as industrial products, home designs, and community designs.* As part of a unit on consumer education, a group of third-grade students decides to compare and contrast the features of three pieces of educational print shop software. They establish a rating sheet for the product, including the quality and variety of the pictures available and the number of different tasks possible (i.e., banner, invitation, greeting card, or letterhead). They compile their data and then, using published software reviews as a guide, write a critique for each product. In this way, the children have gained first-hand experience in evaluation of industrial/technical products.

9. *Engaging in activities that provide opportunities to apply art knowledge and aesthetics to judgment in personal life and in home or community planning.* Ms. Sandstrom has decided that her second-grade classroom needs to be rearranged to accommodate and display some of the students' new projects. One of these projects is a scale model of their main street, because they have been studying simple maps. Rather than reorganizing the room herself after school, she uses this task as an opportunity to build the children's aesthetic judgment. She makes a scale model of the classroom on separate pieces of colored overhead transparencies. The children experiment with many different room arrangements by shifting

the items around on the overhead projector until they decide on the best classroom layout.

Learning About Art

Six-year-old Twila understands how the artwork of others invites us to think and to respond in individual ways. When the teacher asks the children what Van Gogh might be trying to tell us in his painting "Sunflowers," Twila remarks: "It depends on when you see the picture; one picture can mean different things." Henrik, a 5-year-old, has figured out what a painter does: "First, they see their think; then they paint it." Both of these children are developing their vocabularies of art and learning how to discuss art.

Developing a Vocabulary of Art

Developing a child's vocabulary of art involves three things:

1. *Encouraging children to discuss the artwork first in ordinary language.* If children discuss art in their own words first, this permits equal sharing of adult and child perceptions. Five-year-old children who examined a large, colorful book of American artist Mary Cassatt's paintings made interesting observations such as "She must like little kids" and "The pictures look soft." By allowing children to make these observations first, the teacher can follow their lead, briefly presenting facts about the artist's life ("Deidra was right; Mary Cassatt was a mother, and she did love little children. Sometimes she used her own children as models for her paintings"). Teachers might ask questions such as: "What could an artist do to lines to make the picture 'look soft,' as Harrold said? Let's try to make some pictures that way, pictures without dark lines, ones that look softer."

2. *Introducing the vocabulary in context.* If children use new words in conjunction with direct experience, they are more likely to make the words part of their active vocabulary. When Jenny's mother demonstrated her cake-decorating talents to second graders, they used the words *thick, thin, food coloring, pastry bag,* and all of the names for the different metal tips used. They examined a real rose, talked about its parts (petals, leaves), and then watched her create icing roses on the cake. Finally, the children had an opportunity to decorate a cupcake using the pastry tips, techniques, and colors of their choice.

3. *Using accurate, appropriate vocabulary.* Teachers need to provide new vocabulary words quickly and unobtrusively so that they underscore the child's experience rather than impose the teacher's opinions (Dixon & Chalmers, 1990). This may explain why young children tend to prefer abstract works of art to realistic ones; abstract works allow children to suggest a wider range of interpretations for the same work (Bowker & Sawyers, 1988).

Simple materials like cornstarch and water can build the art vocabulary of preschoolers. The recipe for cornstarch and water is simple: 2 cups of warm water plus 3 cups of cornstarch, mixed with the hands (Clemens, 1991). What makes the material interesting is that it is solid when it is left standing but turns to liquid when handled. Rather than simply mixing it and making it available, teachers can turn the experience into an art vocabulary lesson. First, let the children handle the dry cornstarch and describe it. Words like *powder, smooth,* and *silky* may be introduced here. Then, add a little of the warm water and ask the children for descriptors. Words like *lumpy* and *thick* may be introduced here. Next, invite children to hold a chunk of it and watch its transformation from solid to liquid. Add the rest of the water and make statements like "Let your fingers drift down. Try to punch your way down. How do your hands feel now?" Leave the mixture overnight, add water again to watch it change from liquid to solid, and practice the new vocabulary in context again.

"Building a vocabulary of art is important because [we] sometimes take it for granted that children who do not respond verbally are incapable of appreciation or criticism, when in fact they may not have the appropriate words to discuss their own work and involvement or the work of others. Without being able to draw easily on a descriptive vocabulary, children are frequently unwilling to enter into a discussion" (Dixon & Chalmers, 1990, p. 16).

Ways of Discussing Art

In early childhood programs that support children's development in art, young children not only create original art, they respond to the art of others. Figure 3.3 is an overview of discussion strategies to be used in discussing works of art and art reproductions.

Understanding children's artistic development, the role of art in promoting meaningful self-expression, and the basic principles of a high-quality art education are essential to a well-balanced early childhood curriculum. Skillful teachers have learned to use the arts not as an afterthought or add-on, but as a basic foundation of the developmentally appropriate early childhood curriculum.

Critical Issues in Teaching Art

Phyllis is a 5-year-old who has just started kindergarten. One day she comes home from school looking distraught. She bursts into tears, reaches into her pocket, and takes out a tissue with a broken crayon wrapped inside. It seems that the teacher had been especially harsh in cautioning the children about taking care of school supplies and not breaking the crayons. Phyllis knew she had committed the unpardonable sin—"pressing too hard." To avoid punishment, she had resorted to concealing it. Phyllis' experience illustrates how important it is for an art program to (1) respect and encourage children's efforts, (2) give children time to explore and to develop control and sensitivity to materials, and (3) give children independent access to materials (Clemens, 1991).

FIGURE 3.3   Strategies for Discussing Works of Art

Sources for Art and Art Reproductions
Children's picture books, prints of famous works of art borrowed from the library, picture postcards of art, walls of a local gallery, an artist's studio, a display of children's work in a public building, a museum exhibit, a university, slides, art history books, encyclopedias, film.

Types of Questions

Questions on aesthetics: Look at the lines on your paper. On the ceiling. Can you find other lines? Thin lines? Thick lines?

Questions on art criticism: Here are pictures of some famous buildings in the world. If you could choose one to be built in our town, which one would it be? Why?

Questions about art history: Which of these sculptures was made a long time ago? Why do you think so?

Questions on art production: What are some ways artists can make their pictures look smooth? rough?

Questions About a Work of Art

What is this work of art?

What is it made from?

What is the most interesting thing about this work of art?

What is the artist trying to tell us?

Is there a story here? What is it?

Does the artist suggest new ways of seeing things?

How does the work make you feel? Why?

What does it make you think of?

What did the artist use (medium, techniques, tools, methods of organization, effects, composition)?

How is this the same as (or different from) other pieces you have seen? By this artist? By other artists?

What makes a work of art great?

What makes an artist great?

Do you like this work of art? Why or why not?

Source: Adapted from Herberholz (1974) and Rowe (1987).

Selecting and Presenting Materials and Experiences

Although the ownership of art should rest with the child, teachers do have a responsibility to demonstrate the appropriate use of materials. Take, for example, painting at the easel (Herberholz, 1974). When children first begin using paints, a teacher might present the basic concepts of using protective clothing, putting the brush back in the same color, and cleaning up after painting. As they

This is a CAR

made by NiCHAPI

Displaying children's art is one way of respecting and encouraging children's efforts.

gain some experience, the teacher could present the strategy of wiping each side of the brush on the rim of the paint container to avoid drips and grasping the brush with the fingers (rather than the fist) above the metal rim, which increases the child's control over the brush. Next, the teacher could show children how to avoid smearing by letting one color dry before putting wet paint over or very close to it, how to use different-sized brushes for different purposes (narrow/pointed for details, wide/flat for large areas), and how to rinse brushes in cool water and store them with the bristles up. As children gain experience with paints in the primary grades, they can be taught different brush strokes or how to sketch before painting.

Evaluating Materials and Experiences

Walk down the hall of an elementary school, look at children's artwork, and you will see a definite trend. In kindergarten and first grade, there is a freshness and spontaneity to children's work. Most kindergartners and first graders will tackle nearly any illustration challenge—a suspension bridge, a giraffe, or a trailer court. By second or third grade, however, many children have begun to trace and copy rather than create their own drawings. One student teacher even reported that a girl in her class began to cry when a classmate wouldn't share a picture book so that she could trace it too. This is what happens when adults push children in art by comparing, correcting, and making excessive value judgments. Children take the safe route of making their picture look like someone else's rather than creating a new form.

It is particularly important, then, to avoid singling out art that looks like something and identifying it as the only good artwork. When adults do this, children lose confidence in themselves and resort to stereotypes, such as drawing stick figures. A much better strategy is to simply say to the child, "Tell me about your painting." If a 4-year-old says, "I painted it at the easel and the paint ran down the page. Red is my favorite color," then the teacher can reply, "Yes, I see that bright color red. How does red make you feel?"

In many ways, the process of supporting children's art is similar to that of supporting their efforts in writing (Rowe, 1987). Just as teachers maintain a portfolio of children's writing efforts, they should keep a folder of children's artistic efforts. One-dimensional art can be filed or copied for inclusion in the folder, while three-dimensional art such as sculpture or puppets can be photographed.

As teachers, we know we are providing quality art materials and experiences when

- ☐ Children use art materials and request specific materials.
- ☐ Children confidently accept new challenges in art.
- ☐ Children pursue art activities during free time at home and at school.
- ☐ Children express positive attitudes toward art and artistic abilities during class discussions.

Teachers' Roles and Responsibilities

Teachers must do more than go through the motions of offering art; they must fully appreciate its value. One classroom teacher expressed it this way:

> I offer children artwork as a preventive measure, a benign alternative to letting them express themselves in destructive ways. I offer them art because they love it. I offer them art because it makes my survival in the classroom more likely. What we hear from the worst people in our field is that you have to control children, you have to make them behave. The best people will tell you that if you give children interesting choices, your class, home or life will run more smoothly. For all these reasons, art takes a prominent place in my daily class. (Clemens, 1991, p. 4)

Sadly, some teachers miss out on the rich contributions of art to the curriculum. They may rely entirely on work disguised as art or, if they teach in an elementary school, they may delegate all of the responsibility for teaching art to the art teacher. The outcome of both behaviors is that art is further segregated from the child's total life experience. Treating art as a second-class subject contradicts what we know about the holistic learning processes of young children.

Establishing Rules and Limits

As explained in the case study at the beginning of this chapter, teachers sometimes go to one extreme or the other with art, either being excessively controlling or completely laissez-faire. Ideally, teachers should establish rules and limits that enable children to get the most from their art experiences. Figure 3.4 is a suggested list of classroom management considerations in art (Schirrmacher, 1988).

Talking with Children About Their Art

As we have seen, children's drawings may be broadly categorized as nonrepresentational or representational (Kellogg, 1979). Both types of art are authentic means of self-expression. Consider, for example, 2-year-old Katie's drawing of Kirstie, a border collie. She likes to curl up with the dog while they look at a book together. Maybe Katie's scribble goes beyond the visual image that she has of the dog and represents the softness of the animal's fur or the pleasurable feeling of being surrounded by warmth and closeness. The adult who remarks "Very good, but what happened to the dog's tail?" or demands "What is it?" fails to appreciate young children's early forms of artistic expression. The answer, of course, is that it isn't supposed to be anything! Sometimes, children are simply exploring an artistic medium—for example, the sensory pleasure of squishing clay into different shapes or gliding a crayon across the page.

Generally speaking, it is best to rely on artistic elements when discussing art with very young children. You could comment on color ("Look at all that yellow,

FIGURE 3.4   Establishing Rules and Limits in Early Childhood Art Programs

1. Decide upon a few important general rules rather than many insignificant specific rules.
2. Limit the number of children at a center at any one time. This avoids disputes over materials and accidental damage to a child's work caused by overcrowding.
3. Impress upon children the need to wear protective clothing. Provide smocks, aprons, or simply a man's old shirt worn backward with the sleeves rolled up.
4. Teach children how to use and care for art tools, such as rinsing paint brushes, putting the lid on paste, and returning materials to their original location when finished.
5. Model for children the importance of conserving materials and using only what they need. You could give them a dab of white glue on an old margarine tub lid, for example, rather than the whole bottle.
6. Teach children to share supplies and respect others. Model for children asking rather than grabbing ("May I use the stapler next?", "Are you finished with the pink play dough?"). Discuss with children the importance of accepting the art activities of other children.
7. Rather than simply announcing "time to clean up," demonstrate how children are supposed to clean up after each art activity.

Source: Adapted from Schirrmacher (1988).

Ishaka!"), on arrangement ("Lester, you covered the whole page with paint."), texture ("This clay feels smooth now that you rolled it out."), line ("I see the interesting patterns you made with the toothpick and paint on your paper, Claudia."), or shape ("Stevie and Alexei made lots of small, round bubbles. Kerri and Man-Li made one big, long bubble."). For older children who are creating representational art, it is best to follow the child's lead. You might begin by saying, "Tell me about your picture" and then relate subsequent comments to whatever the child says.

Locating Resources and Storing Materials

Few teachers have the luxury of purchasing whatever art materials they please. More often, it is a matter of making choices among many possible alternatives. Materials such as paints, paper, crayons, clay, and wood are usually referred to as *consumable* because they need to be replenished constantly. Often when budgets are tight, the focus is on *nonconsumables,* materials that need replacement less often. Many times, adults are not particularly unhappy to see these messy materials go. But these art materials are a basic means of self-expression and are something that children should have access to every day. Rather than eliminating them altogether, teachers need to be creative problem solvers and seek out art materials wherever they can find them. An added bonus to this approach is that it teaches children the value of responsible recycling.

Art materials should do the following:

Extend Children's Experience. In order to foster creative expression, children need to learn the same elements of design and the principles of design understood by artists. Naturally, it is important that these be presented in developmentally appropriate ways. Figure 3.5 suggests activities that can be used to extend children's experience with design elements and principles.

Be Plentiful. To acquire an ample supply of free paper, all you need to do is find an office and recycle. Newspaper printers will sometimes give away the ends of paper rolls, and wrapping paper from gifts can be saved by everyone in the class. For special papers, make contact with a printer who prints stationery and invitations or a local frame shop. Another way to achieve greater variety in classroom resources is to send home a list at the beginning of the year asking for such things as sewing and craft materials (buttons, trim, pieces of fabric, yarn, and ribbon) and throwaway materials that can be put to another use (plastic bottle caps, detergent bottles, food containers, six-pack holder rings, or foil cannisters of various sizes).

Be Accessible. It is important for children to use materials when they wish, rather than being completely dependent upon the adult for access to them. Be alert to inexpensive or throwaway materials that can be put to another use. An old microwave cart, divided trays, or a lazy susan can all give access to many different materials, keep them organized, and make the collection mobile. One

FIGURE 3.5   Activities to Extend Children's Experiences with Design

ELEMENTS OF DESIGN

Line   *Preschool*—Use an overhead projector to illustrate basic types of lines: fat/thin, straight/curvy, zigzag, wavy. Let children experiment with paint brushes of various widths and markers with different point styles (e.g., chisel point, fine point) to create different lines.

Primary—Use calligraphy markers with special tips (e.g., double, triple, thick and thin) to identify different types of lines; invite children to use the markers to create signs, cards, and bulletin boards. Use cartoon characters to illustrate how a few lines (e.g., mouth, eyebrows) can change the facial expression.

Color   *Preschool*—Use Easter egg dye or food coloring to identify and match primary colors.

Primary—Mix white with colors to form pastels; mix black with colors to darken them. Create a secondary colors wheel through experimentation with color mixing. Use paint samples to arrange primary and secondary colors by hues.

Shape   *Preschool*—Identify basic shapes (circle, square, rectangle, triangle, diamond), read several picture books about shapes and search for examples of those shapes in the environment (e.g., the top of a drum is a circle, a box is a square or rectangle, a sandwich turned sideways and cut diagonally is a diamond and a triangle).

Primary—Help children to discover the properties of less familiar shapes (e.g., using lengths of yarn to create polygons or blocks to create trapezoids). Differentiate between one-dimensional and three-dimensional shapes (e.g., cylinders, pyramids).

Space   *Preschool*—Provide flexible materials, such as collage, and encourage children to experiment before deciding upon a use of space. Give children real experiences in organizing space, such as planning a new arrangement of the housekeeping area on the chalkboard, then rearranging the furniture.

Primary—Invite children to analyze the works of their favorite picture book illustrators in terms of the use of space. Have children categorize the techniques (e.g., words and illustrations on the facing page; illustrations at the top, words at the bottom; words and illustrations interspersed throughout the page).

Texture   *Preschool*—Use real objects, such as the vegetables to be used in cooking or material scraps from an upholsterer, and invite children to describe the textures of each. Experiment with ways of altering the texture of art materials (e.g., adding sawdust to clay, daubing paint on instead of spreading it on).

Primary—Examine the texture of artwork at a museum, in a gallery, or in a schoolwide display of student artwork. Invite children to create a work of art with textural interest.

FIGURE 3.5   *continued*

PRINCIPLES OF DESIGN

Emphasis   *Preschool*—Use several works of art with a clear focal point and ask children: "Where does your eye go first?"

Primary—Ask children to analyze the use of the two-page spread in picture books. How is it used to emphasize something important to the story? Invite children to create original picture books that have a clear emphasis.

Rhythm   *Preschool*—Use unit blocks or plastic beads to develop the concept of a repeated design.

Primary—Using a microcomputer, invite each child to create a repeated design. Children can use their vocabularies of art to describe each one. Using a wallpaper catalog and/or samples, evaluate the rhythm of the designs and compare how often the patterns are repeated.

Balance   *Preschool*—Use flannel shapes on the flannel board to illustrate dramatically the concept of balance in design. Begin with all of the figures piled up at one end; then invite children to come up and create more visually appealing arrangements.

Primary—Develop the concept of symmetry through the use of paper shapes with identical sides cut from folded paper. Use catalogs and magazines to locate fashions and home decorating ideas that illustrate symmetrical and asymmetrical arrangements. Invite children to find examples of balanced designs at home, in books, in storefront displays, and in architecture.

Contrast   *Preschool*—Use photo negatives and the contrast button on the black and white setting of a television set to illustrate the concept of contrast. Make high-contrast pictures using black, white, and gray.

Primary—Present children with several art prints and ask them to categorize them into one of five high-contrast groups: works that use light and dark dramatically, works that use contrasting sizes, works that use contrasting shapes, works that contrast textures, and works that contrast colors. Challenge children to create a high-contrast picture, sculpture, pottery, or fabric.

Proportion   *Preschool*—Use familiar folktales, such as "The Three Bears" and "The Three Billy Goats Gruff" to develop the concept of relative sizes.

Primary—Create illustrated books of comparisons (e.g., big, bigger, biggest); look at grocery store products for words to describe sizes, such as eggs or laundry detergents.

Source: Based upon the Department of Defense Dependents Schools (DODDS) Visual Arts Program Guidelines, Scope and Sequence for Kindergarten–2nd Grade (ERIC Document Reproduction Service No. ED 291 641).

teacher went to a hospital sale and purchased several metal wheeled carts with low, wide shelves that he used to store his art materials; another scavenged a discontinued makeup display from a drugstore that enabled her to hang up children's paintings on hooks.

Be Age-Appropriate.   When a mother volunteered to work in her son Jaime's Head Start classroom, both she and the teacher were surprised to observe the boy take the paper off the easel and put it on newspaper on the floor to paint. Apparently, Jaime's only experience with painting was on a horizontal rather than a vertical surface. This child's behavior illustrates why it is so important to accept children's efforts rather than impose an adult perspective. If the mother had appeared embarrassed or the teacher had reprimanded Jaime, he might have avoided using the materials. But because they both watched and listened, they were gradually able to extend Jaime's experience to painting at an easel.

In providing age-appropriate experiences, it is important to consider whether the child can complete the artwork without excessive adult interference. If the teacher has to draw, cut out, or assemble things *for* the child, then it is not an age-appropriate activity.

Be of High Quality.   As the poet Walter de la Mare once observed, only the rarest and best kind of anything is good enough for the very young. Sometimes tempera paint is thinned to save money, but it is so runny that children have difficulty controlling it. It is better to use a paint extender/thickener, following this recipe:

Powdered Paint Extender
1 cup Bentonite
½ cup Ivory Snow (flakes)
2 quarts warm water

Mix the ingredients well and let them stand in a large jar for about 3 days. Stir the mixture each day. The mixture is jelly-like and can be thinned to the desired consistency. Mix it with water and add powdered paint when you are ready to use it (Clemens, 1991).

Adults sometimes insist that children use crayons rather than markers, but young children often prefer the bright color and control of a water-based marker. True, markers are expensive and can easily be ruined by leaving the caps off or pressing too firmly. But rather than ruling them out, teachers need to demonstrate their use and care. One way to help children with the task of putting on the caps is to make a marker stand by sinking the caps into a lump of wet plaster of paris or clay so that children can recap the markers with one movement (Clemens, 1991).

Displaying Children's Art

Some general guidelines for displaying children's art include placing the work at children's eye level where they can enjoy it, rotating art regularly, and utilizing a variety of spaces—not just walls or bulletin boards, but also cardboard box panels, doors, windows, shelves, and display cases. Frames for children's art can be colored paper, Styrofoam meat trays, plastic microwave food trays, plastic coffee can lids, or boxes and lids of every description. Figure 3.6 presents two pieces of framed art: a picture of three imaginary characters by Sharon Lynn

FIGURE 3.6   Examples of Framed Art

Robin Hood and his horse by Justin, age 5

Three imaginary characters by Sharon Lynn, age 6

(age 6) and a picture of Robin Hood by Justin (age 5). With older children, you may want to develop an art gallery of their framed art, tape-record children's descriptions of their art, or even make a walking tour tape similar to that in a museum.

Remember, displaying art is for everybody, not just the small percentage of children who will become professional artists someday. Rather than functioning as talent scouts who single out only a few pieces of children's work to be displayed, teachers should recognize every child's efforts at self-expression. It is important to respect children's wishes to take their work home and display it there too. Children should be permitted to take their work home immediately or at least within a reasonable period of time. Teachers who care about children's art make sure that the paint is dry before rolling up the picture or, if the art is three-dimensional, plan a way for the child to safely transport the item home. Clean, recycled milk cartons with the lids cut off are good carriers for clay creations, for example.

Child-Centered Art Experiences

The three major considerations in selecting child-centered art experiences are (1) letting children direct their own work, (2) valuing the process more than the product, and (3) encouraging originality rather than conformity. The next section offers several examples of child-centered activities in art.

Paper

Some art activities with paper include the following:

Picture Making

Young children can create pictures with crayons, paints, markers, torn paper of various colors, and colored pencils on large pieces of paper. Primary grade children can use materials that are more difficult to control, such as water colors, and nonwashable colors such as oil pastel crayons, oil paint, or ink. As children gain greater control over their drawing, they can experiment with drawing on different types of paper, such as a mural taped to the wall, tiny cartoon-style pictures on strips of adding machine tape, or pictures drawn on paper plates. You may want to try a pass-it-on picture, in which each child draws something, then turns it over to another child, and so forth, until the picture is complete. Arranging bits of paper into a unified design offers children another opportunity to explore with paper. Generally speaking, preschoolers use larger pieces of paper, while primary grade children have developed the skill and patience to work with smaller, mosaic-like pieces.

Print Making

Preschool children can make simple prints by dipping objects (a bolt, the heel from an old shoe, a plastic cap, Styrofoam shapes) into thin tempera paint and stamping them on paper. Primary grade children can create stamps or gift wrap or monograms by cutting and gluing pieces of Styrofoam or rubber into interesting shapes and using a stamp pad or sponge moistened with tempera. Even very young children can create "marble track pictures." Get an empty paper box and put one sheet of construction paper in the bottom. The child drops a marble dunked in tempera paint into the box and gently rolls it around until the pattern looks pleasing. Children can do crayon rubbing prints by placing a leaf under a sheet of paper and rubbing it with a crayon. Kindergarten or primary grade children can create splatter prints by taping an item to a sheet of paper and dragging a toothbrush dipped in paint over a piece of screen in front of it to create an outline.

Local Art

Use your community resources to give children experiences with art exhibits. In addition to art museums, art exhibits can be seen at shopping malls, colleges, banks and brokerage houses, and many other public buildings. One local chamber of commerce used elementary children's winter scenes to enhance their holiday luncheon. The framed pieces were then transferred to a nearby mall, where everyone in the community could appreciate the winter art for an entire month.

Paper Sculpture

In three-dimensional art with paper, children can experiment with glue and paper and learn simple paper folding (origami). Young children might create hats out of paper. Older children can learn some basic paper sculpture techniques, browse through books illustrating paper sculpture, and watch a person who knows origami demonstrate these skills.

Sculpture and Pottery

Modeling materials such as clay or plasticine are standard items in schools because they introduce children to the basics of sculpting and pottery design. Because these materials are flexible, pliable, and open-ended, they also enable children to start again as they create and re-create using the same material.

Clay

If possible, give children the experiences of digging their own clay out of the earth, seeing a pottery wheel in use, or seeing clay items fired in a kiln. Often these experiences can be arranged in a high school or college art department or at a commercial crafts store.

Wood Sculptures

Children can use scraps of wood, white glue, and a hammer and nails to create three-dimensional wood sculpture. These unified, balanced designs can be fixed (stabiles) or movable (mobiles). Encourage children's inventiveness by adding other materials such as tongue depressors, cotton swabs, toothpicks, popsicle sticks, or milled wooden wheels that can be affixed with one nail and are available from early childhood art supply companies.

Fabric

Textiles include such things as sewing, dyeing, and weaving fabrics.

Sewing

Even preschoolers can begin sewing with plastic needles threaded with yarn if the material being stitched is easy to work with. Squares of burlap or felt with holes punched in them are good materials for early experiences with sewing. Most first graders can stitch various designs on heavy cloth with yarn and work together to create a wall hanging or individually to create a bookmark. With adult supervision, second and third graders can design simple stuffed toy pillows, first on paper, then on fabric. After an adult volunteer stitches the outline on a sewing machine, the children can stuff the toy and stitch the opening closed.

Dyeing

To give children experiences in dyeing fabric using the ancient art of color resist, follow this procedure:

> **Paste Batik**
>
> Mix in a blender:
> ½ cup flour
> ½ cup water
> 2 teaspoons alum

Pour the mixture into squeeze bottles (discarded plastic shampoo or squeeze mustard bottles work well). Tape pieces (8 × 10 inches) of an old white sheet to corrugated cardboard and let children "draw" pictures using the squeeze bottles. Paint the pictures with food dye or deep watercolor wash and let them dry. Remove the paste mixture by chipping and rubbing it off.

Weaving

After children have mastered the under-over aspect of weaving with strips of paper, they can begin weaving with cloth or yarn. Pieces of heavy yarn or string tied to a frame of popsicle sticks can serve as the loom. Plastic rings from a six-pack of soft drink cans can be joined together with yarn, twist ties, or pieces of pipe cleaner. When connected together this way and used by the class as the frame for weaving strips of cloth, these recycled materials become a wall hanging.

Integrating Art Into the Subject Areas

Media and Technology

When children draw on blank slides and then show them on a projector, put on a light show, create puppets and a stage to perform a play, use film, or create imaginative pictures on the computer, they are exploring the media/technology aspect of art.

Ms. Karen's class of 5-year-olds created peep-face boards for their improvised versions of favorite folktales. The teacher used pieces of heavy corrugated cardboard cut large enough to cover the children. She measured and cut out holes for the children to put their faces and hands through. The children painted the boards to represent the characters and used them to enact "Little Red Riding Hood," "The Three Bears," and "The Three Little Pigs."

Mathematics and Science

Mr. Kasatonov's third graders participated in their home state's "Adopt a Highway" program. The goal of the project was for groups of children to assume responsibility for keeping a small portion of the median strip on a highway beautiful by planting flowers and keeping it clean. Before the children decided how to fulfill this responsibility, Mr. Kasatonov took them on a field trip, where they picked wildflowers and used materials from the Agricultural Extension office to label, classify, and learn about them. In art class, the children created vases to display the flowers. Afterward, they used reference materials to find out which flowers were the most colorful, long blooming, disease resistant, and heat tolerant and then tabulated their findings on a chart. The students searched for the best hybrids in seed catalogs. Then they did some test plantings of seeds from different companies in a flower bed in front of the school and graphed the results.

As a culmination of their study and classification of rocks, Ms. Lovell invited a man who makes jewelry out of semiprecious stones to bring his rock-polishing equipment to her kindergarten class. The children had been instructed on how to find small stones with quartz in them that could be put into the polishing drum. In this way, the children had an opportunity to appreciate natural beauty.

Language, Literacy, and Art

When children aged 5 to 9 were interviewed about the connection between their drawing and writing, their responses fell into four basic categories. The children used drawings (1) as objects to label, (2) as catalysts for generating ideas, (3) as a way of making the abstract concrete, and (4) as an aid to their thinking (DuCharme, 1991). Many young children who draw representationally use *narrative art*, pictures that tell a story. Sometimes their storytelling depends entirely on the pictures; sometimes the pictures are combined with captions or complete written stories. Five-year-old Isabell explained the advantage of drawing over writing this way: "I'll draw you what I would write, but drawing is funner." Even before children write alphabetically, teachers can develop the concept of pictures accompanied by print—squiggles, letter-like forms, or letters and numbers that the child happens to know.

Social Studies, Health, and Nutrition

In Ms. Browne's community, a young woman teaches classes on making stained glass. Ms. Browne prepared the children for her visit by going on a "stained glass tour" through an area of town with several churches and old homes. They also looked at some smaller examples of stained glass supplied by the craftsperson, including suncatchers, trinket boxes, and picture frames. When the craftsperson visited the class, she brought a small window she was repairing for a local homeowner, demonstrated the process of putting together the pieces of glass, and talked about the safety measures necessary when working with the material.

Mr. Bleakney's first-grade children were studying Native Americans. After he shared several books about totem poles, the children became fascinated by the concept of a totem pole telling a story. They asked the local ice cream store owner to save his large cardboard containers and used them as the base for their totem pole. The children studied a collection of pictures about totem poles provided by the librarian and then used paper, cardboard, paint, and fabric scraps to produce a simulated totem pole.

Special Populations

There are several important variables that affect children's artistic expression, including the following (Henkes, 1989)

❏ *Prior experience with art materials.* Do children have access to materials and art tools?. Is the range, supply, or quality of materials limited?
❏ *Cultural opportunities.* Do children have the opportunity to see various types of art in their environment? Do they, for instance, visit studios or museums, examine different types of architecture, or appreciate the folk art traditions of their culture and other cultures?
❏ *Family discipline.* How do parents react to the child's artistic efforts? Is the child severely punished for drawing on the wall, for instance? Are boys actively discouraged from artistic pursuits?
❏ *Visual skills, mental capacity, and motor coordination.* What strengths and abilities does the child bring to the art activity? Can the activity be adapted to the physical limitations of the child?

Culturally Diverse Groups

Communication and acceptance are linked to the child's creative expression (Henkes, 1989). In order for all children to flourish as artists, they must communicate about a wide range of artistic styles and forms, see those styles and forms accepted by others, freely experiment with art media, and learn to accept one another's art. Art offers a way of communicating and accepting other cultures. Mexican piñatas, African masks, or Ukranian decorated eggs give children insight into the history, values, and aesthetic sensibilities of others.

It has been rightly said that the language of art is universal. Art gives children an authentic, satisfying form of self-expression. The new immigrant child with limited proficiency in English can express ideas, thoughts, and feelings nonverbally through paper, sculpture, pottery, and fabric.

Children with Disabilities

Creative teachers can adapt art activities to accommodate children with physical impairments. This might mean putting clay on a wheelchair tray rather than on the table or giving the child who lacks the motor control to weave other options with fabric, such as collage. In every case, the key is sensitivity to the child, knowledge of the child's abilities, and creative problem-solving techniques. Art experiences should help all children to see that everyone has different abilities. The visually impaired child, for example, may be more adept than peers with normal vision at discerning different textures through touch alone.

High-Achieving and Low-Achieving Children

Both high-achieving and low-achieving children need the challenge and excitement of working with new art media. It is thrilling to draw with brand new, sharply pointed, soft-leaded, colored pencils or to draw and color a picture with watercolor markers that include unusual colors like silver or gold. Unusual

Skillful teachers adapt art activities to children's developmental levels. These children with Down syndrome are preparing crafts for a parade.

papers are appealing too. Paper that is heavy, embossed, glossy, or foil, such as that used in greeting cards and wrapping paper, can often be recycled to provide a lasting supply of high-quality material. Many children do not have access to art materials (other than crayons and paper) at home. Material like oil pastels, colored chalk, washable acrylic paints, or clay are generally unavailable because parents cannot afford them, do not recognize their value, or are concerned about the mess. Even fewer children have access at home to artists' tools such as an easel and paints, woodworking tools, or crafts materials.

High-achieving primary grade children can use art as a basis for practicing their emerging research skills. A child with an interest in wood carving could, for instance, study different types of wood carvings: those from various regions of the United States, those from different types of wood (e.g., ebony, teak, mahogany), and those from different historical periods.

For low-achieving children who are struggling with academic subjects, art can become a refuge where competition is minimized and self-esteem is built.

Every child, at one time or another, has to deal with angry feelings. Through art, that child can hammer at the woodworking bench or pound clay into a satisfying shape and turn that energy to creative rather than destructive ends. In this way, art offers a medium for expressing powerful emotions and coping with a sometimes confusing or hostile environment. That outlet is particularly important for children with special needs.

Conclusion

Eisner (1976) has defined personal inclinations for the arts as those abilities that enable us "[to] play with images, ideas and feelings, to be able to recognize and construct the multiple meanings of events, to perceive and conceive of things from various perspectives, to be able to be a clown, a dreamer, a taker of risks" (p. vii). As early childhood educators, we need to build these attributes in ourselves, in our colleagues, and, most important, in our students.

Chapter Summary

1. In order for a classroom activity to qualify as art, it must value process over product, emphasize originality rather than conformity, and allow children to retain ownership of their work.
2. Understanding children's art depends upon an appreciation of the child as an artist, knowledge of the developmental sequence in children's art, understanding of the principles of art education, and recognition of the many contributions art makes to children's overall development.
3. In a quality art program, children learn not only to become artists but also to appreciate the artwork of others.
4. To support the goals of art education, teachers should locate quality art and art reproductions from many sources and discuss these works skillfully with

children. Critical issues in art programs for young children include the selection, presentation, evaluation, storage, and display of art and art materials.

5. Teachers in child-centered classrooms believe that quality art experiences with a variety of materials build every child's artistic sensibilities and skills.
6. Art is a true curricular basic.
7. Art must be integrated into different subject areas so that it receives the attention it merits.

Discussion Questions

1. A friend or relative asks you how to tell if his child is artistic. How would you respond, based upon what you have read in this chapter?
2. Reread the quotations that introduced this chapter. How has your understanding of them been enriched?
3. Suppose that a parent volunteers to work in your classroom, and you observe the parent with her hand on top of a child's hand and paintbrush, forcibly showing the child how to paint a flower. After the children leave, the parent tells you that the child was rude and unappreciative. How would you respond?
4. A colleague criticizes you for letting your primary grade children make things out of clay, saying, "I leave that sort of thing to the art teacher." How would you articulate your position on this issue?

—————————— Writing to Learn ——————————

If a classmate mentions that her friend is an art major, does your mind immediately jump to a stereotype? Far too often, we forget that "the artist, no less than the scientist, is the observer/thinker/believer" (Engel, 1983, p. 8). Write in response to one or more of the following questions:

What biases do I have about art and artists? How do I respond to the art I see in my campus or community environment, for instance? How would I describe my background in art? Have I taken a course in art appreciation? Read about famous artists and their works? Visited museums, craft shows, galleries, or other types of art exhibits? What can I do to increase my knowledge of art and use that knowledge to teach more effectively?

—————————— Interview ——————————

Teachers' Beliefs About Child-Initiated Art Activities

Arrange to interview a teacher of young children about the art experiences he or she provides for the child. Write down the teacher's response to each of the following questions:

1. Do you see yourself as being responsible for the child's growth in art? Why or why not?
2. How did your teacher education program prepare you for teaching art? How have you extended your knowledge of art?
3. What kinds of art experiences do you provide for children? Can you describe an activity that was particularly successful?
4. How do you feel about your own artistic ability? How have these beliefs about yourself influenced your ideas about children's art?
5. Have you ever considered a child in your class to be especially artistic? Why did this child impress you with his or her artistic ability?

Observation

Predrawing and Breaking Stereotypes in Art

The purpose of this assignment is to give you some experience in breaking stereotypes in children's art. Just as writing has a stage called *prewriting*, where we draft and revise our ideas, children need *predrawing* activities, warm-ups before they actually draw something. Sebesta (1989) offers the example of the second-grade teacher who invited children to draw the Three Bears' kitchen. At first, they drew kitchens like the ones they had experienced. Then the teacher asked the children to think about how a bear's kitchen would *differ* from a person's kitchen and invited them to draw again. This time, the results were more imaginative. One child drew a scratching board "to make their claws sharp for cutting bread." By breaking stereotypes through a first draft of the drawings, this teacher encouraged creativity.

You can use a similar technique for breaking stereotypes by asking questions that stimulate the child's imagination. Suppose that a child draws the typical tree and flower picture. You might ask:

What makes something a tree? A flower?

What is the strangest tree you have ever seen? The most unusual flower?

What is the wildest sort of tree or flower you can imagine?

You could go outdoors, look at the various types of trees and flowers, and then ask the children to talk about what makes a tree special. A child might say, for instance, that a tree suitable for climbing is best or that a flower with a beautiful scent is favored. Your challenge to them could be first to visualize, then to draft, and finally to refine a form that represents their ideal tree or flower. Ask them to consider, too, which medium and techniques they will choose to communicate their ideas.

Follow these six steps in your observation:

1. Arrange to interview a child or group of primary grade children.
2. Ask them to draw anything that is particularly susceptible to a stereotypic response: houses, trees, pumpkins, or birds, for example.

3. Use the types of questions and procedures outlined above to elicit original, imaginative responses.
4. Transcribe a tape recording of your questions and the children's verbal responses during the activities. Type your experience in the format of a script for a play.
5. Collect both the first drawing and the subsequent drawings. Assure the children that their work will be returned to them. Be prepared to discuss your interview with the entire class.
6. Return the children's work to them.

--- **Controversy** ---

How Basic Is Art?

When describing curriculum, the word *basic* is generally used as a synonym for *fundamental* or *foundational*, something that is an essential component of everyone's educational experience. If we observe young children's behavior, it is clear that art is basic in every sense. Children draw on the sidewalk with chalk, sketch on a steamy window with a fingertip, use wet earth and sand as modeling material, sculpt ice and snow into various forms, and use art materials (such as paints, paper, crayons, scissors, and glue) and other items they find (popsicle sticks, leaves, pull rings from cans, foil, ribbon, fabric, and yarn) to create myriad artistic forms. In elementary school, children make intricate drawings, create three-dimensional objects, design notes and cards, and engage in crafts projects.

On this evidence alone, it is clear that art is basic, especially where young children are concerned. Even before they can communicate through words, children can communicate through art. Yet if we examine a weekly schedule in an early childhood classroom, we often find that there is little time allotted to art; if we talk to some parents, they tell us that art is a "frill"; and if we talk to teachers, we find that they often compromise the goals of art in the activities they select for children by favoring cut-and-paste exercises over authentic artistic expression. Why? Consider these questions:

1. Refer back to your interview on child-initiated art in this chapter. What evidence can you cite to support de Mille's view?
2. What evidence from other courses you have taken substantiates the position that other cultures, either contemporary or historical, have a different perspective on art?
3. What can you do to elevate the status of art in your classroom? To convince parents or administrators that art is a legitimate and appropriate means of self-expression for young children?

As a group, try to develop an action plan for making art basic in your classroom.

—————————————— **Research Highlight** ——————————————

The Effect of Materials on Children's Representations of the Human Form

Summary of Research

Children's emerging ability to represent the human form has been studied extensively. Usually the emphasis in human figure representations by children is on drawing, partly because—unlike painting or sculpting—drawing requires nothing more than ordinary household materials. Golomb (1974, 1988) has studied the human figure drawings of young children and found that they move through clearly distinguishable phases. The first stage is a *scribble*, random markings on paper that the child identifies as a person. Next comes a *contour*, a scribble with curvature. Contours are typically followed by a *global person*, an enclosed, curved space that usually represents the eyes and mouth. In the next stage, children produce a *tadpole person*, a figure that is mostly head with lines for arms and/or legs. Gradually, children begin to represent more of what they know about the person being drawn. The basic body parts are usually added, and features that made a particular impression, such as eyeglasses or long curly hair, are included. By the time most children enter first grade, they are representing people in greater detail and are including most body parts, along with "transparent" clothing (which shows the lines used to draw the person underneath). As children become more skilled at planning their drawings, they can anticipate which portions of the anatomy will be concealed by clothing and draw people with nontransparent clothing.

Golomb's (1988) most recent study found that children's representations of human beings are affected by the materials they use (i.e., clay, wooden pieces, or crayons). Even though a child might be at the stage of drawing tadpole people, he or she usually *does* include the trunk when working with clay. Evidently, the materials children use and the way they use them have a strong effect on the outcome.

Implications for Practice

This research seems to suggest, as Marshall McLuhan once said, that the "medium is the message." What steps could you take to ensure that children have the opportunity to express themselves artistically through a variety of media? What are the implications of this research for the consumables budget of early childhood art programs?

References

Bowker, J. E., & Sawyers, J. K. (1988). Influence of exposure on preschoolers' art preferences. *Early Childhood Research Quarterly, 3,* 107–115.

Brutger, J. H. (1987). Discipline-based art education for early childhood. In J. Sword (Ed.), *Developing social competencies of children in a changing world* (pp. 110–121). Proceedings of the Annual Conference on Early Childhood Education (7th, Duluth, MN, Sept. 25–26). ED 301 529.

Clemens, S. G. (1991). Art in the classroom: Making every day special. *Young Children, 46*(2), 4–11.

de Mille, R. (1967). *Put your mother on the ceiling: Children's imagination games.* New York: Penguin.

Dixon, G., & Chalmers, F. G. (1990). The expressive arts in education. *Childhood Education, 67*(1), 12–17.

DuCharme, E. (1991, April). Paper presented at the Association for Childhood Education International Study Conference, San Diego, CA.

Eisner, E. (1976). *The arts, human development and education.* Berkley, CA: McCuthen.

Engel, M. (1983). Art and the mind. *Art Education, 36*(2), 6–8.

Feeney, S., Christensen, D., & Moravcik, E. (Eds.). (1991). *Who am I in the lives of children?* Columbus, OH: Merrill/ Macmillan.

Gaitskell, C. D., Hurwitz, A., & Day, M. (1982). *Children and their art: Methods for the elementary school* (4th ed.). Dubuque, IA: William C. Brown.

Gardner, H. (1982). *Art, mind and brain: A cognitive approach to creativity.* New York: Basic Books.

Getty Center for Education in the Arts. (1985). Beyond creating: The place for art in America's schools. Los Angeles: John Paul Getty Trust.

Golomb, C. (1974). *Young children's sculpture and drawing.* Cambridge, MA: Harvard University Press.

Golomb, C. (1988). Symbolic inventions and transformations in child art. In K. Egan & D. Nadaner (Eds.), *Imagination and education* (pp. 222–236). New York: Teachers College Press.

Harris, D. B. (1963). *Children's drawings as measures of intellectual maturity.* New York: Harcourt Brace and World.

Henkes, R. (1989). The child's artistic expression. *Early Child Development and Care, 47,* 165–176.

Herberholz, B. (1974). *Early childhood art.* Dubuque, IA: William C. Brown.

Hoffman, S., & Lamme, L. L. (1989). *The expressive arts: Learning from the inside out.* Wheaton, MD: Association for Childhood Education International.

Jefferson, B. (1963). *Teaching art to children: The values of creative expression.* Boston: Allyn & Bacon.

Kellogg, R. (1979). *Children's drawings/ Children's minds.* New York: Avon Books.

Lowenfeld, V., & Brittain, W. L. (1947). *Creative and mental growth.* New York: Macmillan.

National Art Education Association. (1973). Aesthetic education: A social and individual need. St. Louis, MO: CEMBREL.

Rowe, G. (1987). *Guiding young artists: Curriculum ideas for teachers.* Melbourne, AU: Oxford University Press.

Schirrmacher, R. (1988). *Art and creative development for young children.* Albany, NY: Delmar.

Sebesta, S. (1989). The story is about you. In S. Hoffman & L. L. Lamme (Eds.). *Learning from the inside out: The expressive arts* (pp. 22–28). Wheaton, MD: Association for Childhood Education International.

Smith, N. R. (1982). The visual arts in early childhood education: Development and the creation of meaning. In B. Spodek (Ed.), *Handbook of research in early childhood education* (pp. 87–106). New York: Free Press.

Whitehead, A. N. (1967). In G. Selden (compiler). *The great quotations.* New York: Pocket Books.

Children's Books

Ehlert, L. (1989). *Color zoo.* New York: Harper/Lippincott.

Flournoy, V. (1985). *The patchwork quilt.* New York: Dial.

Gackenbach, D. (1977). *Harry and the terrible whatzit.* New York: Seabury.

Hoban, T. (1989). *Colors and things.* New York: Greenwillow.

Hutchins, P. (1985). *The very worst monster.* New York: Greenwillow.

Johnston, T. (1984). *The quilt story.* New York: G. P. Putnam.

Jonas, A. (1989). *The quilt.* New York: Greenwillow.

Keats, E. J. (1962). *The snowy day.* New York: Viking.

Mayer, M. (1968). *There's a nightmare in my closet.* New York: Dial.

Sendak, M. (1963). *Where the wild things are.* New York: Harper.

Walsh, E. S. (1989). *Mouse paint.* San Diego, CA: Harcourt Brace Jovanovich.

Willis, J. (1987). *The monster bed.* New York: Lothrop Lee & Shepard.

Music and Movement in the Early Childhood Curriculum

Of all the gifts with which individuals may be endowed,
none emerges earlier than musical talent.

Howard Gardner, 1983, p. 99

Dance in early childhood provides concrete experiences
in which children become more aware of the movement they see
in their world, try it on for themselves, and notice how it feels.

Susan W. Stinson, 1990, p. 35

After reading this chapter, you will be able to

- ☐ Understand the theory, history, and philosophy of early childhood music education.
- ☐ Appreciate the value of music and movement in children's lives.
- ☐ Describe both traditional and contemporary music programs in early childhood.
- ☐ Identify the contributions that music and movement experiences make to the child's overall development.

❏ Describe a general sequence for young children's development in music and movement.

❏ Understand how teachers, even nonmusicians, can integrate developmentally appropriate music and movement experiences for young children into the total curriculum.

Case Study

When Raphael was a newborn, he could be comforted by nestling against his mother's chest and listening to her heartbeat, something that was familiar to him even before birth. By 3 months, he had a favorite song, "Arorro Mi Niño." When his mother sang it, he listened intently. Often, the song helped him settle down to sleep. At 18 months, Raphael bounced delightedly on his father's knee to the rhythms of marching bands during the "Battle of the Bands," a competition among the area's high schools. At 3 years, he attended nursery school, where he could be observed rocking in the wooden boat with friends, inventing nonsense chants, and giggling. Aunt Otilla brought Raphael a set of brightly painted maracas directly from Mexico when he was 4. When Grandma Diáz babysat, they would listen to her folk music records while Raphael sang, danced, and played his maracas. At 5, Raphael took the maracas to "show and tell," and the teacher invited him to use them while they sang. Later, Raphael taught the class a song in Spanish, "De Colores." By the time Raphael was in first grade, he had learned to sing melodiously and enjoyed singing in church. Uncle Jorge invited 7-year-old Raphael to come up on stage and sing along with the band at their cousin's wedding. As a reward for having done so well in second grade, Raphael's father surprised him with a guitar—the one Uncle Jorge had used as a boy when he first learned how to play.

For Raphael, music is more than listening to prerecorded selections and more than making music. It is a social event: "musical ability is developed in a relationship, in a succession of relationships—musical self in relation to musical selves" (Bernstein, 1990, p. 401).

In recent years, there has been a greater emphasis on music and movement for young children because adults are aware that a child's early musical experiences shape later musical attitudes and abilities. We know that music education is most effective when it is active and interactive, relying upon social activities with family members, teachers, and peers (Boyd, 1989). The remainder of this chapter translates this perception into an early childhood music philosophy and relates that philosophy to professional practice.

Theoretical Framework

Affirming the value of music in children's lives is important, but it is not enough. Educators also need to understand the basic philosophy of music education. In a democratic society, the goal of teaching music is not to single out those who are gifted in music. Rather, the goal is to maximize the musical abilities of every child. Achieving this purpose involves an understanding of (1) the child musician and the musical experience, (2) music development theory, and (3) the connection between music and movement.

Children and the Musical Experience

David Elkind (1987) once noted that if young children could express their feelings, they might well say to adults, "I am not going to be anything. I already am." This sentiment applies to music too. Do we value children's music only for its imitation of adult musical behaviors, or do we appreciate it in its own right? Identifying young children as musicians should not be based on the expectation that they will demonstrate precocious musical behavior (Fox, 1991) or on the hope that they will become concert pianists, rock singers, or ballet prima donnas someday. Rather, the focus should be on music for today and every day, music for everyone.

Too many children's so-called musical experiences are thinly disguised schoolwork. There is drill disguised as music, such as math facts set to music to make practice more palatable. There are ditties that are heavy-handed lessons, such as songs about safety rules. At the other extreme, there are the adult purists who contend that classical/symphonic music is the only music of any value and who try to restrict children's musical experiences to that category. Some adults neglect their responsibility for seeking quality children's recordings and simply use whatever is readily available or heavily advertised. All of these approaches are ill-conceived and inadvisable. As Metz (1989) points out, "Simply using music in an educational setting does not insure that children's musical perceptions are developing . . . we need to focus on music as 'an end in itself' " (p. 89).

Theories of Musical Development

Jerome Bruner (1968) hypothesized that children proceed through three cognitive stages: (1) enactive, (2) iconic, and (3) symbolic. Each of these stages suggests developmentally appropriate music experiences for children.

At the *enactive stage*, physical activity and music are intertwined. Consider all of the rhythmic games that adults play with infants and toddlers and how they combine physical activity with music. We rock babies to sleep with a lullaby like "Rock-a-bye Baby," tickle a child's toes to the chant of "This Little Piggy," or begin sharing simple action songs like "Eency Weency Spider" with toddlers. Bruner's enactive stage relates to Piaget's (1952) sensorimotor stage and Erikson's (1950) trust-building stage. When we think about the enactive music stage of babies and toddlers, it is clear that the activities adults select not only stimulate the child's senses and foster cognitive development, but also build social relationships by communicating warmth and acceptance.

At the *iconic stage,* children begin to use objects and pictures to represent ideas (Bruner, 1968). During preschool, children are highly imaginative (Piaget, 1962) and assert their autonomy, yet want to be accepted by the group (Erikson, 1950). Musical experiences that are appropriate for this stage recognize all of these characteristics of preschoolers. Consider, for example, a teacher who introduces a musical game like "The Farmer in the Dell" with flannel board figures of each character in the song. As Zimmerman (1984) points out, "Singing games and chants are the embodiment of symbolic play and imitation. They help the child move from sensorimotor experience to a symbolic transformation of it" (pp. 6–7).

At the *symbolic stage,* children begin to use abstract symbols, primarily language, to represent ideas. School-age children think more logically and realistically (Piaget, 1952). They also have a sense of industry, which is manifested in their drive to master many different skills (Erikson, 1950). Returning to the "Farmer in the Dell" example, school-age children might interpret the words of this familiar song on a song chart or in a book. As children enter the symbolic stage, they rely less on icons (pictures) and learn to use systems of symbols such as the printed word or musical notation. Illustrated song charts, song collections, and song picture books (illustrated versions of song lyrics) are particularly useful because they link the symbolic stage with the previous iconic stage.

Intellectual development from birth through the school years runs the course of the enactive, iconic, and symbolic systems, "until the human being is able to command all three" (Bruner, 1968, p. 12).

The History of Early Childhood Music Education

Music has a long history in early childhood education. In 1883, Jean Jacques Rousseau invented an "everychild" named *Emile.* When Rousseau wrote about Emile's music education, he recommended that the mother sing simple, interesting, developmentally appropriate songs to "make his voice accurate, uniform, flexible and sonorous; and his ear sensitive to measure and harmony, but nothing more than this." Near the turn of the century, Maria Montessori applied her concept of the prepared environment to the child's music education. She advocated sound exploration activities for children and invented a set of mushroom-shaped bells that helped children to discover musical concepts.

Later in the twentieth century, several music experts designed music programs specifically for young children. Carl Orff, a German music educator, developed creative musicianship by engaging children in producing and creating their own music, rhythmic responses, and imaginative actions. Zoltan Kodaly, a Hungarian music educator, promoted musical literacy through a carefully sequenced program of folk music that began with 3-year-olds. Shinichi Suzuki, a Japanese educator, originated a talent education program that taught very young children to play the violin or cello and required extensive parent involvement.

Today's early childhood educator typically takes an eclectic approach to music that draws upon the best features of each tradition. We recognize the

importance of early experience as Rousseau did, we prepare a musical environment as Montessori did, we emphasize spontaneity and originality as Orff did,
we attend to the developmental levels of children as Kodaly did, and we appreciate the importance of parent involvement as Suzuki did. Even though there
are many comprehensive music curriculum guides (Leonhard, 1968), skilled
early childhood educators use music throughout the day and incorporate a wide
variety of musical experiences rather than slavishly follow a particular program.

The Role of Music and Movement
in Child Development

Music contributes to the child's total development: psychomotor, perceptual,
affective, cognitive, social, cultural, and aesthetic (Gardner, 1973; Greenberg,
1979; Leeper, Dales, Skipper, & Witherspoon, 1974; Zimmerman, 1984). Specific
contributions of music and movement experiences to these areas of development are described below.

Psychomotor Skills

Children are developing psychomotor skills when they strike the keys on a toy
xylophone, interpret the mood of lively music through creative dance, or play a
simple tune on a kazoo. All of these activities involve practice of the large muscle
and small muscle control associated with exploring sounds and making music.

Perceptual Skills

A baby who recognizes her mother's voice or a 3-year-old who requests a favorite action song are demonstrating their ability to perceive music. For the very
young child, sensory perceptions of music are not limited to the auditory chan-
nel. A teacher might play a note on the piano and realize that toddlers are
searching for that note, expecting to see as well as hear it.

Affective Skills

Music evokes emotional responses. A toddler who delights at hearing his name
inserted into a song sung at the day-care center is showing how music affects
him. A kindergartner who remarks that "The Flight of the Bumblebee" sounds
"buzzy" is showing how the music affected him. As children gain experience
with music and language, they can better articulate their emotional responses to
music. A group of primary grade children heard the mournful tune "Ashokan
Farewell," the theme song for the Ken Burns PBS Civil War series. When the
teacher introduced the selection, she asked the children to listen carefully and
explain why it was a goodbye song. The children were quiet, then responded
with statements like "It's kind of slow and sad" and "It makes you feel the way
you feel if your friend moves away."

Cognitive Skills

Understandings about music are a form of intelligence (Gardner, 1983). Musical
intelligence must be nurtured in the same way that we nurture other types of

intelligence, such as the linguistic or logical-mathematical intelligences. Musical intelligence involves children's ability to process mentally the tonal aspects of rhythm and melody. The child who learns to sing "This Old Man," for instance, has learned to focus on a task, sequence material, and link words with actions. Musical experiences, such as creating a tune at a keyboard, can develop all the higher-level thinking skills of application, analysis, synthesis, and evaluation.

Social Skills

Music encourages participation, sharing, and cooperation; it is part of the early bonding process and part of the basic enculturation of childhood (McAllester, 1991). Through a simple musical activity like "London Bridge," children learn to subordinate their individual wishes to the goals of the group—the essence of cooperation.

Cultural Skills

Music familiarizes children with the musical heritage of various geographic regions, cultures, and ethnic groups. A group of second graders who heard the Grammy-award-winning African music group Ladysmith Black Mambazo were captivated by their majestic Zulu harmonies. The children with African roots felt renewed pride in their ethnic heritage, while those with other cultural heritages felt admiration for the music of a culture different from their own.

Aesthetic Skills

When music contributes to the "development of sensitivity for the feelings, impressions, and images that music can convey" (McDonald & Simons, 1989, p. 2), it builds children's aesthetic sensibilities. Aesthetic development is fostered when children consider questions such as these:

How does the music make us feel?

What do we hear in the music?

How can we express the music?

Why do we respond the way we do to music? (Greenberg, 1979)

How Young Children Grow Musically

Children grow musically when adults provide (1) a supportive physical and emotional environment, (2) opportunities for social interaction, and (3) role models to emulate.

A *supportive physical and emotional environment* is in evidence when children feel free to take risks and do not feel pressured to perform. "Musical activities should give pleasure to all who are participating and, if they don't, they are probably worse than useless" (Boyd, 1989, p. 8). It is not enough simply to "bathe" children in music because, to the young child, music is both active (something you do) and interactive (something you share with others).

Early childhood musical experiences maximize *social interaction* when they are adjusted to the particular child's level of development and behavioral re-

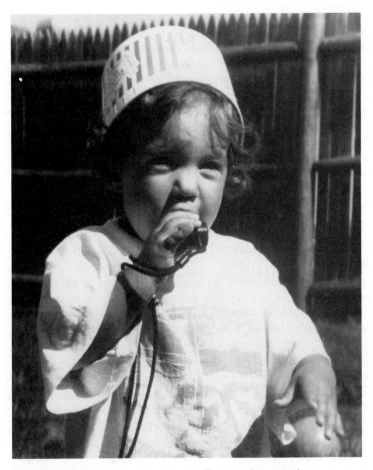

This child's exploration of musical sounds illustrates her emerging understandings about music.

sponses. Think about the traditional singing game "Ring Around the Rosy." As a toddler, Regina's version of the song was simply "rind round . . . pocketful . . . boom," and she participated with her mother by moving in a circle and dropping to the floor at the song's end. In nursery school as a 3-year-old, she mastered all of the words (substituting "Ashes, ashes, we all fall down" for "boom") and learned how to move together with the other children around the circle.

Role models are equally important in the child's overall musical development. Many studies, both of exceptionally talented musicians and of adults in general, suggest that early experiences that were relaxed, informal, and enjoyed in the company of supportive adults contributed to the child's early attachment to music (Wilson & Roehmann, 1990). A team of researchers who studied infant musical development concluded that the parents' own singing might be the single most important variable in an infant's musical activity (Kelley & Sutton-Smith, 1987).

In contrast, when significant others express disdain for certain musical activities, it tends to narrow children's range of interests. Consider the parent who is proud of an inability to carry a tune or a parent who ridicules opera. The child who naturally admires the parent soon devalues these activities too. Clearly, the models we provide at home and at school exert an influence on the child's attitudes about music. A high school stage band, a community barbershop quartet, a college choral group, a group of musical performers from the local senior center, or an organist from the music store at the mall are all potential music role models whom children can listen to and admire, enjoy and emulate.

The Music–Movement Connection

Children naturally connect music with body movement. The direction and flow of music invite children to respond to music with their bodies and to express their feelings and thoughts (Metz, 1989). Music and movement are one of the earliest forms of communication as well: "Movement is the child's first language, reflecting subtleties of thought and feeling not captured by verbal expression" (Metz, 1989, p. 89). When children move their bodies in response to music through creative dance, they use and integrate their bodies, minds, emotions, and spirits (Ririe, 1980). Even babies who have not learned to crawl will usually raise their arms and legs off the floor and make rapid swimming motions in response to lively music.

It is not necessary for teachers to be dancers themselves in order to lead children in movement activities. It is important, however, to include some type of movement activity in every musical experience for young children (Greenberg, 1979). One of the best ways to encourage creative movement is by making comments and asking good questions at the right time.

Werner and Burton (1979) suggest beginning with a word such as *surprise:*

> First show me a surprised face. Then add your arms and your whole body. Show me surprise with whatever word I say. With a jump. With a stretch. With a twist. With fast moves. . . . Next show me how you laugh. With your head. With your whole body. Can you change your level while you laugh? Can you move about while you laugh? Can you laugh a little? Change, show me a big side-splitting belly laugh. (p. 52)

A teacher could stimulate different types of creative movement with questions like these:

> "Can you show me with your body that the music is getting louder? Softer? Higher? Lower? Can you show me with just your hands? Can you show me with your whole body that it is getting faster? With just your head? With just your feet?"

> "Can you show me giant steps as you move around the circle? Baby steps? How would an elephant dance to this music? A mouse?"

"Show me with your whole body how a snowflake moves. Can you show me with a paper streamer? With just your arms?"

The use of simple props is another way to combine music and movement. Toddlers can rock a teddy bear to a lullaby; preschoolers can make "dancing dolls" (using empty detergent bottles and fabric skirts) and swirl them about in response to a Strauss waltz; and primary grade children can lope along to a cowboy song as they hold the reins of their horse (a length of ribbon or yarn encircling the waist of a partner). Naturally, the selection of both music and movement activities depends upon the developmental levels of the children.

Stages in the Development of Music and Movement

As children mature, they attain many milestones in music and movement. Figure 4.1 is an overview of musical development and suitable music and movement activities for each age/stage.

As a result of developmentally appropriate music and movement activities throughout the early childhood years, children should acquire the following attitudes (Hall, 1989):

I can create music—feeling free to explore sounds and confident about their musical intelligence.

I can listen to music—recognizing different ways of using their senses to hear and differentiate among various types of music, such as identifying the music made by different instruments or voices.

I can understand music—using the vocabulary of music to describe experiences with tone, timbre, rhythm, and harmony.

I can write music—knowing that music is a form of creative expression and doing such things as spontaneously creating and singing original songs, inventing new verses for familiar songs, and creating rhythm band compositions.

I can play music—believing that they are capable of producing pleasing sounds and music on homemade or real instruments, such as using "sleigh bells" to accompany a Christmas song or playing a tom-tom to accompany a song.

I can respond to music with my body—knowing that they can use movement as a form of nonverbal communication, like 9-month-old Berkley, who moved animatedly in her car seat and made cooing sounds whenever her favorite Christmas carol, "The Holly and the Ivy," was played on a cassette tape.

Critical Issues in Teaching Music and Movement

Any quality program for young children includes music, and any quality music program has the following five characteristics (McDonald and Simons, 1989):

FIGURE 4.1   Development of Music and Movement

INFANTS

Music
Sensitive to *dynamics,* the loudness or softness of a sound; startle at loud sounds and are comforted by soft, rhythmic, melodious sounds (e.g., those of musical toys and lullabies). Respond to the human voice, especially the primary caregiver's voice. Respond in a more lively way to action songs and in a more subdued way to lullabies.

Movement
Tend to respond to music with the entire body. Babies that are sitting up will bounce to lively music. Babies who are standing may rock from side to side, sway back and forth, or bounce up and down by flexing their knees.

TODDLERS

Music
Discriminate among sounds and may attempt to imitate sounds or to approximate pitches; listen to music and respond enthusiastically to certain songs. Explore sound making with household objects (e.g., hitting a pan with a wooden spoon), musical toys (e.g., a toy xylophone), or musical instruments; express greater interest in recordings. Can demonstrate knowledge of sounds and music by identifying familiar sounds or instruments played on a cassette tape or out of sight. Experiment with songs and voice and gain some control of the singing voice; occasionally match melody and may join in on certain phrases of familiar songs; sing or hum improvisationally during play.

Movement
Use primarily arms and legs, and move in response to the tempo (fast/slow) of a rhythm instrument (e.g., run, walk, "freeze"). Will often dance on request while music is playing and show more control over physical responses. Respond well to large and small motor musical activities that emphasize repetition and rhyme—simple fingerplays and action songs.

THREE-YEAR-OLDS

Music
Have better voice control, rhythmic responses, and mastery of song; in general, have names for favorite tunes, can recognize familiar tunes, and can sing portions of them with a fair degree of accuracy (Day, 1988). With experience, most 3-year-olds can play a simple rhythm instrument in ways that reveal an emerging awareness of beat, tempo, and pitch in response to songs with simple, definite rhythm patterns.

Movement
Move in a more coordinated way to music (usually running) and may experiment with different types of body movements, such as walking on tiptoe; movements tend to be more graceful than previously. Usually try to participate in action songs and fingerplays by doing the gestures; often combine creative drama with song.

FIGURE 4.1 *continued*

FOUR-YEAR-OLDS

Music

Capable of learning some basic musical concepts such as pitch (high/low), duration (long/short), tempo (fast/slow), and loudness (soft/loud), and can use language to express these ideas. Can classify musical instruments by sound, shape, size, pitch, and quality. Sing complete songs from memory with greater pitch control and rhythmic accuracy; sing both original songs and structured songs spontaneously. Vocal range, rhythmic ability, and vocabulary are expanding rapidly; can sing an average of five notes. Usually enjoy group singing games and more complex songs. Longer attention span in guided listening to records.

Movement

Movements that suggest rhythm (e.g., swinging on a swing) are likely to be accompanied by spontaneous song. Master new movements and can switch rapidly from one type of movement to another when the word is substituted (e.g., "Hop, hop, hop to my Lou").

FIVE-YEAR-OLDS

Music

Sense of pitch, rhythm, and melody emerge; usually understand some melodic contours and intervals (skips and steps in a melody); can demonstrate some musical concepts (e.g., fast/slow, high/low, short/long duration) on a small keyboard. Enjoy longer songs with predictable structures (i.e., colors, numbers, repetition, rhyme). Can reproduce the melody in an echo song and have a vocal range of five to six notes.

Movement

Movements have a more rhythmic, interpretive quality than previously. Can march around in a circle while playing in a rhythm band and participate in a variety of group singing games with simple dance movements to songs like "Looby Lou."

SIX-, SEVEN-, AND EIGHT-YEAR-OLDS

Music

Singing voice is nearly at a mature level (Davidson, 1985). Sings in tune, with a vocal range of approximately 8–10 notes; aware of a song being pitched at a comfortable singing level. Sense of harmony is emerging. By second or third grade, can sing a round and may master a simple two-part harmony if given adult direction. Enjoy silliness and begin to understand word play in song lyrics; learn to read song lyrics; able to master songs that place greater demands on memory and sequencing skills. Have greater awareness of printed music and its relationship to the way music is sung or played; usually able to conceptualize musical notes as "stairsteps." Musical preferences are fairly well established; may express an interest in learning to play a musical instrument.

Movement

Able to improvise movements and match movements to the beat of the music (i.e., clapping in time, playing a rhythm instrument to the beat). Capable of following more complex instructions, and can learn simple folk dances with adult direction.

1. *Developmentally appropriate.* We know that children are playful and active, so music activities should build upon each child's natural strengths rather than forcing them to fit an adult's idea of precocity in music. A balance of teacher-facilitated and child-initiated activities is essential (Littleton, 1989).
2. *Pleasurable.* Quality music programs help all children to develop positive attitudes and emotional responses. Early musical experiences should inaugurate a lifelong love of music.
3. *Varied.* Young children need to experience music in all of its forms: listening, moving to music, singing, playing instruments, discussing music, describing music, and representing music using both pictorial and musical symbols.
4. *Individual and social.* Although it is important for children to develop as musical individuals, they should also learn how to participate with others and experience the pleasure of group music making.
5. *Integrated.* Children should experience music throughout the day, not just at designated "music time." Music should become part of daily routines, such as beginning and ending the day or managing transitions from one activity to another; music should also be infused into the various subject areas.

A music program is achieving its goals when children learn to listen appreciatively, sing tunefully, move expressively and rhythmically, play classroom instruments, develop age-appropriate musical concepts, create self-satisfying music, and value music as part of everyday life (Greenberg, 1979).

In high-quality early childhood programs, the emphasis is on children's musical activity. These primary grade children are playing simple instruments and singing with a partner.

Selecting Musical Materials and Experiences

As teachers, we have a responsibility to extend children's music experiences and preferences. This long-term interest in music can be achieved through the careful and balanced selection of materials and provision of experiences.

The general categories of materials that should be part of every early childhood classroom are music-playing equipment such as records and a record player, tapes and a tape recorder; rhythm band materials; visual aids to accompany songs such as song charts, puppets, flannel board figures, rebus song sheets, and simple musical instruments such as bells, xylophones, a recorder, and an autoharp. Figure 4.2 presents a more detailed description.

A well-balanced program contains many different types of music. Research suggests that children generally prefer music and songs that have dominant rhythm patterns, repetition, and nonsense syllables; evoke a mood (e.g., calm, lively); emphasize enjoyment; suggest enactment and movement; and tell a story (Bayless & Ramsey, 1990; Benson & Kates, 1982). Figure 4.3 is an overview of the types of music that ought to be included and examples of each.

Presenting Musical Materials and Experiences

Teachers often have the mistaken impression that they must be able to sing beautifully and accompany themselves on an instrument in order to share music with young children. Actually, very few adults possess such performance skills. It is important to remember that the major focus is on the *children's* musical activity rather than on your talents in music. Some ways to compensate for a lack of musical background are these:

1. *Use your voice.* Judge your voice by your ability to sing *children's songs,* not adult songs. The great majority of songs for preschoolers have a range of about five notes. An ordinary singing voice coupled with extraordinary enthusiasm is perfectly adequate to sing most songs for young children. You probably know many of the songs already or can quickly learn them by singing along with a tape or record.

2. *Use recorded music.* There are many excellent records, tapes, and children's concert videotapes that teachers can obtain through their public library. To avoid fumbling to find a particular selection on a tape or record, make copies on tape containing just the songs you will be using that day or use the counter on the videotape machine and write down the exact location of each song. This will enable you to move smoothly from one selection to another.

   What happens if you find the sheet music to a song in a book but cannot find a recorded version? Have a person who plays an instrument well make a tape for you. You might ask the person to sing it the first time so that you can learn the song and then play just the background music the second time. Videotapes of skilled children's musicians in action are not only for children's viewing but are also a useful self-

FIGURE 4.2   Types of Classroom Instruments

RHYTHM

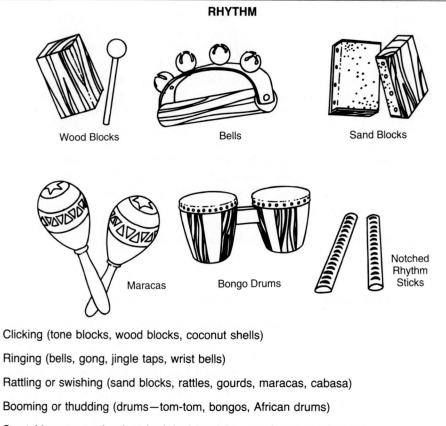

Wood Blocks   Bells   Sand Blocks

Maracas   Bongo Drums   Notched Rhythm Sticks

Clicking (tone blocks, wood blocks, coconut shells)

Ringing (bells, gong, jingle taps, wrist bells)

Rattling or swishing (sand blocks, rattles, gourds, maracas, cabasa)

Booming or thudding (drums—tom-tom, bongos, African drums)

Scratching or scraping (notched rhythm sticks, gourd rasp, washboard)

MELODY

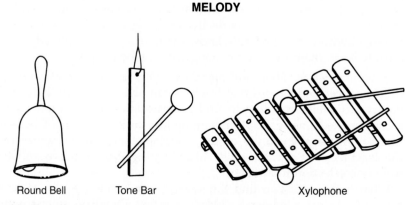

Round Bell   Tone Bar   Xylophone

Hand bells, resonator bells, tone bars, step bells, xylophone

FIGURE 4.2 *continued*

HARMONY

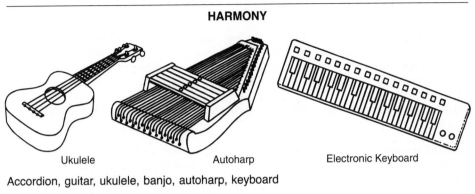

Ukulele   Autoharp   Electronic Keyboard

Accordion, guitar, ukulele, banjo, autoharp, keyboard

Sources for quality classroom instruments: Suzuki, Rhythm Band Inc., and Music for Little People.

teaching tool for early childhood educators. The tapes model the enthusiasm and ways of presenting material that achieve maximum audience participation, such as "A Young Children's Concert with Raffi."

3. *Use simple instruments.* Teachers quickly recognize that any instrument they find difficult to play only diverts their attention from the children and interferes with the musical experience. Perhaps you are familiar with the chorded zither called an *autoharp.* Instead of having to learn the chords by positioning the fingers (as with a guitar), you can simply press a button corresponding to that chord. Place the autoharp on a table or hold it upright against you; then strum down with your thumb and up with your finger in time to the music. The major drawback to the autoharp is the need to tune it. The best way to tune it for nonmusicians is to ask a musician to do it for you or, better yet, learn to do it yourself by matching each string's sound to those on a record or tape (Peterson, 1979). Another alternative is the Omnichord, an electronic version of the autoharp that requires no tuning. All that it requires is pushing a button and stroking a pressure-sensitive keyboard. There are many different models of the Omnichord, and the smaller ones are reasonably priced.

4. *Talk with children about their music.* Leading children to an understanding of musical concepts requires that you identify with the child. Students might be led to understand rests in music by asking them to "freeze" their bodies for a moment when the music pauses. A group of children might understand the concept of rhythm better if it is related to a concrete experience many of them are familiar with: the ticking of a clock. A teacher might pass around a clock, tell the children to listen, and then ask, "How can we make our rhythm sticks sound like a clock?" Alternatively, the children might listen to the song "My Grandfather's Clock"

FIGURE 4.3   Types of Music

LULLABIES—TRADITIONAL AND ORIGINAL, AMERICAN AND MULTICULTURAL

Examples: *Baby's Morning Time* (Judy Collins), *Lullaby Berceuse* (Connie Kaldor and Carmen Campagne), *Star Dreamer* (Priscilla Herdman), *Earthmother Lullabies I, Earthmother Lullabies II* (Pamala Ballingham), *Lullabies for Little Dreamers* (Kevin Roth), *Nitey-Night* (Patti Ballas and Laura Baron)

AMERICAN FOLK SONGS—CHILDREN'S CHANTS, PLAY SONGS AND SINGING GAMES

Record/Cassettes: *Let's Sing Fingerplays* and *Activity and Game Songs* (Tom Glazer), *Circle Time* (Lisa Monet), *Family Tree* (Tom Chapin), *Doc Watson Sings Songs for Little Pickers* (Doc Watson), *Stories and Songs for Little Children* and *American Folk Songs for Children* (Pete Seeger), *The Best of Burl's for Boys and Girls* (Burl Ives), *Come on In* and *Fiddle Up a Tune* (Eric Nagler), *This a Way, That a Way* (Ella Jenkins)

NURSERY TUNES AND SONGS FOR THE VERY YOUNG

Examples: *Mainly Mother Goose* (Sharon, Lois, and Bram), *Singable Songs for the Very Young,* and *More Singable Songs for the Very Young* (Raffi), *Baby Songs,* and *More Baby Songs* (Hap Palmer), *The Baby Record* (Bob McGrath and Katherine Smithrim), *Lullabies and Laughter* (Pat Carfra)

MULTICULTURAL MUSIC FROM AROUND THE WORLD AND MUSIC OF THE CHILD'S ETHNIC HERITAGE

Examples: *Children's Songs of Latin America* and *Cloud Journey* (Marcia Berman), *All for Freedom* (African-American) (Sweet Honey in the Rock), *Family Folk Festival: A Multicultural Sing-Along* and *Mi Casa es Su Casa* (Michele Valeri), *Beyond Boundaries: The Earthbeat! Sampler* (various artists), *Miss Luba and Kenyan Folk Melodies* (Muungano National Choir of Kenya)

HOLIDAY, RELIGIOUS, AND SEASONAL MUSIC

Examples: *Leprechauns and Unicorns* and *Oscar Brand and His Singing Friends Celebrate Holidays* (Oscar Brand), *Holiday Songs and Rhythms* (Hap Palmer), *Songs for the Holiday Season* (Nancy Rover), Mormon Tabernacle Choir, Vienna Boys Choir, Gregorian Chant (Benedictine Monks), Reverend James Cleveland, Mighty Clouds of Joy

---

CONTEMPORARY CHILDREN'S MUSIC

Evergreen, Everblue (Raffi), *Rosenshontz* (Gary Rosen and Bill Shontz), *Sillytime Magic* (Joanie Bartels), *All of Us Will Shine, Hug the Earth,* and *Circle Around* (Tickle Tune Typhoon), *1-2-3 for Kids* (Chenille Sisters), *Little Friends for Little Folks* (Janice Buckner), *Singin' and Swingin'* (Sharon, Lois, and Bram), *Collections* (Fred Penner), *Take Me with You* (Peter Alsop)

FIGURE 4.3 *continued*

POPULAR MUSIC

Examples: *Sebastian the Crab* (from the movie *The Little Mermaid*) (various artists), *Peter and the Wolf Play Jazz* (Dave Van Ronk), *Star Wars Trilogy Soundtrack* (London Philharmonic), *Electronic Music II* (Jacob Druckman), *Really Rosie* (children's musical: Carole King/Maurice Sendak), *Baby Road* (Floyd Domino), *Fresh Aire I* and *Fresh Aire II* (Mannheim Steamroller)

CLASSICAL MUSIC

Examples: *Peter and the Wolf* (Sergei Prokofiev), *Sorcerer's Apprentice* (Paul Dukas), *Carnival of the Animals* (Camille Saint-Saens), *Sleeping Beauty* (Peter Ilyich Tchaikovsky), *The Firebird* (Igor Stravinsky), *Fiedler's Favorites for Children* and *More Fiedler Favorites* (Arthur Fiedler and the Boston Pops Orchestra), *G'morning, Johann: Classical Piano Solos* (Ric Louchard), *Nutcracker Suite* (Peter Ilyich Tchaikovsky), *Symponie Fantastique* (Hector Berlioz), *La Mer* (Claude Debussy), *Mr. Bach Comes to Call* (Toronto Boys Choir and Studio Arts Orchestra)

MUSIC FOR DANCING, PATRIOTIC AND MARCHING SONGS

Examples: *Play Your Instruments* (Ella Jenkins), Sousa Marches, Strauss waltzes, *Swan Lake* (Peter Ilyich Tchaikovsky)

MUSIC FROM VARIOUS HISTORICAL PERIODS

Examples: *Dance of the Renaissance* (Richard Searles and Gilbert Yslas), *Shake It to the One You Love: Play Songs and Lullabies from Black Musical Traditions* (various artists), *Harpsichord Music* (Jean-Philippe Rameau)

MUSIC BY GREAT CONTEMPORARY ARTISTS

Examples: *Who's Afraid of Opera* video (Joan Sutherland), Beverly Sills, Stevie Wonder, Luciano Pavarotti, *Songbird* (Kenny G)

SOURCES FOR CHILDREN'S RECORDINGS

Educational Record Center
Building 400, Suite 400
1575 Northside Drive
Atlanta, GA 30318-4298

(800)-438-1637

Music for Little People
P.O. Box 1460
1144 Redway Drive
Redway, CA 95560

(800) 346-4445

Redleaf Press
450 North Syndicate Suite 5
St. Paul, MN 55104-4125

(800) 423-8309

or the music of "The Syncopated Clock" and move their heads, hands, or feet to the sounds of the clock. If a group of school-age children wants to present a story like "Coppelia" by Leo Delibes (1986) with musical sound effects, the teacher can relate it to their picture-symbol knowledge with questions like "How could you help the players remember when to play?'' Children may decide to provide the director with pictorial cue cards of each instrument, to make a large story chart coded with the symbols, or to provide each child with the text of the story coded with the instrument symbols.

Evaluating Musical Materials and Experiences

Browsing through the display booths at any large professional conference will quickly demonstrate how difficult the job of evaluating music materials can become, particularly for the nonmusician teacher. There are hundreds of records, tapes, and other music materials created for children, and the choice is sometimes overwhelming. Fortunately, there are many sources of support for teachers.

With recorded music, *look for award-winning materials.* Two of the major awards in children's recordings are the Parent's Choice Award and the American Library Association's Notable Recording. Look, too, for favorable reviews in newspapers and endorsements from various professional organizations. Where musical instruments or sound exploration equipment is concerned, *deal with reputable manufacturers and school supply companies.* Fisher Price, for example, has an all-in-one rhythm band that is reasonably priced, durable, and versatile. *Use the library* to locate professional journal and magazine articles about music, curriculum guides for early childhood music, song books, music methods textbooks, and children's picture books that contain songs. Finally, *talk with teachers,* both music specialists and regular classroom teachers, about early childhood music materials that they have found particularly useful.

Teachers' Roles and Responsibilities

The teacher's role involves far more than merely dropping the needle of a record player or pushing the button on a tape player at various times of the day (Brand & Fernie, 1983). Teachers fulfill their musical roles and responsibilities when they function as motivators, planners, co-participants, and observers.

Motivator

Too often, teachers assume that they have done their part when they set up a music center with some rhythm instruments and a listening station. But children need to be introduced to musical experiences in an engaging way, just as they do to a story or lesson. The motivation for a music activity should include a concrete object, thought-provoking questions, and active participation. Ms. O'Malley introduced a new song to her kindergarten class by placing a four-sided wooden object with one pointed end and a stem in the center of the circle. The children were not sure what it was or why it had unusual markings on it. When she gave it a twirl and it began to spin around, they called out delightedly ''a top!'' Ms.

O'Malley then explained that it was a special type of top, a *dreidel*, that it was a traditional toy of Jewish children, and that the markings on the top were Hebrew letters. Then the children learned to sing "My Dreidel" while each child took a turn spinning the top. Additional motivational ideas include introducing *The Teddybears' Picnic* with a picnic basket, arranging chairs in bus seat formation to introduce *The Wheels on the Bus* (Zelinsky, 1990), or singing "I'm Being Swallowed by a Boa Constrictor" with a snake sock puppet.

Providing simple rhythm band instruments for children to play is naturally motivating. Even if resources are limited, rhythm sticks can be made from dowel rods, sandpaper blocks from scraps of wood and sandpaper, and drums from pieces of innertube stretched over coffee cans. For many ideas on making simple instruments, see *Listen!* (Wilt & Watson, 1977).

Planner

Planning a musical experience involves preparation, pacing, and providing variety. *Preparation* includes identifying your purpose, deciding what to include, and assembling your materials. If you are using recording equipment, make certain that it is in working order. Careful preparation will enable you to keep attention on the children rather than on the book, musical instrument, or recording equipment (Benson & Kates, 1982). Another aspect of preparation is getting the children assembled and ready. The children should be seated comfortably where they all can see. A circle is usually the best arrangement. Teach the children a signal indicating that it is music time, such as a clang of the finger cymbals or an introductory song. Strive to reduce background noise and other distractions before beginning.

Pacing is important too. Do not drag out an activity or race through it. It is generally best to alternate "mostly listening" activities with "mostly movement," to limit the amount of unfamiliar material at any one session, and to conclude with a quiet song or a song that leads into the next activity planned. If children ask to sing a song again, honor their request but stop before interest wanes.

Variety is another consideration. Give children a variety of opportunities to participate by listening, singing, using creative movement, and playing rhythm instruments. Remember that the goal is to extend and balance children's musical experiences, so include many different types of musical selections (see Figure 4.3), not only during music time but also throughout the day.

Co-Participant

The best early childhood teachers of music recognize that they are co-participants. These teachers share and enjoy music *with* children rather than perform *for* them. "Teachers who enjoy music and sing with enthusiasm, regardless of ability or training, are the ones who receive the greatest response and involvement from children" (Eliason & Jenkins, 1977, p. 245).

Observer

When sharing music with young children, answer these questions (Jalongo & Collins, 1985):

1. *What parts of the activity generate the most response?* Without prompting, children may clap, sway from side to side, bounce up and down, or associate specific words with actions. When singing, children do not usually sing every word. They may join in by singing just one word, a phrase, the first word of a verse, or the chorus.

2. *When do children follow along best?* Experiment with different methods of presenting concepts to children and note which ones are most effective. Try to relate explanations to something that the children have all experienced, asking, for example: "Can you make your coconut shells sound like the clip-clop of a horse's feet?"

3. *How do children use music spontaneously?* Note when and where children burst into song, dance around, or use musical instruments. If talk with a parent reveals that a child who never sings at circle time is singing away as she rides home in the car, an audiotape of the class singing might be sent home to build the child's confidence. If children seldom engage in song outdoors, teachers might plan an outdoor music activity, like singing "The Bear Went Over the Mountain" while climbing an obstacle course. If children seek a quiet corner in the classroom to play their instruments, a new music center and a better room arrangement might be the answer. By keeping in mind that the purpose is to support children's growth, teachers can provide the best possible experiences for their students.

Locating Resources

The local record store or bookstore probably will not carry the high-quality music resources that teachers need for their classrooms. Usually the best ways of locating these products include the following:

1. *Use the library.* Many of the most popular children's musicians, such as Ella Jenkins, Hap Palmer, Wee Sing, Tickle Tune Typhoon, Sharon, Lois and Bram, and Raffi have concert tapes that you can borrow from the public library. Weston Woods has several song picture books on tape, including Pete Seeger's *The Foolish Frog*, Aliki's *Hush Little Baby* and Maurice Sendak's *Really Rosie*, and some commercial videotapes, like Walt Disney's *Fantasia*, are of good quality. With videotapes becoming more affordable, your school may want to invest in some of these materials.

   Another possibility is to tape quality children's television programs. *Reading Rainbow* often includes songs, and there are musical programs for children like *The Elephant Show*. Occasionally there are children's concerts or seasonal music specials for children.

2. *Attend professional conferences.* At conferences, you can often attend music workshops by children's musicians. Usually, there are display booths where you can listen to a record or tape, assess the quality of rhythm instruments, or look over song picture books or song collections before investing in them.

3. *Contact children's music distributors.* One important resource for quality children's recordings and musical instruments is the catalog. Usually, the catalogs will indicate which records have earned awards. These catalogs often include authentic music from other lands and simple instruments from around the world that children can play (see Figures 4.2 and 4.3 for sources).

4. *Read the professional literature.* Publications such as *Booklist*, published by the American Library Association, regularly review picture books, videotapes, and records for children. Each year, they publish a "Nonprint Editor's Choice." They also feature special listings periodically, such as "Best in Kidvid."

After teachers have located high-quality materials, the next step is to place music and movement activities throughout the curriculum.

Integrating Music and Movement into the Subject Areas

As long as music is kept separate from academic subjects, it will be considered a "frill" and will remain neglected. By integrating music into all subject areas, teachers provide richer music and movement experiences for young children.

In general, appropriate music activities include singing songs together, playing and listening to records and tapes, learning the names and uses of musical instruments, discovering ways of making sounds, experiencing the different ways that music makes us feel, learning to participate with music through physical action and song, discovering rhythms in everyday life, observing different instruments being played, and playing simple musical instruments (Taylor, 1991). Activities that integrate music, movement, and all other areas of the curriculum are suggested below.

Mathematics, Science, and Technology

There are many ways of integrating mathematics, science, and technology into music activities.

Musical Sets

In mathematics, children can seriate instruments from large to small; they can also classify instruments into sets and subsets (e.g., woods, metals, drums, sticks). The teacher can provide experience with one-to-one correspondence by asking a child to distribute one rhythm band instrument to each classmate or create a momentary rhythm instrument shortage to get across the idea of unequal sets.

Sounds of Nature

In science, children can listen to nature's music: bird songs, the rhythms of the ocean, or the sounds created by whales and dolphins. A good follow-up to identifying the song of a real mockingbird on tape is learning a song like "Mockingbird Hill" (Muldaur, 1990).

Sound Shake Match

Use empty potato chip or 35mm film cannisters and make two cans that contain distinctive-sounding materials such as popcorn, rice, beans, and sand. The children can listen to the sounds and try to find the matching pairs.

Sound Quality

Children can conduct simple sound vibration experiments: listening to and observing the vibrations of rubber bands stretched across cardboard, experimenting with tuning forks, or trying different ways of beating a drum (with the fingertips, with the palm, with a stick). In technology, children might compare/contrast symphonic and synthesizer versions of the same selections, produce different types of sounds on a computer or electronic keyboard, or compare the sound of the same recording played on a record player or cassette player and a portable compact disc player.

Language, Literature, and Literacy

The child's growth in music and the language arts of listening, speaking, reading, and writing are connected in that both are symbolic systems. Some child-centered experiences that connect these systems include the following:

Musical Storytelling

Storytelling often lends itself to musical accompaniment. We can read "Jack and the Beanstalk" and use a slide whistle to represent characters' ascent and descent on the stalk, drums of different sizes to represent Jack's and the giant's footsteps, or set "Fee Fi Fo Fum . . ." to music. Most high-quality recordings for young children contain at least one story with sound effects and music, such as "Bear Hunt" (Bayes, 1983).

Song Picture Books

One category of picture book for young children is the *song picture book,* an illustrated version of a song (Jalongo, 1984; Jalongo & Renck, 1985). Often these books contain the music for the song, like *On Top of Spaghetti* (Glazer, 1982); sometimes they are accompanied by a record, like *Over in the Meadow* (Keats, 1965); and sometimes they tell the history of the song, like *Follow the Drinking*

Gourd (Winter, 1988). Of course, teachers and/or children can also design original illustrations to accompany song charts.

Creative Movement and Literature

A teacher might connect music with stories or picture books by asking:

> "Can you show me how Baby Bear might go for his walk as you move around the circle? Now let's see Papa Bear's walk. Now Mama Bear's."
>
> "Which rhythm instrument will you choose for each billy goat? Who can show me how the little billy goat would cross our balance beam bridge to this music?"
>
> "In the book *Color Dance* (Jonas, 1989), the dancers made colors with their scarves. Can you mix the colors while you dance, too?"

Song Parodies

A teacher might invite children to invent new verses for a song, beginning with simple substitutions like "If you're happy and you know it, _____", then listening to a parody of "She'll Be Comin' Round the Mountain," "All for Freedom" (Sweet Honey in the Rock, 1989). Teachers in the primary grades might ask children to create an entirely new version, as Raffi did for "Old MacDonald Had a Band" or "Baa Baa Black Sheep," in which he sings "One for your sweater, one for your rug. One for your blanket to keep you warm and snug." In order for children to accomplish this task, they must synthesize and evaluate what they know about lyrics, melody, rhythm, and rhyme. Writing a song parody is a complex, intellectually demanding activity (D'Angelo & Jalongo, 1984).

Vocabulary Enactment

The language of creative dance includes words that describe the body, space, time, energy, and relationships (Stinson, 1990). Combining concrete physical movements with abstract verbal symbols helps to build children's active vocabularies. It is one thing to use descriptors like *flexible, energetic, agile, graceful,* or *powerful* and quite another to see these attributes in action. By looking at several different types of movement on tape, such as those of a gymnast, a tap dancer, a modern dance troupe, and a scene from a ballet, children can incorporate these words into their vocabularies and then respond to them through dance.

Social Studies, Health, and Nutrition

The music of a culture communicates information about that culture because every social group uses music to celebrate, to worship, and as a vehicle for creative expression.

Restaurant Play

A teacher who transforms the housekeeping area into a Mexican restaurant with authentic music, a menu, and equipment is extending children's understandings about other cultures and building the self-esteem of those children who are already familiar with the materials and theme.

Visiting Musician

Teachers should use community resources to extend children's concepts about music. One Head Start teacher, for example, invited an African college student to her class. He arrived in traditional costume, taught the children a simple game from Nigeria, played the mbira (a thumb piano made of graduated metal strips over a wooden sound board), and taught them to sing a Nigerian children's song.

Health and Nutrition Songs

Practically every activity has a musical component if you look for it. As part of a dental health unit, teachers might use a chant like Raffi's "Brush Your Teeth." One teacher used the song "Today Is Monday" as a culmination to her unit on the four food groups. Each child created a version of the song by drawing pictures using different healthful foods for each day of the week.

Special Populations

When sharing music with special populations of young children, it is imperative that teachers first understand each child's strengths and limitations (McDonald & Simons, 1989).

Culturally Diverse Groups

Oscar Wilde once said, "Art says nothing, art expresses everything." Throughout history and in every culture, music and movement have been regarded as an art form, a part of religious rituals, a type of recreation, and a form of therapy (Schwartz, 1989). As a result, music and movement provide a common vehicle for children to know about, understand, appreciate, and preserve cultural traditions. Children can respond to dances from other cultures through recordings like *Dances of the World's Peoples* (Folkways 6501, 6503, 6504). Simple dances from the Far East, India, Africa, the Americas, and continental Europe can be taught using the Nonesuch Explorer series (Numbers 7–11) as a guide. Songs like *Tortillitas Para Mama* (Griego, 1980), a Spanish work song, or *Moonsong Lullaby* (Highwater, 1981), a Native American lullaby, expose children to the language and music of other cultures.

Children with Disabilities

A condition like cystic fibrosis can cause a deterioration in breath control and affect singing. Cognitive limitations can make it difficult for the child to recall words and melodies, and to focus on the music activity, or lead to problems in following directions to an action song (Darrow, 1985). Cerebral palsy affects the child's motor skills and may prevent participation in certain movement activities. Hearing impairments of various types obviously affect listening capacities.

Although we can make these general statements about limitations, each child is an individual. Teachers should check with specialists to determine each child's particular capabilities. You may find, for instance, that the hearing-impaired child has enough residual hearing to hear a song played on earphones or has low-frequency acuity and can hear low-pitched sounds like a bass drum. Even a child who is deaf can feel the rhythm of the vibrations by gently touching the speakers of the record player.

You could help the child with cognitive difficulties by using visual, verbal, and physical cues; providing more repetition; reducing distractions and background noise; breaking tasks into smaller segments; and ritualizing procedures (Darrow, 1985). For the child with attention disorders, creative dance is a highly motivating way to concentrate because "dancing involves making movement significant in and of itself. The first step in making movement dance is to pay attention to it" (Stinson, 1990, p. 35).

A child with cerebral palsy sometimes has more motor control on one side of the body than on the other and can therefore participate to some extent in motor activities. Likewise, you may find that a child with cerebral palsy can participate in singing if given an opportunity to rest for a moment. Often, children with special needs are so motivated to participate in music that they function at the highest possible level.

Music often motivates the child with a physical disability to function at the highest possible level.

High-Achieving and Low-Achieving Children

Music and creative dance should not be available only to the privileged child whose parents can afford private lessons or to the child who is gifted in music and movement (McLaughlin, 1988). Some low-achieving children recall and retain information better when they use more than one modality (e.g., visual, auditory, tactile). Music and movement offer multimodal approaches to learning and enable children to practice and solidify information and concepts.

Sometimes, the learning problems of low-achieving children are more social and emotional than cognitive. Socioemotional difficulties can be addressed through music as well. Psychologists have found that music is especially useful for children who have difficulty gaining social acceptance from peers, such as children who are aggressive and uncontrolled and those who are timid and withdrawn (Hughes, 1991). Creative dance in response to music builds self-esteem because a young child who moves in response to music does not move the wrong way or take the wrong step (Stinson, 1990). High-achieving children may or may not be gifted musically. If they are, they may be ready for somewhat more formal musical experiences, such as leading a group of classmates as they play pitched bells or composing original songs at an electronic keyboard. If these children are not musically gifted, it can be an opportunity for them to fully appreciate the fact that each person has unique strengths and talents.

Conclusion

There are some music and movement activities suitable for every child, regardless of age, talent, or physical limitations. Leading children to music and movement is also for every early childhood educator, regardless of his or her performance skills in music or dance. When teachers make music and movement an integral part of the school day, children's development in all areas—emotional, social, physical, and cognitive—is supported and enriched.

Chapter Summary

1. Children develop their musical abilities through interaction with significant others and enjoyment of music activities.
2. The goal of early childhood music and movement is to support every child's growth in music and movement from the earliest days of life.
3. Children proceed through the enactive, iconic, and symbolic modes in their understandings about music.
4. Music and movement activities have a long tradition in early childhood education and contemporary programs tend to be eclectic.
5. Factors that contribute to the child's growth in musicality are a supportive physical and emotional environment, opportunities for social interaction, and adult role models.

6.   Teachers fulfill their roles and responsibilities in music education when they select, present, and evaluate musical experiences effectively; when they function as motivators, planners, co-participants, and observers; and when they integrate music throughout the school day and across various subject areas.

Discussion Questions

1.   Compare and contrast the beliefs, values, and attitudes that underlie a program to maximize *every* child's musical talent with those that seek to identify precocity in music. Use your readings to support the philosophy of building every child's abilities.
2.   A parent tells you, "I don't sing to my child because I never learned to play an instrument, but I play his song tape for him at night." How would you respond? Why?
3.   An administrator observes the children briefly during your lesson and then asks, "Why are they having music during social studies?" How would you support your decision without becoming defensive?

Writing to Learn

Imagine that you are responsible for planning a thematic mini-unit for a group of children. The unit must include all of the traditional academic subjects (language arts, mathematics, science, social studies, health/nutrition), as well as sociodramatic play, art, and music. Begin with the music and movement characteristics of a particular age group of children (see Figure 4.1). Sketch out a plan for your theme and unit.

Interview

Children's Favorite Songs

The purpose of this assignment is to study young children's musical preferences. Arrange to interview the parents of a young child (5 to 8 years old) and the child individually. Try to interview a child who knows you well and who will not be too shy to sing on tape. Ask the parent about the child's favorite lullaby, nursery rhyme, children's song, or popular song at various times during the child's development. Then interview the child and invite the child to name, describe, and/or sing some of the songs he or she prefers today. (If the child is uncomfortable doing this, you might ask the parent to do it.) Tape-record the child's responses. Ask the child to tell you what he or she likes about each song.

In class, make a list of the songs selected by children. What categories of music are generally preferred? What features do they tend to have in common? Are there any surprising choices? Which songs are mentioned most often?

Observation

Children's Responses to Music

Arrange to observe a group of children in a singing, listening, or movement activity. Describe the setting, time, and activity. Watch the group carefully and record what you see in three columns. The first column should describe the teacher's activity. The next column should describe the group's general response—their observable behaviors (e.g., "everyone is marching around in a circle"). The final column should list specific behaviors by individual children, such as psychomotor behavior (e.g., "M. makes the gestures that go with the song but does not sing") and language behavior (e.g., "J. calls out, 'Can I have the tambourine this time'?"). In your summary, look for connections between the teacher's behavior and the children's responses. Is there anything that you would have handled differently? What? Why? How?

Controversy

Is Musicality Natural?

Many music experts have concluded that children have a natural propensity for musical behavior. Howard Gardner (1983) contends that musical intelligence is the first form of intelligence to develop. This contention is supported by work with premature and newborn infants suggesting that they are immediately responsive to music (Fox, 1991). In a study of the musical perception skills of newborns, for example, their facial expression, body movement, and alertness differed dramatically during a play song and a lullaby (Lopez, Dixon, Schanberger, & Fairweather, 1989).

There is evidence of a natural response to music in older children too. A toddler will naturally move more rapidly to fast music than to music with a slower pace. The research literature on early musical development suggests that children have a genetic predisposition to be musical, meaning that they are born with the means to respond to the music of their culture (Hodges, 1989).

Studies like these have led some researchers to believe that infancy may be a critical period for musical development, meaning that it is the optimal time to influence musical potential (Scott, 1989; Smardo, 1984). If early childhood is a prime time in the development of musical abilities, what implications does this have in terms of time, environment, and nature of activities for parents? For teachers?

Research Highlight

The Music Laboratory

Summary of Research

The modern version of Montessori's "prepared environment" is the music laboratory. A music laboratory functions much like a scientist's laboratory—providing the equipment, time, and opportunity to investigate. Recent research with toddlers, preschoolers, and school-age children (Fox, 1989; Upitis, 1990) suggests that one of the best ways of leading children to music is to provide a comparable environment where children have the materials, time, and opportunity to discover and build their own knowledge about music.

A music laboratory has these features

❏ *Active involvement.* Children explore and experiment with sounds and classroom musical instruments in an environment that supports their play.
❏ *A teacher/facilitator.* Teachers observe, model, support, and make comments or ask questions about the child's activities.
❏ *A balanced program.* There is a balance between unstructured music play and teacher-facilitated music and movement activities; a balance between individual activity (e.g., experimenting with bells) and group music making (e.g., playing in a rhythm band).
❏ *Attention to the child's developmental level.* Music and movement activities are adjusted to the child's developmental level (e.g., moving from primarily enactment to iconic representations and, finally, symbols).

Implications for Practice

Children are accustomed to *hearing* music—at shopping malls, in a radio jingle, or from a musical toy—but these experiences do not teach children to really *listen* to music. In fact, these experiences may be doing just the opposite: teaching children to disregard music by bombarding them with poor quality. Furthermore, as the research from the music laboratory suggests, even high-quality background music is not enough. Young children need opportunities to create, produce, and respond to music at an early age. Classroom teachers who bring relevant broad and varied musical elements into the curriculum are affecting children's musical behaviors throughout life.

How will you go about creating a music laboratory in your class?

If money were available through the budget, a donation or a small grant, what materials would you purchase first for each age group? Why?

References

Andress, B. (1989). Music for every stage. *Music Educator's Journal, 76*(2), 22–27.

Barr, K. W., & Johnston, J. M. (1989). Listening: The key to early childhood music. *Day Care and Early Education, 16*(3), 13–17.

Bayless, K. M., & Ramsey, M. E. (1990). *Music: A way of life for the young child.* New York: Macmillan.

Benson, A., & Kates, D. (1982). *Child care: Volume II. Vocational home economics education.* Stillwater, OK: Oklahoma State Board of Vocational and Technical Education. ERIC Document Reproduction Service No. ED 226 168.

Bernstein, P. (1990). On breaking 100 in music. In F. Wilson & F. Roehmann (Eds.), *Music and child development: Proceedings of the 1987 Denver Conference* (pp. 400–419). St. Louis, MO: Mosby.

Boyd, A. E. (1989, July–August). Music in early childhood. (Paper presented at the 21st International Conference on Early Education and Development (Hong Kong, July 31–August 4). ERIC Document Reproduction Service No. ED 310 863.

Brand, M., & Fernie, D. (1983). Music in the early childhood curriculum. *Childhood Education, 59*(5), 321–326.

Bruner, J. (1968). *Toward a theory of instruction.* New York: W. W. Norton.

D'Angelo, K., & Jalongo, M. R. (1984). Song picture books and the language disabled child. *Teaching Exceptional Children, 16,* 114–120.

Darrow, A. A. (1985). Music for the deaf. *Music Educator's Journal, 71*(6), 33–35.

Davidson, L. (1985). Preschool children's tonal knowledge: Antecedents of scale. In *The young child and music.* Reston, VA: Music Educator's National Conference.

Day, B. (1988). *Early childhood education creative learning activities.* (3rd ed.). New York: Macmillan.

Dugard, M. C. (1984, June). Musical movement: From slithering to galloping through music. In J. Boswell (Ed.), *The young child and music: Contemporary principles in child development and music education* (pp. 82–97). Proceedings of the Music in Early Childhood Conference, Provo, UT (June 28–30). ERIC Document Reproduction Service ED 265 949.

Eliason, C., & Jenkins, L. (1977). *A practical guide to early childhood curriculum.* St. Louis, MO: Mosby.

Elkind, D. (1987). *Miseducation: Preschoolers at risk.* New York: Knopf.

Erikson, E. (1950). *Childhood and society.* New York: W. W. Norton.

Fox, D. B. (1989). Music time and music times two: The Eastman infant-toddler music program. In B. Andress (Ed.), *Promising practices in prekindergarten music* (pp. 13–24). Reston, VA: Music Educators National Conference.

Fox, D. B. (1991). Music, development, and the young child. *Music Educator's Journal, 77*(5), 42–46.

Gardner, H. (1973). *The arts and human development.* New York: Wiley.

Gardner, H. (1983). *Frames of mind: The theory of multiple intelligences.* New York: Basic Books.

Greenberg, M. (1979). *Your children need music.* Englewood Cliffs, NJ: Prentice-Hall.

Hall, M. A. (1989). Music for children. In B. Andress (Ed.), *Promising practices in prekindergarten music* (pp. 47–57). Reston, VA: Music Educators National Conference.

Hodges, D. A. (1989). Why are we musical? Speculations on the evolutionary plausibility of musical behavior. *Bulletin of the Council for Research in Music Education, 99,* 7–22.

Hughes, F. (1991). *Children, play and development.* Boston: Allyn & Bacon.

Jalongo, M. R. (1984). The top ten: Song picture books. *The Bulletin* (Children's Literature Assembly of the

National Council of Teachers of English), *10*, 4–5.

Jalongo, M. R. (1991). *Developing children's listening skills*. Bloomington, IN: Phi Delta Kappa.

Jalongo, M. R., & Bromley, K. D. (1984). Developing linguistic competence through song picture books. *The Reading Teacher, 37*, 840–845.

Jalongo, M. R., & Collins, M. (1985). Singing with young children! Folk music for nonmusicians. *Young Children, 40*, 17–22.

Jalongo, M. R., & Renck, M. A. (1985). Stories that sing: A storytime resource. *School library journal, 32*(1), 42–43.

Kelley, L., & Sutton-Smith, B. (1987). A study of infant musical productivity. In J. C. Peery, I. W. Peery, & T. Draper (Eds.), *Music and child development* (pp. 35–53). New York: Springer-Verlag.

Leeper, S. H., Dales, R., Skipper, D., & Witherspoon, R. (1974). *Good schools for young children* (3rd ed.). New York: Macmillan.

Leonhard, C. (1968). *Discovering music together: Early childhood.* Chicago: Follett.

Littleton, D. (1989). Child's play: Pathways to music learning. In B. Andress (Ed.), *Promising practices: Prekindergarten music education* (pp. ix–xiii). Reston, VA: Music Educators National Conference.

Lopez, S., Dixon, S., Schanberger, P. N., & Fairweather, P. D. (1989, July). The effects of lullabies and playsongs on newborn infants. (Paper presented at the 19th Congres Internationale de Pediatrie, Paris, July 23–28.)

McAllester, D. (1991). *Becoming human through music*. Reston, VA: Music Educator's National Conference.

McDonald, D. T., & Simons, G. M. (1989). *Musical growth and development: Birth through six*. New York: Schirmer/Macmillan.

McLaughlin, J. (1988). A stepchild comes of age. *Journal of Physical Education, Recreation, and Dance, 59*(9), 58–60.

Metz, E. (1989). Music and movement environments in preschool settings. In B. Andress (Ed.), *Promising practices in prekindergarten music* (pp. 89–96). Reston, VA: Music Educators National Conference.

Music Educators National Conference (1986). *The school music program: Description and standards.* Reston, VA: Music Educators National Conference.

Peterson, M. (1979). Stay in tune (record/cassette). Summit, NJ: Meg Peterson Enterprises.

Piaget, J. (1952). *The origins of intellect.* New York: International Universities Press.

Piaget, J. (1962). *Play, dreams and imitation in childhood.* C. Gategno & F. M. Hodgson (Trans.). New York: W. W. Norton.

Ririe, S. R. (1980). Individual arts: Dance. In J. J. Hausman (Ed.), *Arts and the schools* (pp. 270–279). New York: McGraw-Hill.

Rousseau, J. J. (1883). *Emile, or treatise on education.* W. H. Payne, (Trans.). New York: Appleton.

Schwartz, V. (1989). Dance for all people. *Journal of Physical Education, Recreation, and Dance, 60*(9), 49.

Scott, C. R. (1989). How children grow—musically. *Music Educators Journal, 76*(2), 28–31.

Smardo, F. (1984). Using literature as a prelude or finale to music experiences with young children. *The Reading Teacher, 37*(8), 700–705.

Stinson, S. W. (1990). Dance for education in early childhood. *Design for Arts in Education, 91*, 34–41.

Taylor, B. (1991). *A child goes forth.* New York: Macmillan.

Upitis, R. (1990). *This too is music.* Portsmouth, NH: Heinemann.

Werner, P. H., & Burton, E. C. (1979). *Learning through movement: Teaching* cognitive content through physical activities. St. Louis, MO: Mosby.

Wilson, F., & Roehmann, F. (Eds.) (1990). *Music and child development: Proceedings of the 1987 Denver Conference.* St Louis, MO: MMB Music.

Wilt, J., & Watson, T. (1977). *Listen!* Waco, TX: Creative Resources.

Zimmerman, M. (1971). *Musical characteristics of children.* Washington, DC: Music Educator's National Conference.

Zimmerman, M. (1984). *State of the art in early childhood music and research.* Paper presented at the Music in Early Childhood Conference, Provo, UT. ERIC Document Reproduction Service No. ED 250068

Children's Books and Records

Aliki. (1968). *Hush little baby.* Englewood Cliffs, NJ: Prentice-Hall.

Bayes, L. (1983) "Bear Hunt" on *Circle Around.* Seattle, WA: Tickle Tune Typhoon.

Beale, P. C., & Nipp, S. H. (1983). *Wee sing silly songs.* Los Angeles: Price/Sloan/Stern.

Child, L. (1974). *Over the river and through the woods.* New York: Scholastic.

Collins, M. (1982). *Sounds like fun.* Rochester, NY: Sampler Records.

Delibes, L. (1986). Coppelia. In M. Greaves, *Petrushka (A little box of ballet stories).* New York: Dial.

Glazer, T. (1982). *On top of spaghetti.* New York: Doubleday.

Griego, M. (1980). *Tortillitas para mama.* New York: Holt, Rinehart & Winston.

Highwater, J. (1981). *Moonsong lullaby.* New York: Morrow.

Jonas, A. (1989). *Color dance.* New York: Greenwillow.

Keats, E. J. (1965). *Over in the meadow.* New York: Scholastic.

Kennedy, J. (1983). *Teddy bear's picnic.* La Jolla, CA: Green Tiger Press.

Muldaur, M. (1990). *On the sunny side.* Redway, CA: Music for Little People.

Pearson, T. C. (1983). *We wish you a merry Christmas.* New York: Dial.

Peek, M. (1981). *Roll over! A counting song.* New York: Houghton Mifflin.

Raffi (1987). *Down by the bay.* New York: Crown.

Seeger, P. (1973). *The foolish frog.* New York: Macmillan (also on Weston Woods video).

Spier, P. (1961). *The fox went out on a chilly night.* Boston: Little, Brown.

Sweet Honey in the Rock (1989). *All for freedom.* Redmond, CA: Music for Little People.

Wescott, N. B. (1980). *I know an old lady who swallowed a fly.* Boston: Atlantic/Little.

Winter, J. (1988). *Follow the drinking gourd.* New York: Knopf.

Zelinsky, P. (1990). *The wheels on the bus.* New York: Dutton.

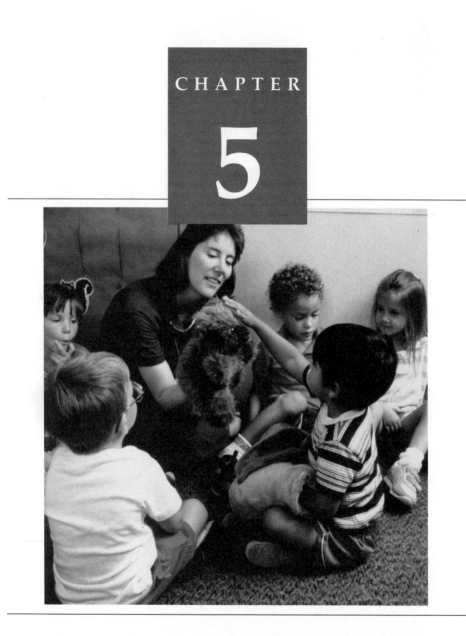

Creative Drama in the Early Childhood Curriculum

Of all of the arts, drama involves the participant most fully: intellectually, emotionally, physically, verbally, and socially. As players, children assume the roles of others, where they learn and become sensitive to the problems and values of persons different from themselves. At the same time, they are learning to work cooperatively in groups, for drama is a communal art, each person necessary to the whole. As spectators, children become involved vicariously in the adventures of the characters on stage.

Nellie McCaslin, 1990, p. 2

After reading this chapter, you will be able to

- ❑ Explain how creative drama contributes to children's learning.
- ❑ Identify criteria for integrating creative drama into the curriculum.
- ❑ Design and implement appropriate creative drama experiences for all young children.
- ❑ Analyze the controversial issues in teaching creative drama.

Case Study

It is February in Ms. Clark's inner-city, first-grade classroom, and five children have asked to enact "The Little Red Hen." Florence, a nonreader, has volunteered to be the narrator. Jesse, a shy, obese African-American boy, has asked to play the role of the hen. When Ms. Clark comes by, she helps them plan by asking good questions:

Ms. Clark: Let's do some brainstorming about what we might need for costumes, and I'll write it down.

Jesse: I need some feathers.

Ms. Clark: How do you want to do the feathers? How would you put them on? (Tory holds up a fringed red scarf and says) We can use this for the head part.

(Ms. Clark writes down what each child chooses to wear, how each will invent a simple costume and props, and then announces) I need to know what you're going to work on tomorrow so that I can have my supplies ready.

This group of students is ethnically diverse and lives in a low-income area of the city. Why would Ms. Clark devote time to drama?

Ms. Clark knows how important child-initiated activity is for young children. Her first graders initiated the idea of dramatizing a favorite, familiar story. They also selected and negotiated roles, jointly planned costumes, and chose their audience. Rather than giving her students seatwork to complete after reading the story (such as cutting and pasting pictures in the correct sequence), Ms. Clark capitalized on their interest, involved them in purposeful and meaningful activities, and supported their learning through dramatization. A simple enactment activity like dramatizing "The Little Red Hen" enables children to learn about themselves and others, to develop a sense of belonging in a community of learners, to gain self-confidence, and to master skills and concepts in meaningful situations. Observing these children reveals how important these goals are in any classroom.

Remember Jesse? He usually speaks softly and does not enunciate clearly, but because he wanted to be the Little Red Hen, he practiced and refined his communication skills. Florence is not yet reading, but her role as narrator has prompted her to learn and apply the strategies necessary to decode print.

Theoretical Framework

When most adults think about drama, they think about formal productions: a small group of performers who memorize lines and use props and costumes while entertaining an audience. Formal drama often causes both teachers and students to feel anxious, self-conscious, and uncreative. Consequently, many teachers are reluctant to integrate drama into their classrooms (Fox, 1987).

Formal drama differs significantly from creative drama. In creative drama, children can spontaneously invent, enact, and interpret familiar situations and themes for themselves rather than memorizing a script for an audience (McCaslin, 1990). Experiences with enactment belong everywhere in the early childhood curriculum (Fox, 1987; Hennings, 1990).

The Meaning of Enactment

Three-year-old Haley has heard the story of *Perfect the Pig*. In this story a homeless, flying piglet is loved and cared for by a young woman, stolen and abused by a man, and happily reunited with the woman when a judge awards her custody. As she pretends to be Perfect, she experiences the feelings and thoughts of the pig during the story. She also decides which props and behaviors she needs to enact that role and experiments with ways of creating oinks.

Enactment occurs when children adopt the actions, feelings, thoughts, and behaviors of people in particular situations. This ability emerges at about age 3 and signals the child's developing imagination. Enactment is "potentially the most powerful kind of learning" (Dillon, 1988, p. 7) because children can

- ❏ Assume roles, create dialogue, feel emotions, use their bodies, and make decisions.
- ❏ Use their past and present experiences to talk about and solve problems.
- ❏ Develop knowledge of appropriate roles, actions, and behaviors.
- ❏ See others' points of view.
- ❏ Try out new and emerging skills.
- ❏ Explore the forms and functions of language (Shaftel & Shaftel, 1983; Dillon, 1988).

Children learn about their physical and social worlds, not only from their interactions with these worlds, but also from the way these worlds interact with them. These concrete, personal experiences provide the basis for their developing abstract, interpersonal knowledge that comprises much of the learning that goes on in schools today. Because drama is always concrete, specific, and personal, it helps children more easily understand how their physical and social worlds work (Dillon, 1988). In other words, it is a powerful way of knowing.

Preschool and kindergarten children most often enact situations based upon real or imaginary roles they have experienced, such as preparing meals for a family or taking care of a baby. Primary grade children most often imagine themselves in real-life, problem-solving situations like controlling a space shuttle in outer space. Through enactment, all children stretch their imaginations, share experiences that help them understand their world in a low-risk setting, and explore feelings, emotions, and ideas in socially acceptable ways (Erickson, 1988).

Forms of Enactment

Enactment occurs in four forms in the early childhood years: dramatic play, informal drama, story or interpretive drama, and formal or scripted drama. These drama forms can be differentiated according to their level of spontaneity versus formality (Tompkins & Hoskisson, 1991). Following are the characteristics and an example of each form.

1. *Dramatic play*, the earliest and most informal type of enactment, is typical of preschool children. In dramatic play, children spontaneously take on a role or behavior of someone else (such as pretending to direct traffic as a police officer), use an object to stand for something else (such as sitting on a block and driving a "tractor" around the fields), and use make-believe to act out familiar events (such as going to a fast-food restaurant). In dramatic play there is no audience, and the teacher serves as an observer or facilitator.

2. *Informal drama* is also spontaneous and process oriented. It is typical of 5- to 8-year-old children who create and enact their own scripts based on familiar life, literature, or media experiences. Pantomime (such as eating a dripping ice-cream cone) and movement (such as walking like an elephant) are types of informal drama activities.

3. *Story or interpretive drama* involves inventing an *interpretation* of someone else's ideas and words rather than creating new ones. Children in the primary grades often enact favorite stories they have heard and read, or they create original stories. Take, for example, the picture book *Amazing Grace*. Grace is an African-American child with a flair for drama who pretends, among other things, to be a nurse whose patients' lives are in her hands. When the class decides to enact Peter Pan, her peers tell Grace that she cannot play the lead role because she is female and black. But with her mother's and grandmother's support, she *does* pursue her dream. This story readily lends itself to interpretation and readers theater because Grace is practicing some form of enactment on every page. Story drama is particularly valuable in stimulating children's oral language. At the end of this chapter, there is a selective list of picture books that lend themselves to dramatization.

4. *Formal or scripted drama* is the most structured form of drama. It involves a polished production of a prepared script before an audience (McCaslin, 1990). In scripted drama, the children memorize lines and the teacher directs. Because scripted drama is product oriented, it focuses on technique rather than expression (Bolton, 1985). Current thinking in the field of early childhood education is against the use of formal or scripted drama for young children unless they choose to create and produce their own plays. Otherwise, it is not considered a form of creative drama for this age group (Schickedanz, York, Stewart, & White, 1991). Table 5.1 compares and contrasts these types of enactment in terms of level of formality, preparation time needed for each form, the role of the players and audience, materials needed and implications for teachers.

TABLE 5.1 Four Types of Drama Activities

Dramatic Play	Informal Drama	Story or Interpretive Drama	Scripted Drama
Least Formal – – – – – – – – –			– – – Most Formal
CHARACTERISTICS			
Unrehearsed, spontaneous enactment of roles and behaviors of familiar people or characters; important first step in uses of enactment; most characteristic of 3-, 4-, and 5-year-olds.	Spontaneous, improvised, invented enactments; includes verbal and nonverbal activities (facial expressions, gestures, body movements, and vocal changes) to enact feelings and ideas. Typical of 5- to 8-year-olds.	Invented interpretation of ideas and stories using voices, gestures, and facial expressions. Involves some rehearsal and is more formal.	Memorizing a written script; performing polished plays before an audience.
PREPARATION TIME			
Minimal: children initiate roles and behaviors; teacher prepares setting; provides enriching experiences and materials.	Minimal: children invent actions, dialogue, and movements based on knowledge of the world and/or a familiar story.	Moderate: children rehearse reading; interpret story and enact roles.	Extensive: children memorize parts, dialogue, and gestures.
ROLES OF PLAYERS AND AUDIENCE			
Active: all children are players and audience at the same time.	Active: children move freely from role of audience to that of player; not designed for an audience.	Active: children read parts individually or as members of a group.	Passive: roles must be rehearsed to play; audience watches.
MATERIALS			
Simple, familiar props; some realistic.	None required; some may be used.	Simple props.	Elaborate costumes, prop, scenery.
IMPLICATIONS FOR THE CLASSROOM			
Exerts powerful influence on children's social and cognitive understandings; children practice these understandings and begin to see others' points of view.	Naturally extends children's dramatic play skills; can be used with children's favorite or original stories; children practice both verbal and nonverbal communication.	Increases children's confidence in using scripted drama; allows for cooperative work with peers.	Not applicable.

Dramatic play, informal drama, and story drama are the only forms of creative drama that belong in the early childhood curriculum. They offer purposeful ways to develop children's oral language, imagination and thinking, nonverbal communication, and self-confidence.

The Importance of Creative Drama in the Curriculum

Creative drama meets the needs of all children in four main ways.

1. *It values and respects children's individuality and creative expressiveness.* Drama builds positive self-concepts in children as they participate in experiences that have no right or wrong answers (McCaslin, 1990). Each child's interpretation of a role is unique and enables the child to feel good about involvement in a group experience.

2. *It offers a means for cooperative learning and teamwork through shared experiences* (Erickson, 1988; McCaslin, 1990). Two third graders wanted to use a secret code to "put on a show" for their friends. During recess, they decided on the theme of eating and sleeping in space and then figured out a code based on colors. After collecting props like sleeping bags, Ziploc plastic bags, and a pillow, they invited some of their peers to watch their skit and try to figure out their code.

3. *It enables children to construct meanings from abstract situations and personalize real-life situations* (Verriour, 1985). After 4-year-old Mary's puppy died, she initiated an animal rescue theme play. In her dramas, unlike the real-life situation, Mary always saved the animal's life.

4. *It provides opportunities to be spectators and actors.* Whether children are enacting or watching others enact, they are simultaneously imagining the situations and problems of others (McCaslin, 1990). After hearing a story about a Kwanzaa celebration, a group of kindergartners imagined and enacted African-American children's use of dance, poetry, songs, and food to celebrate the bounty of the earth.

In the following enactment of a restaurant theme, Kellie and Tammie, 4-year-old twins, and Brenda, a college student, are co-playing. Consider how this dramatic play episode contributes to the twins' developing imaginative thinking; problem-solving ability; language, and listening skills; perspective-taking ability; and appreciation of drama as an art form.

Kellie: Oh, here's your table. (She gestures toward the table.)

Brenda: Well, what should we eat, Tammie? What do you have here, Kellie?

Kellie: Well, we have pork chops, lima beans, and fish sticks.

Tammie: That sounds good. We'll take it.

Some creative drama activities provide opportunities for children to be both actors and spectators.

(Kellie exits and returns with a "tray"—two parts of a plastic sweater-drying rack.) The girls continue their play, name their restaurant "King's," order drinks, and then ask for a check.

Tammie: I want my check to be five dollars.

Kellie: Five dollars . . . and eighty-six cents.

Tammie: Okay.

Brenda: Do you have any money?

Tammie: Oh, yeah. I have a lot of money. Oh, I forgot. I don't have any money. (Starts rummaging through her purse and begins to giggle.)

Creative drama develops children's *imaginative thinking*. In the restaurant scene, Kellie and Tammie needed a strong mental image of a restaurant in order to create the roles of customer and waitress in ways that satisfied their self-expression.

When Kellie needed a tray to serve the food in the restaurant, she was *problem solving* as she used two parts of a plastic sweater-drying rack for this prop. Through drama, children relive their experiences by creating their own worlds in order to experiment with solutions to real-life problems (McCaslin, 1990).

Drama also enables children to practice *literacy skills* in meaningful contexts. In dramatic play, younger children generate more verbal play and richer language than in any other setting (Christie & Johnson, 1983), develop narrative competence by inventing stories that contain essential story elements, and display their knowledge of the functions of reading and writing (Roskos, 1988). In other forms of drama, they gain confidence in their ability to speak and begin to value language. In the restaurant episode, Kellie and Tammie communicate verbally about what to order and how to pay. Kellie also uses nonverbal communication as she gestures toward the table. Play episodes like this one give children opportunities to use the forms and functions of language (Halliday, 1975).

When children actually become someone else, they learn the behaviors and feelings of that character or role, as well as how people affect other people. Role enactment enables children to develop their *perspective-taking ability*. Even very young children may glimpse insights that help in understanding people and, therefore, in living (McCaslin, 1990). In the restaurant episode, Kellie and Tammie practiced appropriate behaviors for eating in a restaurant. They also watched Brenda, the college student, model the customer role by asking, "Well, what should we eat, Tammie? What do you have here, Kellie?"

For children to *appreciate drama as an art form* and become our future audiences and players, they must experience drama early. School provides an important context for children, not only to be actors but also to gain understanding of what drama is and how it comes into being (Jacobs, 1988). According to drama expert Nellie McCaslin (1990), drama activities "offer children their first taste of the magic and make-believe of the theatre" (p. 16). Moreover, when children dramatize stories, they walk in someone else's shoes—a critical opportunity to experience the feelings and behaviors of others (Jacobs, 1988).

Drama, in its many forms, is an important stimulus for children's healthy growth and development. It enables them to express their thoughts, feelings, and ideas in both verbal and nonverbal ways. As so poignantly stated by Gavin Bolton (1985), an authority in drama education: "Drama allows children to experience the complexities of today's world and to be prepared to live in the twenty-first century" (p. 156). Therefore, its place in the early childhood curriculum is essential.

Criteria for Integrating Drama into the Curriculum

Teachers possess the most powerful influence over children's dramatic expression. An early childhood curriculum must contain a variety of opportunities for children to enact familiar experiences and to share information through their interactions with both peers and adults (Nelson, 1986). Openness to their creative efforts and the establishment of a supportive, child-centered environment are crucial in selecting and presenting opportunities for creative drama (Edwards, 1990).

Selecting and Presenting Experiences and Materials

Some considerations that enhance creative drama include space, materials, and an enthusiastic teacher (McCaslin, 1990). To release creative potential through drama, children need

- ❑ *Large, pleasant spaces.* How space is arranged sends strong messages about how to use that space for drama. Providing specific space for dramatic activity, as well as clear pathways to enter and exit those spaces, is important.
- ❑ *A large assortment of open-ended materials.* Materials influence the content of children's enactments and support their ability to initiate and sustain them. A group of first graders was playing in a spaceship they had constructed with blocks. Using the accessible props of buttons, plastic cups, and a steering wheel, they took their spaceship into outer space and used their control panel to communicate with mission control.
- ❑ *Accessible and easily stored materials.* Three first-grade children were role-playing in their classroom grocery store and decided to make signs for the "weekly specials." Their teacher provided folders and table easels to save or reuse their work. Prop boxes, discussed in the section on dramatic play in this chapter, offer another type of accessible storage. Accessible and easily stored material gives children autonomy with drama.
- ❑ *Adequate time.* Children need ample time to plan, carry out, and sustain their dramatic activity. Drama requires recruiting players, locating materials and props, negotiating roles and plots, and carrying out joint ideas. In order to do this, we, as teachers, need to schedule lengthy periods for creative drama (Johnson, Christie, & Yawkey, 1987).
- ❑ *Personal involvement.* Students' level of personal engagement in drama is important (Morgan & Saxton, 1987). For drama to be an effective learning medium, children must be interested, engaged, and committed to the enactment.

Let's look at Mr. Manley's kindergarten class, which is enacting a camping theme. Think about the five considerations for selecting and presenting drama experiences—space, materials, storage, time, and personal involvement. How did these variables affect the children's enactments?

Because camping is a relatively inexpensive family vacation, many children have had some direct experience with this activity. In planning a camping theme corner, the children designed a campground with tents, a campfire, trees, a lake, and trails. Following a few days of play, Mr. Manley observed the children repeatedly re-enacting the same sequence of putting up and taking down their tents. After talking with them about other camping activities, such as what they were using for food and how they were getting their meals, he decided to add some cooking equipment and empty boxes from real food for a camp store. He also read them several camping stories, including *Bailey Goes Camping* (Henkes, 1985) and *Three Days on the River in a Red Canoe* (Williams, 1981) to help them elaborate their dramatic play. Clearly, this episode illustrates the importance of the teacher with creative drama in the classroom.

Teachers' Roles and Responsibilities

Teachers often wonder how much, if at all, they should intervene in children's enactments. As facilitators who enhance and encourage drama and dramatic play, teachers assume a role in the preparation and follow-up to children's dramatizations (Shaftel & Shaftel, 1983). One common error is for teachers to become too intrusive, to act as "directors" who disrupt the children's spontaneity.

The following strategies will help extend drama throughout your classroom.

1. *Ask thoughtful questions that provoke creative thinking.* Before any drama activity, find out what children know or want to know about the content and roles. During the activity, infuse curiosity and exhibit a real desire to hear children's responses. When Mr. Manley's kindergartners were planning their camping theme corner, he asked them to talk about what they knew about camping. He also asked them questions such as "Where will you all sleep?", "How will you get your food?", and "What will you do for fun on your trip?" Through knowledge of the children in his class, Mr. Manley challenged children's thinking that helped them enact more complex camping themes.

2. *Reflect with children.* Talking about specific roles and situations during and after the drama helps children clarify their thoughts and feelings. Ms. Wengel's second graders had created a shoe store as part of their unit on clothing. The store contained various styles of shoes, such as slippers, boots, running shoes, ballet shoes, and photos of old-fashioned shoes and boots that the children used to sort, classify, measure, and make purchases. Ms. Wengel helped the children reflect on their play by asking them to imagine what old shoes looked like and what shoes would look like when they were adults. By reflecting on their enactments, the children thought about new uses for shoes, generated new ideas about shoes, and listened to other children's ideas and responses, which they then incorporated into future dramatizations in the shoe store.

3. *Model a behavior or attribute.* One of the most effective strategies for empowering children through drama is to model certain behaviors for them. Watch, however, for the appropriate moment to do this (Morgan & Saxton, 1987). In creative drama, teachers should not impose their ideas on children. Rather, they should encourage children to develop their own ideas, value their responses, support their improvisations, and encourage them to believe in themselves and their abilities (Shaftel & Shaftel, 1983). When Mr. Sargent's first graders wanted to enact a firefighting scene, they needed a prop to use as a firehose. He invited

them to problem-solve, asking, "What should the object do?" Children suggested that it should be long, rounded, skinny, and sort of stretchy. They decided to use a plastic Slinky.

Talking with children about their drama, assuming different roles, and providing time, space, and resources are the building blocks of the early childhood drama program. This foundation provides children with the needed opportunities to explore appropriate drama activities.

Appropriate Creative Drama Activities and Experiences

Informal, unrehearsed, process-oriented drama activities are most appropriate for the early childhood years (Tompkins & Hoskisson, 1991). Some of these activities include dramatic and sociodramatic play, pantomime, puppets, story drama, and readers theater. These drama activities help children to

1. Develop improved skills in reading, listening, speaking and writing.
2. Develop skill in thinking analytically, in acting decisively and responsibly.
3. Increase and sustain the ability to concentrate and follow directions.
4. Strengthen self-concept by cooperative interaction with others.
5. Increase motivation to learn.
6. Develop individual and group creativity. (Joint Committee on the Role of Informal Drama in the Classroom, 1983, pp. 370–371).

Dramatic and Sociodramatic Play

Three-year-old Michelle dons a surgeon's cap, hangs a stethoscope around her neck, and examines Spotty, a large teddy bear. She uses a spoon to give her patient a shot and scribbles a prescription on a scrap of paper located in the play area.

A group of kindergartners are being air traffic controllers and helping planes land during a blizzard. Their conversation includes negotiations and decisions about how many controllers can fit in the control tower and which planes belong to which controller. These children are engaged in dramatic play.

Why Use Dramatic and Sociodramatic Play?

Dramatic and sociodramatic play contribute to children's enactment abilities. In this kind of drama, children can be both actors and directors. As actors, children experience the actual feelings, thoughts, and behaviors of the roles they are playing. As directors, they imagine the thoughts, feelings, and behaviors associated with a role and coach the actors. Playing both roles in dramatic and sociodramatic play helps children

❑ Construct their own understandings of how the world works (Donoghue, 1990).

❑ Act out social situations requiring negotiation with players with different needs and views (Donoghue, 1990).

❑ Express their inner feelings (Mayesky, 1990).

❑ Communicate in meaningful ways and develop social skills by negotiating roles, locating props, and agreeing on a common theme (Tompkins & Hoskisson, 1991).

❑ Develop the confidence to explore freely and imaginatively the more structured forms of drama (Shaftel & Shaftel, 1983).

Suggestions for the Classroom

Ms. Senack has set up a beach theme center that includes assorted, related materials like a large ocean poster, a child-sized beach chair, a small umbrella, a collection of shells, water toys, and casette tapes for her 4-year-old class. Ari spreads his towel on the sand and checks his bag for sunglasses and sand toys. Shayna locates her portable radio and skips over stations until she finds the appropriate music. "Hey, Ari!", Shayna asks, "do you like this song? Let's pretend we are teenagers!" Eventually, they use towels to bury themselves and call themselves "Dancing Sand People." At the sand table, they engage in the following dialogue:

> Ari: Put all the shells you want in your pile. Don't get them mixed up. These are mine! (Gets a magnifying glass from the science table.) Look, this one is really dirty!
>
> Shayna: Let me see! (Ari hands her the magnifying glass, and Shayna examines the shell.) That's not dirt! That's the way the shell is. It comes like that! You just don't know 'cause only if you have a 'fying glass can you see what it looks like underneath.
>
> Ari: My mom sometimes uses shells for plates. She has really big shells and puts all our food on it.
>
> Shayna: Here's some macaroni and cheese! (Hands Ari a shell with some sand on it.)

This beach theme play illustrates two strategies for enhancing dramatic play—prop boxes or dramatic play kits and theme corners.

Prop Boxes and Dramatic Play Kits.   Prop boxes or dramatic play kits contain a collection of real items that are related in some way, such as a picnic basket, plastic food, a tablecloth, and plastic ants. Using real items can foster and extend children's play with particular ideas and concepts in all curricular areas. Prop boxes

❑ Promote experiences with real materials and tools related to a theme (e.g., a toolbox).

❑ Extend interest so that children can sustain their theme play (e.g., books, posters, records, and tapes related to the theme).

In dramatic play, children experience the actual feelings, thoughts, and behaviors of the roles they enact.

❑ Provide opportunities to enact familiar roles (e.g., deposit slips and checks for a banker or boots, a net, and a fishing pole for a fisherman).
❑ Develop career awareness (e.g., a medical kit or a briefcase).

Younger children need adequate props, space, and time to pursue dramatic play even though their roles and themes shift frequently. Older children, who are more sophisticated in their play, can plan their theme and often negotiate roles and responsibilities. At all ages, children use the props in many different ways.

The basic procedure for creating and using prop boxes and dramatic play kits to extend units of study and to support children's enactments is as follows

❑ *Brainstorm themes that most interest your children.* Then choose some that are very familiar (e.g., a grocery store), others that are somewhat familiar (e.g., a gas station), and still others that are less familiar to children (e.g., a travel agency). Be certain to provide adequate background experiences that will support their play in theme centers.

❑ *Collect strong boxes with lids such as those that contain photocopy paper (17 × 11 inches).* Label the outside of the box with the theme (e.g., "The Three Bears" or "Chinese New Year").

❑ *Generate with your children a list of possible items to include in the prop box.* Ask children, parents, and colleagues to contribute items. Clothing, especially old uniforms and costumes, and recycled materials such as old toys and household articles, are generally useful.

❑ *Think about your goals for the theme or unit.* What vocabulary could children be using in their drama? How will you introduce the center and related activities so that they capitalize on children's previous experiences? Record these ideas and tape them inside the cover of the prop box to serve as a guide for parents, substitute or student teachers, or administrators. These ideas will help keep the dramatic play well connected to the goals of the unit. Figure 5.1 shows a properly labeled prop box containing an assortment of related items. Appendix A shows how to use a dance prop box and contains ideas for additional prop boxes.

FIGURE 5.1 Properly Labeled Prop Box

Information to be taped inside the lid or cover of the prop box	Theme:_____
	Goals for Center:_____
	Vocabulary:_____
	Introduction of Center:_____
	Field Trips and Resource People:_____
Information on the outside of the prop box	Theme:_____
	Props: (costumes, real things, objects)_____
	Materials in Box:_____
	Suggested Supplements:_____
	Child-Made Materials:_____

Theme Corners or Play Centers. Theme corners or play centers contain materials focused on a topic familiar and interesting to a particular group of children. They encourage children's spontaneous interactions with a variety of roles (Woodward, 1985). Theme corners make a unit of study, such as nutrition, more real to children and add to their interest.

The following five guidelines encourage children's powerful enactments using theme corners.

1. Provide a variety of background experiences through pictures, stories, and discussion centered on the theme. Children need to be familiar with roles in order to enact them.

2. Create an attractive physical setting with posters, books, and materials. The physical setting conveys a powerful message that can invite or discourage children from entering the area.

3. Provide simple, durable props. They help children enact desired roles and behaviors.

4. Intervene only when necessary. When introducing a new theme corner, jointly establish limits such as the number of children who can be there at any one time.

5. Encourage children to suggest ideas for themes and plan new theme corners periodically. Children can make and collect the necessary props. (Adapted from Woodward, 1985, pp. 291–295)

Figure 5.2 shows a theme corner for a fast food restaurant that incorporates goals, materials, and related activities. Figure 5.3 lists other ideas for theme corners.

Pantomime

Pantomime, a type of spontaneous or informal drama, is a good starting point for creative drama. In pantomime, children use gestures and movement to communicate ideas, feelings, and actions without words. As part of their unit on the circus, a group of second graders were pantomiming eating cotton candy. Some children were holding their hands in front of their faces and biting off chunks of the cotton candy; others were pulling some off the cones with their hands and eating it; still others were just licking their hands and fingers. Both the second graders and their teacher found pantomime a satisfying means of self-expression.

Why Use Pantomime?

Pantomime helps children feel comfortable with their bodies while interpreting ideas, feelings, and actions. Because it begins with physical experience, it makes concepts more concrete. More specifically, it helps children

FIGURE 5.2   Theme Corner for a Fast Food Restaurant

Goal	Vocabulary	Teacher-Provided Props
To increase children's ability to choose and enact roles	Restaurant Drive-through Cashier Cook Menu Boot Hamburger Customer Trash can Cash register Tables and chairs	Uniforms Play money Trash can Stove Cups, straws, trays Assorted containers Cooking utensils Pencils Cards for taking orders

Child-Provided Props	Introducing the Corner	Related Activities
Hats Aprons Menus Signs Decorated car made from box Price list	1. Discuss experiences of eating in a fast food restaurant. 2. Discuss roles of workers and customers. 3. Discuss appropriate behavior in restaurant. Introduce imprinted items from different restaurants and have children sort and classify them.	1. Take a field trip and eat in a fast food restaurant. 2. Invite employees to talk with the children about their work. 3. Collect cups, napkins, hats, and other objects. 4. Cook and taste different kinds of potatoes.

Source: Adapted from Isbell, Floyd, Peters, and Raines (1988).

FIGURE 5.3   Suggestions for Theme Corners

Bank	Frozen yogurt shop
Bakery	Hospital or clinic
Birthday party	Library
Chinese New Year	Music store
Drugstore	Office and office supply store
Farmer's market	Science laboratory
Fix-it shop (appliance, car)	Travel agency
Flower shop	Truck stop

1. Develop the confidence needed for later story dramatization.
2. Handle nonverbal communication.
3. Combine thought and action, because they must think about how to use their bodies to convey their feelings or actions.
4. Develop skills in listening, language, remembering, actions, and a sense of the audience (Hennings, 1990; McCaslin, 1990).

Because mime uses no words or dialogue, it is particularly valuable for children who are nonnative English speakers; who have speech or hearing problems; or who are very shy. It helps them develop confidence in their ability to express themselves through body language. In pantomime, all children can be successful because they do not have to be concerned about verbal communication. "Learning that takes place in words alone, without the foundation of understanding derived from experience, is in fact too rote and superficial to be called 'learning' " (San Jose, 1989).

Suggestions for the Classroom

Younger children need help getting started with pantomime. The less experienced children are, the more background and modeling they need to stimulate their imaginations before they can create their own interpretations. Children respond positively to teachers' suggestions like "Show me with your body" or "Show me with your face."

Older children enjoy group pantomime. They explore sophisticated variations of actions or feelings and respond favorably to teachers acting as choreographers in changing their actions (Hennings, 1990). One third-grade class, for example, was pantomiming ways of walking in response to these directions by the teacher: "You are walking—on slippery ice, through the muddy jungle, in the very hot desert, and in a very dark alley." As the context changed, the children interpreted and invented the appropriate movements, such as tiptoeing and sliding.

Here is an example of a beach activity that children of all ages like to pantomime.

THE BEACH

Let's pretend we're at the beach at lunchtime. It's hot! The sun is right overhead. Put on some sunburn lotion. Don't lose the top of it in the sand. Put the top on and rub in the lotion. What about some for your nose? Pick up the tube and squeeze out some lotion. Smear it over your nose and under your eyes. Super!

It's too hot for me! We don't want to get burned, so let's put up an umbrella—a striped beach umbrella. Ooh, it's heavy and it's difficult to put up. There! I've done it. Mine is red and orange. What color is yours? And yours? And yours?

(Ask some of the children to tell you the colors of their umbrellas.)

Look at the shadow that the umbrella's made. Let's all lie down in it. Aah, that's better.

Come and sit by me. Wasn't it great at the beach? (Fox, 1987, pp. 64–65)

Because all children like to make and do things, miming actions interest them. Children will be most able to mime those actions they have experienced and can easily imagine. Some appropriate mime activities for young children are

1. Acting out familiar nursery rhymes such as "Jack and Jill" and "One, Two, Buckle My Shoe."
2. Showing what it is like to do your favorite after-school activity, such as riding a bike or working in the family garden.
3. Being a character or an animal in your favorite song. Short songs, such as "I'm a Little Teapot," are a good introduction to mime and song.
4. Modeling familiar actions such as brushing teeth, washing hands, riding on a crowded bus, or eating in the school cafeteria. Have the children try to model the action after they guess it. Children also like to mime throwing balls of different sizes, eating a dripping ice cream cone, washing dishes, and making cakes.
5. Imagining that they are a tiger stalking through the jungle looking for food, a kitten lapping some milk, or a wriggling worm.
6. Asking children to pretend that it is their birthday. Show what it is like to eat ice cream and cake. Make a wish and blow out your candles. Talk to your grandmother on the telephone. Write thank-you notes for your presents.

Older children who have had little experience with mime also need practice and modeling before they feel free enough to mime. Group experiences of the same action convey the message of multiple interpretations, with no right or wrong response.

Puppets

Puppets make powerful teaching tools. Even though the word *puppet* comes from the Latin word for doll, puppets are more than dolls. They invite children to explore their imaginations and share their imaginings with others. Puppets are the perfect props for all forms of creative drama.

Why Use Puppets?

Puppets add life to the classroom and are a natural vehicle for creativity, imagination, and self-expression. In today's product-oriented world, they help children convey feelings, emotions, values, and ideas.

For children, the process of creating and using puppets makes learning valuable rather than focusing on the puppet as a finished product. Teachers can also use puppets to enhance their own creativity, view children in different roles, and nurture affective development (Hunt & Renfro, 1982).

A puppet can become a nonthreatening vehicle for

❏ Self-expression, storytelling, improvisation, and enactment (Hunt & Renfro, 1982; Mayesky, 1990).
❏ Risk taking and building confidence in speaking abilities (Donoghue, 1990).
❏ Social negotiation (McCaslin, 1990).
❏ Releasing emotions, distinguishing between reality and fantasy, and practicing life experiences (Hunt & Renfro, 1982).

Many puppets are simple, safe, and easy for children to create and use. A wooden spoon easily becomes a person when given a face; a mitten can be transformed into an animal by adding eyes and a nose. If puppets are to become real tools for unlocking children's creative potential, they must be easily accessible. Consequently, storing puppets is an important consideration. Figure 5.4 lists materials for making and storing puppets.

Suggestions for the Classroom

Here are some suggestions for classwork with puppets.

1. Provide many opportunities for children to experiment with different puppets before creating their own. Have them hold the puppets in front of them or over their heads. Introduce a mirror so that they can explore the puppet's movements, voice, and gestures. Young children find it easiest to manipulate puppets with moving mouths so that they can use dialogue if they choose (Hunt & Renfro, 1982).

2. Create a puppet center with a box of puppet-making materials such as scraps of fabric, paper tubing and plates, and recycled buttons, yarn, and popsicle sticks. Locate the center away from the normal traffic pattern so that children can gather and use their puppets in informal enactments (Hunt & Renfro, 1982). First-grade children often use the puppet center to create silhouette stick puppets of favorite book characters to share informally with each other. Preschoolers enjoy creating paper plate puppets for the sheer enjoyment of inventing.

3. Use puppets to help children express feelings with their voices, such as fear, high- or low-pitched voices, or animal sounds such as squeaking, growling, or chirping (Hunt & Renfro, 1982). A kindergarten teacher uses paper plate puppets with happy, sad, surprised, and frightened faces on them. She tells a short story, stops, and asks a child to respond, using one of the puppets and an appropriate voice.

4. Suggest that children audiotape a story if they are going to do a puppet show. Primary grade children often have difficulty manipulating puppets and saying the words at the same time.

Story Drama

Story drama, a type of interpretive drama, is based upon the reenactment of familiar stories, poems, fables, or original stories. It often consists of a teacher-

FIGURE 5.4   Creating and Storing Puppets

TYPES OF PUPPETS

Hand and Finger	Face	Body
Bandanas	Paper plates	Grocery bags
Cups	Eye masks	Large carton with opening in
Gloves		sides for head and arms
Mittens		Pillow cases
Paper lunch bags		
Small boxes (gelatin, pudding, hamburger)		
Socks		
Stapler		
Straws		
Stuffed animal with cut-off bottom		
Throat sticks		
Toilet paper		
Rolls		
Wooden spoons		

MATERIALS

Assorted fabric scraps of different textures; assorted sticks; button eyes; colored paper; crayons; markers; egg cartons; felt; glue; old panty hose; pompoms; rubber bands; sequins; scissors; stapler; Styrofoam balls and packing materials; tape; wire hangers; yarn.

Storage: Using common recyclable materials enhances children's play with puppets and makes storage attractive and accessible. Teachers have successfully used the following items: aprons with pockets; cardboard six packs; egg cartons; expanding hanging baskets; hat or wine rack; photocopy paper boxes; multiple skirt hangers; plastic gallon containers or 2 liter plastic bottles; shoe box, bag, or rack.

Styrofoam Ball Stick Puppet   Clothespin Puppet   Box Puppet   Body Puppet

FIGURE 5.4 *continued*

Paper Plate Puppet (front view)

Paper Plate Puppet (back view)

Paper Plate Frog Puppet

Face Puppet

Sock Puppet

Stick Puppet

Finger Puppet

Animal Face Puppet

led group experience, with children creating scenes from familiar literature that use both dialogue and movement (Tompkins & Hoskisson, 1991). Younger children enjoy dramatizing cumulative tales like *Henny Penny* by Paul Galdone (1968) or *Over in the Meadow* by O. A. Wadsworth (1986). Older children enjoy dramatizing scenes from longer stories like *Ramona the Brave* by Beverly Cleary (1975).

Why Use Story Drama?

Story drama supports children's understanding of story structure and helps them see how language affects others (Jacobs, 1989). Research shows that enacting stories (1) improves reading comprehension by enabling readers to clarify concepts and gain a deeper understanding of the literature (Donoghue, 1990; Kukla, 1987; San Jose, 1988) and (2) promotes speaking, listening, critical, and creative reading skills by interpreting familiar material (Cunningham, 1981; Ross & Roe, 1977).

Suggestions for the Classroom

When choosing and adapting stories to dramatize, think about the following characteristics.

1. Choose stories with *immediate action, a simple plot, few characters, and appealing dialogue* that children can easily put into their own words.

Students must be familiar with the story and characters if they are to re-create the plot and the conversation (Donoghue, 1990). Folktales, like *How Many Spots Does a Leopard Have* (Lester, 1990) or fables (Lobel, 1981) fit this criterion.

2. *Involve children* actively in the selection of the story. Allowing them to choose stories to enact will build interest in dramatization.

3. *Adapt familiar stories* and enthusiastically support children's spontaneous interpretations. Young children will have simple and often loose interpretations; older children will have more sophisticated understandings and a more coherent plot (Jacobs, 1989).

4. *Be a facilitator*. Prepare questions in advance to help children focus on story elements and to gain distance from the story. For example, in re-enacting the story of "The Three Bears," you might ask, I wonder how Goldilocks got into the bears' house? How do you suppose the bears felt when they came home and saw their porridge, chairs, and Goldilocks sleeping in their bed? If you were Goldilocks, what would you have done? Why?

5. *Provide ample time and space for children to plan the dramatization, decide which parts to read or enact, and explore the dimensions of their characters.* Each child must determine how a character feels and thinks before trying to act like that character. Children can ask each other such questions as these to help them better understand a character: Where do you live? What do you do in your free time? What are your favorite foods? Do you watch television?

6. *Evaluate the reenactment*. By second grade, children can evaluate their story dramatizations. Always begin with the strengths of the drama. What did you see that you liked? Then ask questions that will help children reexamine the drama elements of voice, action, diction, and movement of the characters.

Readers Theater

Readers theater, another form of interpretive drama, is a presentation of a story or script by a group of readers. Readers assume a role, read, and interpret the parts of the script that relate to their particular role. This form of drama enables children to develop oral language abilities. In readers theater, children use facial and vocal expressions and gestures to interpret a play or story in a nonstaged performance. Sometimes a narrator sets the tone, but this is not necessary. Because readers theater usually incorporates practice before presentation, less proficient readers can often be successful in oral reading and interpretation (Pappas, Kiefer, & Levstik, 1990). Although readers theater was designed for older children, it is adaptable to primary grade children as well.

Why Use Readers Theater?

In readers theater, both the audience and the readers use their imaginations. Participants practice different ways to use their voices, gestures, and nonverbal language to communicate shades of meaning (Bromley, 1992). Children focus only on the oral interpretation of the material and are not pressured to memorize lines, as in formal, scripted drama. The audience receives information and responds to the participants.

Suggestions for the Classroom

Here are some suggestions for the appropriate use of readers theater in primary classrooms:

1. Have readers sit on the floor or stand, with their books in front of them, while they read and follow along with the material.
2. Make sure that children can read the material without help (Bromley, 1992). Many of the stories children use as big books or language experience stories from their reading program are a rich source for readers theater.
3. Select material that is action based, exciting, and capable of interpretation in a dramatic fashion (Bromley, 1992). Folktales such as "The Three Little Pigs" and "The Little Red Hen," and stories in verse such as "The Cat in the Hat" and "Taxi Dog," are appealing and meet the criteria for readers theater. For a more complete list, see Busching (1981). In addition, the Readers Theatre Script Service provides scripts for readers theater at the elementary level such as "The Tale of Peter Rabbit" and "The Emperor's New Clothes." Information about this service is provided at the end of the reference list in this chapter.

Creative drama experiences during early childhood develop children's understanding of the forms and functions of language, nonverbal communication, self-esteem, and self-confidence. These activities can be used across the curriculum to enhance and reinforce learning in all subject areas.

Integrating Creative Drama into the Subject Areas

Drama experts (Bolton, 1985; McCaslin, 1990) recommend that drama activities be infused into the subject areas. In this way, children come to understand abstract ideas by enacting them concretely. The activities that follow are grouped by subject area and may be adapted to various ages and subject areas.

Mathematics, Science, and Technology

Preschool and kindergarten children enjoy creative drama activities that focus on mathematics and science. Some examples of these activities are:

Bodyplays and Fingerplays

Three-year-olds are particularly fond of these activities. While studying animals, they enjoy acting out rhymes such as this one about an elephant:

His name is Elmer elephant, (Point to elephant)
His lip and trunk are one. (Put two fists in front of mouth)

And when I went to pick him up, (Bend way down)
I knew he weighed a ton! (Lift up arms enclosed in a semicircle and make facial gestures)

Identifying and Expressing Feelings

During a unit on pets, preschool and kindergarten children enjoy enacting how a pet feels when it is hungry, hurt, afraid, lonely, or tired. Using a mood cube made from a box like the one in the illustration that follows, have children roll the cube and enact a situation that elicits this emotion.

Theme Corners

As part of a grocery store theme corner, children's dramatic play can include counting items on the shelves, sorting and classifying empty boxes and containers of different foods, counting money and making change, or designing a recycling bin for clean, used grocery bags. Environmental awareness can be introduced through questions such as "Do you want plastic or paper bags?"

Primary grade children enjoy some of these activities:

Pantomime

As part of their study of life cycles, primary children can cooperatively plan a pantomime of the life cycles, for example, of the caterpillar and the frog. Their classmates may provide feedback.

Readers Theater

In a unit on time, one third-grade class invented their own story of the future and presented it as readers theater.

Movement

One teacher had her children develop rhythmic patterns to different number bases in mathematics. Divided into different bases, the group rhythmically

These children enjoy enacting their original stories as part of their study of animals.

grouped and regrouped themselves according to their base. They enjoyed working with the concept on paper after they had interpreted it physically (Stewig, 1984).

Language, Literature, and Literacy

Try these language and literacy activities with preschool and kindergarten children:

Pantomime

Ms. Poretz's 2-year-olds like to act out action words. They choose an action picture from her shoebox collection and then do what they see in the picture.

Some popular pictures include a child jumping, an airplane flying, a kitten lapping up milk, a horse galloping, and a mother cuddling a baby.

Role Play and Dramatic Play

Many teachers place real telephones in the theme or housekeeping area for children to converse freely with an imaginary person. Encourage children to create situations where they have to relay messages, such as taking a sick child to the doctor, asking for information about a movie, or making a reservation at a restaurant.

Storytelling

Second and third graders enjoy inventing bean bag stories. With children sitting in a circle, a child begins to tell a story. After a few sentences, the storyteller stops and throws a bean bag to another child, who continues the story. When no more ideas can be generated, another child starts a different story.

Characterization

With their favorite story in hand, third-grade children like to create a "Literature Talk Show" and become the host. Other children call in and ask questions about the characters in the book, their feelings or actions, or the resolution of the problem.

Pantomime

First-grade children respond positively to pantomiming action words that relate to favorite books or book characters, feelings, and skill lessons in which they are engaged. They like unusual words like *glide, hammer, inside out, jiggle, knead, limp, meander, nod,* and *quake.* Older children can do more complicated charades based on poetry, folktales, and fairytales such as "The Cow Jumped Over the Moon" or "Fee Fi Fo Fum."

Social Studies, Health, and Nutrition

Creative drama helps to solidify the concepts that are taught in each of these subject areas:

Role Playing

Using gestures, facial expressions, intonation, and movement, young children can communicate social studies concepts (e.g., enacting mothering behaviors), health and safety concepts (e.g., dramatizing safe and unsafe ways to cross the street), and nutrition (e.g., a puppet play about balanced meals and the four food groups).

Prop Boxes

As part of her unit on the post office, Ms. Packer and her kindergarten children prepared a prop box. They located scales, stamps and stamp pads, mailers, wooden mail boxes, a mail carrier's bag, and a cap. The children enacted the roles of the postal worker, mail carrier, and customer, and wrote letters and cards to mail at the post office.

Try these activities for the primary grades:

Role Playing

Mr. Kang's first graders are comparing the similarities and differences between Japanese and American families. After extensive background experiences, including reading "The Boy of the Three Year Nap" (Snyder, 1988), Mr. Kang observed the children dramatizing scenes from each culture's home life and enacting different ways of sleeping, eating, and greeting people.

Body Movement and Nonverbal Communication

While studying maps, second and third graders can use body movements to demonstrate map symbols and directions. One child becomes the hands of the compass, pointing north; another lays down and faces east. They can also use their bodies to show such map symbols as mountains, roads, and railroads.

Puppetry

Following a unit on careers and vocations, children can use puppets to interview each other about their careers. Using simple hand, finger, and face puppets, create a set of interview questions such as: Why did you choose this career? What do you do in your job? How long does it take you to get to work? What do you like about your work? Is your boss nice? What is the hardest part of your work?

Special Populations

Creative drama is inclusive (Stewig, 1984), meaning that all children have the opportunity to participate, portray, and react spontaneously to an idea. Creative drama has been used positively with learning-disabled students (Snyder, 1977), second-language students (Turkewych & Divito, 1978) and timid, fearful, and aggressive children (Stewig, 1984). Since the goal of drama is to release children's creative potential, children can choose how they will participate.

Culturally Diverse Groups

Drama enables all children to work together in groups or teams to create, direct, and interpret meaningful situations. Because of its social nature, drama provides opportunities for children with limited proficiency in English to initiate and engage in conversation with fluent English speakers, to improve their oral language skills, and to develop positive attitudes toward each other. According to McCaslin (1990), "the most common error in dealing with [limited English-speaking] children is underestimating their ability and overestimating their verbal skill" (p. 339).

The following suggestions use drama as a foundation for developing children's oral language ability while simultaneously improving their self-image.

1. *Use body movement, choral speaking, and pantomime to develop vocabulary.* These activities force children to concentrate without the added pressure of verbalization. Movement activities, like folk dances or responding to music, require a physical response to oral language; pantomime connects actions to words when the spectator guesses what the person is doing; and choral speaking provides practice in oral interpretation and pronunciation without identifying a less capable speaker (McCaslin, 1990).

2. *Use children's literature to enhance oral language development.* It is well known that reading aloud to children is a powerful way to expand their language. With children from all cultural groups, extend read-aloud sessions with creative drama activities such as puppetry, story drama, and dramatic play. The younger the children, the more quickly they acquire and expand their language. Cumulative folktales and fables, such as *Millions of Cats* by Wanda Gag (1956) or *The Very Hungry Caterpillar* by Eric Carle (1969), are good for younger children to enact because they are repetitive and predictable. Older children can dramatize scenes from *Mrs. Frisby and the Rats of NIMH* (O'Brien, 1971) or important events from famous people's lives using *Columbus* (d'Aulaire & d'Aulaire, 1955).

3. *Immerse children in oral language.* Drama is one of the most natural means of bathing young children in oral language. In dramatic play, children have the richest opportunity to use language. Provide daily experiences in which children can create and interpret familiar situations, character roles, and events.

Children with Disabilities

Alicia was a hearing-impaired third grader who used sign language to communicate outside of school. Mr. Ubek, her teacher, invited Alicia to share her knowledge of sign language using pantomime. Her hearing peers acted as spectators as they interpreted the signs that Alicia shared. For the hearing-impaired child, pantomime and movement are the easiest media with which to achieve success (McCaslin, 1990).

Children with other physically disabling conditions can still participate in drama activities. Often, these children can be assigned the role of the narrator in a retelling, the puppeteer in a dramatization, or a member of a group in choral speaking.

Children with disabling conditions can participate in and feel successful in drama activities. They, too, must experience the rewards of creative drama.

High-Achieving and Low-Achieving Children

High-achieving children learn quickly and easily and often see many possibilities in their activities. They need an environment that encourages risk taking, opportunities to be producers rather than consumers of information, and varied formats for project work (Cohen, 1987). The following example involving third graders illustrates how drama, with its many possibilities, challenges high-achieving children's thinking skills while meeting these basic needs.

A group of third graders had been learning about basic concepts of economics—the study of choices and decision making in their own daily lives. For their project, they brainstormed, created, and enacted two different mini-puppet skits about decision making in their classroom. One play told the story of planning an entire day with playing games, watching movies, listening to music, and eating snacks as children's only choices; the other skit described a day with more variety in activities. The children incorporated sign language, jokes, and vocal changes as they applied creative problem-solving processes to their decision making. The skits ended with the puppets discussing the impact of three major economic concepts on their lives: how choices affect the quality of life; the impact of limited resources on our choices; and the need to give up something in order to choose something else.

Low-achieving students benefit from relevant, meaningful learning activities that focus on intensive oral language experience and use imagination to deal with abstract ideas (McCaslin, 1990). Drama provides many opportunities for meaningful language learning and for developing imagination through dramatic play, role playing, and story reenactments. Sensitive and knowledgeable teachers use dramatization to establish a positive learning climate for all children, but especially for low achievers.

Conclusion

Creative drama nurtures children's expression from within. Concrete enactments of people, roles, actions, and feelings help children learn about themselves and their world in significant, personal, and lasting ways.

Chapter Summary

1. Creative drama contributes to every child's learning and is an essential part of a child-centered early childhood curriculum. Enactment enhances the development of children's imaginative thinking, problem-solving, communication, and perspective-taking abilities, as well as their appreciation of drama as an art form.
2. Creative drama focuses on children's natural expression of thoughts, feelings, and ideas enacted for themselves rather than on a polished theatrical performance.

3. Drama activities can be characterized on a continuum from least to most formal. Dramatic play uses children's natural pretend behavior to enact roles, behaviors, and actions; informal drama relies upon participants' inventions or creations in such activities as pantomime. Story or interpretive drama involves some rehearsal, and participants use voice, gestures, and facial features to interpret someone else's ideas and words. Scripted or formal drama uses a memorized script performed for an audience.
4. Teachers possess the most powerful influence over children's dramatic expression. How teachers select and present drama activities and experiences significantly influences how children will develop their creative potential.
5. Appropriate creative drama experiences and activities for children include dramatic and sociodramatic play, pantomime, puppets, story drama, and readers theater. All of these drama forms can be integrated with every subject area.

Discussion Questions

1. Many educators and parents believe that the answer to our educational problems is a "back to basics" philosophy. What arguments would you put forth to convince other educators that drama is basic to the early childhood curriculum?
2. The teacher has an important role in developing and sustaining creative drama as an integral part of the curriculum. What teaching behaviors would you expect of a teacher who supported children's growth through drama?
3. All children have the propensity to play and mime. Why do you think this is the case? Of what value is it? Can you recall some episodes in which children were engaged in these activities? What was happening?
4. Review the opening case study of first-grade children preparing to enact the story "The Little Red Hen." Why do you think Ms. Clark devoted one week to this activity? If a colleague of Ms. Clark's criticized her for "wasting time," how might she respond without being overly defensive?
5. Have you ever performed a scripted drama on stage in front of an audience? Describe your feelings. How do you think children feel when engaged in this kind of activity?
6. As a beginning teacher, how much experience with drama do you need to have? What are the minimum skills and values you will need to incorporate drama successfully into your curriculum?
7. In the Research Highlight, Lee Galda describes the effects of dramatization on children's reading comprehension. What stories would be appropriate for children at different age levels to re-enact? Why did you select these particular stories? With what age group would you use them? Why? How can teachers encourage the use of story drama in their classrooms?

---------------------------------- **Writing to Learn** ----------------------------------

As a second-grade teacher who integrates drama experiences in all subject areas, you have been asked by your building principal to share your ideas and beliefs about drama in the curriculum with your grade level colleagues. Do some free writing in which you explore how you will share these ideas, what your main points will be, and how you will function as a resource person for your peers. Then share your reading with a partner and plan to share your main points with the rest of the class.

---------------------------------- **Interview** ----------------------------------

Teachers' Beliefs About Drama

Experts in creative drama agree that classroom teachers must value creative drama for it to be integrated into the curriculum (Stewig, 1984). In light of this conclusion, arrange to interview an early childhood teacher about his or her beliefs concerning creative drama in the classroom. Ask the following questions and record the teacher's responses. You may want to tape-record your interview and transcribe the responses afterward.

1. What types of dramatization do you use in your classroom? Could you provide an example of a drama activity your children enjoy?
2. How did your teacher education program prepare you to teach drama in the classroom?
3. How do parents and principals react to your efforts to use drama? Could you give an example?
4. In an ideal curriculum, how much importance would you attach to drama in the curriculum?
5. What factors discourage teachers from using more drama in the classroom?

Note: You may find yourself interviewing a teacher who is totally uninvolved in drama. Think about how you will conduct your interview if you are in this situation. Try role-playing various possibilities prior to conducting this interview.

---------------------------------- **Observation** ----------------------------------

Values of Creative Drama

Drama expert Nellie McCaslin (1990) asserts that all children gain important values from creative drama activity, regardless of age, circumstance, or previous experience. Nevertheless, few teachers utilize its potential.

The purpose of this assignment is to help you observe creative drama and to articulate the values and opportunities children receive from them. Arrange to observe a group of children engaged in creative drama. Observe them for at least 10 minutes. Write down a description of the setting, the number and ages of the children involved, their ethnic backgrounds, any special needs they may have, the kind of activity in which they are engaged, the available props, how the activity was initiated, and any dialogue.

Next, expand your notes immediately after the observation. Document your answers by providing an example of each of the following values discussed in this chapter

❑ *Imaginative thinking.* How is children's imaginative thinking enhanced in this episode?

❑ *Problem solving and decision making.* How did the children develop the ability to formulate and choose alternatives? How did they evaluate their dramatizations?

❑ *Language and listening skills.* How did the children express emotions, frustrations, or excitement?

❑ *Perspective-taking ability.* How did the children modify their ideas and plans as they worked together?

❑ *Appreciation of drama as an art form.* Were there children in the roles of players and spectators? How did that occur?

Bring your written transcript and analysis to class and be prepared to share your findings with the group. We will generate a portrait of how dramatic activities include all children, yet enable every child to participate in his or her own way.

Controversy

Is Drama Developmentally Appropriate?

Jennifer's kindergarten teacher produced an annual school "musical revue." The children, dressed in elaborate teacher-made costumes, performed popular show tunes. Before her performance, Jennifer told her grandmother, "I think I'll stand behind all the tall people, so no one will see me if I make a mistake. I'm scared!" Jennifer's mother reported that during the show, the children looked stiff—almost puppet-like—and had anxious looks on their faces.

Jennifer's experience reveals what happens when teachers make developmentally inappropriate choices in drama activities for young children. Why the controversy?

Increasingly, drama experts suggest that creative drama is the *only* appropriate form of drama for children in the primary grades (Bolton, 1985; Donoghue, 1990; McCaslin, 1990; Tompkins & Hoskisson, 1991). Through creative drama, children generate their own questions and problems in ways that make sense to them. One of the best ways for them to gain insights about their lives and their world is through a range of drama experiences (Hennings, 1990; McCaslin, 1990).

Despite the recognized importance of creative drama, it is not uncommon to witness young children who are forced into formal drama by some misguided adult. What is obvious in the performances is the emphasis on the production. Educators have long argued against such performances for elementary school children (Stewig, 1984).

Some children naturally express interest in doing a play, and it is all right to support their choice. Teachers' primary concern, however, is to develop children's self-expression. They should not succumb to pressures from parents, principals, or colleagues to mount a production for an audience. "For the younger child, public performance is undesirable; for the older child, under the right conditions, it may do no harm" (McCaslin, 1990, p. 28).

To illustrate the difference between developmentally appropriate and inappropriate practice where drama is concerned, consider two different approaches to sharing the story of Rosa Parks. In the first classroom, the children listen to the story about Mrs. Parks' valiant refusal to move to the back of a segregated bus in Birmingham, Alabama, in the 1950s; then they enact the scene, using their own words. The focus is on the essence of the story—emotion and injustice (Paley, 1981). In another classroom, the teacher gives the children a prepared script to rehearse their lines before performing in the school auditorium. The focus here is on memorization, making mistakes, and stage fright.

Research Highlight

Playing About a Story: Its Impact on Comprehension

Summary of Research

Research in the last decade shows the strong influence of story dramatization on children's comprehension. In Lee Galda's (1982) study, conducted with 108 kindergarten, first-grade, and second-grade children, she found that those children who played with story reenactment had better story comprehension than those who only participated in discussion or drawing as a follow-up to the story.

After listening to a familiar folktale in small groups, children either drew a picture about the story; talked about the story by responding to such questions as "Why do you think this was a good story?"; or enacted it with encouragement and support from the researcher. Results indicated that the enactment group was better at "remembering, understanding, solving, and analyzing questions" (p. 53) and better able to retell the stories in a more sequential order.

Why did enactment facilitate children's comprehension? Galda suggests the following explanations:

1. To dramatize a familiar story, children must engage in discussion and dialogue about the roles, props, and setting. This verbal interaction

helps them become "aware of aspects of the story which they individually might not have noticed" (p. 53).

2. Children who are most actively involved in reenactment must reconstruct the story mentally. This improves their retellings and develops their sense of story. To reenact a story effectively, "children must understand characters and their motivations, events as cause and effect, and the logical order of beginning, middle and end" (p. 54). Story drama aids literary awareness and appreciation.

Implications for Practice

How can teachers encourage the use of story drama in the classroom? Galda suggests two basic ways that teachers support children's reenactments—either from *outside the play* (suggesting props, role behaviors, or feelings and asking questions about the character) or as a participant *within the play* (enacting a specific role or character within the story and exiting the role as soon as children are able to carry on independently). Clearly, story drama is an important way to build understanding and appreciation of literature.

References

Bolton, G. (1985). Changes in thinking about drama in the classroom. *Theory into Practice, 24*(3), 151–157.

Bromley, K. D. (1992). *Language arts: Exploring connections.* Boston: Allyn & Bacon.

Busching, B. A. (1981). Readers theatre: An education for language and life. *Language Arts, 58*(3), 337.

Christie, J. F. (1990, April). Dramatic play: A context for meaningful engagement. *The Reading Teacher, 43*(8), 542–545.

Christie, J. F., & Johnson, E. P. (1983). The role of play in social-intellectual development. *Review of Educational Research, 53*(1), 93–115.

Cohen, L. M. (1987). Thirteen tips for teaching gifted students. *Teaching Exceptional Children, 20,* 34–38.

Cunningham, P. (1981). Story dramatization. *The Reading Teacher, 34,* 466–468.

Dillon, D. (1988). Dear readers. *Language Arts. 65*(1), 7–9.

Donoghue, M. (1990). *The child and the English language arts* (5th ed.). Dubuque, IA: W. C. Brown.

Edwards, L. C. (1990). *Affective development and the creative arts: A process approach to early childhood education.* Columbus, OH: Merrill/Macmillan.

Erickson, K. L. (1988). Building castles in the classroom. *Language Arts, 65*(1), 14–19.

Fox, M. (1987). *Teaching drama to young children.* Portsmouth, NH: Heinemann.

Galda, L. (1982, October). Playing about a story: Its impact on comprehension. *The Reading Teacher, 55,* 52–55.

Garvey, C. (1977). *Play.* Cambridge, MA: Harvard University Press.

Halliday, M. A. K. (1975). *Explorations in the functions of language.* London: Edward Arnold.

Hennings, D. G. (1990). *Communication in action. Teaching the language arts* (4th ed.). Boston: Houghton Mifflin.

Hunt, T., & Renfro, N. (1982). *Puppetry in early childhood education.* Austin, TX: Nancy Renfro Studios.

Isbell, R., Floyd, S., Peters, V., & Raines, S. (1988). *Ideas to stimulate sociodramatic play.* Paper presented at the Play Leadership and Animation

Conference, November 2–4, Washington, DC.

Jacobs, L. B. (1988). The play's the thing. *Teaching Pre–K–8. 19*(3), 26–29.

Jacobs, L. B. (1989). Dramatizing literature. *Teaching Pre–K–8. 19*(6), 33–35.

Johnson, J. E., Christie, J. F., & Yawkey, T. D. (1987). *Play and early childhood development.* Glenview, IL: Scott, Foresman.

Joint Committee on the Role of Informal Drama in the Classroom of the National Council of Teachers of English and the Children's Theatre Association. (1983). Forum: Informal classroom drama. *Language Arts, 60,* 370–371.

Kukla, K. (1987). David Booth: Drama as a way of knowing. *Language Arts, 64,* 73–78.

Mayesky, M. (1990). *Creative activities for young children* (4th ed.). Albany, NY: Delmar.

McCaslin, N. (1990). *Creative drama in the classroom* (5th ed.). New York: Longman.

Millward, P. (1990). Drama as a well made play. *Language Arts, 67*(2), 151–163.

Morgan, J., & Saxton, J. (1987). *Teaching drama: A mind of many wonders.* Portsmouth, NH: Heinemann.

Nelson, K. (1986). *Event knowledge.* Hillsdale, NJ: Erlbaum.

Paley, V. (1981). *Wally's stories.* Cambridge, MA: Harvard University Press.

Pappas, C. C., Kiefer, B. Z., & Levstik, L. S. (1990). *An integrated language perspective in the elementary school: Theory into action.* New York: Longman.

Renfro, N. (1979). *Puppetry and the art of story creation.* Austin, TX: Nancy Renfro Studios.

Roskos, K. (1988). Literacy at work in play. *The Reading Teacher, 41*(6), 532–566.

Ross, E. P., & Roe, B. D. (1977). Creative drama builds proficiency in reading. *The Reading Teacher, 30,* 383–387.

San Jose, C. (1988). Story drama in the content areas. *Language Arts, 65*(1), 26–33.

San Jose, C. (1989). Classroom drama: Learning from the inside out. In S. Hoffman & L. Lamme (Eds.), *Learning from the inside out* (pp. 69–76). Wheaton, MD: Association for Childhood Education International.

Schickedanz, J. A., York, M. E., Stewart, I. S., & White, D. A. (1991). *Strategies for teaching young children* (3rd ed.). Englewood Cliffs, NJ: Prentice-Hall.

Seefeldt, C., & Barbour, N. (1990). *Early childhood education: An introduction* (2nd ed.). Columbus, OH: Merrill/Macmillan.

Shaftel, F. R., & Shaftel, G. (1983). *Role playing in the curriculum* (2nd ed.). Englewood Cliffs, NJ: Prentice-Hall.

Smilansky, S. (1968). *The effects of sociodramatic play on disadvantaged preschool children.* New York: Wiley.

Snyder, A. B. (1977, Spring). Let's do drama. *The Pointer, 21*(3), 36–40.

Stewig, J. W. (1984). Teachers' perceptions of creative drama in the elementary school. *Children's Theatre Review, 33*(2), 27–29.

Tompkins, G. E., & Hoskisson, K. (1991). *Language arts: Content and teaching strategies* (2nd ed.). Columbus, OH: Merrill/Macmillan.

Turkewych, C., & Divito, N. (1978, Summer). Creative dramatics and second language learning. *TESL Talk, 9*(3), 63–68.

Verriour, P. (1985). Educating through drama. *Theory into Practice, 24*(3), p. 150.

Woodward, C. (1985). Guidelines for facilitating sociodramatic play. In J. Frost & S. Sunderlin (Eds.), *When children play* (pp. 291–295). Wheaton, MD: Association for Childhood Education International.

Children's Books

Blevgach, E. (1980). *Three little pigs.* New York: Atheneum.

Carle, E. (1969). *The very hungry caterpillar.* Cleveland, OH: Collins-World.

d'Aulaire, I., & d'Aulaire, E. P. (1955). *Columbus*. New York: Doubleday.

Gag, W. (1956). *Millions of cats*. Coward, McCann (Putnam Publishing Group).

Henkes, K. (1985). *Bailey goes camping*. New York: Greenwillow.

Lester, J. (1990). *How many spots does a leopard have? and other tales*. New York: Scholastic.

Lobel, A. (1981). *Fables*. New York: Harper & Row.

O'Brien, R. (1971). *Mrs. Frisby and the rats of NIMH*. New York: Atheneum.

Seuss, Dr. (1957). *The cat in the hat*. New York: Random House.

Snyder, S. (1988). *The boy of the three year nap*. New York: Scholastic.

Williams, V. B. (1981). *Three days on the river in a red canoe*. New York: Greenwillow.

Picture Books for Dramatization

Andersen, H. C. (1982) *The emperor's new clothes*. *New York:* Crowell.

Butterworth, O. (1978). *The enormous egg*. New York: Dell.

Carle, E. (1990). *The very quiet cricket*. New York: Putnam.

Cauley, L. B. (1981). *Goldilocks and the three bears*. New York: Holt, Rinehart and Winston.

Cauley, L. B. (1986). *Puss in boots*. San Diego, CA: Harcourt Brace Jovanovich.

Cleary, B. (1975). *Ramona the brave*. New York: Morrow.

Degen, B. (1983). *Jamberry*. New York: Harper & Row.

Domanska, J. (1973). *The little red hen*. New York: Macmillan.

Flack, M. (1932). *Ask Mr. Bear*. New York: Macmillan.

Galdone, P. (1968). *Henny Penny*. New York: Seabury.

Galdone, P. (1973). *The three billy goats gruff*. New York: Seabury.

Galdone, P. (1975). *The gingerbread boy*. New York: Seabury.

Hawkins, C. (1988). *I know an old lady who swallowed a fly*. New York: Holt, Rinehart and Winston.

Hoban, R. (1970). *A bargain for Frances*. New York: Harper & Row.

Hutchins, P. (1972). *Goodnight owl*. New York: Macmillan.

McGovern, A. (1967). *Too much noise*. New York: Scholastic.

Piper, W. (1945). *The little engine that could*. New York: Platt & Munk.

Schmidt, J. (1985). *The gingerbread man*. New York: Scholastic.

Sendak, M. (1963). *Where the wild things are*. New York: Harper.

Slobodkina, E. (1947). *Caps for sale*. New York: Scott.

Thurber, J. (1974). *Many moons*. New York: Dutton.

Viorst, J. (1972). *Alexander and the terrible, horrible, no good very bad day*. New York: Atheneum.

Wadsworth, O. A. (1986). *Over in the Meadow*. New York: Penguin Puffin.

Wells, R. (1973). *Noisy Nora*. New York: Dial.

Readers Theatre Script Service
P.O. Box 178333
San Diego, CA 92117
(619) 276–1948

Contexts for Creative Expression and Play

Planning and Arranging the Creative Environment

. . . teachers can use physical setting as an active and pervasive influence on their own activities and attitudes as well as on those of their students.

Lesley Mandel Morrow, 1990, p. 538

After reading this chapter, you will be able to

- ☐ Consider the effects of the physical environment on children's and teachers' behavior.
- ☐ Identify the characteristics of creative indoor environments.
- ☐ Plan and use room arrangements, centers, transitions, and routines to enhance children's creative expression and play.
- ☐ Identify the characteristics of creative outdoor environments.
- ☐ Plan creative outdoor experiences.
- ☐ Analyze the roles and responsibilities of a teacher in a creative environment.

Case Study

When Ms. Ring had surgery, she missed 2 weeks of school and a substitute taught her kindergarten class. On the day Ms. Ring returns to her classroom, she is shocked by what she sees. There may be a place for everything, but nothing is in its place. Puzzle pieces are in the toy box, on the floor, and buried in the sand table. Dolls and stuffed toys are sticky with glue, raisins are squashed into the carpet, and crayons are mixed in with the woodworking tools. The substitute had brought in sieves, sifters, and soil so that the children could categorize and label them as rocks, gravel, or sand. Now those materials are everywhere. Before Ms. Ring took sick leave, she conferred with the substitute and felt confident that she was a creative teacher. Now Ms. Ring has doubts. Her classroom is no longer a context for creative expression and play. It is, in her words, a "disaster area"—unsupervised, unstructured, and unplanned.

This scenario dramatically highlights how a classroom can become a poor context for learning. Teachers who design creative environments do more than supply a setting for learning. They view the environment as a "participant in teaching and learning" (Loughlin & Suina, 1982, p. 1). The creative classroom is carefully planned and supervised; it encourages children's self-expression; builds upon children's natural curiosity and joy of learning; and allows personal initiative to flourish, yet develops respect for others.

The choices teachers make in planning and arranging the environment strongly affect children's interactions with each other, with materials, and with the learning experience. If we compare Ms. Ring's concept of a creative environment with that of the substitute, it is easy to see how contexts for creative expression and play reveal our own beliefs, values, and attitudes about creativity. Planning and arranging the classroom is as important as planning for instruction. Both must harmonize with the goals of the program.

Theoretical Framework

There are three basic features of creative environments: climate, space, and time (Garreau & Kennedy, 1991; Jones, 1977; Phyfe-Perkins, 1980).

Climate

Climate refers to the feeling one gets from the environment and dictates to what extent children can be productive, engaged learners. In many ways, the child's environment can be compared to the adult's work environment (Jones, 1977). Young children respond best to classrooms that have

- ❏ *Design features* that evoke a warm, homelike quality, such as carpeted surfaces and soft furniture.
- ❏ *Materials* that capture and sustain children's interest and imagination.

- ❏ *Teachers* who show genuine interest in children's activities and support children's efforts.
- ❏ *Children* who are absorbed in learning, have choices, and make decisions about work to be done.

On the other hand, classrooms that hinder creative expression are product-oriented and have

- ❏ *Design features* that evoke an institutional feeling, such as neutral colors or unmovable furniture.
- ❏ *Materials* that elicit one correct answer and suggest a hands-off approach to learning.
- ❏ *Teachers* who have little physical contact with children and strive for complete control through numerous verbal commands.
- ❏ *Children* who are passive learners, have few choices, and rarely make their own decisions.

Consider these characteristics as you think about the feeling emanating from two second-grade classrooms. In Mr. Kaminsky's class, desks are aligned in neat rows; children are quiet and work individually on the same tasks while the teacher reads with a reading group in the back of the room. Teacher-made bulletin boards, cartoon figures, and posters of classroom rules dominate the room. Mr. Kaminsky divides his daily schedule into five subject area time blocks. When he rings the bell, the children move quietly to the next activity.

In the class across the hall, Ms. Reiks arranges her classroom into learning and interest centers, each identified by inviting and colorful hanging signs. When the children arrive each morning, they talk with each other and plan their instructional day with selections on a planning board. They move easily and freely around the room, independently accessing materials and placing completed assignments in designated, labeled boxes. Active and quiet activities are occurring simultaneously. Some children are reading to each other in the library corner; others are constructing scenery for a play they have created; still others are working with Ms. Reiks on a three-dimensional community map. Displays of children's original work fill the room and are placed at the children's eye level. At planned times during the day, they gather together for group experiences and sharing.

Clearly, Ms. Reik's classroom has a climate that is more conducive to creativity. The context she has created is more child-centered, more responsive to children's needs and interests, and more respectful of children's ability to participate in making decisions.

Classroom climate is also influenced by an environment's aesthetic appeal. Classrooms for young children should be beautiful places to learn. One Head Start teacher played soft audiotaped classical music in the dramatic play area each day and placed fresh flowers at her work stations. She also organized her interest areas by color-coded shelving, and plastic baskets held the materials neatly on the shelves. These containers gave her storage system an appealing, uncluttered look. The message to children in her classroom was one of warmth and beauty.

There are published rating scales and guidelines that support teachers' design of appropriate environments for children of all ages. Using one or more of them will provide the salient criteria needed to arrange and assess children's creative environments. Appendix B lists and describes several such scales.

The process of planning and arranging the environment is not completed by the previous teacher or finished before school begins. Rather, it is a continuous process based on the children's and teacher's changing needs and interests. Environments that are responsive to children can and should be modified periodically.

Space

Space includes the degree to which the physical environment is arranged to develop active, creative thinkers. In good early childhood classrooms, teachers use easels, movable cabinets, storage shelves, and tables to define areas so that children can work individually, in small groups, or in a large group at circle time. Well-balanced classroom space separates quiet and boisterous activities and creates safe traffic patterns. It gives both children and teachers more control over and choice regarding the arrangement of the physical setting (Kritchevsky, Prescott, & Walling, 1977; National Academy of Early Childhood Programs, 1984).

Teachers sometimes underestimate the young child's need for private space. Some children need a periodic rest from the action and interaction of the classroom in a place to restore energy or to think quietly before resuming classroom activity. Certain activities, such as listening to a story tape, are enjoyed more fully in a secluded place. If classrooms lack such places, children often create their own. One first-grade teacher who seldom used her desk put it in the corner and found that the space underneath it was a favorite place to read. When teachers insist upon private behavior in a nonprivate space, such as demanding absolute quiet at work tables, it is often stressful for young children (Jones, 1977).

How children use materials within arranged spaces can also enhance or inhibit original thinking. One preschool teacher modeled different uses of materials by moving her easel outdoors in good weather and moving the tricycles indoors when the weather was inclement. A kindergarten teacher placed the workbench near the art center, encouraging the children to build, glue, and paint their constructions. Children could then see materials being used in a variety of settings and in a variety of ways rather than being limited to a single setting or use. Even though room size and shape are important, how space is arranged is even more important.

Time

Time conveys a clear message about the importance of an activity. When children have long blocks of time, their play is more constructive, cooperative, and expressive than with short, interrupted time periods. In a full-day preschool or kindergarten, 60 minutes per day of play is a minimum (Peters, Neisworth, & Yawkey, 1985). Time exerts an important influence on two dimensions of creative behavior—self-expression and self-directedness. These two dimensions affect overall attention span.

❑ *Time influences children's self-expression and self-direction.* Mr. Moore, a teacher of 4-year-olds, planned his schedule to meet his goal of developing children's imagination. He provided a long block of time each day during which children were free to select dramatic play activities, among others. Knowing that there would be time each day to act out familiar roles and events such as playing house, doctor, or restaurant without interruption contributed to children's *creative and playful expression.* When children are continuously interrupted by many teacher-directed activities in short time blocks, they lose valuable time waiting and are disengaged in learning (Perlmutter, 1990).

In contrast, when children have enough time during the school day to choose some learning activities, they become more *self-directed learners.* Effective early childhood teachers plan creative environments that have a comfortable climate, flexible space, and ample time to foster children's imaginative spirit.

❑ *Time affects children's attention span.* Early childhood teachers often refer to children's short attention spans when describing children who are not interested in or motivated to complete a project. Many teachers erroneously believe that because children have short attention spans, activities must be changed constantly. When young children are engaged in meaningful activities, however, they are capable of concentrating for long periods of time.

Consider how long a child can sustain interest in an activity that is particularly interesting and meaningful to him or her (Garreau & Kennedy, 1991). Robin, a 4-year-old Sioux girl, is a good example. Her favorite game is "Pow," short for "powwow," and she has participated in a number of these Native American gatherings. Powwows usually last for a few days and include such experiences as dancing, storytelling, selling wares, and judging costumes. In her lengthy play scenarios, Robin takes her daughter (a Native American doll) to see the "powwow" events and invites her friends to play the roles of dancer and storyteller (Jalongo, 1992). Because Robin's teacher provides large blocks of time for Robin to pursue her activities in a meaningful and responsible fashion, she is motivated, interested, and has a longer attention span. (Garreau & Kennedy, 1991).

Planning for the physical environment is equal in importance to planning the instructional setting and cannot be overlooked. When the physical environment supports children's creative expression, it has many benefits for children's learning and development. Elizabeth Jones (1977) describes five teaching-learning dimensions that affect children's learning and influence the arrangement of the environment. These dimensions are described in Figure 6.1.

FIGURE 6.1   Dimensions of Teaching and Learning Environments

---

1. **SOFTNESS**   **HARDNESS**

   This dimension describes the feeling of the environment.

   Carpeted Areas   Hard surfaces (wood or linoleum)
   Soft, comfortable, and mobile furniture   Immobile furniture
   Animals to hold   Drab colors
   Messy materials (water, sand)
   Laps for sitting
   Warm, soft vocal tones

2. **OPEN**   **CLOSED**

   This dimension describes how much materials, storage patterns, and program
   structure restrict children's creative interactions with materials and with each other.

   Open materials offer unlimited   Limited alternatives (e.g., puzzles and
   possibilities for use (e.g., collage and   matching games)
   water)

   Relatively open materials offer a number   No visible or reachable storage
   of possibilities (e.g., construction
   materials)

   Visible and accessible storage

3. **SIMPLE**   **COMPLEX**

   This dimension describes the extent to which materials and equipment sustain
   children's interests. Simple environments encourage children to focus on task
   completion; complex environments contribute to children's imagination.

   Single use not fostering manipulation   Combine two different materials (e.g., art,
   (e.g., slides, puzzles)   dramatic play); supercomplex materials:
                                                   combine three or more materials (e.g.,
                                                   sand, tools, and water)

4. **HIGH MOBILITY**   **LOW MOBILITY**

   This dimension concerns the degree of children's physical activity.

   Gross motor, active physical activities   Small motor, sedentary activities (e.g.,
   (e.g., climbing, jumping)   drawing, writing)

5. **INTRUSION**   **SECLUSION**

   This dimension concerns boundaries.

   Adds new people and materials to the   Defined private spaces
   environment; children free to move
   about; cross-age grouping and teachable
   moments

Source: Adapted from Jones (1977).

Arranging the Indoor Environment

In creative environments, children engage in a balance of self-selected, self-directed, and teacher-selected activities. Picture these two kindergarten environments in which the daily schedule is posted. In Mr. Klick's room, the day begins with centers containing thematic activities and projects. After cleanup, the children gather together as a group. Mr. Klick places traditional, interesting whole-group activities (e.g., story, calendar, sharing) after cleanup to reserve the morning for creative expression and play activities and to capitalize on children's high interest in starting to learn early in the day. Across the hall in Ms. Gorman's room, the children spend the first hour and a half of each day in circle activities. They are required to remain seated on a piece of masking tape that marks their place on the rug. Each day begins with a good-morning song, attendance, the calendar, and the weather. This is followed by a lesson and a lengthy period of teacher's questions to individual children about the lesson. Children are constantly reminded to pay attention, and several are isolated from the group by being sent to the "thinking chair" as punishment for becoming distracted.

Notice how, in Mr. Klick's room, the arrangement is flexible, interest centers are provided, transitions are managed well, and routines are established to meet children's needs. In Ms. Gorman's room, on the other hand, the room arrangement is invariant, there are no interest centers, one activity blurs into another, and routines are established for the teacher's convenience. Ms. Gorman's teacher-directed environment does not provide opportunities for children to assume responsibility for their own learning, while Mr. Klick's arrangement encourages and supports child-initiated learning.

Room Arrangement

Room arrangement refers to the way space is organized for children's learning and movement. It can be planned, such as the art center and the area around it, or unplanned, such as a cubbyhole between two shelving units that attracts children. Space also affects both children's and teacher's behaviors and attitudes (Kritchevsky et al., 1977).

When children use space in ways that do not occur to us as teachers, it is time to reexamine the room arrangement. One kindergarten teacher who observed her students using the coat room for a play space realized this. She responded to their discovery by converting empty space, first dividing the space with a screen and then adding dramatic play materials (Loughlin & Suina, 1982). Now, when the children entered the coat room, their activity was primarily guided by the materials available in that area.

When arranging or rearranging the environment, keep in mind the following principles:

1. *Consider how the environment communicates messages about appropriate behavior.* If you are invited to dinner, you would behave differently at a

cookout with paper plates and plastic utensils than at a formal dinner party with china, silver, and crystal. Space works in the same way with children. It dictates how they may interact and use materials and affects their work pace (Loughlin & Suina, 1982). Well-organized space facilitates freedom of movement, creative expression, and learning. In contrast, poorly organized space invites ongoing interruptions, decreases children's attention spans, increases the likelihood of conflicts, and demands more teacher direction about rules and regulations (Kritchevsky et al., 1977).

2. *Space must be easy to supervise* (Kritchevsky et al., 1977). When children are involved in a variety of activities simultaneously, teachers must be able to scan the room from all vantage points. Carefully arranged space enables teachers to observe and monitor children's behavior. In this way, teachers can facilitate behaviors that support program goals and redirect those behaviors that do not.

3. *Materials must be accessible and easy to use.* Ms. Elverenli arranged the manipulative toys in her class of 2-year-olds—like large tinkertoys, puzzles, shape sorters, rings, and links—on low open shelves that faced a carpeted area away from the traffic flow. In this class, the children's typical behavior dictated the room arrangement. Because toddlers usually dump manipulatives on the floor to play with them, Ms. Elverenli provided the space. From a developmental perspective, it is unrealistic to expect every 2-year-old to carry materials to a table, so this teacher made her toys easy to use. When materials are accessible to children, they enhance children's sense of ownership of the classroom, encourage creative problem solving, and foster exchanges of materials from one part of the classroom to another.

4. *Be alert to behaviors that conflict with your goals.* Sometimes children's behaviors do not match teachers' intentions. When that happens, think about whether the problem lies with the children or with the room arrangement (Loughlin & Suina, 1982). For example, when Fernando, a kindergartner, repeatedly ran through the dramatic play center to feed the guinea pig, he disrupted the ongoing play. Upon observation and questioning, his teacher discovered that the easiest and fastest route to the guinea pig cage went directly through the dramatic play area. Together, they figured out a different location for the guinea pig, and the problem of using the dramatic play area as a thoroughfare was solved.

5. *Distinguish between the child's and the adult's environment.* Teachers and children view their surroundings from different perspectives. Both usually attend to what is at their eye level. Obviously, that space is different for adults and children due to differences in their height, experience, and movement patterns. The best way to understand the child's environment is to kneel down and view the space from the child's perspective (Loughlin & Martin, 1987; Loughlin & Suina, 1982; Moyer, Egerston, & Isenberg, 1987). Adopting a child's-eye view can enable you to plan a more child-centered room arrangement.

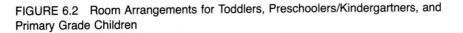

FIGURE 6.2   Room Arrangements for Toddlers, Preschoolers/Kindergartners, and Primary Grade Children

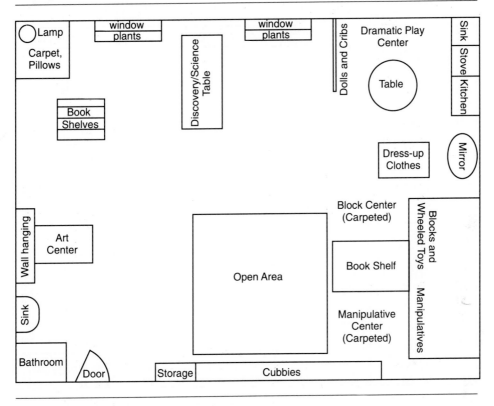

6. *Be alert to traffic patterns.* Well-arranged rooms provide clear pathways for a smooth and easy flow of traffic throughout the room. A path is visible: empty floor space through which people move from place to place. When activity centers are too close to each other and children cannot move freely from one to another, they interfere with each other. This usually causes conflict. To maintain freedom of movement, paths should not be used for any other purpose. Unclear paths often distract children on their way to a space or disrupt others' activities by intruding in their ongoing play or by accidentally knocking over materials.

Room arrangement is a powerful tool in the creative environment. It requires a knowledge of how space affects behavior and how to design space for special purposes and interests. Figure 6.2 shows room arrangements for toddlers, preschoolers and kindergartners, and primary grade children.

Centers

Most creative environments for children organize space into well-defined, thematic interest areas or centers. Centers are a valuable educational tool, enabling

FIGURE 6.2   *continued*

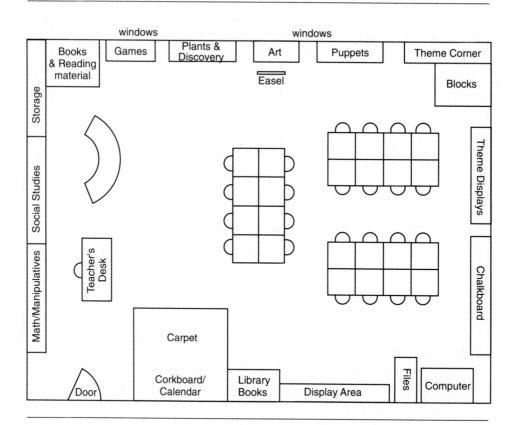

teachers to integrate the curriculum, overlap subject areas, develop multicultural awareness, and nurture children's spontaneity and originality (Casey & Lippman, 1991). Carefully designed centers contain a variety of books and real and manipulative materials that

❑ Promote active learning, planning, decision making, problem solving, originality, and interaction throughout the subject areas (Casey & Lippman, 1991; Nash, 1976; Seefeldt & Barbour, 1990).

❑ Increase social and verbal interaction and various forms of play among peers (Bredekamp, 1987).

❑ Require children to make choices on how to spend and manage their time and decide when to move to another activity.

❑ Reflect children's interests and cultural backgrounds.

Arranging Centers for Different Age Groups

A center arrangement is appropriate for children of all ages, as well as for children with special needs. Some adaptations, however, must be made to meet the needs and interests of children at different ages.

FIGURE 6.2 *continued*

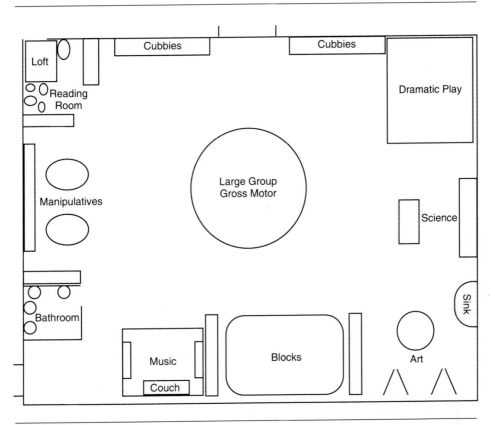

Toddlers need centers that contain a variety of play materials with different levels of complexity, as well as time for exploration (Caruso, 1984). They must

- ❑ Have low, open shelves to display and help them find materials.
- ❑ Have materials that reflect familiar people and places matched to their developmental level to encourage and extend play (Caruso, 1984).
- ❑ Encourage exploration and large motor development with climbing, push-pull, and ride-on toys.
- ❑ Provide a private space to watch others play or to rest with a soft toy.
- ❑ Offer sensory and creative experiences with music, science, dramatic play, construction, manipulatives, and sand and water. Chapter Seven details the variety of developmentally appropriate materials toddlers can use in these areas (Leavitt & Eheart, 1985).

Preschool children and kindergartners need centers that meet all of the requirements for toddlers and contain a variety of interesting materials and supplies that can be used to role-play pretend games (e.g., hats, shoes) and to construct objects (e.g., wood and glue, wooden blocks). The materials must reflect the expanding world of their community and their increasing interest in all subject areas (Seefeldt & Barbour, 1990).

School-age children need centers that support their need to develop logical thinking skills, create an orderly environment, belong to a peer group, and demonstrate competence in a particular area (Hughes, 1991).

Types and Uses of Centers

Indoor areas may include some of the following centers commonly found in all creative early childhood classrooms.

Art center. The art center enables children to investigate and create using a wide variety of materials. Some teachers even display works from famous artists in or near the center to enhance aesthetic appreciation. The art center should be located near a water source. If not, use plastic sheeting to cover carpeted areas or tables when children are using messy materials.

Most art materials should be organized and accessible on low, open shelves. This arrangement enables children to use them in other centers as needed. For example, in one first grade classroom, two children were designing a menu and a cover for their Mexican restaurant theme center. They used the menu to elaborate on their play. In a third-grade class, Horace used the art center to create a glove finger puppet as a prop for his story on dragons. In these rooms, the centers provided a vehicle for integrating the curriculum while supporting children's creative expression. Chapter Three contains a detailed list of appropriate uses of art materials.

Block center. Blocks help children develop essential classification and seriation skills and concepts, as well as increase their social and problem-solving skills. The block center should be located away from busy traffic areas and in an area where there is ample space for construction. It should contain a wide assortment of blocks and accessories (such as human figures, road signs, and small wheeled vehicles). Literacy materials and tools are another important addition. Children may want to sketch their "blueprints" on paper, label a building they've created, or write a story about their experience. Blocks should be accessible on open shelves marked with paper silhouettes of each block size and shape. Placing the center adjacent to the dramatic play center increases the interchange among centers (Kinsman & Berk, 1979). Chapter Seven contains more detailed information on blocks.

Discovery and science center. In this center, children actively explore materials that help develop scientific and conceptual understandings, such as shape, size, number, and volume. Children gain firsthand experiences with, for example, animals, vegetation, minerals, and the equipment used to study them such as scales, magnets, and simple measurement tools. Materials for experiments include boxes of collected items (such as shells or rocks) for sorting, classifying, comparing, and contrasting. Literacy materials and tools also support reading and writing across the subject areas. Often children use these materials for ongoing projects in other centers. One kindergartner took the magnifying glasses from the discovery center to examine sick animals she was tending in the dramatic play area. A second grader added information about his plant's growth to the classroom graph.

The discovery and science center also includes experiences with sand, rice, and water. Appropriate tables or plastic tubs with plastic containers and tubing of all shapes and sizes provide opportunities for scientific exploration of such concepts as volume, buoyancy, and displacement.

Dramatic play center.   The dramatic play center offers a rich setting for children's exploration of roles, behaviors, social skills, and language. It also promotes career and cultural awareness as children explore various occupations and cultures. Dramatic play centers are often transformed into thematic units of study such as a bakery during a unit on economics, a shoe store during a unit on measurement, and a photographer's studio during a unit on colors and shapes. Prop boxes, described in Chapter Five, are appropriate in this center and enhance children's play.

Library and literacy center.   This center invites children to read a variety of print materials in a relaxing way and should be located in a quiet area of the classroom. It should be a soft, cozy place. Some teachers use a rocking chair, a seat removed from a car, or an old bathtub filled with pillows in their literacy centers. A variety of familiar and interesting books should be displayed on book

Children can develop scientific understandings through exploration with a variety of plastic containers and tubing and a large water table.

shelves. There should also be books in different formats such as story and information books, wordless and predictable books, riddles, rhymes, and child-made books. The center should also contain printed signs and questions that invite children to explore the book selections. Some teachers include the Sunday comics, old catalogues, puppets and prop boxes for retelling stories, recycled copies of children's magazines, and mobiles of information about a featured author. Interesting writing materials, such as recycled colored paper from a print shop and unusual pens and pencils, should be available. For young children, this center encourages early literacy play—an important precursor to learning to read and write.

Manipulative and math center. Manipulative materials, such as colored blocks, buttons, and cubes, encourage children's growing mathematical understandings of number, classification, ordering, comparing, measuring, estimating, and counting. It needs to be located near low, open shelves that contain an organized system for storing manipulatives and math games like dominoes. Writing materials, a chalkboard, and a flannel board should also be available for children to create their own math stories and to explore and practice mathematical skills and concepts. Chapter Seven contains an extensive list of appropriate manipulative materials for different ages.

Media and music center. This center uses electronic media (e.g., computers, audio- and videotapes, records) as vehicles for play and as objects of playful expression. The media and music center needs to be located away from extreme heat, cold, and glare and near an electrical outlet. Many teachers find that laminated posters with rebus-type instructions on operating the equipment are useful. Computers should be placed on table tops at the children's eye level and should be arranged so that two or three children may work together at any one time (Hohman, 1985). The media and music center should be as open and accessible as other centers so that children can use the equipment for play and investigation. It should also contain a variety of music for children to listen to, simple musical instruments that enable children to create their own music, and experiences with music from other cultures.

Writing center. In this center, children experiment with writing, ranging from scribbling or drawing to composing poems and stories. Sometimes they come here from other centers to make signs or captions for their work. Good writing centers contain chalkboards, a stapler, glue, pencils, markers and crayons, and an assortment of papers in various sizes, shapes, and colors for writing and illustrating. Magazines, newspapers, old catalogues, scissors, and glue should also be available for children to illustrate stories or add to their creations. Some teachers have children keep a box of children's drawings for others to use to create stories (Loughlin & Martin, 1987).

A Center-Based Classroom

Consider how Mr. Kennedy uses centers in his first-grade classroom. There are two large child-created displays relating to their unit on insects. One display contains a variety of three-dimensional, imaginative insects created by the children at the art center. Another presents children's illustrated stories about their creations. Mr. Kennedy's centers contain interesting and accessible materials that invite children's participation. They are attractively stored in color-coded plastic baskets and tubs and have pictures to assist children in keeping them properly organized.

Mr. Kennedy has placed centers for dramatic play, blocks, and the workbench near each other because children's play here is often noisy; he has grouped the discovery and art centers next to the sink because they need water; and he has clustered the literacy, writing, and listening areas together because they demand a quieter environment. He has even arranged a small, cozy corner with a beanbag chair and colored pillows for those times when children seek solitude. Because of these groupings, children commonly use materials from one center as they work in another (e.g., using pots and pans from the dramatic play center in the "trailer" they constructed from blocks in the block center).

Mr. Kennedy stores his materials in cabinets close to the center where they will be used. This enables him to add new materials quickly and efficiently as he

A workbench and tools are an important part of a center-based classroom.

observes children's use of existing materials. He also organizes children's work in individual mailboxes made from recycled 2-liter or gallon jugs with the tops cut off, uses an egg carton as a scissors holder, and uses a clothesline to display children's art.

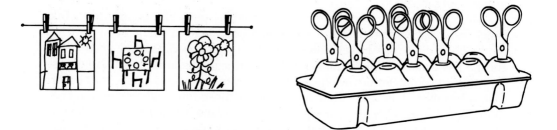

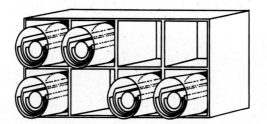

In arranging his centers, Mr. Kennedy considered the essential spatial aspects of the environment—clear, visible, defined areas; clear pathways created by using the backs of large pieces of furniture; private space by providing a cozy area; centers arranged by type of activity (e.g., large or small group, active or quiet play); special requirements such as water, electricity, large floor space, or privacy; and supervision by organizing materials close to their appropriate centers and maintaining a proper vantage point for observation (Loughlin & Suina, 1982).

Mr. Kennedy's environment has been prepared to foster children's learning through play and creative expression. Through active, concrete experiences and numerous opportunities for peer and adult interactions, these first graders can express themselves in developmentally appropriate ways (Bredekamp, 1987).

Transitions and Routines

Transitions are those times during the day when children move from one activity to the next. In a classroom with centers and choices, each transition requires children to make a decision (Vartuli & Phelps, 1980). Routines are regular and predictable activities that form the basis of the daily schedule; they help children sense the passage of time (e.g., snack follows cleanup) and enable them to anticipate events (e.g., playing a musical selection at the end of each day) (Alger, 1984).

Transitions and routines consume 20 to 35% of the preschooler's day (Berk, 1976) and are an integral part of the day for school-age children. Unless planned well, they can be difficult and stressful periods for both children and teachers. Failure to plan for transition times encourages inappropriate behaviors, boredom, and increased dependence on the teacher. Planned transitions and routines

☐ *Facilitate children's control over the environment.* One beginning second-grade teacher was having difficulty with classroom management. It seemed that each time the children moved from one activity to the next, they playfully pushed each other, tripped or knocked over materials, and constantly interrupted and asked her what to do. What was happening in her classroom? The daily schedule consisted of a series of whole group activities requiring children to spend an inordinate amount of time waiting for a turn. Little attention was given to transitions. The teacher's mentor suggested examining the organization of the day, starting with planning for routines and transitions. The teacher replied, "It never occurred to me that I should even think about those times in the day. I just assumed children knew what was expected of them when they finished. Now I realize that I must plan for transitions, just as I plan for the rest of the instructional day."

☐ *Must be child-centered* (Garreau & Kennedy, 1991). A first-grade teacher opens his morning group time with the whole class clustered around him in a large space. Following group time, the children sing a special song or chant some poetry (such as "A Wiggle in My Toe" to move from one activity to the next.

☐ *Help children make connections to their ongoing, thematic activities.* During a unit on transportation, Ms. Plate sang the song "Riding in an Airplane," by Raffi, with the children. At the end of the song, she suggested that the children pretend to fly to the prepared art tables and make appropriate airplane noises along the way. This tied their study of transportation to music and art and ensured a positive transition. Figure 6.3 lists common routines and transition times and provides ideas for turning them into learning opportunities.

Planned transitions and routines are essential for children of all ages. They differ from other activities in purpose, length, and frequency and depend upon the age of the children and the available physical facilities. Adequate planning enables children to take charge of the day easily and comfortably (Hildebrand, 1981).

Arranging the Outdoor Environment

Many teachers still view the purpose of outdoor play as a release of tension and excess energy. This narrow view perpetuates the neglect of the outdoor environment as an important setting for children's creative growth and development. Outdoor environments need the same systematic attention to space, ma-

FIGURE 6.3   Ideas for Routines and Transitions

Routines are an integral part of learning and offer both children and teacher more control over their environment.

ARRIVAL

❑   Prepare materials and activities before children arrive.
❑   Be available to greet children.
❑   Prepare engaging and interesting activities that attract children's attention and are easy to monitor.
❑   In extended day settings, be certain to communicate any unusual behaviors or concerns to staff and teachers who follow you.
❑   Ask parents who want to talk to stay for a moment, if feasible, or call them later to arrange a time.
❑   Construct an attendance chart and a center planning board so that children can sign in and choose activities as they arrive.

OPENING GROUP TIME

❑   Begin this part of the day after children have had a chance to explore the environment.
❑   Introduce available choices for the day and ask children to make decisions about what they will do.
❑   Use this time to review or create any classroom rules related to using a particular center or piece of equipment. When children help set these limits, they are more apt to internalize them.
❑   Demonstrate the appropriate use of new materials.

CLEANUP

❑   Give notice. Children need a 10-, a 5-, and then a 1-minute warning to begin cleanup.
❑   Play tape-recorded music and have children listen for something special as they put away materials.
❑   Use a song to announce that cleanup time is approaching and sing while cleaning up.
❑   Organize a precleanup circle. Decide how to divide the tasks so that each child picks up a certain number of objects or a particular kind of object (e.g., everything that is smaller than a shopping bag; everything that has a metal part) or use a cleanup helpers' board.
❑   Model the behaviors you want to see from the children.
❑   Prepare an interesting activity to follow cleanup that children can anticipate with enthusiasm.
❑   Create rhymes to familiar tunes that refer to putting away materials or helping ("This is the way we clean up our room . . .").

FIGURE 6.3 *continued*

DEPARTURE

☐ Establish a departure ritual such as hearing a story or enjoying a song together.
☐ Briefly preview some of the interesting things that will take place the next day or later that week.
☐ Encourage children to bring tote or paper bags for papers, newsletters, and other forms of communication.
☐ Be available to say good-bye.

TRANSITIONS FROM ONE ACTIVITY TO ANOTHER

☐ Develop a repertoire of songs and fingerplays to be used as children move from one place to another. Use a song or fingerplay (e.g., "Two little blackbirds"; ask one child to name another by color of clothing, kinds of fasteners on shoes, or name card).
☐ Have books ready for children to read while others finish their activities and get ready to join the group.
☐ Use a mystery box, puppets, a riddle ("I see something red, white, and blue with stars on it"), fingerplays, or quiet songs.

For primary grade children:

☐ Review the day and talk about tomorrow.
☐ Plan ahead on how to move from one activity to another.
☐ Have materials ready for the next activity.

Source: Adapted from Alger (1984).

terials, and equipment as indoor environments. The best outdoor environments provide children opportunities to engage in all forms of play—exercise, dramatic and constructive play, and games with rules in an environment with natural features (Frost, 1986, 1988; Wortham & Frost, 1990).

Think about Ms. Ogur's beliefs about her preschooler's outdoor environment. Ms. Ogur was concerned about the quality of the play on the playground. In her school, the playground equipment included three tricycles, two balls, and a combination swing set/climbing apparatus for 15 children to share. The children were continuously fighting over the materials. She knew that this was the year to address and solve this problem. She also knew that the children's disputes were caused, in part, by not having enough challenging materials and equipment.

After talking with other colleagues and reading professional literature on outdoor play for preschoolers, she discovered that some materials have different levels of complexity. Kritchevsky et al. (1977) classify materials as

☐ *Simple units* that have a single use, with no subparts for children to manipulate or create (e.g., swings, tricycles).
☐ *Complex units* that have subparts of two very different kinds of material for children to manipulate or invent (e.g., water and plastic containers, sand and digging tools).

❑ *Supercomplex units* that have three or more subparts that children can juxtapose (e.g., sand, digging tools, and water).

Supercomplex units hold children's attention and interest the longest because of the many opportunities children have to manipulate and juxtapose the parts and integrate them into their play themes. Simple units, on the other hand, are necessary but typically hold interest and attention for only a short period of time because they are often played with by one child in just one way, such as a Hot Wheels toy.

Ms. Ogur then decided to expand children's play by adding some complexity to the environment. She brought out a wagon; created an obstacle course from old, worn tires obtained free from the local junk yard; and made some simple traffic signs out of scrap lumber and paint. She also brought out the police officer's hat from the dramatic play center and markers and scrap paper from the literacy center. From these simple additions, the children created elaborate play themes or scenarios about accidents, traffic, parking, and speeding. Some children even created and handed out parking tickets. On other occasions, the children used the wagon as an ambulance to transport an accident victim to the hospital, where another elaborate scenario was enacted. Ms. Ogur even used the traffic signs to reinforce bicycle safety practices.

Ms. Ogur illustrates what a resourceful teacher can do to make the outdoor environment more stimulating and challenging even with limited financial resources.

Types of Playgrounds

Basically, there are three types of playgrounds: traditional, adventure, and creative (Frost, 1988).

Traditional playgrounds originated early in this century. They contain large, steel, immovable equipment (e.g., climbing bars, slides, swings)—mostly simple units—that are designed for physical exercise. Traditional playgrounds are often not well maintained or supervised, are built on dangerously hard surfaces, and are not consistent with what we know about children's learning and development, yet they are prevalent in elementary school playgrounds (Frost, 1988). Since the late 1970s, wooden superstructures with a variety of apparatuses have replaced some of this steel equipment.

Adventure or "junk" playgrounds, originating in Denmark in the middle of this century and uniquely European, were designed to provide supervised, creative play opportunities for urban children. They contain unconnected tools and materials that enable children to build, create, and pretend with their own play structures, using materials in a free and open atmosphere. Varying in size, they offer children a variety of options (e.g., building, gardening, using sand or water, cooking). Each adventure playground contains a large hut filled with a variety of typical indoor materials (e.g., art, dramatic play materials, and music) that children choose to use. Adults function as play leaders, people who support

The sand area should contain an assortment of digging and molding materials that invite children's experimentation and exploration.

children's ideas and act as facilitators. Adventure playgrounds support children's freedom to learn through discovery in an enriched environment.

Creative playgrounds, adapted in this century from the adventure playground concept, contain a superstructure with movable parts (e.g., boards, ramps, wheels), are action oriented, provide safe underneath surfaces, and promote all forms of play (e.g., functional, constructive, dramatic, and games). "Loose parts provide for flexibility, diversity, novelty and challenge which are all important ingredients for creativity, socialization, and learning. They are also adaptable for use with fluid materials (sand and water) and with larger structures" (Frost, 1988, p. 13).

Playgrounds that provide many play possibilities for children are important learning environments. These environments stress integrated rather than isolated equipment and extend learning to the outdoor environment. Their design has certain features that enhance all forms of children's play.

Characteristics of Outdoor Play Environments

Outdoor play provides many benefits for children of all ages and should be planned to be utilized year round (Isenberg & Quisenberry, 1988). There are three primary characteristics of high-quality outdoor play environments: equipment and materials, safety, and storage (Frost, 1986; Frost & Klein, 1979).

Equipment and Materials

Equipment and materials in high-quality outdoor play environments hold children's interest over time and enable them to engage in all four forms of play (Frost, 1986; Frost & Klein, 1977). They feature loose parts; a combination of simple, complex, and supercomplex materials; a wide range of experiences and activities; and well-defined spaces.

Loose parts are movable pieces in the play area that children can manipulate and use to improvise. Lightweight objects of different sizes, shapes, and textures; movable boards or ramps; and organic materials like sand and water can be moved from place to place as children choose. They also add complexity to the environment.

Complexity refers to the number of possibilities the material offers children. The more possibilities the material has, the more likely it is to hold children's interest and attention because children can do more with it (Kritchevsky et al., 1977). If too much of the play equipment is designed to be used by one child at a time or to be used in just one way, it severely limits the play area's complexity. For example, a large tire swing that can hold two or more children offers more options for play than a swing on a swing set.

Diversity or *variety* refers to the number of ways materials can be used, regardless of their complexity. It influences how children get started in their play (Kritchevsky et al., 1977). A wide slide, for example, has more possibilities than a narrow one.

Defined spaces include both the amount and arrangement of space to facilitate children's play patterns. A minimum of 200 square feet per child is required on playgrounds attached to early childhood centers (Esbensen, 1990). Both open and partitioned spaces need to be available in the outdoor environment.

Figure 6.4 is a checklist of criteria to use in planning and arranging high-quality outdoor play environments. When the outdoor space is designed using these criteria, children retain ownership over their play, communicate and express thoughts and feelings, and develop feelings of satisfaction and competence. Well-planned outdoor environments meet all of their needs—physical, social, emotional, and intellectual.

FIGURE 6.4   Checklist for Planning and Arranging the Outdoor Environment

Adequate Space

Does the environment

- ❏ Stimulate all four types of play—exercise, constructive, dramatic, and games with rules—through appropriately arranged space and traffic patterns?
- ❏ Provide appropriate spaces for individuals and small groups of children according to their ages, physical sizes, interests, and abilities?
- ❏ Develop play areas (zones), so that activities such as tricycle riding and climbing do not occur in close proximity to one another?
- ❏ Ensure that movement from one zone to another will be safe and manageable?
- ❏ Offer a visually pleasing area in which the natural elements and fabricated structures complement each other?
- ❏ Provide overall cohesiveness rather than discrete, unconnected objects or structures?
- ❏ Foster a sense of flow from one activity to another?
- ❏ Provide varied ground surfaces such as hardtop for games and vehicles, grass, water, or soft mulch or sand, hilly or mounded areas, flat areas, construction areas, sunlight, and shade?
- ❏ Offer easy access to coats, toilets, and drinking fountains?
- ❏ Define areas for exercise, dramatic, constructive, and games-with-rules types of play?
- ❏ Provide protected storage for equipment?
- ❏ Contain space for walking, running, and skipping?
- ❏ Include a shaded area with tables and benches to be used for art activities, table games, or snacks?

Materials

Does the environment

- ❏ Offer ample opportunities for children's physical, cognitive, and social development through a dynamic, challenging, age-appropriate environment with complex materials?
- ❏ Promote independent and creative uses of flexible materials such as sand, water, dramatic play, and superstructures with room for many children?
- ❏ Contain equipment for active and quiet play and for solitary, parallel, and cooperative play?
- ❏ Contain materials for dramatic play (e.g., car, boat, house)?
- ❏ Contain materials for constructive play and experimentation (e.g., boards, ramps, tires, tools, nails)?
- ❏ Provide materials for gross motor development (e.g., climbers, wide slides)?
- ❏ Provide a sand area located away from people, with proper covering to protect it from inclement weather and animals?
- ❏ Include a water area located near an outdoor water supply with a variety of materials for experimentation, problem solving, and exploration?

FIGURE 6.4 *continued*

___

☐ Contain a variety of balls?
☐ Contain nonlocomotor materials for stretching, carrying, and swinging?
☐ Contain manipulative materials for throwing, kicking, and catching?

Activities and Experiences

Does the environment

☐ Provide for children's interactions with materials, peers, and adults through proper storage, defined spaces, and interest areas?
☐ Offer a range of activities, experiences, and equipment with "loose parts" that children can adapt to their own play schemes?
☐ Provide large equipment for gross motor development; loose parts and natural materials for constructive play; enclosed structures for dramatic play; linked platforms for social play; semiprivate spaces for hiding; and nature areas for gardening?

Safety

☐ Are adults actively supervising the play area?
☐ Is the equipment in good repair, in working order, and free of sharp edges?
☐ Are there fences at least 5 feet high with lockable gates that work well?
☐ Are there 8–10 inches of sand, mulch, or pea gravel under climbing and moving equipment?
☐ Is there some type of edging (e.g., railroad ties) to contain the cushioning materials?
☐ Is the area free of litter (e.g., broken glass)?

___

Source: Adapted from Frost (1986), and Frost and Wortham, (1988).

Safety and Supervision

A safe, well-supervised outdoor environment is an important part of the early childhood environment. Yet, national survey data reveal that today's preschool and public school playgrounds are "unconscionably bad" (Frost et al., 1991, p. 179). They

☐ Are poorly designed, antiquated, and inadequately maintained (Thompson, 1991; Wortham & Frost, 1990).
☐ Lack storage facilities (Bruya, 1988).
☐ Neglect features children prefer such as dramatic play materials and nature areas (Bruya, 1988; Wortham & Frost, 1990).
☐ Focus entirely on motor activity (Bruya, 1988).
☐ Are developmentally inappropriate (Wortham & Frost, 1990).
☐ Are used without safety orientation for staff or children (Bruya, 1988; Wortham & Frost, 1990).

We suggest the following guidelines for better safety and supervision in outdoor settings:

1. Circulate around the area rather than standing in a group and talking.
2. Decide on supervision of areas in advance. Give special attention to swings or climbers, where there is a lot of activity and potential for injury.
3. Place 8–10 inches of fall-absorbing material, such as pea gravel, bark mulch, or shredded tires, under and around all moving equipment (e.g., swings and rotating devices) because falls from high places are the number one cause of playground injuries to children (USCPSC, 1981). Be certain to include a retaining border to hold the material and replenish it frequently (Frost, 1986).

Storage

Storage facilities are essential on playgrounds for young children. They house the materials children use to develop and extend their play.

The location of the storage area is critical. Storage that is accessible to the immediate play area saves time in transporting toys and encourages responsibility in children themselves. Think about storage that is

- ❏ Child-scaled to facilitate taking out and putting away equipment.
- ❏ Weathertight and vandalproof to protect the equipment.
- ❏ Multipurpose, contains space for teacher storage, and allows childen to play on the structure.

These characteristics of high-quality outdoor environments apply to children of all ages. However, some adaptations need to be made according to children's needs, interests, and abilities.

Outdoor Environments for Children of Different Ages

Like indoor environments, outdoor environments must be adjusted to the child's development level.

Infants and Toddlers

Playgrounds for infants and toddlers should be arranged to meet their rapidly increasing motor and social development, as well as their clear need for autonomy. They need opportunities for experimentation and exploration with a few simple, safe, age-appropriate choices. Adding sensory materials, such as clear pathways of different textures, enhances their play. They need equipment that is stimulating and close to the ground; dramatic play options; loose parts for stacking, gathering, and dumping; and natural experiences with living plants and animals.

Some interesting additions for toddler outdoor play include

- ❏ Hanging large, inflatable balls or characters from a tree and having children try to "catch one" with a cardboard tube.
- ❏ Painting the pathways, equipment, or fence with small buckets of water and large brushes.

❑ Washing dishes and furniture with pans of warm, soapy water, sponges, and scrub brushes (Miller, 1989).

Preschoolers and Kindergartners

Playgrounds for preschoolers and kindergartners should promote all four forms of play—functional, constructive, dramatic, and games with rules. Preschool structures must develop a wide range of skills and abilities while emphasizing dramatic play. They should contain a convenient and accessible storage facility for portable materials, a grassy area for group games, a place for privacy to accommodate children's need for solitary and parallel play, and a variety of child-sized equipment for motor development (Wortham & Frost, 1990). The best outdoor environments for preschool and kindergarten children include a complex superstructure with a combination of loose parts (e.g., raw materials such as sand, water, lumber, tires, and discarded telephone cable spools).

Try some of these activities to add novelty and complexity to the outdoor environment:

❑ Turn wheeled vehicles into a fire engine, ambulance, or tractor by adding appropriate props nearby and stimulating dramatic play.

❑ Use a large, empty carton and other appropriate props to create a service station area for wheeled vehicles, a bank drive-through, or a roadside produce stand.

❑ Have a car wash for the wheeled vehicles. Use large buckets of warm, soapy water and add other appropriate props to stimulate imaginative play outdoors.

❑ Mix bubbles from ¼ cup dishwashing detergent and 1 gallon of water. Use an assortment of recycled materials, such as berry baskets and straws, for bubble wands.

❑ Encourage children to paint along the fence. Clip clothespins and easel paper along the fence and use cardboard six-packs to hold paint containers in recyclable plastic containers. Leave the paintings up for an art show.

❑ Read *A Rose for Pinkerton* by Steven Kellogg (1981) and *Pet Show* by Ezra Jack Keats (1972) and then have a pet show with children's stuffed animals. Make judges' clipboards out of cardboard and clothespins, stands for the animals out of recycled ice-cream tubs, and prize ribbons out of used gift wrap.

❑ Create nature collages. Use shoebox lids and white glue to make collages of natural materials located on or near the playground, park, or nearby woods (Miller, 1989).

School-Age Children

Environments for school-age children should encourage natural investigation and challenge the imagination. School-age children prefer structures that feature numerous physical challenges such as climbers, equipment for social development, and safe places for group games. Following are some suggestions that challenge school-age children in outdoor areas.

- ❏ Plan and conduct a scavenger hunt. Use a variety of clues that incorporate riddles, listening, or writing. Tie the scavenger hunt to the unit of study where possible.
- ❏ Provide plenty of chalk so that the children can make outdoor games such as hopscotch or four square or create shadow drawings.
- ❏ Do some tie-dyeing. Tie old t-shirts with rubber bands and dip them into fabric dyes. Hang the shirts to dry along the fence. Repeat the process with another color for more complex and symmetrical designs (Miller, 1989).
- ❏ Do a shadow play in the afternoon. Invite children to enact various roles, and use cardboard silhouettes for props. The audience watches the show on the ground rather than the players themselves.

The outdoor environment can be arranged to foster children's creative growth and development through a variety of planned uses of space, activities, experiences, and materials. Teachers who believe in the power of both the indoor and outdoor environments for learning must assume roles that guide children's creative growth.

Teachers' Roles and Responsibilities

What teachers believe about creativity and play influences a vision of a creative environment. We, as teachers, would be wise to keep in mind the words of Danette Littleton (1989) as we plan and arrange creative environments:

> It is our own playfulness that links the child within each of us to the child we teach: the feeling child, the thinking and reasoning child, the creative child, the compassionate child. All of these are a whole fabric woven of the unending thread of play. (p. xiii)

The following suggestions can foster a dynamic, creative environment.

1. *View yourself as a creative teacher.* Ask yourself, how creative am I? What efforts do I make to support children's creativity and build a creative learning environment? Do I have original ideas? How do I solve problems and make decisions? Do I accept children who respond in unusual ways? Could I identify the most creative children in my class? Creative teachers exhibit spontaneity, sensitivity, open-mindedness, and a high tolerance for ambiguity. They support child-initiated learning, encourage children to "live the question," reward imaginative ideas, and believe in children's self-evaluation (Dacey, 1989).

2. *Maintain an orderly environment.* An orderly environment gives children control over activity choices, helps them carry out their ideas, and builds responsibility for the care and storage of materials. Materials for children

of all ages should be neatly arranged and pleasantly displayed. When children have access to materials, they must also assume responsibility for returning them to their place when finished. This means that the materials must be organized so that children understand where they belong. Most teachers separate materials by type in simple labeled containers so that children can take responsibility for keeping them organized.

3. *Use a planning or choice board.* Planning or choice boards encourage children to recognize the beginning and end of an activity, develop planning and organizational skills related to their own activities, manage their time, work independently and with others, assume responsibility for their own activities, and reflect on their decisions (Casey & Lippman, 1991; Garreau & Kennedy, 1991). They also help teachers limit the number of children in a center or activity at any one time, evaluate and change centers as needed, and observe children's choices. Planning or choice boards provide teachers with a great deal of flexibility.

    A planning board can be easily constructed from pegboard or any freestanding object (such as a bulletin board), pictures or labels for centers, and name tags. Some teachers use a magnetic board with small magnets or magnetic tape strips on the board and paper clips glued on the backs of cards. For preschool and kindergarten children who are emergent readers, children's names and the names of the centers can be illustrated pictorially. Figure 6.5 illustrates a planning board used with preschoolers and a planning sheet used with kindergartners and first graders.

4. *Consider the environment a powerful instructional tool.* When teachers are knowledgeable about space and materials, they can often anticipate how children will use them. Predicting behavior in this way promotes children's independence, active involvment, and sustained attention.

    The environment can also be used to *manage tasks*. Carefully arranged and displayed materials invite children to participate in appropriate ways with a minimum of adult intervention. One preschool teacher uses children's photographs for taking attendance and rebus recipes for preparing snacks. Such tools reduce the amount of time teachers devote to routine administrative tasks, freeing them to focus on children's creativity and learning.

5. *Plan for diversity.* Just as individuals differ in developmental level, differences in abilities or interests also influence how subject matter affects thinking. It is important to have a variety of materials and subject areas to stimulate children's imagination and diverse use of materials. Be innovative in your use of the physical environment, but keep your purpose in mind. Sometimes you might want to use an area to stimulate aesthetic appreciation; at other times, you might change the area to provide use of complex materials. Planning for diversity means providing a variety of center materials that respond to children's cultural backgrounds, interests, and ability levels, a balance of teacher-directed and child-initiated activities, and flexible grouping.

FIGURE 6.5   A Planning Board and Planning Sheets

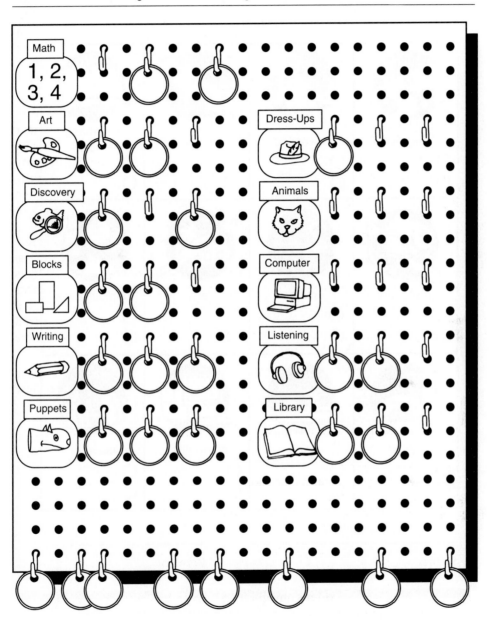

FIGURE 6.5   *continued*

puzzles ○ ○	playhouse ○ ○	writing ○ ○	homebase reading ○ ○
discovery ○ ○	math ○ ○	art ○ ○	manipulatives ○ ○
blocks ○ ○	sand ○ ○	computer ○ ○	listening ○ ○

Name   Week of

FIGURE 6.5   *continued*

Name _____   Week of _____

Art	Math
_____ ○	_____ ○
_____ ○	_____ ○

Writing	Discovery
_____ ○	_____ ○
_____ ○	_____ ○
_____ ○	

Skill Group

Lunch 	Story	Recess			
Blocks	○ ○	Homebase reading	○ ○		
Manipulatives	○ ○	Sand	○ ○		
Listening	○ ○	Puzzles	○ ○		
Playhouse	○ ○	Computer	○ ○		

Special Populations

Most early childhood classrooms have children with special needs. Teachers' awareness of these needs is particularly important during the early years because many of these special needs have not yet been identified. Adapting the environment for special populations means that we as classroom teachers determine how to use the basic characteristics of the creative environment— climate, space, and time.

Children with Disabilities

Some simple adjustments in equipment, materials, and room arrangement are necessary for children with disabling conditions in both the indoor and outdoor environments. The first step in adapting both environments to these children's needs is to understand fully the nature and extent of each child's limitations. The next step is to adapt the environment so that each child can participate in a meaningful way, ideally in a way that emphasizes abilities rather than disabilities.

Hearing-impaired children often feel frustrated and socially isolated from other learners. Hallahan and Kaufman (1991) suggest adapting the environment for them by

- ❏ Seating them away from noisy backgrounds such as windows, doors, and heating and cooling systems.
- ❏ Allowing them to move about freely so that they can position themselves to hear better and see the faces of their peers.
- ❏ Reducing classroom noise with carpeting and corkboard walls.
- ❏ Minimizing classroom activities in large, echoing rooms.

Visually impaired children always require a physical orientation to the classroom, including the location of materials, centers, and exits. They need

- ❏ An orientation to the classroom from a single focal point such as their table or desk.
- ❏ An orientation to the school after they are familiar with the classroom (Ashcroft & Zambone-Ashley, 1980).
- ❏ Information about any changes in the physical arrangement.
- ❏ A designated sighted guide for special activities like fire drills.
- ❏ Lighting that does not cast shadows or glare on their work and allows them to move so that they can comfortably see each activity.
- ❏ Traffic patterns and pathways that are clear and free.
- ❏ Simple room arrangements.

Physically impaired children have problems with either large or small muscles and have a slower reaction time than other children. The adaptations vary according to the severity and type of disability. They can benefit from

❑ Taking apart movable playground equipment and laying it flat on the ground. Children who otherwise cannot use parts of play structures can practice walking across them when they are on the ground.

❑ Modifications for writing such as computers, felt tip rather than soft lead pencils, and pads rather than sheets of paper.

❑ Playground designs that use smooth pathways and ramps to help them gain access to play areas.

❑ Wheelchair-height tables and trays so that they can use water tables and manipulatives.

High-Achieving and Low-Achieving Children

High-achieving children need environments that foster self-directed learning in which they can "initiate plans for their own learning, identify resources, gather data, and develop and evaluate their own products and projects" (Hallahan & Kaufman, 1991, pp. 437–438). They need environments that

❑ *Contain interest or learning centers to promote self-directed learning and independence.* These centers should provide a variety of manipulative, media, and print materials for exploration, experimentation, and long-term research (Hallahan & Kaufman, 1991). One teacher, for example, developed an interest center about bicycling with materials for children to create bicycle paths and gain permission to build and install bicycle racks in public places (Burns, 1985).

❑ *Use contracts to guide independent study and promote autonomy.* Contracts allow children to make choices about what work to do, when to work, with whom to work, and where to work. After studying the habits of different animals, some second graders contracted to extend their knowledge through art by making drawings or models of their favorite animal; others wrote original stories; still others created original play scenarios, such as "Meet My Pet Boa Constrictor." Contracts help children take responsibility for their own learning and free teachers to facilitate that learning.

Low-achieving children also can participate in self-directed learning activities that challenge them at their own level. Contracts help these children feel successful and offer them opportunities to choose what work to do, when to work, with whom to work, or where to work. Using this model provides more flexible grouping for all children.

Conclusion

Planning and arranging a creative environment fosters learning, responsibility, and self-direction in the early childhood classroom. In a creative environment, the emphasis is on learning, not teaching; a variety of opportunities for child choice; and invitations to children that unlock creative potential. The creative environment involves children in planning, provides a wide range of materials and equipment, and has appropriate, predictable routines and transitions.

Chapter Summary

1. Planning and arranging the creative environment is as important as planning for instruction.
2. There are three basic features of creative environments: climate, space, and time. Climate is the feeling emanating from the environment; space includes the degree to which the physical environment contributes to active, creative thinking; and time encompasses the influences of the classroom schedule on children's expression, attention span, and self-directedness.
3. Room arrangement is the way space is organized for children's learning and movement. When arranging the classroom environment, consider what it communicates to children; how easily the space can be supervised; how accessible the materials are; and how you feel about unpredictable behaviors. Teachers also need to distinguish between the child's and the adult's environment and be alert to traffic patterns.
4. There are various types and uses of centers. Centers organize space and promote active learning, planning and decision making, problem solving, originality, and interaction. All early childhood classrooms should have the following centers: art, blocks, discovery/science, dramatic play, library/literacy, manipulative/math, media/music, and writing.
5. Transitions are times during the day when children move from one activity to another. Routines are activities that occur regularly and form the basis of the daily schedule. Planned transitions and routines are essential for children of all ages.
6. What teachers believe about creativity and play influences how they prepare the environment, as well as their vision of a creative environment. Teachers need to be creative themselves, maintain an orderly environment, use a planning or choice board, and consider the environment as an instructional tool.
7. Outdoor environments need the same systematic attention to space, materials, equipment, and safety as indoor environments. They need simple, complex, and supercomplex units to hold children's interest over time and challenge their imagination.
8. There are three types of playgrounds—traditional, adventure, and creative. Action-oriented playgrounds containing a superstructure with movable apparatus, loose parts, and safe underneath surfaces promote all four forms of play.
9. Adapting the environment for special populations of children means adjusting the basic characteristics of climate, space, and time to the particular needs of each child.

Discussion Questions

1. Reread the quotation that introduced this chapter. How has your understanding of it increased since reading this chapter?
2. Think about your most pleasurable play environment as a child. How does this relate to what you know about the importance of environments to support creative growth?
3. Visualize your ideal classroom, both indoors and outdoors. In what ways do you think your beliefs about creativity influence your mental view of the indoor and outdoor environments?
4. Refer back to the case study at the beginning of the chapter. What behaviors did Ms. Ring demonstrate that influenced her environment? Were her reactions justified? On what basis? How will she go about re-creating a creative environment? If Ms. Ring's substitute asked you how she could improve her classroom, what would you suggest?
5. Some teachers admit that they never think much about children's play on the playground. What do you think of this practice? Why?
6. In planning and arranging your creative environment, think about how you would respond to a parent or colleague who said "But they are just playing! When are they going to *learn* something?" What would you say? Why?

──────────────── **Writing to Learn** ────────────────

Select an age group—infants/toddlers, preschool/kindergarten, or primary. You have just been transferred to a brand new school where you will be teaching. Your principal has given you 2 weeks to purchase equipment and materials for your teaching-learning environment. Using the criteria for creative environments discussed throughout the chapter, create a working schedule and develop a floor plan for the room arrangement. Justify your selections. Present and discuss these ideas in a small group. What revisions, if any, would you make now that you have heard others' ideas?

──────────────── **Interview** ────────────────

How Teachers Plan Their Classroom Environments

Arrange to interview a teacher of an infant/toddler, preschool/kindergarten, or primary class about the way he or she plans and arranges the environment. Ask the following questions and record the teacher's responses. You may wish to tape record the responses and transcribe them immediately after the interview. Bring your responses to class to compare and contrast the findings by teacher and by age group.

1. How was the environment arranged in your classroom when you first began teaching? Did you make any changes in the indoor or outdoor environment? Please describe and explain why those changes were necessary or desirable.
2. What do you think about when you arrange the environment?
3. Could you please share your views about centers as a part of the learning environment?
4. What features of the indoor environment are most interesting and challenging for your children? What do you suppose is the reason? Do you think room arrangement has any influence on these interests? In what ways?
5. Could you describe how you handle transitions and routines with your class?

———————————— **Observation** ————————————

Evaluating a Play Space

The purpose of this assignment is to give you an opportunity to evaluate an early childhood outdoor environment according to the criteria described in this chapter. Too often, early childhood teachers underestimate the importance of the outdoor environment or do not think they have any control over what occurs there. During the last decade, we have come to understand that the best early childhood outdoor environments include natural materials, as well as opportunities to engage in all forms of play (Wortham & Frost, 1990).

Using the criteria presented in Figure 6.4, evaluate a local early childhood playground. Choose one item from each of the broad categories (space, materials, activities and experiences, and safety) and provide a detailed description of what you see. What changes would you make in each of these areas to make them appealing to children over time? In small group discussions, compare your findings of what exists and envision some realistic changes you could make as the classroom teacher.

———————————— **Research Highlight** ————————————

Preparing the Classroom Environment to Promote Literacy During Play

Summary of Research

In this study of 13 different suburban preschool classrooms, Morrow (1990) investigated whether preschool children's voluntary literacy behaviors could be increased by adding reading and writing materials to the dramatic play area and rearranging space. No classroom had intentionally included literacy materials in the play areas. One group incorporated a teacher-guided introduction of books, paper, and pencils into the dramatic play area. Another used teacher-guided thematic play with books, paper, and pencils in a veterinarian's office. In both groups, teachers suggested various ways children could use the literacy material—reading to dolls, taking telephone messages, writing prescriptions, and making appointments. A third group added books, paper, and pencils to the dramatic play area with no teacher guidance.

Results indicated that adding literacy materials to the dramatic play centers with teacher guidance increased children's voluntary use of literacy behaviors. Children in the thematic setting produced more literacy behaviors than those in other groups. Moreover, these behaviors continued over an extended period of time after the intervention. Anecdotal observations revealed that children in the thematic play center interacted with each other extensively in their literacy play and engaged in more elaborate cooperative play sequences. They read to themselves or their pets in the waiting rooms; made appointments with a receptionist, who recorded them in the appointment book; or examined pets and made notes in the folder. Literacy materials, when combined with teacher guidance, lead to more voluntary use of literacy behaviors during dramatic play (Morrow, 1990).

Implications for Practice

This study clearly demonstrates the impact of the physical environment on changing literacy behavior. Literacy materials can be added to particular themes and units of study (e.g., safety signs, boarding passes, and magazines for transportation) to enhance literacy development. Teachers who not only add materials but also coach children in their use have the greatest impact on children. What other classroom examples of the "materials plus modeling" strategy can you envision?

References

Alger, H. A. (1984). Transitions: Alternatives to manipulative management techniques. *Young Children, 39*(6), 16–25.

Ashcroft, S. C., & Zambone-Ashley, A. M. (1980). Mainstreaming children with visual impairments. *Journal of Research and Development in Education, 13,* 22–35.

Berk, L. (1976). How well do classroom practices reflect teacher goals? *Young Children, 32,* 64–81.

Bredekamp, S. (Ed.). (1987). *Developmentally appropriate practice in early childhood programs serving children from birth through age 8* (exec. ed.). Washington, DC: National Association for the Education of Young Children.

Bruya, L. D. (Ed.). (1988). *Play spaces for children: A new beginning.* Reston, VA: American Alliance for Health, Physical Education, Recreation and Dance.

Burns, D. E. (1985). Land of opportunity. *Gifted Child Quarterly, 43,* 41–45.

Caruso, D. A. (1984). Infants' exploratory play: Implications for child care. *Young Children, 40*(1), 27–30.

Casey, M. B., & Lippman, M. (1991). Learning to plan through play. *Young Children, 46*(4), 52–58.

Dacey, J. S. (1989). *Fundamentals of creative thinking.* Lexington, MA: D. C. Heath.

Esbensen, S. (1990). Play environments for young children: Design perspectives. In S. Wortham & J. Frost (Eds.), *Playgrounds for young children: National survey and results* (pp. 49–68). Reston, VA; American Alliance for Health, Physical Education, Recreation and Dance.

Frost, J. (1986). Planning and using children's playgrounds. In J. S. McKee (Ed.), *Play: Working partner of growth* (pp. 61–67). Wheaton, MD: Association for Childhood Education International.

Frost, J. (1988). Child development and playgrounds. In L. D. Bruya (Ed.), *Play spaces for children: A new beginning* (pp. 3–28). Reston, VA: American Alliance for Health, Physical Education, Recreation and Dance.

Frost, J. L., Bowers, L. E., & Wortham, S. C. (1991). The state of American preschool playgrounds. In K. M. Paciorek & J. H. Munro (Eds.), *Annual editions: Early childhood education 91/92* (pp. 177–181). Guilford, CT: Dushkin.

Frost, J., & Klein, B. (1977). *Children's play and playgrounds.* Boston: Allyn & Bacon.

Frost, J. L., & Wortham, S. (1988). The evolution of American playgrounds. *Young Children, 43*(5), 19–28.

Garreau, M., & Kennedy, C. (1991). Structure time and space to promote pursuit of learning in the primary grades. *Young Children, 64*(4), 46–51.

Hallahan, D. P., & Kaufman, J. M. (1991). *Exceptional children.* Englewood Cliffs, NJ: Prentice Hall.

Hildebrand, V. (1981). *Introduction to early childhood education.* New York: Macmillan.

Hohman, C. (1985). Getting started with computers. *High Scope Resource, 4*(3), 11–13.

Hughes, F. P. (1991). *Children, play and development.* Boston: Allyn & Bacon.

Isenberg, J., & Quisenberry, N. (1988). Play: A necessity for all children. *Childhood Education, 64*(3), 138–145.

Jalongo, M. R. (1992). Children's play: A resource for mulitcultural education. In E. B. Vold (Ed.), *Multicultural education in the early childhood classroom* (pp. 55–63). Washington, DC: National Education Association.

Jones, E. (1977). *Dimensions of teaching-learning environments.* Pasadena, CA: Pacific Oaks.

Kinsman, C., & Berk, L. (1979). Joining the block and housekeeping areas: Changes in play and social behavior. *Young Children, 35,* 66–75.

Kritchevsky, S., Prescott, E., & Walling, L. (1977). *Planning environments for young children: Physical space* (rev. ed.). Washington, DC: National Association for the Education of Young Children.

Leavitt, R. L., & Eheart, B. K. (1985). *Toddler day care: A guide to responsive caregiving.* Lexington, MA: D. C. Heath.

Littleton, D. (1989). Children's play: Pathways to music learning. In B. Andress (Ed.), *Promising practices: Prekindergarten music education* (pp. ix–xiii). Reston, VA: Music Educator's National Conference.

Loughlin, C. E., & Martin, M. D. (1987). *Supporting literacy: Developing effective learning environments.* New York: Teachers College Press.

Loughlin, C., & Suina, J. (1982). *The learning environment: An instructional strategy.* New York: Teachers College Press.

Miller, K. (1989). *The outside play and learning book. Activities for young children.* Mt. Rainier, MD: Gryphon House.

Morrow, L. (1990). Literacy during play. *Early Childhood Research Quarterly, 5*(4), 537–554.

Moyer, J., Egerston, H., & Isenberg, J. (1987). The child-centered kindergarten. *Childhood Education, 63*(4), 235–242.

Nash, C. (1976). *The learning environment.* Toronto: Methuen Publications.

National Academy of Early Childhood Programs. (1984). *Accreditation criteria and procedures.* Washington, DC: National Association for the Education of Young Children.

Perlmutter, J. (1990). Fostering children's fantasy play. *Dimensions, 18*(3), 23–24.

Peters, D. L., Neisworth, J. T., & Yawkey, T. D. (1985). *Early childhood education: From theory to practice.* Monterey, CA: Brooks/Cole.

Phyfe-Perkins, E. (1980). Children's behavior in preschool settings: The influence of the physical environment. In L. G. Katz (Ed.), *Current topics in early childhood education* (vol. 3, pp. 91–125). Norwood, NJ: Ablen.

Seefeldt, C., & Barbour, N. (1990). *Early childhood education: An introduction* (2nd ed.). Columbus, OH: Merrill/Macmillan.

Thompson, T. (1991, April). Play it safe: A parent's guide to playground safety. *PTA Today,* pp. 8–10.

U.S. Consumer Product Safety Commission. (1981). *A handbook for public safety. Volume 1: General guidelines for new and existing playgrounds.* Washington, DC: U.S. Government Printing Office.

Vartuli, S., & Phelps, C. (1980). Classroom transitions. *Childhood Education, 57*(2), 94–96.

Wortham, S. C., & Frost, J. L. (1990). Introduction. In S. C. Wortham & J. L. Frost (Eds.), *Playgrounds for young children: National survey and perspectives* (pp. 1–4). Reston, VA: American Alliance for Health, Physical Education, Recreation and Dance.

Children's Books

Keats, E. J. (1972). *Pet show.* New York: Macmillan.

Kellogg, S. (1981). *A rose for pinkerton.* New York: Dial.

Materials for Creative Expression and Play

*All young children, boys, girls, and those with special needs
and abilities, develop in the same way and have the same need
for play and for carefully chosen play materials. Children need
good toys just as adults needs good tools to do their work well.*

Stephanie Feeney
and Marion Magarick
1984, p. 21

After reading this chapter, you will be able to

- ❏ Describe the history of toys and playthings.
- ❏ Identify divergent and convergent play materials.
- ❏ Provide age-appropriate materials and games.
- ❏ Discuss the appropriate roles of the adult.
- ❏ Incorporate invented games into the curriculum.
- ❏ Use play materials to nurture creative expression in all populations.

Case Study

In the housekeeping area, three 4-year-old children are putting on dress up clothes, while another is moving pots and pans around on the stove. They are talking about who is going to wear what. In the block area, five boys and girls are constructing a pirate ship from hollow wooden blocks. In the absence of pirate garb, the children make do with cowboy boots, vests, and construction worker hard hats. One child, sitting in front, steers the ship, while the "lookout" paces about.

A child dashes in from the block area and quickly carries away the "jewelry case."

Suddenly, the cry goes up: "Jewels! We've found the treasure! We're rich! Jewels, jewels, jewels!" With great noise and excitement, the pirates display their necklaces, bracelets, and rings. In the days that follow, the children extend this theme by adding a treasure map to assist with their forays and decorating boxes to use as treasure chests.

In these pretend play scenes, 4-year-olds used objects symbolically to initiate and carry out their pirate play theme. Their responses to materials revealed original uses of common materials (using the jewels as a treasure), role playing (acting as a lookout) and problem centeredness (how to create a treasure chest). As this play episode illustrates, environments that foster creative expression and play support children through the careful selection of materials (Isenberg & Jacobs, 1982; Sutton-Smith, 1986).

Theoretical Framework

For teachers, three concepts are important to understanding self-expressive materials—their historical development, their convergent or divergent nature, and children's responses to them.

History of Toys and Playthings

Children's toys and playthings have a long history in early childhood education. In fact, the materials we provide for children are a reflection of social, political, and cultural issues. In colonial America, for example, boys played with simulated hunting and fishing materials, and girls played with corncob dolls. Near the turn of the century, construction toys were strictly for boys; homemaker's toys were strictly for girls (Hewitt & Roomet, 1979).

During the Industrial Revolution in the mid-1800s, toys specifically designed for children became industrialized as well. When wheeled toys, board games, dolls, and doll furniture first appeared, they were mass produced on the assembly line (Auerbach, 1986). At the turn of the century, during the child study movement, childhood was recognized as a distinct period of development and children were no longer viewed as miniature adults. As a reflection of this movement, toy manufacturers began producing educational toys. During this time, Dr. Maria Montessori also introduced an array of sensory materials for retarded children. Lacing frames, knob puzzles, and graduated cylinders were just a few of Montessori's contributions to educational toys. She is also credited with originating the concept of "self-correcting" toys, which are used in a particular sequence and a specified way. These materials slowly became part of some early childhood programs.

In the 1920s, toy manufacturers invited early childhood educators to help develop educational materials that would stimulate children's imagination and self-expression. Influenced by the ideas of child development specialists and educators such as John Dewey, early childhood educators provided firsthand experiences for children with concrete, self-expressive materials such as blocks, clay, paint, and wood. Additionally, they encouraged children under the age of 6 to play with language and rhythms and to invent their own games instead of playing games with rules (Monighan-Nourot, 1990).

Today, the same child may play with an heirloom set of nesting dolls from a great-great-grandmother's era, a Raggedy Ann doll from her great-grandmother's day, a Barbie doll from her grandparent's era, and anatomically correct dolls of boys and girls from her parents' day.

As a stroll through a toy store or a look at an early childhood materials catalogue will attest, teachers and parents need to make literally thousands of choices among materials for young children. The next section will outline some basic considerations in selecting materials for creative expression and play.

Convergent and Divergent Play Materials

The materials children use influence the possibilities of their play and expression of ideas. Some materials lead to single or prescribed uses and encourage convergent thinking. Wind-up toys, talking dolls, and coloring books are generally considered *convergent* materials. These materials lead children to think about a single or correct way to use them.

Other materials lead to multiple uses and are more open-ended. Blocks, sand, and water encourage thinking about many possibilities or uses and are considered *divergent* materials (Guilford, 1967). Divergent materials invite children's exploration, experimentation, and original thinking.

Think about Amy, a 4-year-old who watched with great interest as her teacher was preparing to give away some materials. Among them was a baby carriage with wobbly wheels, prompting Amy to ask, "Could we have the wheels from the carriage to play with?" What appealed to her were the divergent properties of the wheels—the endless possibilities for expressive play. In the weeks that ensued, the wheels became a steering wheel for a camper, a home for wooden animals, and a tray for food in the children's restaurant play.

Divergent or open-ended materials—blocks, carpentry tools, dress-up clothes, paints and markers, modeling dough, mud, sand, and water—are usually the most valuable (Hendrick, 1988; Isenberg & Quisenberry, 1988; Kamii & DeVries, 1980; Sutton-Smith, 1986; Tegano, Sawyers, & Moran, 1989). These materials

❑ *Enable children to use their imaginations in original and satisfying ways.* After 3-year-old Melissa had eye surgery, she used a spoon from the housekeeping area to operate on the eyes of a toy dog and wrapped the dog in bandages made from paper towels. She created a new use for the spoon and paper towels while reliving what she knew about surgeons.

❑ *Offer children latitude for creating, manipulating, and experimenting.* When 5-year-old Ted painted subway stops on a class mural illustrating different types of transportation, he investigated the properties of art— color, line, form. When he added a ticket booth, an engineer, and shapes for subway seats, he created what he knew about subways.

❑ *Encourage children to work cooperatively.* In Ms. Anderson's second-grade unit on the community, the children used blocks to build a city, sand to sculpt the terrain, and earth-moving toys to create roads. They learned more from their experience than Mr. Smith's second graders, who completed dot-to-dot papers and worksheets on community helpers.

❑ *Have no right or wrong uses, are failure-proof, and build self-esteem.* When 5-year-old Taso carefully dressed up as a cook and proudly stood before a long mirror, he exuded a sense of self-confidence and competence.

❑ *Are process-oriented rather than product-oriented.* After hearing the rhyming verse of *Jamberry*, a bear who rejoices in finding all kinds of berries, a group of kindergartners repeatedly chanted "One berry, two berry, Pick me a blueberry." Their sheer delight in the rhythm and rhyme produced giggles and laughter as they elaborated and created other silly Jamberry rhymes. Here their play with language illustrates their interest in process over product.

Children's Responses to Materials

How children respond to divergent materials depends on their familiarity with them. When first exposed to unfamiliar materials, children typically progress through the following developmental sequence:

1. *Exploration and manipulation.* If children are introduced to an unfamiliar material, they usually investigate what the object(s) can do and inspect its properties (Hutt, 1979). With blocks, for example, very young children initially examine them, touch them, and carry them around but *do not actually use* them to build.

2. *Nonrepresentational use.* Once children have information about what objects can do, they become interested in what they can do with the objects (Hutt, Tyler, Hutt, & Christopherson, 1989). Preschool children usually explore different ways of using blocks, including horizontal or vertical rows, bridges, and enclosed space (Apelman, 1984).

3. *Representational use.* School-age children intentionally plan and carry out ideas and actions that resemble their world. They often use elaborate verbal descriptions of their actions instead of actual objects in their play (Smilansky, 1968; Smilansky & Shefatya, 1990). Block play during this stage usually involves planning and building symbolic structures, along with dramatic play and verbal interactions to sustain the play.

Divergent play materials offer children unlimited possibilities. To capitalize on this potential, children must have opportunities to investigate and use all types of materials.

Types of Materials

Two-year-old Allysun clutches a fat red crayon and vigorously scribbles on a large piece of paper. She is absorbed with her markings and with the gliding movement of the crayon across the paper's smooth surface.

Four-year-old children of migrant workers in a Head Start classroom pack, unpack, and repack boxes with dishes and food and talk about where they will live next.

Six-year-old twins, Carla and Carlos, are building tunnels and bridges with blocks as part of their unit on transportation.

Eight-year-olds Kim and Brady are engrossed in a game of checkers. They carefully contemplate their next strategic move.

Each of these children is using different types of materials in age-appropriate ways. It is important for teachers to support children's growth by providing a range of materials. The following section describes different types of materials, including skill/concept, gross motor, manipulative, construction, and self-expressive materials, as well as natural and everyday objects (Johnson, Christie, & Yawkey, 1987).

Skill/Concept Materials

Materials that emphasize skill and concept development are prescriptive and product-oriented (Johnson et al., 1987). Children commonly practice skills like eye-hand coordination, sorting, classifying, or counting with them. Typical materials in this category consist of board games like Picture Lotto; simple card games like Go Fish; picture books; and perception materials like lacing beads and puzzles. These structured materials have limited possibilities for creative and divergent thinking in play.

Gross Motor Materials

Gross motor materials stress large muscle activity. Children use them primarily to explore and practice motor abilities. Typical gross materials include balls, climbers, pull toys, and riding toys. As motor development increases due to activity, these materials have the potential for encouraging divergent and inventive thinking when used in supportive environments.

Manipulative Materials

Manipulative materials develop small muscles, basic concepts, and eye-hand coordination (Feeney & Magarick, 1984). Typical fine motor materials include beads, building sets, crayons, dough, markers, lacing and sewing frames, pegs, pencils, pop-up boxes, and scissors. They provide a foundation for early literacy and numeracy development.

Construction Materials

Construction materials have separate pieces that can be combined in different ways. These materials include blocks (e.g., units, parquetry), building sets (e.g., Lincoln Logs, tinkertoys), and woodworking materials (e.g., hammer, nails, wood scraps, white glue). They offer endless possibilities and support coordination and inventive thinking (Feeney & Magarick, 1984). The number of pieces influences how children choose to combine pieces and determines when their product is finished.

Self-Expressive Materials

Self-expressive materials encourage children to experiment with different roles and express them through drama, music, and art. Materials in this category include dolls, dress-up clothes, housekeeping toys, markers, miniature life toys like Weebles or bendable people, musical instruments, and puppets. Children determine how the materials will be used, invent personalities and roles, and respond imaginatively.

Natural and Everyday Objects

Everyday objects can be natural and/or household materials that have specific nonplay purposes (Johnson et al., 1987). Children decide how to use them, employ imaginative and divergent thinking, and imitate and model adult roles with them. Materials in the household category include buttons, carpentry tools, and pots and pans. Natural materials include sticks, twigs, leaves, rocks, pine cones, sand, mud, and water. Table 7.1 describes the range of materials and their specific uses, lists the child's role, and gives the potential play possibilities for the child within each category.

   To make the most of each material, teachers need to consider other possibilities. This might involve altering the object in some way or adding materials to it. For example, think of an empty detergent bottle. A toddler might fill and

TABLE 7.1 Materials for Divergent Thinking

Type of Material	Skill/Concept	Gross Motor	Manipulative	Construction	Self-Expressive	Natural and Everyday Objects
Illustrative Examples	Card and board games; lacing, sorting, and stacking materials.	Balls, indoor/outdoor climbers, pull and riding toys.	Puzzles, interlocking plastic and wooden sets; nuts and bolts; table blocks.	Blocks, interlocking building sets, markers, paper, scissors.	Dolls, dress-ups, housekeeping toys, markers, musical instruments, puppets.	Buttons, natural materials, pots and pans, carpentry tools.
Intended Use or Purpose	Teach skills and concepts. Structured and outcome-oriented.	Emphasize large muscle development.	Emphasize small muscle development and eye/hand coordination.	Contain materials with separate parts to make things.	Relate to child's role or identity and creative expression in art.	Have clear nonplay uses in the adult world.
Child's Role	Responds to material with senses, both physically and intellectually.	Responds, explores, and practices gross motor skills.	Responds, explores and practices fine motor and perception skills.	Creates with multiple pieces. Determines beginning and end of project.	Decides how to use material. Invents situations, personalities, and roles. Responds imaginatively to materials.	Determines use and incorporates into activity.
Potential for Divergent Thinking	Limited number of uses. Structure imposed by material. Little opportunity for creative expression.	Some opportunity for creative and imaginative input in language, depending upon the environmental conditions and the role of the teacher.		Multiple combinations possible, depending upon number of pieces available.	Multiple possibilities to respond and invent scenes and express language and ideas.	Self-motivating and versatile materials encourage children to imitate and model adult roles and behaviors.

empty it; a preschooler might experiment with the number and location of holes punched in it and the rate of water flow out of it; a first grader might add plastic tubing and create a siphon. In this way, one recycled piece of plastic has become challenging yet appropriate for each child.

Developmentally Appropriate Materials

Developmentally appropriate materials are concrete, real, and meaningful to children (Bredekamp, 1988). They are basic to the early childhood program because they support child-initiated and child-directed learning and stimulate the imagination. Through extensive play with real materials and interactions with others, children through the primary grades come to understand the people, events, and things in their world. In contrast, "workbooks, worksheets, coloring books and adult made models of art products for children to copy are *not* appropriate for young children, especially those younger than 6" (Bredekamp, 1988, p. 4). In the following sections, we describe developmental characteristics and age-appropriate materials for infants/toddlers, preschoolers/kindergartners, and school-age children. We also suggest how teachers can use these materials appropriately with children of different ages.

Infants and Toddlers

Infants and toddlers learn by sensory exploration and social interaction. Toddlers actively struggle with issues of independence and show great interest in children of their own age. Materials for them must be carefully matched to their needs and abilities. Infants and toddlers need materials for looking, feeling, listening, sucking, grasping, and moving. Toddlers also prefer

- ❏ Action toys that *they* can make produce sounds or movements.
- ❏ Toys that fit together and pull apart.
- ❏ Building toys like blocks, reading materials, and musical toys.
- ❏ Toys that stimulate make-believe play.
- ❏ Gross motor toys to pull and push (Hughes, 1991).

Although a variety of toys is necessary, infants and toddlers need only a few at one time. Tables 7.2 and 7.3 list examples of developmentally appropriate materials for infants (birth–age 1) and toddlers (ages 1–3).

Teachers' Roles and Responsibilities

The following guidelines will help teachers and caregivers enhance infants' and toddlers' self-expression with materials.

1. *Use only toys that meet safety standards.* Avoid toys and materials that have sharp points or edges, as well as nails, wires, or pins that can be swallowed or have parts that can lodge in children's ears and throats. Be sure

TABLE 7.2 Developmentally Appropriate Play Materials for Infants (Birth–Age 1)

Type of Material or Activity	Appropriate Materials	Examples
Skill/concept	Books/records and tapes	Soft cloth and thick cardboard books; lullabies, voices of familiar caretakers
	Games	"Peek-a-Boo," "So Big," "Where Is the Baby?" and other socially interactive games
Gross motor	Active play	Push/pull toys; large balls, infant bouncers
Manipulative	Fine motor	Simple rattles, teethers, sturdy cloth toys, squeeze and squeak toys, colorful mobiles, activity boxes for the crib; clutch and texture balls; stacking toys; containers to fill and dump
Construction	Blocks	Soft rubber blocks
	Puzzles	Two- to three-piece puzzles of familiar objects
Self-expressive	Dolls and soft toys	Soft baby dolls; plush animals
	Puppets	Soft hand puppets
	Dramatic play	Large, unbreakable mirrors attached to the crib or wall
	Sensory	Tactile toys like soft plush animals and pillows; colorful visuals like pictures of babies; auditory toys like a music box; suitable teethers
Natural and everyday objects	Household	Pots and pans; plastic containers

Note: For further information, see Feeney and Margarick (1984), Isenberg and Jacobs (1982), Johnson et al. (1987), and McKee (1986).

that toys are painted with nontoxic or lead-free paint, do not require electricity, can be easily cleaned, and cannot pinch fingers or catch hair.

2. *Provide a rich sensory environment.* Infants and toddlers need to experience materials with all of their senses. The teacher who creates a "crawling trail" made from scraps of fabrics with distinctively different textures, such as satin, lace, corduroy, and flannel, is providing a sensory environment that intrigues and involves infants and toddlers.

3. *Have plenty of materials available.* Infants who use a variety of materials perform better on cognitive tasks than those who do not (Gottfried,

TABLE 7.3   Developmentally Appropriate Play Materials for Toddlers (Ages 1–3)

Type of Material or Activity	Appropriate Materials	Examples
Skill/concept	Books/records and tapes	Simple picture books and poems about familiar places and people; records and tapes of children's songs, folk songs, nursery rhymes, popular songs, songs from other cultures; movement and exercise music
	Games	Social interaction games with adults like "Pop Goes the Weasel," "Ring-a-Round-a-Rosy," "Round and Round the Garden"
Gross motor	Active play	Toys to push and pull while walking; doll carriage, wagon, toys with objects; Ride-on toys allowing the child to move the self along
	Outdoor	Low slides and climbers, tunnels of oversized cardboard boxes for crawling, variety of balls; sand and water materials
Manipulative	Fine motor/perception	Colored paddles, dressing dolls, activity boxes, pop-up-toys operated by pushing a button, nesting and stacking toys; toys to put together and take apart; large colored beads and spools, sewing and lacing cards, large shape sorters, pegboards with a few large pegs, frames for zipping and snapping
	Puzzles and form boards	Simple two- to three-piece puzzles and form boards with familiar shapes and objects; puzzles with books
Construction	Building sets	Small, lightweight sets of 15–25 pieces before 18 months; solid wooden unit blocks (20–40 pieces); wooden hollow blocks and accessories; interlocking building sets
	Carpentry	Assorted pounding toys with large wooden pegs or balls, plastic hammers, plastic pliers, thick Styrofoam boards
Self-expressive	Dolls and soft toys	Soft-bodied or rubber dolls; simple caretaking accessories
	Dramatic play	Toy telephone, full-length mirror for self-awareness; miniature dishes, pots and pans; dress-up clothes; shopping cart
	Sensory	Soft, cuddly, easy-to-hold, safe toys; modeling dough; visual and auditory stimuli; sensory games and boxes
	Art/music	Rhythm instruments, bells, large crayons, markers, unlined paper
	Sand and water	Sponges, small shovel, pail, cups, plastic containers for dumping and filling, baster, molds
Natural and everyday		Pots and pans, plastic containers, cooking utensils; real objects appeal to children's imagination for all categories of play and suit many types of materials

Note: For further information, see Feeney and Margarick (1984), Isenberg and Jacobs (1982), Johnson et al. (1987), and McKee (1986).

1986). Toddlers need plenty of materials and containers to collect, fill, dump, and stack objects. Simple, small plastic containers of all sizes and shapes, cloth sacks, a variety of cardboard tubing, and empty wooden spools are necessary for water, sand, and manipulative play.

4. *Use appropriate social games.* Infants and toddlers respond positively to "Peek-a-Boo," "So Big," "Trot, Trot to Boston," and other familiar social routines. These highly repetitive games have simple rules through which infants learn the beginning of turn taking, the rhythms of conversation, and the bonds of social relationships.

5. *Provide attractive, everyday, safe objects.* Infants and toddlers like to use one object to represent another. Blocks, water, sand, dress-up clothes, and carefully selected, safe jewelry appeal to toddlers' imaginations.

Preschoolers and Kindergartners

Preschoolers and kindergartners show an increasing interest in make-believe play that peaks at about age 5. Their simple, unstructured play includes family roles such as Mommy, Daddy, and Baby, and roles of familiar people outside the family, like a supermarket checker or truck driver. These children use both realistic and nonrealistic props and accessories.

Materials for preschoolers and kindergartners should support their developing social skills and interest in adult roles, their growing imaginations, increasing motor skills, and rapidly expanding vocabularies (Hughes, 1991). They need

❑ Dramatic play props like discarded adult clothes, props from familiar adult roles, and literacy tools to write.
❑ Realistic replicas of models like telephones and cars.
❑ Construction materials, like simple building sets, to create products.
❑ Sensory materials, like sand and water, to explore.
❑ Manipulative materials, like simple puzzles, to test.
❑ Wheeled vehicles to demonstrate gross motor skills and to facilitate social interaction.
❑ Books that capitalize on familiar themes.
❑ Everyday objects.

Table 7.4 lists a variety of developmentally appropriate materials for preschool and kindergarten children.

Teachers' Roles and Responsibilities

Teachers need to keep in mind the following guidelines when providing materials for preschoolers and kindergartners:

1. *Include adequate props and materials.* Younger children and less skilled players need more realistic props (like miniature cars, people, or tools) to support and sustain their play. Older children and more advanced

TABLE 7.4 Developmentally Appropriate Play Materials for Preschool and Kindergarten Children (Ages 3–5)

Type of Material or Activity	Appropriate Materials	Examples
Skill/concept	Books/records and tapes	Picture books; simple and repetitive stories and rhymes, animal stories, pop-up books, simple science or information books, wide variety of musical recordings
	Games	Socially interactive games with adults like "What If", matching and lotto games based on colors and pictures like picture bingo or dominoes; games of chance with a few pieces that require no reading like "Chutes & Ladders" and "Go Fish"; flannel board with pictures, letters, storybook characters
Gross motor	Active play	Push and pull toys like wagons, wheelbarrows, doll carriages; ride-on toys like tricycles, three-wheeled vehicles, cars, trucks, balls of all kinds; indoor slide and climber; rocking boat
	Outdoor	Climbers, rope ladders, balls of all sizes, old tires, sand and water materials
Manipulative	Fine motor/ perception	Dressing frames; toys to put together and take apart; cookie cutters, stamp and printing materials, fingerpaints, modeling dough, small objects to sort and classify; bead stringing with long, thin string; pegs and small pegs; colored cubes, table blocks, magnetic board/letters/numbers and shapes; perception boards and mosaics
	Puzzles/form boards	Fit-in or framed puzzles For 3-year-olds: from 4 or 5 to 20 pieces For 4-year-olds: from 15 to 30 pieces For 5-year-olds: from 15 to 50 pieces Large, simple jigsaws; number/letter/clock puzzles
	Investigative	Toys, globe, flashlight, magnets, lock boxes, weather forecasting equipment, scales, balances, stethoscopes
Construction	Building sets	Small and large unit blocks; large hollow blocks, interlocking plastic blocks with pieces of all sizes from age 4
	Carpentry	Workbench, hammer, preschool nails, saw, sandpaper, pounding benches, safety goggles

TABLE 7.4 *continued*

Type of Material or Activity	Appropriate Materials	Examples
Self-expressive	Dolls and soft toys	Realistic dolls and accessories; play settings and play people (e.g., farm hospital)
	Dramatic play	Dress-up clothes, realistic tools, toy camera, telephone, household furniture
	Puppets	Simple sock/mitten puppets; finger puppets; simple puppet theater
	Sensory	Tactile boxes; auditory and musical materials like smelling and sound boxes; cooking experiences
	Art/music	All rhythm instruments, music boxes, large crayons, paint, paste, glue, chalkboard and chalk, sewing kits, collage materials, markers, modeling dough, blunt scissors
	Sand and water	Sandbox tools, bubbles, water toys
Natural and everyday objects		Old clocks, radios, cameras, telephones; telephone books, mirrors, doctor kits, typewriter, magazines, fabric scraps, computer, cash register and receipts, measuring cups and muffin tins

Note: For further information, see Feeney and Margarick (1984), Isenberg and Jacobs (1982), Johnson et al. (1987), and McKee (1986).

players need less realistic materials for variety and flexibility of play themes, although they still enjoy realistic props. One preschool teacher noticed, for example, that a bridal veil, a bouquet of plastic flowers, and an old tuxedo jacket that she found at a secondhand store stimulated considerable excitement and elaborated play in the dress-up corner. Be certain to include natural and everyday objects like puppets, hats, and boxes for children to represent their understandings. Use items that are likely to have personal significance for the child, like a stuffed toy dog with a bowl, leash, brush, and bone.

2. *Model the use of open-ended materials when necessary.* As children use more highly developed make-believe skills, encourage them to use less realistic props. Bringing a square block to the post office theme corner, one kindergarten teacher suggested: "Let's pretend this is a package that just came in the mail" or "Look what the UPS driver delivered today!" Be certain to leave the play once interactions are established.

3. *Use technology as an integral part of the learning environment.* Quality educational software is fun and easy to use, has several levels of difficulty,

and encourages children to work together. In Ms. Hicks's preschool classroom, the children were fascinated by different animals, so she added the program *Fantastic Animals* to the computer center. In pairs or triads, the children playfully selected a body, head, tail, and legs to create an animal that danced across the screen. Ms. Hicks also noticed that the children were using *Delta Draw* to create their own fantastic, mixed-up animals. Some of them even invented pretend scenarios for their animals. Ms. Hicks's use of technology illustrates how the computer can be appropriately integrated into the play environment.

4. *Develop your own imagination.* One of Mr. Phelps's kindergartners brought in a pith helmet and sombrero to add to the dress-up corner. Rather than simply leaving the gear on a hat rack, Mr. Phelps thought about the possibilities and created a game that the children loved called "Expedition." He put a piece of blue cloth on the floor and put the balance beam over it with a rubber crocodile below. He strategically positioned other animals around the room, too. Soon the children's activity took on many new dimensions—sinking into the quicksand, swinging from a pretend vine, and getting lost in the jungle. Each time Mr. Phelps introduced a new picture book, such as *Junglewalk* (Tafuri, 1988), new themes were introduced.

School-Age Children

School-age children are refining skills and talents, relying on support from their peer group, and becoming more organized and logical thinkers. Materials for them should reflect their need for realistic, rule-oriented, and peer activities. They need

❑ *Organized educational or physical games with rules.* Card and board games enable them to practice school skills, strategic thinking, decision making, and problem solving. Games like "Red Rover" and tag enable them to practice physical skills and teamwork.

❑ *Construction materials.* School-age children usually have something in mind when they begin building. They often create useful items like a puppet stage and typically engage in cooperative group projects like building a space shuttle (Seefeldt & Barbour, 1990).

❑ *Props that enhance fantasy play.* School-age children's fantasy more closely resembles the reality of adults than the fantasy play of preschoolers. During the school years, children often collect their own props, create hideaways (like treehouses) and social clubs with friends, and develop secret codes (Seefeldt & Barbour, 1990).

❑ *Songs, chants, word games, and rituals.* Play with language and its rhythm is a hallmark of the school-age child. Games like "Scrabble," "Boggle," or "Word Yahtzee," as well as jokes, riddles, and tongue twisters, appeal to what Piaget called *cognitive conceit,* helping children to feel "in the know" and superior to those who are not so well informed. Mastery of games with rules also teaches a child how to follow instructions and preserve moral order (Hughes, 1991).

❏   *Puzzles.* Puzzles with 50 to 500 pieces interest school-age children. Larger puzzles make excellent long-term cooperative projects and provide opportunities for extended conversation. Table 7.5 lists a variety of developmentally appropriate materials for school-age children.

Teachers' Roles and Responsibilities

As elementary teachers, we must also carefully consider how to use materials to foster children's divergent thinking. Use the following guidelines to think broadly about how to use materials.

1.   *Arrange the classroom in interest centers.* As part of an integrated curriculum in one inner-city second-grade class, children used a sandbox as the centerpiece of the language arts center. Through their reading about knights and castles, they used the sand table to construct their own interpretation of elaborate sand castles. They also used materials in the art center to illustrate more detailed aspects of the medieval environments they were learning about (Barbour, Drosdeck, and Webster, 1987).

2.   *Use projects and investigative activities.* In their unit on the circus, a group of first graders worked together for several days planning and practicing circus acts and designing their outfits from available resources. Matt created a flaming hoop with a hula hoop and crepe paper streamers. Shy Sherree became a roaring lion by putting a nylon net tutu around her neck and using a knit belt as her tail. Reginald became the strong man by putting inflated balloon muscles under his T-shirt and making a barbell from a yardstick with balloons tied on each end. Later they performed circus acts for their peers.

3.   *Integrate technology into the curriculum.* Many early childhood teachers have mixed feelings about using computers with young children, yet computers are part of our daily lives. Children see their use in the grocery store, the bank, and the service station. During dental health week, one second-grade teacher introduced the software program *Explore-a-story: Where Did My Toothbrush Go?* Some of the second graders manipulated scenic backgrounds, animated characters, and composed texts about toothbrushes as part of their study. They also used the program *Color Me* to create bright illustrations for their original stories about healthy teeth. Using developmentally appropriate software in the curriculum enables children to be active learners, set their own learning pace, test alternative responses, and develop social interaction skills.

4.   *Use developmentally appropriate materials.* Developmentally appropriate materials take into account children's ages, needs, interests, abilities, and cultural backgrounds. They also challenge children's creative think-

TABLE 7.5 Developmentally Appropriate Play Materials for School-Age Children (Ages 6-8)

Type of Material or Activity	Appropriate Materials	Examples
Skill/concept	Books/records	Books on different cultures, recipe books, Caldecott and Newberry Award books and tapes, folktales, fables, historical fiction books in a series, biographies, jokes, riddles, tall tales; music of all types
	Games	Strategy and memory games like checkers, tic-tac-toe, and multiple-digit numbers; more complex board and card games for problem solving and decision making, sports games like bocce, tetherball, soccer; word games
Gross motor	Active play	Organized group games like "Simon Says" and "Red Rover"
	Outdoor	Jump ropes, flying disks, bicycle, rope ladders, wagon, bear bags, assorted balls, sports sets like badminton
Manipulative	Fine motor/perception	Gardening equipment, canister of buttons to sort and classify, weaving looms, Perception sewing kits, combination locks, pick-up sticks, spirograph
	Puzzles	More complex puzzles with 50-100 pieces; puzzles of reproductions of paintings; form boards by famous artists
	Investigation	Science materials like prisms, bionuculars, microscope; printing sets, terrariums and aquariums to create and observe, various science kits (e.g., rocks)
Construction	Building sets	Sets with realistic models; additional unit blocks, shapes, and accessories; props for roads and towns
	Carpentry	Add screwdriver, vices, and accessories
Self-expressive	Dolls	Dolls from other cultures, more detailed, smaller dolls; varied play settings (e.g., office, gas station) and action figures
	Puppets	Head and arm puppets; puppets with links, finger puppets and marionettes
	Dramatic play	Storybook masks and costumes, walkie-talkie
	Sensory	Collecting toys in sets; clay and clay tools
	Art and music	Small crayons, chalk, watercolors, hole puncher, stapler, all musical instruments, basket-making materials, pottery wheel, stencil and craft kits
	Sand and water	Add food coloring, funnels, pumps, hoses, plastic tubing, and assorted containers and utensils
Natural and everyday objects		Simple camera and film, typewriter, paper and pencil

Note: For further information, see Feeny and Margarick (1984), Isenberg and Jacobs (1982), Johnson et al. (1987), and McKee (1986).

Using developmentally appropriate software enables children to be active learners and develop social interaction skills.

ing and self-expression within familiar contexts. In the following sections, we describe specific divergent materials that should be available to children of all ages in every early childhood classroom, regardless of resources.

Other Divergent Play Materials

There are certain, divergent materials that are basic for all children—blocks, modeling materials, sand, and water. These materials offer many possibilities for children to express their ideas and feelings and grow naturally with children.

Blocks

In his autobiography, Frank Lloyd Wright (1932) enthusiastically recalled his kindergarten experiences with blocks: "The smooth, shapely maple blocks with which to build, the sense of which never afterward left the fingers: so form became feeling" (p. 11). With blocks children are free to release their imagination and inventiveness. Ms. Mitsoff rearranged her entire first-grade room to double the block-building space. Throughout the year, her first graders used the blocks as the focal point for their units of study. In their unit on the farm, for example, the children conceptualized, built, and played in a farm containing stalls for cows, a hen house, a main farmhouse, and a barn. They also assumed different farmworker roles, including those of the farmer, milker, and egg collector. Ms. Mitsoff noticed her children practicing the following concepts:

❑ *Science concepts* as they observed, compared, and interpreted findings on ways to collect, store, and deliver milk.

❑ *Math concepts* as they estimated the length of the path needed to get from the farmhouse to the hen house.

❑ *Social studies concepts* as they re-created the roles of the farm workers.

❑ *Language arts concepts* as they named and labeled their structures and considered books as references.

❑ *Art concepts* as they repeated patterns in their symmetrical buildings.

Types and Uses

There are many different types of blocks—hollow blocks, unit blocks, and table blocks. Hollow blocks are large wooden blocks that have an opening for carrying. Children often use these blocks to build large structures. Unit blocks should be made from hard wood; have smooth and rounded corners and edges; and be accurate so that children can build without frustration (Maxim, 1989). To build structures, children need precisely measured unit blocks including units, double units, quadruple units, wedges, triangles, cylinders and half-rounds. Figure 7.1 illustrates the various unit block shapes. Table blocks are small, colored, cubed blocks that children use alone or in pairs around a table. They often include unusual shapes that stimulate children's inventiveness.

There are stages that children pass through in block building. Apelman (1984, pp. 193–200) summarized Harriet Johnson's seven stages as follows:

Stage 1.   Blocks are carried around but are not used for construction. This applies to the very young.

Stage 2.   Building begins. Children make mostly rows, either horizontal (on the floor) or vertical (stacked). There is much repetition in this early building pattern.

Stage 3.   Bridging: two blocks, with a space between them, connected by a third block.

Stage 4.   Enclosures: blocks placed in such a way that they enclose a space.

Stage 5.   When facility with blocks is acquired, decorative patterns appear. Much symmetry can be observed. Buildings generally are not yet named.

Stage 6.   Naming of structures for dramatic play begins. Before this stage, children may also have named their structures, but the names were not necessarily related to the function of the building.

Stage 7.   Children's buildings often reproduce or symbolize actual structures they know, and there is a strong impulse toward dramatic play around the block structures.

FIGURE 7.1   Illustrations of Block Shapes

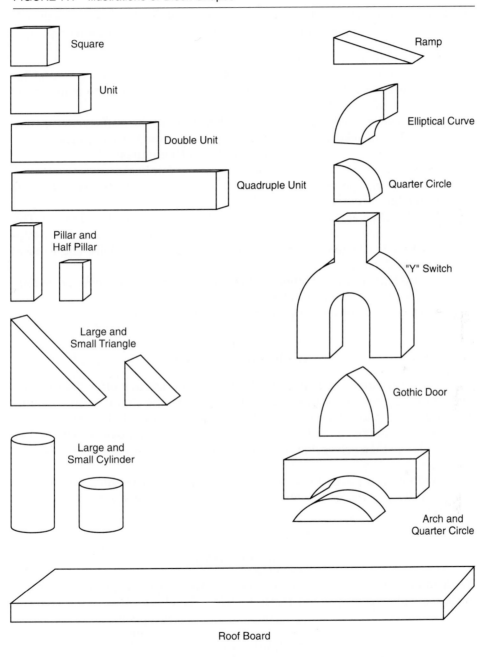

Square

Unit

Double Unit

Quadruple Unit

Pillar and
Half Pillar

Large and
Small Triangle

Large and
Small Cylinder

Roof Board

Ramp

Elliptical Curve

Quarter Circle

"Y" Switch

Gothic Door

Arch and
Quarter Circle

Teachers' Roles and Responsibilities

Block play is central to children's learning. The following guidelines will help teachers maximize the potential learnings in block play for children of all ages.

- ❏ Store blocks on low, open shelves for easy access.
- ❏ Provide an adequate supply of blocks—211 blocks for a group of ten 3-year-olds. A complete set of over 750 blocks is not too many for an older group of 20 children.
- ❏ Allocate enough floor space for building out of the traffic patterns, next to the housekeeping area, and away from a quiet activity area.
- ❏ Provide enough time for building (45 to 60 minutes).
- ❏ Provide props and accessories like cars and animals.
- ❏ Maintain a periodic physical presence in the area to attract children to the block center.
- ❏ Label shelves, with the shape of the long side of the block in view. This helps children to locate materials quickly, to perceive the relationships of the blocks to each other, to practice classification skills, and to assist with cleanup.
- ❏ Use blocks in ways other than building, such as a matching or measuring game with blocks of a specific size.
- ❏ Develop a genuine appreciation for block playing.

Modeling Materials

Dough and clay are three-dimensional sensory materials that offer children possibilities for expression of thoughts and feelings. Young children enjoy pounding, squeezing, and rolling these materials. Older children do the same but also represent and/or create familiar objects or people. Where possible, let children mix the dough themselves. Figure 7.2 contains some simple recipes for modeling materials.

Children need plenty of dough for modeling to be satisfying. Be certain to focus on the process of the material and avoid pushing children to create a product.

Sand and Water

Sand and water are readily available, inexpensive, satisfying resources that help children explore concepts and release tension. Children learn science concepts like the effects of objects dropped on water, math concepts like estimating how much water is needed or volume by guessing the number of cups of water needed to fill a larger container, and social interaction skills.

Sand and water are particularly absorbing and relaxing materials for children. Children can release tension as they pour water back and forth in containers or let sand gradually sift through their fingers. When children use sand

FIGURE 7.2   Recipes for Modeling Materials

Clay Substitutes

1 cup flour
½ cup salt
⅓ cup water

Mix the ingredients and knead with fingers. Add 1 teaspoon sodium benzoate as a preservative. Refrigerate.

Vegetable Dye

1 cup flour
½ cup salt
1 teaspoon powdered alum
½ cup water

Mix together. Color with food coloring or vegetable dye. Keep in a covered container.

Sawdust Dough

2 cups sawdust
3 cups flour
1 cup salt
water as needed

This dough dries very hard and is not as breakable as other three-dimensional materials.

Cornstarch Dough

1 cup cornstarch
2 cups baking soda
¼ cup cold water
food coloring

Combine cornstarch and soda. Add water and coloring. Stir until smooth. Cook to boiling point over medium heat for 1 minute. Cool and knead. Dries very hard.

Play Dough

1 cup salt
½ cup cornstarch
½ cup boiling water

Knead ingredients and place in a plastic bag for storage.

Peanut Butter Dough (edible)

1 cup honey
1 cup peanut butter
2 cups dried milk

Mix ingredients together. Form into various shapes. Add additional dried milk if too sticky.

and water, their social interactions are often quite calm and cooperative (Hendrick, 1988).

Play with sand and water should occur both indoors and outdoors. Some teachers place the sand or water in large plastic tubs or in specially prepared tables. Other teachers substitute rice, shelled corn, or birdseed for indoor sandboxes when sand is unavailable. The inside of an old truck tire laid flat makes a serviceable outdoor sandbox. Be certain to cover the sandbox when the children are not using it so that stray animals do not foul it. Check outdoor sandboxes frequently for insect infestations, too.

Water is a particularly absorbing and relaxing material for children of all ages.

Teachers' Roles and Responsibilities

When using sand and water, consider the following:

- ❑ Use sand and water together so that children can mold the mixture.
- ❑ Vary the equipment so that children are continually challenged to think of new uses. Some common materials for sand and water play include various sized molds, sponges, plastic bottles and containers of assorted sizes, flexible plastic tubing, measuring cups and spoons, and small replicas of cars, buildings, and boats. Plastic aprons are also useful.
- ❑ Ask open-ended questions like "Why do you think the water is coming out so slowly?" or "I wonder what would happen if you added water to your sand mound?"
- ❑ Decide in advance on simple rules so that water and sand do not get tracked around the classroom. Have materials available so that children take responsibility for cleanup.

Materials need to be matched to individual abilities. They are children's tools for understanding their world. Teachers have a key role in ensuring a balance of appropriate materials for the release of children's creative expression. They provide a different experience from games.

Organized Games

In the following scenario, think about the triplets playing games at different ages.

Tanya, Dolly, and Norman attend an inner-city elementary school. When they were toddlers, their caregiver played social interaction games with them like "This Little Piggy" and "Hide the Keys." In the Head Start program, they played running and chasing games and simple spinning games of chance like "Hi Ho Cherry-O." In these games, rules did not matter. Now they are in third grade. Tanya plays soccer on the school team and practices soccer skills wherever she can; Dolly, intrigued by all sorts of card and board games, actively seeks friends to play strategy games like "Rummy" and "Clue." And Norman thrives on memory games like "Twenty Questions" and word games like "Scrabble."

The games Tanya, Dolly, and Norman played are typical of those that are popular during the early childhood years. Although games broaden the curriculum for children of all ages (Bredekamp, 1988), many teachers believe that games with rules foster a competitive rather than a cooperative spirit, question the value of such games, and view them as frivolous.

What Is a Game?

A *game* is a form of play in which children follow a set of rules, predetermine an outcome, and assign players specific roles (DeVries with Kohlberg, 1987; Kamii & DeVries, 1980). Dictionary definitions usually include the elements of rules, competition, and winning.

Most children's games involve physical skill, chance, strategy, or some combination of these elements to determine the outcome (Sutton-Smith & Roberts, 1981). In games of physical skill, such as jump rope or stick ball, motor skill is essential. Games of chance, like the simple board game "Winnie the Pooh," rely on dice or a spin of the wheel. And games of strategy, like "Checkers" or "Boggle," require decision-making skills and compel players to take turns, follow complex directions, and employ complicated strategies. Organized sports are often considered strategy games because they require a player to plan strategies and imagine oneself in the opponent's role (Hughes, 1991).

Competition versus Cooperation

How games are presented influences their degree of competition versus cooperation. If teachers make it clear that the goal of a game is to do as well as each child can, then games can enhance cooperation. Ms. Ake's second graders were involved in relay races. When she reminded them that the goal of these races was to do their best, she noticed how they urged each other on in their "Three-Legged Races" as they figured out ways to get quickly to the other side of the room.

Cooperation means operating together. It involves negotiating to arrive at an agreement that is acceptable to all. As a result, some disputes and conflicts are inevitable (Kamii & DeVries, 1980). When children play games cooperatively, they construct rules for themselves as they begin to experience others' viewpoints. An emphasis on cooperative games encourages children to play together rather than against each other by focusing on group participation, sharing, giving each player an opportunity to play, and making rules that suit the players (Sobel, 1983). Cooperative games help children develop a sense of teamwork, loyalty to the group, and knowledge of how to get along with others. Because Western culture is inherently competitive, it is a challenge for teachers to handle competition constructively in classrooms.

The Value of Games

Some early childhood educators believe that organized games for young children are developmentally inappropriate, thwart creativity and encourage competition (Hendrick, 1988; Hildebrand, 1990). Others believe they can be appropriate if teachers positively confront the competitive element (DeVries with Kohlberg, 1987; Kamii & DeVries, 1980; Hughes, 1991). When group games match children's developmental levels, children

- ❏ *Develop cooperation and strategic thinking* by learning to understand others' thinking and relate it to their own. One second grader talked about setting up a "double jump" in checkers, indicating her understanding of her thoughts in relation to her actions.
- ❏ *Practice autonomy* by choosing whether or not to play the game and to follow its rules. When Carmella's kindergarten friends wanted to play "Shadow Tag," she chose another activity because she did not want to be "it."
- ❏ *Engage in problem solving* by deciding how to follow rules and play fairly. A group of first graders was trying to start a game of "Go Fish" but could not begin their play until they solved the problem of who was to go first.

Games suitable for young children have one or two simple rules, include all children who want to participate, encourage children to figure things out for themselves, and do *not* stress being first, winning, or losing. Children like noncompetitive guessing games like "I'm thinking of something in the room that is," simple sorting and matching games, simple board games (if they can change the rules), and basic running and chasing games (Sawyers & Rogers, 1988).

Older children need strategy games that develop problem-solving and decision-making abilities while encouraging them to think about others' thoughts and feelings. Board games and active outdoor group games are typical of school-age children. Today children of both sexes engage equally in these games.

When games focus on playing together rather than against each other, each player becomes important. With an emphasis on involvement, mutual enjoyment, and respect, appropriately played group games can promote basic intellectual and social skills in school-age children.

Teachers' Roles and Responsibilities

Consider this group of first graders playing "Marble Run," a commercial game in which children combine small blocks with slides and intricate grooves into a course for the marble. As the first graders excitedly invented new courses, they exclaimed, "Now, let's try this" or "Look at it go!" Their teacher commented, "This is their favorite game because it has so many possibilities and combinations. When I now say 'It's game time', I have to be sure to say 'Only four children can use Marble Run.' It is truly the favorite game in our classroom."

The teacher's role, in this case, was that of observer and manager as she freed the children to utilize the many available combinations. There was no correct way to play the game. The children constructed the rules in ways that made sense to them (Kamii & DeVries, 1980).

When using games in the classroom, teachers must provide opportunities for children to modify rules and create their own games (Kamii & DeVries, 1980). That way, games such as "Marble Run," as it was being played, become a powerful vehicle for developing intellectual and social autonomy. Teachers can help children modify game rules by

- ❑ *Supporting their initiatives in games.* The first graders playing "Marble Run" were encouraged to play the game in many different ways. Sometimes the game involved races; at other times it turned into a maze. Each group of players could initiate the way to play the game and then negotiate rules for it.
- ❑ *Introducing noncompetitive games.* Children who compete can and do also cooperate in games, as well as other activities. Appendix C describes appropriate, noncompetitive ball games, quiet games, singing games, running games, and partner games that can be introduced into the curriculum to enhance cooperation.
- ❑ *Allowing children to modify rules during the game.* Even though the first graders started one of the "Marble Run" games with a race of some kind, they often decided to change it in midstream to a different game. Their teacher encouraged their ideas about all the variations they invented.

Games are useful for active and quiet times, for transitions from one activity to another, and for fostering specific learning outcomes. Teachers must develop a repertoire of games that foster a cooperative spirit in children that will last through their lives.

Child-Constructed Games

Child-constructed games promote children's understanding and acceptance of rules, as well as their ability to cooperate and compete (Berns, 1985). Unfortunately, children in today's world spend less time spontaneously inventing games and more time using prepared commercial games with predetermined instructions, rules, and outcomes or in organized team sports. This limits their opportunities to make, revise, and follow their own rules with their peers and to control their social interactions (Berns, 1985; Piaget, 1962; Sutton-Smith, 1979). In the next section, we describe the power of children's invented games.

Invented Games

Kathryn Castle (1991) suggests that inventing games makes rules meaningful and relevant for children. Invented games help children

- ☐ *Become autonomous learners.* Second grader Andy made a simple baseball game from oak tag, markers, and colored dots. When other children were excited about using it and helped him to modify and perfect the game, Andy gained confidence in his ability as an independent yet collaborative learner.
- ☐ *Practice ongoing basic skills.* Julia wanted to create her own version of hopscotch on the playground outdoors. She practiced writing to label the asphalt with chalk and to write the game's rules; she used reading skills to read her rules to a friend; and she incorporated mathematics when figuring out the procedures and format of her hopscotch game.
- ☐ *Develop organizational skills.* In invented games, children plan, construct, play the game with others, discover its problems, and make changes. Some of Mr. Spencer's third-grade girls invented a board game called "Shopping." The object was to move along a path to purchase various department store items. While playing the game, they discovered that their rule of getting the exact number on the dice as the number of spaces remaining on the game board left them sitting for many turns waiting to complete the game. So they agreed to change the rules.
- ☐ *See others' ideas and points of view and develop ways to solve disagreements.* Should differences occur, children need to compromise and negotiate to reach a consensus with their peers. Children need opportunities to problem-solve and negotiate without adult interference and intervention.

Invented games encourage mutual self-interest in rules and rule making and differ greatly from teacher-imposed rules. They provide an appealing and satisfying vehicle for children to apply skills, increase their understanding of rules, and improve their social interaction skills. Think about the following second graders in Mr. Green's inner-city classroom. Paolo, Kristin, and Sarah are slow readers and have some difficulty with basic arithmetic operations. For 1 hour every Wednesday afternoon, Mr. Green expects all of his second graders to invent their own games, using assorted available materials. They choose to create a game either alone or with a partner.

Let's look at the games of Kristin, Sarah, and Paolo.

Kristin made the "Go Here and There Game" alone and then taught it to her friend. Her simple path game included starting and finishing points, some obstacles along the way, a few game cards and an individual card for rules. During play her friend asked, "Where are the place cards?" Kristin said, "Ooops, I forgot them" and went back to make them.

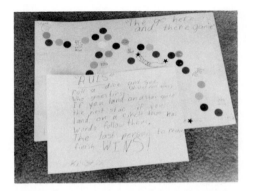

Sarah's game reflects the solar system unit her class is studying. It includes all the planets, Saturn's three rings, a darkened background indicating night, and the sun and stars. She made cards for the number of spaces to move forward and back, as well as outer-space instructions like "Tack a peas [take a piece] of the moon rock and stay." She used existing dice to designate turns and dried beans for markers. Her simple rules read as follows: "RULES: Start from the moon go to the Erath and the frist person to get there wen's." When she tried to teach it to a friend the next week, she quickly discovered that she had no labels on the dots telling players when to choose a card. As a result, the game could not begin. Sarah then made the necessary modifications.

Paolo's game, "Colorland," is also a simple path game containing a clear beginning and end, periodic spots to pick cards, a place labeled "card," and many cards sending players to jail or helping them escape from jail. Two of his cards read "brach owt of jail [break out of jail]" and "Go 5 steps forword." Paolo has played his game several times with his classmates. His final version evolved from the many questions his friends asked while playing.

Notice that in all three cases, children were refining the format or organization of their games, practicing skills in context, and collaborating with peers. Child-constructed games provide children with the opportunity to construct and use rules in relevant ways, to see others' points of view, and to figure things out autonomously or cooperatively.

Making Games with Children

The following guidelines will help you include game making in your curriculum.

1. *Make the game.* Have a variety of free and inexpensive materials available, such as file folders, poster board of all sizes and colors, beans, markers, sticky dots, labels, plastic bread ties, old magazines, calendar numbers, and assorted plastic bottle caps. Expect children to decide on the type of game to make (board, card, motor) and invent it. Their games will usually look like games that are familiar to them, yet the content and the play of the game will vary.
2. *Play the game.* Playing games helps children notice problems and pitfalls. Children "go back to the drawing board" willingly to produce a playable game.
3. *Modify the game to achieve more accurate representation. Revision* means literally "to see again." As children revise their games, they resee and rethink them until they achieve excellence in the finished product. Because there is no correct way to make games, they provide multiple opportunities for creative expression, constructive conflict resolution, and practice in self-evaluation. By observing, recording, and comparing children's progress with their invented games throughout the year, teachers have a powerful learning, teaching, and assessment tool that appeals to children of all ages (Castle, 1991).

Special Populations

In every classroom, children from different cultures, children with disabling conditions, and high- and low-achieving children need their creative expression nurtured.

Culturally Diverse Groups

Play is a powerful vehicle for multicultural education because it enhances awareness of others' feelings, behaviors, and traditions. Play materials, therefore, can
enhance children's awareness of cultural diversity when teachers provide

- ❏ Interest centers that reflect not only the cultural backgrounds represented in the classroom but also other cultures, like a celebration of the
  Chinese New Year.
- ❏ Literature to enrich children's understanding of cultural pluralism, such
  as *Mufaro's Beautiful Daughters* (Steptoe, 1987) or *I Hate English!* (Levine,
  1990).
- ❏ Quality puzzles, books, songs, games, puppets, and dances from other
  cultures or eras.
- ❏ Dark and light colors for painting and bulletin boards. Refer to darker
  colors as positively as you do to lighter colors. Be certain not to call
  brown "yucky" or "muddy" (Whaley & Swadener, 1990).
- ❏ Art projects including jewelry making and ethnic clothing (Jalongo,
  1991; Morrison, 1991).

To help children express themselves through materials, teachers need to
make children from other cultures feel welcome and safe in their classrooms;
promote their own intercultural understanding through knowledge of their students and their cultural backgrounds; help children believe in their own worth
and abilities; and provide children with many opportunities to use real, concrete, and culturally relevant, divergent materials in their play and in their
projects.

Children with Disabilities

Children with disabling conditions need materials that encourage them to feel
comfortable in the classroom and able to communicate their feelings and ideas
(Yawkey, Dank, & Glosenger, 1986). Visually impaired children, for example,
need tactile and auditory materials. Tactile maps for exploration, large-type print
kits, and braille materials such as a braille menu for the housekeeping area might
be welcome additions for these children (Sheridan, 1988).

Children with language delays need opportunities to communicate about
familiar people, events, and objects. Pretend play offers an appropriate context
for children to communicate with their peers. Often the child who is reluctant to
talk to another person directly will use the toy telephone or respond to a puppet.

High-Achieving and Low-Achieving Children

Both high-achieving and low-achieving children are, first and foremost, children. Materials for them should be the same as those of their peers, with some
additional emphasis. Infants and toddlers need materials that spark their emerg-

ing imaginative play. Preschool and school-age children need materials that capitalize on their unique interests and abilities and foster their sociodramatic play and role-taking abilities to develop the "social skills and tolerance needed to live with others who have a different world view" (Roeper, 1987, p. 165). Because of their often exceptional verbal ability, high-achieving preschool children need to use more language play like riddles, jokes, and poems and more logical, rules-oriented games.

Conclusion

In every early childhood classroom, children need a variety of materials for self-expression. Developmentally appropriate materials for children of all ages provide important opportunities for children to use divergent thinking.

Chapter Summary

1. Throughout history, children in all cultures have played with materials. The types of play materials available are affected by economic, cultural, and political issues and strongly influence children's self-expression, inventiveness, and divergent thinking.
2. Materials that hold the most promise for creative expression and play have multiple uses, encourage inventiveness and problem solving, and are process-oriented. Playing with these materials fosters children's inventiveness.
3. Children should experience a balance of materials, including skill/concept, manipulative, construction, and self-expressive materials, and natural and everyday objects.
4. Developmentally appropriate materials, which are real, meaningful, and stimulating to the imagination, should be available to children of all ages. Young children need sensory materials to explore and investigate using dramatic play, art, music, construction, and manipulative play. School-age children also need realistic, rule-oriented materials.
5. Organized games can be a significant aspect of the early childhood curriculum if presented and played appropriately. They can encourage autonomy, decision making, cooperation, and an understanding and use of rules.
6. Teachers should provide opportunities for children to invent, teach, and play their own games as part of the curriculum.
7. It is important to nurture creative expression in special populations. Using a variety of open-ended materials and activities is one of the best ways for teachers to adapt the curriculum to a wide range of children's abilities, interests, and cultural backgrounds.

Discussion Questions

1. Select, investigate, and explore a child's play material from the classroom in which you are now working. Think about the possible ways children could

use it. If you can, observe different children using the same material. Keep a list of your ideas and the children's uses. Compare your list with those of others who selected a similar material. How did infants/toddlers, preschoolers/kindergartners, and school-age children use the material?

2. In some classrooms, war toys and war play are banned, yet children still manage to find ways to play war. Discuss the implications of and reasons for teachers' decisions and children's responses.

3. Incorporating invented games into the curriculum provides children many opportunities for learning. Discuss these opportunities and suggest ways to include them as part of a thematic unit.

4. Why should children use self-expressive materials? List as many types of these materials as you can think of and briefly state a rationale for including each in the curriculum.

5. Refer to the case study at the beginning of the chapter. Why was it important for the children's teacher to provide these materials? What was her role in this play? Why do you think so?

6. Observe a child who is introduced to a play material for the first time. Refer back to the discussion of the uses of materials in this chapter and describe his or her behaviors. How do the behaviors fit the progression?

Writing to Learn

You are a teacher who believes in nurturing creative expression and play in all young children. However, a group of parents has complained to your principal and to other parents that "there is too much creativity in your room." Write down your thoughts about this allegation. Explore the significance of creative expression through materials, why you use divergent materials, and how they support children's learning and development. Share your writing in a small group and record the group's responses on a chart to report them to the whole class.

Interview

Play Materials: A Cross-Cultural Perspective

Throughout history, children in all cultures have played with different kinds of materials. These materials often reflect social, political, and cultural values and provide an important avenue for discovering others' behaviors (Auerbach, 1986; Mergen, 1982). Given this information, arrange to interview a person whose background is different from yours to discover the types and uses of play materials in his or her childhood years. Ask the following questions and record the responses. You may want to tape-record your interview and transcribe your responses immediately thereafter.

1. Describe the types of play materials you used as a child. In what ways did they reflect certain values and beliefs in your culture?
2. Did you have a favorite play material? Could you describe how you used it? Why did you find it satisfying?
3. In your culture, did boys and girls use similar or different play materials? Could you give me some examples of what materials each preferred?
4. What kinds of games did you play? Were they mostly indoor or outdoor games? Do you recall ever making up your own games? What were they like?
5. Do you know what kinds of play materials children from your cultural background use today? Could you elaborate?

Observation

Organized Sports or Activities and the Young Child

Many American parents want their children to have a "head start" on adult challenges. They enroll them at very early ages in structured group activities organized and maintained by adults (Isenberg, 1987).

Advocates of organized activities for young children believe they build character and foster self-discipline. Critics assert that children are being pushed too soon into activities coached by adults who pressure children to perform like adult sports stars. This "premature structuring" stems from adults' needs rather than children's needs and interests, and causes stress in young children (Elkind, 1984, 1986).

This assignment will help you apply your knowledge of children in observing a structured activity (e.g., soccer, gymnastics, infant swim classes) and analyzing it according to the adult–child or child–child interactions you observed.

1. Arrange to observe an organized physical activity for young children for at least 10 minutes. Write down a description of the setting, the number and ages of the children involved, their ethnic backgrounds, and any special needs they may have. Did any of the children seem upset or reluctant to begin the activity? What was the adults' dominant role?
2. Expand your notes immediately after your observation. Provide detailed descriptions of the following characteristics:

Divergent thinking: How much latitude is there for children to vary, manipulate, and experiment with the skill?

Self-expression: Can the children improvise and use innovative strategies or must they conform to the coach's instructions?

Internal control: Is there evidence that the children can control any part of the activity? Do children appear to be gaining confidence and competence?

Adult role: Does the adult allow children to figure things out for themselves, provide for active participation and involvement, and encourage children to work cooperatively? How does the adult handle failure? How does the adult handle success?

Share your observations in class. What conclusions about organized activities for young children do you draw? What conclusions does the group draw? As a teacher, how do you think you will now respond to parents who seek your advice on enrolling children in a structured physical activity?

Controversy

War Toys and War Play

Three boys whose fathers are stationed overseas with the military are playing "Scud Missile Attack." They have built a square enclosure out of blocks and are using a flat board over a triangular block as a fulcrum. When a plastic block is launched by dropping a weight on one end of the "Scud launcher," the child who is controlling the Patriot missile estimates the trajectory and intercepts it with a plastic tray. Then all three boys cheer.

This kind of war play immediately raises questions: Do children whose country is at war usually play war games? Should we allow or prevent such play in the classroom?

Each era has its wars and warrior-superheroes—Superman, Ninja Turtles, Rambo, He-Man, Transformers, or Gobots. Teachers anguish over the effects of war play and war toys on young children's play and social interactions. They are concerned that it usurps children's needed control from their play, and they express ambivalence and frustration about how to handle war play and war toys in the classroom.

In the current debate about the role of war play and war toys in the classroom, disagreement abounds. Teachers who have banned war play, stating the typical "no guns in school" rule, say that it doesn't work. There is increased tension in dealing with children, and they find means of getting around the rule. On the other hand, teachers who permit war play report that "the play is getting out of control and stretching their management skills to new levels" (Carlsson-Paige & Levin, 1987, p. 8).

Two different perspectives on war play, developmental and sociopolitical, fuel this debate about early childhood teachers. Developmentalists believe that war play is an important way for children to deal with their fears and concerns. It meets their developmental needs to control impulses, separate reality from fantasy, understand others' points of view, feel empowered, and understand world events surrounding them. However, simply playing war does not guarantee the satisfaction of children's needs (Carlsson-Paige & Levin, 1987, 1990).

On the other hand, sociopolitical supporters believe that children *should not* be allowed to engage in war play. It contributes to the early formation of militaristic values and condones violent, aggressive ways of solving disagreements. These early understandings of aggressive conflict resolution, of friends and enemies, and of power and subservience strongly influence children's developing political learning. Sociopoliticalists argue that war play and war toys glamorize fighting and killing, promote excessive materialism, and foster unnecessary aggression.

There are no clear-cut solutions to the dilemma of war play and war toys. Teachers can, however, help children learn to solve problems peacefully as they meet them in their everyday encounters (Rogers & Sharapan, 1991). They must also help children develop skills in (1) refocusing war play from shooting and killing to perhaps building hospitals for the sick and wounded, (2) creating school policies that reflect thoughtful consideration of both perspectives on war play, and (3) advocating for government regulation of industries that market simulated weapons to young children. Where do you stand on this issue and why?

———————————— **Research Highlight** ————————————

Clay in the Classroom: Helping Children Develop Cognitive and Affective Skills for Learning

Summary of Research

In this cross-cultural study, Smilansky, Hagan, and Lewis (1988) investigated what works best for children when using clay. Approximately 1,600 preschoolers and kindergartners in 53 different classrooms in Tel Aviv, Israel, and Columbus, Ohio, used clay for 16 weeks as part of their daily curriculum. Using three different teaching methods—observation/discussion, encouragement, and a control group—the researchers sought to discover the potential of clay in children's creative expression and cognitive development.

The researchers chose real clay over other modeling materials, for its responsiveness, manageability, flexibility, malleability, and low cost. Because clay is three-dimensional, it invites children to manipulate and freely try out possibilities that challenge their intellectual and language abilities, as well as to find methods of self-expression.

Results indicated that both experimental groups made significantly more improvements in clay manipulation, drawing, and language development compared to the control group. The findings clearly support growth in cognitive abilities and in verbal and artistic expression. The most effective strategy for the majority of preschoolers was the one in which the teachers provided technical assistance, encouragement, and a range of observation and discussion opportunities. A further significant discovery was the effectiveness of clay for preschool boys who began school "less prepared and experienced for the schooling process" (pp. 18–19).

Implications for Practice

Classroom teachers need to re-examine their use of clay in the classroom. Based on this research, we know that clay helps the young child

❑ Acquire abstract concepts through a concrete medium.
❑ Transfer new understandings to other curriculum areas.
❑ Improve motor skills and eye-hand coordination by manipulating, smoothing, and pressing the clay.
❑ Increase imagination and imaginative play.
❑ Develop understandings of size, shape, and quantity.
❑ Develop and express nonverbally concepts that can later be expressed verbally.

This medium is particularly important for children whose cultural backgrounds are different from those of their teachers, who have difficulty understanding new or abstract concepts, or who need other forms of communication of ideas and feelings.

References

Apelman, M. (1984). Appendix 1: Stages of block building. In K. Hirsch (Ed.), *The block book* (2nd ed.) (pp. 193–200). Washington, DC: National Association for the Education of Young Children.

Auerbach, S. (1986). *The toy chest: A sourcebook of toys for children.* Secaucus, NJ: Lyle Stuart.

Barbour, N., Drosdeck, S., & Webster, T. (1987). Sand: A resource for the language arts. *Young Children, 42*(2), 20–25.

Berns, R. M. (1985). *Child, family, community.* New York: Holt, Rinehart & Winston.

Bredekamp, S. (1988). NAEYC position statement on developmentally appropriate practice in the primary grades, serving 5- through 8-year-olds. *Young Children, 43*(2), 64–84.

Carlsson-Paige, N., & Levin, D. (1987). *The war play dilemma: Balancing needs and values in the early childhood classroom.* New York: Teachers College Press.

Carlsson-Paige, N., & Levin, D. (1990). *Who's calling the shots?* Philadelphia: New Society Publishers.

Castle, K. (1991). Children's invented games. *Childhood Education, 67*(2), 82–85.

DeVries, R., with Kohlberg, L. (1987). *Programs of early education.* New York: Longman.

Elkind, D. (1984). *All grown up and no place to go: Teenagers in crisis.* Reading, MA: Addison-Wesley.

Elkind, D. (1986). *The miseducation of children: Superkids at risk.* New York: Knopf.

Feeney, S., & Magarick, M. (1984). Choosing good toys for young children. *Young Children, 40*(1), 21–25.

Gottfried, A. W. (1986). The relation of play materials and parental involvement of young children's cognitive development. In A. W. Gottfried & C. C. Brown (Eds.), *Play interactions: The contribution of play materials and parental involvement to children's development* (pp. 327–334). Lexington, MA: D. C. Heath.

Guilford, J. P. (1967). *The nature of human intelligence.* New York: McGraw-Hill.

Hendrick, J. (1988). *The whole child* (4th ed.). Columbus, OH: Merrill/Macmillan.

Hewitt, K., & Roomet, L. (1979). *Educational toys in America: 1800 to the present.* Burlington, VT: Robert Hall Fleming Museum/University of Vermont.

Hildebrand, V. (1990). *Guiding young children* (4th ed.). New York: Macmillan.

Hughes, F. P. (1991). *Children, play, and development*. Boston: Allyn & Bacon.

Hutt, C. (1979). Exploration and play. In B. Sutton-Smith (Ed.), *Play and learning* (pp. 175–194). New York: Gardner Press.

Hutt, S. J., Tyler, S., Hutt, C., & Christopherson, H. (1989). *Play, exploration, and learning: A natural history of the preschool*. New York: Routledge.

Isenberg, J. P. (1987). Societal influences on children. *Childhood Education, 63*(5), 341–348.

Isenberg, J. P., & Jacobs, J. E. (1982). *Playthings as learning tools: A parents' guide*. New York: Wiley.

Isenberg, J. P., & Quisenberry, N. L. (1988). Play: A necessity for all children. *Childhood Education, 64*(3), 138–145.

Jalongo, M. (1991). Children's play: A resource for multicultural education. In E. B. Vold (Ed.), *Multicultural education in the early childhood classroom* (pp. 55–63). Washington, DC: National Education Association.

Johnson, J. E., Christie, J. F., & Yawkey, T. D. (1987). *Play and early childhood development*. Glenview, IL: Scott, Foresman.

Kamii, C., & DeVries, R. (1980). *Group games in early education: Implications of Piaget's theory*. Washington, DC: National Association for the Education of Young Children.

Kendall, F. E. (1983). *Diversity in the classroom: A multicultural approach to the education of young children*. New York: Teachers College Press.

Maxim, G. W. (1989). *The very young. Guiding children from infancy through the early years*. Columbus, OH: Merrill/Macmillan.

McKee, J. S. (1986). Play materials and activities for children birth to ten years: People, play, props and purposeful development. In J. S. McKee (Ed.), *Play: Working partner of growth* (pp. 47–61). Wheaton, MD: Association for Childhood Education International.

Mergen, B. (1982). *Play and playthings: A reference guide*. Westport, CT: Greenwood Press.

Monighan-Nourot, P. (1990). The legacy of play in American early childhood education. In E. Klugman & S. Smilansky (Eds.), *Children's play and learning: Perspectives and policy implications* (pp. 59–85). New York: Teachers College Press.

Morrison, G. (1991). *Early childhood education today* (5th ed.). New York: Merrill/Macmillan.

Piaget, J. (1926). *The language and thought of the child* New York: Harcourt Brace and World.

Piaget, J. (1962). *Play, dreams, and imitation in childhood*. New York: Norton.

Piaget, J. (1965). *The moral judgement of the child* (M. Gabain, Trans.). New York: Free Press.

Roeper, A. (1987). Play and gifted children. In D. Bergen (Ed.), *Play as a medium for learning and development: A handbook of theory and practice* (pp. 163–165). Portsmouth, NH: Heinemann.

Rogers, F., & Sharapan, H. B. (1991). Helping parents, teachers, and caregivers deal with children's concerns about war. *Young Children, 46*(3), 12–13.

Sawyers J. K. & Rogers, C. S. (1988). *Helping young children develop through play*. Washington, DC: National Association for the Education of Young Children.

Seefeldt, C., & Barbour, N. (1990). *Early childhood education: An introduction* (2nd ed.). Columbus, OH: Merrill/Macmillan.

Sheridan, M. D. (1988). *Spontaneous play in early childhood from birth to 6 years*. Windsor, Berkshire, England: Nfer-Nelson.

Smilansky, S. (1968). *The effects of sociodramatic play on disadvantaged preschool children*. New York: Wiley.

Smilansky, S., Hagan, J., & Lewis, H. (1988). *Clay in the classroom: Helping children develop cognitive and affective skills for learning*. New York: Teachers College Press.

Smilansky, S., & Shefatya, L. (1990). *Facilitating play: A medium for promoting cognitive, socio-emotional, and academic development in young children.* Gaithersburg, MD: Psychosocial and Educational Publications.

Sobel, J. (1983). *Everybody wins: Noncompetitive games for young children.* New York: Walker.

Sutton-Smith, B. (1986). *Toys as culture.* New York: Gardner Press.

Sutton-Smith, B. (1979). *Play and learning.* New York: Gardner Press.

Swedlow, R. (1986). Children play—children learn. In J. S. McKee (Ed.), *Play: Working partner of growth* (pp. 29–34). Wheaton, MD: Association for Childhood Education International.

Tegano, D. W., Sawyers, J. K., & Moran, J. D. (1989). Problem-finding and solving in play: The teacher's role. *Childhood Education, 66,* 92–97.

Torrance, E. P. (1983). Preschool creativity. In K. D. Paget & B. A. Bracken (Eds.), *The psychoeducational assessment of preschool children* (pp. 509–519). New York: Grune and Stratton.

Whaley, K., & Swadener, E. B. (1990). Multicultural education in infant and toddler settings. *Childhood Education, 66*(4), 238–240.

Wright, F. L. (1932). *An autobiography.* New York: Longman.

Yawkey, T. D., Dank, H. L., & Glosenger, F. L. (1986). *Playing inside and out: How to promote social growth and learning in young children including the developmentally delayed child.* Lancaster, PA: Technomic Publishing.

Children's Books

Degen, B. (1983). *Jamberry.* New York: Harper & Row.

Levine, E. (1990). *I hate English!* New York: Scholastic.

Steptoe, J. (1987). *Mufaro's beautiful daughters.* New York: Lothrop, Lee & Shephard.

Tafuri, N. (1988). *Junglewalk.* New York: Greenwillow.

Children's Software

Color Me. Mindscape. 3444 Dundee Rd., Northbrook, IL 60062; (800) 221-9884

Delta Draw. Spinnaker Software Corp., One Kendall Square, Cambridge, MA 02139; (800) 826-0706.

Explore-a-Story: Where Did My Toothbrush Go? D. C. Heath. 125 Spring St., Lexington, MA 02173; (800) 225-1149

Fantastic Animals: Mix-Up Puzzler. Bantam Electronic Publishing, 666 Fifth Ave., New York, NY 10103; (212) 765-6500.

PART

4

Child-Centered Teaching
for
Today and Tomorrow

Guiding Young Children's Creative Growth and Communicating with Families

If we have cultivated the art of play early in our lives, we are likely to hold onto our self-initiating behaviors, our capacity for risk-taking, our inventiveness as adults.

Selma Wasserman, 1990, p. 19

Unfortunately, our knowledge about parent involvement far exceeds the average taxpayer's, legislator's and school person's enthusiasm for doing something about it.

Polly Greenberg, 1989, p. 68

After reading this chapter, you will be able to

- ❏ Name and describe three theoretical perspectives that guide creative growth.
- ❏ List and discuss three styles of guidance and their influences on children's creative growth.
- ❏ Describe the characteristics of a creative teacher.
- ❏ Explain the roles and responsibilities of the teacher in a creative classroom.

❑ Discuss the role of the teacher in managing children's conflicts.
❑ Apply strategies that support children's divergent thinking and problem-solving ability.
❑ Communicate with families about creative expression.
❑ Adapt child-guidance strategies to special populations of children.

Case Study

It is center time in Ms. Manning's first-grade classroom. Daniel and Donald are making puppets so that they can dramatize their original stories about farm animals. When their puppets are finished, they begin tugging on each other and wrestling with their puppets. The boys become increasingly boisterous, so Ms. Manning comes over and says:

	Pardon me, Daniel and Donald. Please talk with me over here. (She goes to a quiet corner, kneels down, and talks to them at their eye level.) What was in your story that made you pull on each other so roughly? (She listens intently to their responses.)
Donald:	Playing pigs and robbers. The robbers were getting my pigs, and we needed to catch them to get our pigs back. (Daniel nods in agreement.)
Ms. Manning:	Daniel, tell me in your own words about what you were doing.
Daniel:	Playing pigs and robbers. But I was done with the game and didn't want to be the robber anymore, and Donald kept pulling on me.
Ms. Manning:	You were done playing with your puppets for your story. Do you think when you're playing like that, when you might be wrestling or pulling, that you need to tell each other when you stop playing? (Daniel nods.) Daniel, did you tell Donald when you wanted to stop? (Shakes head no.) You know, you could say in your own words, "Donald, I don't want to play this game anymore." (Daniel looks down and shakes his head.) Look at my eyes, Daniel. How will Donald know that you want to stop the game if you don't tell him? Remember to use your words the next time. When you leave the game, tell the person you're playing with so that they know. All right? Let's go back to finishing your puppet stories about the farm animals. (All three get up and leave.)

In this scenario, Ms. Manning is guiding the behavior of two first-grade boys. She knows that Daniel has difficulty verbalizing his needs and that conflict with peers often results. She uses this incident to provide a meaningful discussion (talking about the need to communicate wishes), model appropriate verbal behavior ("You could say in your own words, 'Donald, I don't want to play this game anymore' ''), and expresses confidence in Daniel's ability to take charge of his own behavior ("Remember to use your words the next time"). Her appropriate guidance techniques reveal her underlying belief that children can guide their own behavior and become fully functioning individuals (Rogers, 1961).

Guiding children's creative growth can be accomplished both indirectly and directly. Indirect guidance influences children's behavior by the strategies teachers use to manage and arrange the classroom space, materials, and schedule. These strategies were explained in detail in Chapters Six and Seven. Direct guidance includes teachers' physical, verbal, and affective strategies (Hildebrand, 1990) designed to shape children's behavior. This chapter explores the important role of creative growth in preparing children with real-life skills.

Theoretical Framework

There are three fundamental theoretical perspectives about guiding children's creative growth: constructivism, humanism, and behavioral-social learning.

Constructivism

Constructivists, like Piaget (1952), view children as active agents in their own development. They study creativity as a mental process (e.g., how a task is approached) and are interested primarily in how children come to understand their world rather than the specific types of behaviors they demonstrate (Papalia & Olds, 1990). Constructivists assume that

- ❏ Creative growth refers to concept building and problem solving, which are dependent upon a child's level of intellectual development.
- ❏ Children are doers—constructors or builders of understandings of their world.
- ❏ Children think differently from adults and gradually come to understand the viewpoints of others.

Developmentally appropriate child guidance is based on these principles of constructivism. Appropriate adult–child interactions include

- ❏ Adapting to children's different styles.
- ❏ Providing many opportunities to communicate thoughts and feelings.
- ❏ Facilitating and supporting children's investigations and experimentation with tasks and materials.
- ❏ Providing a respectful, comfortable, and accepting environment for all children.
- ❏ Facilitating the development of self-control (Bredekamp, 1987).

Classroom teachers who use constructivist theory to guide children's creative growth are most effective when they understand children's social and intellectual development; encourage children's interaction with others to increase their perspective-taking ability; and probe children's thinking and reasoning about ideas.

Humanism

Humanists like Carl Rogers and Abraham Maslow believe that people are capable of controlling their lives. They do this positively through "choice, creativity and self-realization" (Papalia & Olds, 1990, p. 30). How people feel about themselves exerts a strong influence on how they approach and resolve problems.

From a Rogerian perspective, human beings strive to become fully functioning individuals. Such an individual possesses four characteristics:

- ❏ Positive self-regard.
- ❏ Awareness of personal feelings and those of others.
- ❏ Acceptance of responsibility for decisions.
- ❏ Ability to solve problems (Rogers, 1961).

Children who interact with supportive, accepting adults learn to view themselves positively. In contrast, children who are deprived of accepting, supportive adults seek approval in inappropriate ways. When teachers draw upon Rogerian traditions, they foster children's creative growth by allowing them to think about and investigate problems, by encouraging them to express a range of feelings, and by accepting a range of solutions to problems.

Supportive, accepting, resourceful teachers facilitate children's investigative capacity. They provide activities that appeal to children's natural inclination toward problem solving (MacDonald, 1991).

Behavioral/Social Learning

Behaviorists view the environment as the single most important variable in shaping development. Consequently, they are concerned with observable, measurable behaviors. From this perspective, children react to the forces in their environment. Behaviorists assume that

- ❏ All behavior is learned. Learned behavior, shaped by external influences, causes development.
- ❏ All children gradually learn how to respond to environmental influences, regardless of age and developmental level (Marion, 1991).
- ❏ Adults in the environment are the major catalyst in changing or shaping children's behavior.

The behavioral perspective has provided the foundation for behavior modification programs. Teachers who rely extensively on this perspective use it to modify children's behavior. The danger, of course, is that overreliance on these intrusive methods may make children more dependent upon adults to resolve problems. For example, using time-out repeatedly to allow children to gain self-control often does not achieve the desired behavior. Rather, children perceive it as an opportunity to gain additional attention.

Social-learning theorists view social interaction as the major influence on learning and development. They hold that children learn socially appropriate behavior by observing and imitating others in a social setting as they respond to their environment. Social-learning theorists assume that children learn socially appropriate behavior by imitating models in their world (Papalia & Olds, 1990).

An Eclectic Approach

Most early childhood educators rely on the assumptions and practices of several theoretical perspectives for guidance techniques. In other words, our philosophy of child guidance tends to be eclectic. Deciding which strategy to use is affected by the child's characteristics, the adult's values and background, and the social context.

To understand how an eclectic philosophy operates, picture two scenarios. Mr. Keller is a substitute teacher who discovered that Lisa, a child in his class for the day, had Tourette's syndrome. Some symptoms of this poorly understood medical condition are tics, repeated tongue clicking, eye blinking, and uncontrollable verbal outbursts. Experts liken the uncontrollable nature of Tourette's syndrome to the involuntary response of sneezing; we can feel a sneeze coming on and can sometimes suppress it, but it is involuntary. During one of these episodes, Lisa suddenly shouted out in class, "Everybody, pick your nose!" Mr. Keller adopted a very humanistic view of Lisa's behavior and did not reprimand her because he knew that this disruptive behavior was out of Lisa's control.

Ms. Olson taught a class of 4-year-olds and was challenged by Yvonne's consistently aggressive behavior when she doesn't get her own way. She had been patiently but unsuccessfully trying to help Yvonne use words to express her wishes. Yvonne was building a trailer in the block center and needed a large, hollow block for a door. When she grabbed one from Joseph, he took it back. She then hit Joseph with a different block, drawing blood from an area near his eye. After Ms. Olson removed Yvonne from the block area, she decided to start her on a behavior modification plan.

Teachers often underestimate the influence of their own upbringing and value system on child guidance. Is the child who takes "silverware" from the housekeeping area to use it with clay breaking the rules or being creative? To a considerable extent, our orientations derive from our experiences. We need to be aware of how the social context often determines the child guidance strategy we select.

As teachers, we must avoid dealing with all children in exactly the same way. Each child brings a rich history of experiences, cultural backgrounds, and personality traits to the classroom. As teachers, we view children as individuals and must be as flexible as possible in guiding their creative growth.

Like an artist who selects particular paints, colors, and paper to convey an idea or image, teachers must select the most appropriate approaches and strategies to guide each child. The more teachers understand the different child guidance perspectives, and their own beliefs and values about creative growth, the more able they will be to respond appropriately to children's creative ideas and behaviors. Figure 8.1 presents different classroom teachers' views on creative behavior. Consider these responses. Which ones reflect your current views of creative behavior?

Teachers' Roles and Responsibilities

Consider the different responses of these second graders to their teachers' invitation to use a blank piece of corrugated cardboard to make something. Each teacher gave the children an 8 ½ × 11 inch piece of cardboard, asked them to think of any way to use it, and then share how they made their creation. Becky quickly saw the possibility of folding it and turning it into a bird feeder. She then decorated it with birds, flowers, and seeds. Sam looked longingly and sadly at the blank cardboard, with tears welling up in his eyes. When his teacher asked him what the problem was, he said, "I can't do this. I don't know what you want me to make." He refused to think of any way to use the cardboard. Andrea hastily folded her piece of cardboard into a "crayon box," but after a few un-

FIGURE 8.1   Classroom Teachers' Views on Creative Behavior

successful attempts to figure out how to get it to stay closed, she left the project unfinished on the table.

Clearly, children respond to creative tasks in very different ways. The teacher's interaction style exerts a major influence on the way children express creative behavior. A teacher who tells Sam "You're just not trying hard enough. Put on your thinking cap" may be providing choices and freedom, but without support. Teachers who are warm, accepting, and supportive guide children's positive creative growth. A sensitive teacher realizes that Andrea needs encouragement and recognition of her efforts to persist at a task. She might encourage Andrea with a statement like "I like your idea of a crayon box. I wonder if this stapler would help you close those edges." On the other hand, teachers who are not accepting or supportive make it difficult for children to develop a creative, problem-solving approach to ideas and tasks.

Adult–Child Interactions

There are three basic styles of adult–child interactions—autocratic, permissive, and democratic (MacDonald, 1991). Each refers to how demanding or responsive teachers are with children; each also cultivates typical behaviors and approaches to problem solving.

Autocratic Interactions

Autocratic teachers demand children's obedience to an inflexible set of rules and standards. The autocratic teacher

❑ Maintains stern and formal interactions with students.
❑ Devalues adult–child verbal interactions in which there are disagreements.
❑ Emphasizes a no-nonsense classroom environment.
❑ Discourages individuality or autonomy in children (Baumrind, 1967; MacDonald, 1991).

When teachers are autocratic, children are often resentful and rebellious. Autocratic methods tend to develop children who have difficulty with peer relations, lack initiative, and tend to be anxious, withdrawn, and apprehensive (Baumrind, 1967; MacDonald, 1991). Because the teacher is so controlling, children do not learn self-control. For example, when an autocratic teacher leaves the room, children often become unruly and out of control. This behavior is children's way of expressing resentment of controlling interactions.

Permissive Interactions

Permissive teachers have an "anything goes" orientation. They place few demands and controls on children's decision making and problem solving in a poorly organized environment with unclear and inconsistent standards for behavior. The permissive teacher

❑ Projects a laissez-faire, uninterested attitude.
❑ Presents an inconsistent, unpredictable environment.
❑ Fails to set clear, firm limits on behavior (Baumrind, 1967).

The methods of permissive teachers tend to create children with little self-control, self-reliance, or exploratory or investigative behavior. Because the standards for behavior are so inconsistent and the environment is so unpredictable, children cannot anticipate that their rights will be protected or even clearly determine what their rights are.

Democratic Interactions

Democratic teachers believe that children need firm but reasonable limits for behavior, as well as opportunities for choice, verbal negotiation, and decision making. The democratic teacher

- ❑ Exhibits confidence in his or her ability to guide children.
- ❑ Understands children's development, limits, and potentials.
- ❑ Really listens to children and respects their ideas and opinions.
- ❑ Has high expectations for all children.
- ❑ Responds to children's initiatives and suggestions.
- ❑ Prepares the environment with choices, age-appropriate activities and materials, and plenty of time for interaction.
- ❑ Expects students to be responsible for the consequences of their decisions.

Children who live and work with democratic teachers appear to feel secure, know what is expected of them, and are self-sufficient, self-controlled, and self-assertive. They also tend to be self-starters who are capable of initiating and completing projects independently of adults. Democratic teachers do more than cover material. They develop concepts and problem-solving skills in children by engaging them actively in learning and empowering them to accept responsibility for their own learning and actions (MacDonald, 1991).

The Creative Teacher

Ms. Mason has been teaching kindergarten for 10 years and is now enrolled in a graduate program in early childhood education. During a class session on environments that foster competent children, Ms. Mason was silent. After class she talked with the professor, and emotion overcame her as she said: "I was a child who felt I could never do anything without help, and now I'm the same kind of adult! How can I ever help kindergartners grow into competent, autonomous children? What do I need to do?"

Before Ms. Mason can guide children's creative growth, she needs to determine what beliefs, values, and abilities she brings to the classroom. Ms. Mason is right; negative teachers do not exert a positive influence on children's creative growth. Rather, it is the positive, confident teacher, who understands and accepts herself or himself, who can bring out the best in children (Hildebrand, 1990).

Guiding children's creative growth requires two criteria—the teacher's desire and competence.

Democratic teachers really listen to and respect children.

Desire

Teachers who desire to be creative see themselves as decision makers. They provide materials and experiences that challenge children's problem-solving ability, divergent thinking, and social skills because they respect children's ability to think creatively. They do this with full understanding of the goals and objectives of their curriculum and knowledge about their children.

Conversely, teachers who believe that play and creative expression are frivolous, unimportant, and nonessential aspects of the curriculum lack the desire to guide children's creative growth. Teachers who go by the book—the teacher's manual—and are unwilling to make decisions about appropriate curriculum also lack the basic desire to try.

Teachers in child-centered classrooms believe in the importance of setting the stage for learning. They wish to develop competent children by respecting children's choices and providing active, challenging, investigative play opportunities in which children test hypotheses (Wasserman, 1990). These teachers set the stage for children's learning with self-expressive experiences that allow children to explore and investigate meaningful concepts in cooperative learning groups. The desire to teach this way is very different from the *banking model* (Freire, 1983, p. 58) of teaching, which views the child's head as a sort of savings account in which teachers deposit facts. Although it may be more efficient to employ the banking model, it does not promote child-centered growth and learning.

Creative teachers view themselves as problem solvers, risk takers, and decision makers. They expect children to share responsibility for their own learning, value their ideas, and guide children's inquiry, exploration, and experimentation with materials and ideas. In this way, they act as facilitators and are more likely to create classrooms in which creativity can thrive.

Competence

Guiding children's creative growth requires a basic *knowledge of how children grow and develop.* Such knowledge helps teachers make appropriate decisions about children's interpersonal skills, their methods of communication, their approach to problem solving, and their developing self-control (Hildebrand, 1990). Knowledge of child development is essential to competent teaching in an early childhood classroom.

Teachers must also be willing and able to support children's *choices and decisions.* All children should have many opportunities to choose whether to work alone or with another child; whether to use manipulatives or play in the dramatic play area; or what message to write in a note to a sick classmate. As a group, young children have less experience in making choices. Therefore, they need to begin with two or three alternatives so that they are not overwhelmed by the possibilities. The range of choices can be increased as children gain self-confidence and experience with decision making. This gradual introduction enables students to learn quickly how to make decisions about how to use materials and to determine which materials would work best for a particular project (Krogh, 1990).

Creative teachers want their students to become competent problem solvers, decision makers, communicators, and collaborators. They themselves are not content to use a single source for information but synthesize from many sources—their personal experiences, the community, print and nonprint media, and children's experiences and ideas—to guide children's creative growth. When children are able to explore and investigate ideas and concepts that are linked to their experiences, they connect new knowledge to prior knowledge. In this way, children learn to be responsible for their own learning, work on teams, and share the excitement of learning.

Creative teachers guide children's growth in classrooms where students are actively engaged in a variety of real, firsthand learning experiences such as enactments, projects and thematic units, field trips, and community resources. Creative teachers use developmentally appropriate guidance techniques to foster children's creative growth.

Developmentally Appropriate Guidance

Three-year-old Hans is confined to a wheelchair, but he wants to participate in a movement activity. Justine suggests that he can be the engine when the group sings "Little Red Caboose."

Five-year-old Sandy is trying to make her picture "look snowy" after the first snowfall. After listening to Sandy and realizing that it is the blanket of glistening snow that Sandy wants to re-create, Ralph remembers that they used a mixture of soap flakes, water, and silver glitter in his Sunday School class. He asks the teacher if they can try the recipe at after-school care, too.

Seven-year-old Monica helps Jeffrey rig a pulley system to send messages across the room. Later, Jeffrey sends a note to Monica: It reads: "Thank you to Monica. Your friend, Jeff."

These children are all engaged in *prosocial behavior—spontaneously sharing with another child.* Prosocial behavior develops in children who live and work in supportive environments where adults model cooperative, helping behaviors (Hildebrand, 1990; Kostelnik, Stein, Whirren, & Soderman, 1988).

Fostering Prosocial Behavior

In child-centered environments there is mutual respect between teachers and children. When children see adult models of prosocial behavior, they develop cooperative, helping, and responsible behaviors themselves (Marion, 1991).

Picture the following scenario in Ms. Payne's class of 4-year-olds. After a few days of playing in the camping center, Ms. Payne introduced the idea of fishing. She added a pup tent, a blue paper lake, and a small grill filled with crumpled black and orange paper to represent a glowing charcoal fire. She developed the fishing theme by including fishing licenses, some magnetic fishing poles, a bucket, and some paper fish shapes with paper clips attached to the ends. She stimulated the children's interest in the idea by relating that she noticed people fishing nearby, so that the pond was probably well stocked with fish. In the following play text, see if you can identify examples of prosocial behavior in the 4-year-olds. What role did the teacher have in fostering such behavior? Look at the photo to better understand the children's interactions.

Katie, Steven, and Harold were fishing excitedly at the pond.

Katie: I need a fish. (Fishing.) Is this real water?

Ms. Payne: No, it is blue paper, but we are pretending it is a lake.

Katie: (At the lake.) Got the fish. One, two, three . . .

Steven: I need a fish. That one. (Points to the big one.) I caught a fish for myself. Look how big!

Harold: Here's a fish.

Katie:	Pick it up. (Says to Harold.) Put it over here. (Points to the bowl.) I caught that one for you.
Steven:	(Cutting the fish and eating.) That was good. I need more.
Katie:	Hey, all the fish are gone. (Everyone has caught all of the fish.)
Steven:	We have to put some back.
Harold:	We have to catch them all over again. (They put some of the fish back. Katie catches one and starts to put it back in the water.)
Steven:	Don't throw *him* back!
Harold:	We have to put them back after we catch them.
Ms. Payne:	(Passes by the camping center and adds ideas about baiting the hook to catch the fish, cleaning the fish before cooking and eating them, and throwing back the ones that are too small.)
Katie:	I am the mother, and I am going to cook everything.
Melanie:	No, I am the mother. I want to cook.
Katie:	No, you can be the grandma and help me cook, but we can have only one mother.
Melanie:	Okay. (They both go over to the grill and start to cook the fish.)
Katie:	Is the grill hot? Why don't we cook the fish on it?
Melanie:	Yes. (She puts a plastic tub on it and pretends to cook.)
Katie:	If you put the plastic on there, won't it melt? The grill is real hot. Why not cook the fish right on top of the grill? Then you won't melt the plastic. (Steven and Harold bring some more fish over to the grill for Katie and Melanie.)
Katie:	Hey, you [to the fish]. Don't burn! Are you done? I need a fork and a cup.
Melanie:	I'll get one. (Returns with a long stick.) We have to turn the fish with a fork. I think I burned my finger. Ouch! Ouch! (Blows on finger.)
Katie:	Come over here, Grandma. I can put a bandage on it, and it will make it feel real good. (Pretends to take out some bandages and fix the finger.)
Steven:	I want pink fish. They taste better.
Harold:	I have a pink one, and I have a big fish.
Steven:	Can I have the pink one?
Harold:	I'll give you another one. You can have two, and I'll have two.
Steven:	Okay. Hey, Grandma, where are the fishies? Are they done yet?
Melanie:	No, I burned them. So, now I have to clean the grill because the fish are burnt on it. (She takes the sponge and pretends to wipe the grill.) All clean.
Katie:	Dinner today will be fish, macaroni, and juice.

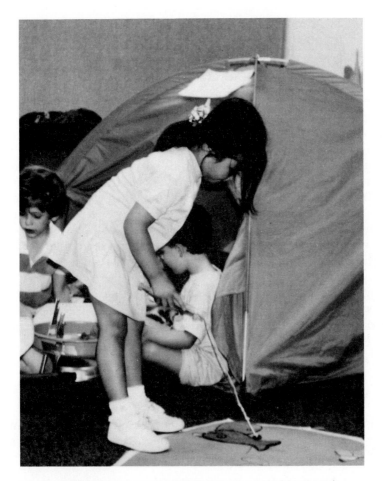

In play, children use their imaginations to solve problems and practice social skills.

Harold: Mom, is it okay if we go play ball?

Katie: Yes.

Harold: We will probably be late for dinner.

Steven: (Starts setting up for dinner. Then goes back to fish with Melanie. They fish and put the fish in bowls for dinner.) Mom, can I help you with dinner?

Katie: Sure, just give everybody fish. Put two fishies on each plate.

Steven: I passed out the fish.
(The children all sit down for a fish dinner.)

Katie: Wait until everyone comes. We don't want to be rude. (Other children come by to join the fish dinner feast.) Is everyone hungry? Boy, I sure am. Melanie, please pass the corn. (Melanie passes the corn.) Harold, do you want some?

Harold: No, I want some fish. (Katie passes Harold some fish.)

Steven: Pass me a napkin and cup, please. (Harold passes them to him. All the others are eating, passing different containers around, and pretending to eat and drink.)

While this play scene may seem unimportant to the novice, it is actually rich with examples of creative and prosocial behavior. All of these children are not only drawing upon their experiences, but also using their imaginations to solve problems and practice social skills. From an experiential perspective, they took part in a common episode—helping to prepare, cook, and eat food together with family and friends. They used their imaginations as they solved problems—how to cook fish on the grill and what to do when the fish were gone from the lake. They practiced social skills as they negotiated who was to play the mother when both Katie and Melanie wanted the role. In this 45-minute play episode, the children were responsible for the contents, roles, and sequence of events. After the play began, Ms. Payne intervened only once with a comment about catching, cleaning, and cooking the fish.

Using the above play text and the guidelines for creative growth that follow, identify which episodes of the play supported children's prosocial behavior. Cite specific passages from the play text. What was the role of the teacher in this play scene?

Guidelines for Creative Growth

The National Association for the Education of Young Children recommends the following developmentally appropriate guidelines to foster children's creative growth (Bredekamp, 1987):

1. All children need adults' respect and acceptance to nurture their self-esteem. Understanding and accepting the child even when his or her *behavior* may be unacceptable demonstrates this respect.

2. Adults play a key role in helping children develop self-control. Children learn self-control through positive guidance techniques, such as setting clear limits for younger children and helping older children set their own limits, modeling appropriate behavior, and redirecting inappropriate behavior.

3. Teachers must prepare interesting and challenging activities that promote prosocial behavior and independence of thought. Through projects, investigative play experiences, and divergent materials, children develop social skills such as cooperation, negotiation, problem solving, and perseverance.

Although it is important to recognize and respect positive behaviors in children, teachers must also prepare children to cope with the conflicts that inevitably arise. How teachers interact with children in conflict situations largely determines how children will approach problem solving as adults (Hildebrand, 1990).

Understanding Children's Conflicts

In Ms. Balboa's Head Start classroom, Juanita joins Erik at the playdough table. Within a few minutes, she rolls out a large, thick pancake shape, and the following dialogue occurs:

Juanita: Look at my big thing! (Points to a long, snake-like shape.)

Erik: Oh man! That's big!

Juanita: I'm gonna get it even bigger. (She picks it up and shows Erik the thumbprint on the bottom.) See, on the back, Erik?

Erik: Whoa! (Erik leans on his rolled-out playdough, making a "tummy print." Juanita cuts biscuit shapes with a plastic cup.)

Erik: Hey, I need that cup!

Juanita: NO!

Erik: (In increasingly loud, angry tones.) *I* need that cup! I need it. I need it. I'm gonna make balls and put the balls in it. So, gimme it. Gimme that. Teacher! Juanita won't let me have the cup.

A dispute over a toy like Juanita's and Erik's is a leading source of conflict among preschool children. Consider the different strategies you might use to respond to this dispute. Perhaps you could try to ignore it, deeming it unworthy of your attention. You also might insist that Erik and Juantia share the cup. Or you might observe the situation, suggest that Erik try another container on the table, and leave after a suitable replacement is found.

Without a doubt, conflicts hold significance for the teacher. In fact, children's inappropriate behavior is a major concern of educators, both novice and expert. But what about the children? What causes conflict? What are the consequences of various types of conflict resolution for their social and cognitive development? And what are some guidelines for conflict resolution?

Causes of Conflict

Children's conflicts are a natural part of their lives. Conflict occurs when one person does something to which a second person objects. Underlying reasons for the conflict may be either intentional or unintentional (Hay, 1984).

Types of conflict that dominate various age groups tend to follow a developmental sequence. Toddlers tend to have conflicts over possessions or toys because sharing toys and materials is an essential part of group functioning in classrooms (Eisenberg-Berg, Haake, & Bartlett, 1981). Preschool children's conflicts continue to focus on play materials but also include struggles over playing roles; gaining access to an ongoing group, space, or number of players allowed in a space; and conflicts about whether the player fits the ongoing play needs by gender, size, or dress (Corsaro, 1985; Isenberg & Raines, in press). For example, a preschool child expects a baby to act in certain ways. When a child does not conform to the role expectations and fails to act like a baby, peer criticism and conflict are often the result.

Primary grade children often disagree with their peers over rules for games, initiating interactions, and maintaining relationships (Asher & Hymel, 1981). They tend to be inflexible in thinking about rules and often find themselves involved in disputes over them.

Most teachers are anxious to stop conflicts at all costs as soon as they arise or try to prevent them from occurring. Yet, conflict has a positive side. It is a form of interaction that offers children the opportunity to deal with their thoughts and feelings in social situations. Successful conflict resolution helps young children to develop the skills and attitudes needed for group living, to form friendships with peers, and to perceive others' behavior and ways of thinking (Feeney, Christensen, & Moravcik, 1991). As teachers, we need to guide conflict to enhance children's social and intellectual development.

Guidelines for Resolving Conflicts

The following guidelines will help children resolve conflicts in developmentally appropriate ways.

1. *Allow children to work through conflicts on their own, where possible, before intervening.* If teachers are to develop children who are responsive to the needs of others, they must design environments that guide children toward caring about and helping others. Classrooms that encourage children's cooperative conflict resolution promote children's prosocial understandings (Isenberg & Raines, in press).

2. *Help children find solutions to problems.* Children's actions indicate their understanding of others' behavior. In conflict situations, focus on *what can be done* rather than unraveling the complex *causes* of the dispute. Taking action will enable children to resume their activity, and this, in itself, is reinforcing. Eventually, children learn that making a few concessions can keep their play going instead of bringing it to an abrupt halt.

3. *Help children understand the consequences of their behavior* (Kostelnik et al., 1988). Children need to understand the conflict from their own and another's perspective. Very young children do not understand how others feel or think. It is important, therefore, to let each child present his or her perspective on the conflict. Teachers' comments like "Sarah is crying now" or "How do you think she feels after you took her doll?" give children information about the feelings of others. Older children need to be reminded of others' feelings in a conflict situation.

4. *Encourage children to generate alternative solutions to the conflict* (Kostelnik et al., 1988). A variety of alternative solutions to the conflict may be generated by the participants, peers, or adults in the setting. The adult acts as a mediator, restating the suggestion for the children involved (e.g., suggesting that a child use words instead of crying when he or she needs a toy or suggesting a role for someone who has been denied access to a play situation).

5. *Differentiate between intentional and unintentional behavior.* Young children do not distinguish between intentional and unintentional behavior, but older children do. Teachers may help young children understand behavior by explaining unintentional behavior (e.g., "Selma did not mean to drop your cards, Harriet. It was an accident").

6. *Teach specific social skills to children who are aggressive, unpopular, and rejected by their peers.* Unpopular children often suffer peer rejection because they lack the skills for gaining entry into existing play groups or dominate the entire play scene. Consider, for example, a kindergarten classroom where children have been assigned to small groups to reenact "The Three Little Pigs." Dana takes *total* control. She shoves the other children around and berates them if they deviate from her planned script. Just as the group is about to perform, a shy child named Rolando, who has been completely excluded by Dana's stage-mother presence, says quietly to his teacher, "But I was supposed to be the narrator."

    Dana is desperately in need of guidance. She needs to see that she can experience success in the group without being overbearing. Rolando needs to have his rights protected as well. If the teacher ignores this peer conflict, neither child's social skills are enhanced.

Children's conflicts present important opportunities for developing positive social interaction skills and creative growth with both peers and adults. In the classroom, there are some strategies that are particularly well suited to fostering children's creative growth.

Strategies for Guiding Creative Behavior

A major goal of the early childhood curriculum is to enable children to become creative thinkers. Strategies designed to meet this goal include cooperative problem solving (Tudge & Caruso, 1988), investigative play (Wasserman, 1990), and project work (Katz & Chard, 1989).

Cooperative Problem Solving

Cooperative problem solving occurs when there is a shared goal or interest, a difference of opinion, and an active exchange of ideas. Collaboration in real, shared, firsthand experiences exposes children to different points of view, enhances their perspective-taking ability, and increases their social interaction skills (Tudge & Caruso, 1988). Cooperative problem solving supports divergent thinking abilities, especially for minorities and women (Johnson & Johnson, 1989).

Children solve problems regularly through their cooperative play as they decide how to bridge two blocks, fit two children on a swing, or balance objects on a balance beam. However, not all problems lead to cooperative problem solving. Cooperative problem solving is enhanced when there are good problems to solve. Figure 8.2 describes the characteristics of good problems.

Tudge and Caruso (1988) and Atkinson and Green (1990) suggest the following guidelines for cooperative problem solving in the classroom:

1. *Plan activities with a common goal.* A group of kindergartners were building a school bus to enact the song "The Wheels on the Bus." Before they began, their teacher encouraged them to discuss their ideas and agree on how to build the bus and to decide what to include on it (e.g., steering wheel, seats, horn, driver, steps, a door). Helping children work together on a common goal encourages cooperative problem solving.

2. *Encourage children's free exchange of ideas.* As part of a unit on environmental responsibility, a second-grade teacher invited children to collect clean, recyclable materials and encouraged them to use them as they wished. Nothing much came of her suggestion. Later, she decided to try the same activity with small groups. Most children responded more favorably to this activity because they were able to build upon one another's ideas as well as suggest their own.

3. *Help children agree upon common goals.* Preschool and kindergarten children are action-oriented; they do something first and then think. Two 4-year-olds at a water table illustrate this point. They were struggling to pump water from one container to another when the teacher came by and said, "I see. You're trying to get this water over there by using the

---

FIGURE 8.2   Characteristics of Good Problems

Good problems

☐ Are relevant and interesting to children.
☐ Involve real or simulated materials and/or people.
☐ Require the child to modify, move, or transform the materials.
☐ Elicit many possible solutions.
☐ Can be solved by the child, yet provide interesting challenges.
☐ Help the child believe in his or her own problem-solving abilities.
☐ Encourage children's sharing of differing points of view.
☐ Occur spontaneously in children's free play.
☐ Occur in open-ended, content-specific, planned activities.

Source: Atkinson and Green (1990), Tudge and Caruso (1988), Wasserman (1990).

tubes and funnels" (Tudge & Caruso, l988). After the teacher had ver-
balized their common goal for them, the children tested different ways
to pour water from one container to another using the tubes and funnels. Their play then centered on pumping water through them.

4. *Expect all children to participate in problem-solving groups.* Marcus is a third
   grader who stutters and is reluctant to share his ideas in a large group.
   Cooperative problem-solving groups provide a less intimidating setting
   for Marcus to test his ideas.

Children can engage in cooperative problem-solving activities during spontaneous play; planned, open-ended activities; or planned activities that are content specific, such as science investigations. Through shared exchanges of ideas,
children explore new possibilities together and enhance their thinking.

Investigative Play

Mr. Yoon's first graders are exploring the effect of different formulas on soap
bubbles. Five groups of children are experimenting with different solutions of
food colorings, liquid detergents, corn syrup, and glycerin and are using other
materials—straws, lids, a plastic tennis racket, plastic tubing attached to a fun-
nel, the plastic rings from a six-pack of soda cans—to produce bubbles of various
sizes. Mr. Yoon has given them an activity card with the following guidelines:

Find out everything you can about bubbles.

What did you observe about the different formulas? Colors?

What solution made the biggest, strongest bubbles?

What materials can be used to make many small bubbles? To make one huge
bubble?

Talk about what you noticed.

One group of children added glycerin to see if they could get stronger
bubbles. They started with one teaspoon and then increased it to two, three,
four, five, and six. Another group tried different ways of making different-sized
bubbles. In both groups, there was laughter and interaction. All the children
were involved in the tasks, either as investigators or as observers. Mr. Yoon
functioned as a facilitator, encouraging and supporting the children's investigations with such comments as "I see you are now going to try a new color of
bubbles."

This activity illustrates a three-step model for organizing instruction and
challenging primary grade children's divergent thinking called *play-debrief-replay*
(Wasserman, 1990). Each step is explained below.

Play

During play, children investigate and explore materials to make predictions,
observe and classify information, and make both individual and collaborative

decisions. Investigative play builds children's conceptual understandings about materials and ideas and enables them to examine actively key curriculum concepts such as "Plants are living things" and "The work different people do requires special abilities and talents." In play, teachers set the stage and challenge children's learning, while children control their own learning. Wasserman reports that teachers using this model "feel exhilarated, energized and empowered" (1990, p. 28). Mr. Yoon's first graders were testing hypotheses about the "perfect" soap bubble formula. They were learning about viscosity, pressure, air velocity, colors, and light—all basic concepts of physics.

Debrief

In the second step, investigative play becomes the common base for children's reflections. In either small or large discussion groups following exploratory play, Mr. Yoon asks the children questions that encourage them to reflect upon their experiences, such as "What did you notice about the bubbles?" and "How did you figure that out?" Good questions cause children to think carefully and to add their understandings to others. In the hands of a skillful teacher, debriefing play empowers children as thinkers, invites new ideas, builds self-esteem, and provides the foundation for future play with the same concept (Wasserman, 1990).

Replay

Replay occurs after debriefing. Some replay may involve the same materials; other replay may involve some new materials to move the inquiry along. A teacher might invite children to figure out the best way to transfer a bubble from one person to another without breaking it or might ask children to introduce some new ways of blowing into the bubble makers. Replay provides additional practice with the concept or skill and an opportunity to replicate and verify findings. As a result, replay gradually builds children's conceptual understandings.

Project Work

Another powerful strategy for enhancing creative growth is the project approach. According to Katz and Chard (1989), a project is a focused study of a particular subject or theme undertaken by one or more children for as long as children remain interested.

Projects are an important teaching strategy because they foster meaningful learning. Think about the possibilities for children's engagement in learning in the following description of project activities related to construction.

All of the children were at the window watching. They had many questions, including "Why do they dig a hole first?", "What happens next?" and "How do they know what to do?" In response to their questions, Ms. Hartman develops a project on construction.

She locates several picture books that illustrate basic building principles, including Byron Barton's *Building a House*. They look at a real blueprint, take a walking tour of the community to look for different building styles, and interview an architect. Ms. Hartman also brings in picture postcards of famous buildings and lavishly illustrated books from the library. It turns out that one of the teachers built a house last year and has a set of photographs that document each building stage.

In this scenario, Ms. Hartman initiated the construction project in response to children's interest and questions. She began with a class discussion about what children already knew about construction and what they were interested in finding out. Through their investigation of books, examination of postcards and real materials like a blueprint, and a walking tour of the community, the children developed their own construction site to build a "class house" from blocks and boxes. Through their project and dramatic play, the children became actively engaged in understanding the interdependence of the roles of architect, builder, and construction worker. They also developed clearer concepts of the complexities of building a house.

Project work can enhance creative growth by

- ❏ Responding to children's questions.
- ❏ Fostering children's independent, creative thinking.
- ❏ Enabling children to be involved at different levels.
- ❏ Providing diverse cognitive challenges so that all children can experience success.
- ❏ Utilizing academic skills in relevant, highly motivating contexts.
- ❏ Encouraging cooperation to ensure successful completion of the project.
- ❏ Providing opportunities to increase knowledge, understandings, and interpretations (Katz & Chard, 1989; Webster, 1990).

Teaching strategies like the project approach, investigative play, and cooperative problem solving make learning meaningful by relating what children are learning to what they already know. Keeping children engaged in learning makes further learning possible. In the next section, we present some ideas on communicating concepts of creative expression and play to families.

Communicating with Families

As early childhood teachers, we have many occasions to communicate with families about their children's creative growth and development. The nature of the interaction between teachers and families makes a great difference in children's creative growth, self-esteem, aspiration level, motivation, and view of themselves as learners both in school and outside (Berger, 1991; Greenberg, 1989; Kagan, 1989). One of the challenging roles early childhood teachers encounter is a changing view of working with families. To communicate best with families, teachers need to understand the obstacles to good communication and to develop effective strategies for enhancing communication with families.

Obstacles to Communication

Communicating with families about children's creative expression and play is important because these forms of self-expression are the vehicles for developing children's divergent, creative, and imaginative thinking. The key to communicating with families is to help them understand how creative expression and play contribute to children's physical, intellectual, social, and emotional development.

There are four obstacles that prevent teachers from communicating effectively with parents about children's creative growth.

1. *They do not know how to work with families.* Many classroom teachers feel unprepared to respond to parents' comments that play and creative activities are frivolous. They blame their lack of preparation in working with parents on teacher education institutions. Although it is not possible to reach all parents, classroom teachers must learn new ways of reaching and working with them (Greenberg, 1989).

2. *Working with families has never been a priority.* Even though school systems give lip service to working with families, they rarely provide the support teachers need to develop the skills to do so. Helping parents understand the role of play and self-expression in children's lives involves an ongoing dialogue because these experiences cannot be transported home in worksheet form. Rarely do schools reward teachers for outstanding communication with parents about creative expression and play.

3. *Some families do not respond to invitations to come to their child's school.* One inner-city teacher wondered why she should make the extra effort to reach her students' families when so many of them never came to meetings or conferences. Such a negative view reveals a lack of understanding of different kinds of families. Some family members feel anxious about meeting teachers at school to discuss their children's progress. When parents have less formal education or feel less competent than teachers, they often appear passive during parent–teacher meetings or they do not bother to come at all. Classroom teachers must develop a new mindset that accepts the inherent strength of families and allows parents to feel comfortable with teachers (Davies, 1991; MacDonald, 1991).

4. *Some parents are adversarial, uncooperative, and defensive.* Many parents view teachers as harsh judges of themselves—especially if they had a negative school experience—and as harsh critics of their child. Quite often, these parents convey negative feelings about school to their children, and children who fear failure are reluctant to try something. As we have seen, without trial and error and without risk taking, learning and creative expression are thwarted (Greenberg, 1989).

When teachers make a serious commitment to communicating with parents, they enhance every child's chances for success in school, meet the needs of the whole child, and share responsibility for their creative growth with their families (Davies, 1991). There are many strategies teachers can adopt to overcome the barriers to communication they face.

Strategies for Communicating with Families

Communicating with families means establishing a partnership built upon mutual trust and respect. The strategies that teachers adopt to enhance communication naturally depend upon their individual beliefs and attitudes about a commitment to such communication. The following suggestions for building home–school partnerships are grouped according to one-way communication—informing parents about the school's and children's plans—and two-way communication—inviting family members to share their knowledge, interests, and concerns about their children and the school (Berger, 1991).

One-Way Communication

One-way communication flows from the schools to the families. Four one-way communication strategies are recommended:

1. *Newsletters* communicate school events or projects to parents. They are well suited to conveying information. One first-grade teacher's monthly newsletter included excerpts from professional publications related to children's self-expression and play. She also included examples of particular projects children created with blocks, puppets, or music. As a result, parents came to expect information about creative arts as well as basic skills in the monthly newsletter.

2. *Handbooks* provide information about school policies and procedures and available resources. A kindergarten teacher developed a special one-page insert in which she explained her emphasis on creative expression and its importance to children's overall growth and development (Berger, 1991).

3. *Notes* can and should communicate children's positive creative growth experiences. When teachers take the time to send such notes home, it enhances communication and boosts children's self-concept. Be certain to keep paper handy to record any significant incident that illustrates creative growth, such as playing with language or resolving a conflict in a constructive manner (Kuschner, 1989).

4. *Photo albums* documenting the processes of children's activities are especially useful to validate the importance of children's play and to give children's creative projects a sense of ownership and permanence (Kuschner, 1989). Ms. Alvarez photographed her preschoolers' block structures and dramatic play episodes and placed them in a class album. The children took turns bringing the album home on weekends and sharing it with their families.

Two-Way Communication

Two-way communication encourages dialogue between families and schools. Four recommended two-way communication strategies follow.

1. *Meetings,* such as back-to-school nights, provide an opportunity for both teachers and parents to share general information about what and how

the child is learning. They provide a good opportunity for teachers to emphasize the creative aspects of their program and for parents to ask general questions. Ms. Daniels, a preschool director, had struggled to find a way to convince parents of the importance of play in the curriculum. She recently opened her parent meeting with the story of Richard Feynman, the physicist who won a Nobel Prize. In his autobiography, *Surely You're Joking, Mr. Feynman* (1985), he tells the story of how he played with physics concepts at Cornell University. At dinner in the cafeteria, he played with dinner plates—tossing them in the air to observe their "wobble rate." In his words, "There was no importance to what I was doing, but ultimately there was. The diagrams and the whole business that I got the Nobel Prize for came from that piddling around with the wobbling plate" (p. 174).

Ms. Daniels invited the parents to think about some creative problem solving they had experienced, such as reinventing a new recipe because some ingredients were missing or figuring out a temporary solution to a mechanical problem.

2. *Conferences* provide private opportunities for teachers and parents to share information and feelings about a child's progress. Many teachers include the child in the conference, thus making it three-way communication. One second-grade teacher helped families to prepare for upcoming conferences and set the tone for the meeting by sending home a note. She invited the parents to share examples of their child's creative behavior at home. Parents responded favorably to this invitation and became more focused on their children's creative behavior.

3. *Telephone calls,* like notes, provide another vehicle for sharing information briefly with parents. In the case of creative behavior, calling a parent to describe a child's success story sets a positive tone and keeps the lines of communication open.

4. *Parent visits and participation* in the classroom enable them to observe the classroom and their child. When parents do visit or volunteer to help in the classroom, invite them to participate in the children's typical activities. Select activities that require no particular preparation and contribute to the overall flow of the day (Berger, 1991).

Understanding how to communicate with all kinds of families establishes a foundation for building strong school–family interactions. Parents and teachers have a shared responsibility in the education of their children. As teachers, we need to determine how to create comfortable relationships.

Special Populations

Guiding children's creative growth is important for all children, not only those who are gifted. However, there are specific curriculum adaptations that encourage creative problem solving in special populations of children.

Culturally Diverse Groups

Children from different cultural groups need many opportunities to express themselves creatively. Penny Low Deiner (1983) suggests the following adaptations for these children:

1. In a social studies unit on animal families, children can role-play different behaviors of animals, such as conflicts over materials and looking for food. Talk with children about the similarities and differences between animal families and children's families. Children from other cultures can share a variety of family styles.

2. Develop a collection of pictures depicting problem situations (e.g., two children arguing over a toy or a child locked out of the house). Have children generate many solutions to the problems and perhaps role-play some of them. Children from other cultures can discuss why some solutions would be more appropriate in some contexts than in others.

3. Adapt existing games (e.g., Lotto, Bingo, Memory) with words, numbers, or significant pictures representing the cultural backgrounds of the children in your class. Invite children and their families to supply materials to adapt classroom games.

4. Prepare the dramatic play area with props and clothing from different cultures represented in your room. Try to find children's clothing, adults' clothing, jewelry, scarves, and pictures representative of these cultures. Include overnight bags for children to take pretend trips to a variety of places. Get travel folders and posters. Encourage children to decide how to get there, what to take, what to do there, and what language to speak. Children from other cultures will be able to share traditions and special cultural practices. Figure 8.3 suggests additional resources for obtaining information about culturally diverse groups.

Children with Disabilities

1. In a project on the community, have children decide what kinds of buildings they wish to construct with blocks (e.g., firehouse, townhouse, prison, hospital). Define building areas with strips of masking tape. Continue this project over the course of a few days to maximize children's sense of community. *Visually impaired* children can feel their own work area and keep their blocks in a container to make it easier for them to build in a group. *Physically disabled* children can use light or small blocks to build their section of the community or build on a board at a table or wheelchair tray, then move the structure to its location on the floor.

2. Try an art activity of string painting in which children dip yarn of various thicknesses into paint and make designs on paper. *Visually impaired* children can participate in the process and feel the effects when the

FIGURE 8.3   Additional Teaching Resources for Culturally Diverse Groups

The following resources provide free information for classroom teachers.

African American Institute
School Services Division
833 United Nations Plaza
New York, NY 10017

Afro-American Publishing Co.
1727 S. Indiana Avenue
Chicago, IL 60616

Alternatives
1924 East 3rd Street
Bloomington, IN 47401
(provides information about Native Americans)

Asian-American Studies Center
3232 Campbell Hall
University of California
Los Angeles, CA 90024

Hispanic-American Institute
100 East 21st Street
Austin, TX 78705

picture is dry. *Physically disabled* children may find it easier to grip an empty spool with the yarn pulled through it rather than trying to grip the yarn itself.

3. Have children close their eyes as they paint to music to support an ongoing theme (e.g., friends, circus, music from other cultures). This activity will give the entire class practice in interpreting auditory stimuli and a better understanding of visually impaired children's abilities.

High-Achieving and Low-Achieving Children

1. In the same project on the community listed above, high-achieving children can help become city planners who evaluate the community's needs, such as a recycling center or a traveling library, and create possible ways to meet those needs. Low-achieving children can select and build the necessary buildings, make signs for the community areas, make drawings of the types of buildings and equipment needed, or plan a playground.

2. In the unit on animal families, high-achieving children can locate more in-depth information about animals and animal behavior. They can also use imagination and fantasy to create or enact their own interpretations of particular animals. Language-delayed children can participate in role enactment and can produce animal sounds. Children with adjustment problems can discuss problems and feelings in a supportive setting.

3. Have a cooking activity and make two batches of Jell-O, using cold water in one and ice cubes in another to figure out which jells sooner. High-achieving and low-achieving children may chart their predictions about the jelling process and compare their predictions to what actually happened. Have them engage in a group discussion, articulate what they observed, and give reasons why one batch jelled more quickly.

Conclusion

Guiding children's creative growth and working with families are essential aspects of the early childhood curriculum. To provide such guidance, teachers must understand their own creative behavior in order to nurture it in children. As teachers, we must find ways to provide children with opportunities for divergent thinking, investigative activities, self-selected activities, reflective discussions, and probing questions. Perhaps most important, we must develop ways to communicate these values to families.

Chapter Summary

1. There are three fundamental theoretical perspectives that guide children's growth: constructivism, humanism, and behavioral-social learning. Constructivists view children as active agents in their own development. Humanists assume that people are capable of controlling their own lives. Behavioral-social learning theorists view individuals as products of their environment.

2. There are three basic styles of adult–child interactions—autocratic, permissive, and democratic. Each refers to how demanding or responsive teachers are with children. Each also cultivates typical behaviors and approaches to problem solving.

3. Creative teachers view themselves as decision makers, risk takers, and problem solvers. They also expect children to be responsible for their own learning, value their ideas, and guide children's inquiry with materials and ideas.

4. Guiding children's creative growth includes facilitating the development of prosocial, cooperative, and helping behaviors. Democratic teachers use positive guidance techniques that help children become more caring and responsible.

5. Children's conflicts are a natural part of their lives. Most conflicts among toddlers concern possessions; most preschoolers' disputes are over role

playing; and many primary grade children's disagreements with peers are over rules and social interactions.

6. Helping children learn to resolve their own conflicts encourages their cognitive and social development.

7. Three strategies to help children become better thinkers are cooperative problem solving, investigative play, and project work.

8. Communicating with families is fundamental to early childhood programs. Teachers should use both one-way and two-way communication strategies to help families understand the value of play and how children grow creatively.

Discussion Questions

1. Refer to the chapter-opening case study, in which Ms. Manning intervenes in Daniel and Donald's play. Think about the consequences of her actions. Suppose she had said, "Boys, stop that fighting right now!" What difference would that have made in their future ability to negotiate or to express feelings?

2. Imagine that you are responsible for making a presentation on parent's night that explains child guidance or the development of creativity to parents. How would you show parents what these concepts mean and get them to become active participants?

3. Brainstorm different curriculum projects that would be appropriate for collaborative problem solving. Select one project and figure out ways to identify the common goal, find the problem, test hypotheses, and provide feedback.

4. Refer to the chapter-opening quote by Wasserman. After having read and discussed the material in this chapter, discuss your own capacity for risk taking and inventiveness. Give some examples from your own experience. If you wish to cultivate the art of risk taking, what are some of the steps you might take?

5. Using Ms. Hartman's construction project as a model, collaborate with several classmates to sketch out a 2-week project for preschoolers or a 3-week project for primary grade children. How would you communicate with parents about the class project? Which strategies would you select? Why?

——————— Writing to Learn ———————

Encouraging children to figure out answers for themselves is an essential aspect of guiding creative thinking. Recall an incident that happened to you or that you observed in a classroom where children were encouraged to solve a problem. Think about the following: What did the teacher do? How did the children go about solving their problem? Write about what implications this incident has for you as a teacher. Share your writing in small groups, and compare the teacher's behavior to the characteristics of a creative teacher described in this chapter.

--- **Interview** ---

Levels of Concern About Communicating with Families

Early childhood educators have always considered linkages between the home and school to be important, yet many teachers are uncomfortable about communicating with parents. Interview at least two other students during class and articulate concerns about communicating with parents. Ask the following questions and record your responses to share with the group. Brainstorm ways in which you could begin to address these concerns to improve communication with parents.

1. Have you had many opportunities to communicate with parents? Describe them.
2. What concerns you most about communicating with parents? Why do you think this concerns you?
3. Have you ever observed (conducted) a parent–teacher conference? If so, how were children's strengths shared? How were problems or difficult areas handled?
4. Would you feel comfortable explaining your views on creative expression and play to parents in a public meeting? How would you approach such a challenge?
5. Have you ever been concerned about including parents in your program or using them as volunteers? What concerns you?

--- **Observation** ---

Children's Conflicts and Resolutions

A major goal of the early childhood program is to help children learn to get along with other children. When children learn to cooperate, they feel good about themselves, make friends easily, and use different means for getting what they want from other children. No child, however, comes to school each day with all of these skills. Thus, we see a variety of naturally occurring conflicts over possessions, space, roles, and rules.

This assignment will help you identify different kinds of children's conflicts and analyze their resolution.

1. Arrange to observe at least one of the following situations in an early childhood classroom for 20 minutes:
   - ❏ A conflict between a child and another child.
   - ❏ A conflict between a child and a parent.
   - ❏ A conflict between a child and a teacher or aide.
2. Describe the setting and the age of the child. Record the dialogue between the persons.

3. Analyze the conflict. What was it about? How long did it last? What initiated the incident? What happened in the middle? How did it end? What was the role of the adult? What message did the incident and its resolution convey?

Share your observation in class. Synthesize your findings about typical conflicts by age and identify common resolution patterns.

--- **Controversy** ---

Home–School Partnerships: Why Have Them?

As part of the restructuring of public education, the idea of families as partners in their children's education is assuming a central role. Federal, state, and local initiatives (e.g., Head Start, Chapter I, P.L. 99-457) all include families as integral to their children's education (Epstein, 1991). No longer do we view parents' involvement as simply baking cookies, chaperoning a field trip, or making a costume for the class play. Today there are increased efforts to include families as equals in the education of their children (Kagan, 1989). Families and schools together help achieve the larger goals of providing success for all children, educating the whole child, and sharing educational responsibility (Davies, 1991; Epstein, 1986). Early childhood teachers have a long, rich history of working with families, offering a child-centered curriculum, and providing integrated learning—all key components of contemporary school reform.

Not all school professionals support increased home–school collaboration, however. Critics believe that educational goals for children can best be attained when education and families remain separate because "professional status is in jeopardy if parents are involved in activities that are typically the teacher's responsibilities" (Epstein, 1986, p. 227).

These conflicting notions about the appropriate role of parents in children's education have often separated early childhood education from elementary education (Kagan, 1989). Whatever their grade level assignment, teachers who believe in collaboration between the home and school find a variety of ways to communicate with families, respect parents' knowledge of their own children, and celebrate the different strengths each brings to the education of children. Teachers who do not fundamentally believe in such partnerships place the blame on parents and continue to perpetuate myths about uninterested, stressed, and isolated families who express no interest in their children's education. Why is there such a difference? Think about these questions:

❏ What evidence can you cite that supports or rejects the notion of home–school partnerships?
❏ How could a teacher's attitudes about families be subtly communicated, even though the teacher is using a recommended parent involvement strategy (e.g., newsletter, conferences, notes).

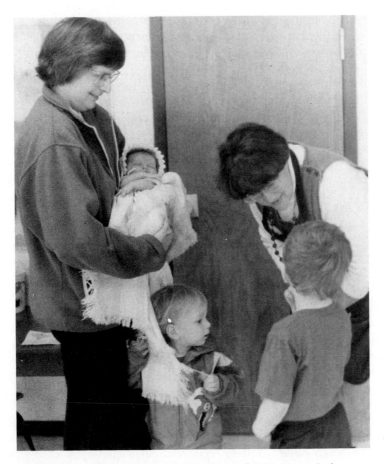

Families and schools together help achieve the larger goal of providing success for all children.

❑ What can teachers do in their own classrooms to improve collaboration between the home and the school?

❑ How would you develop a group plan for involving families more fully in their children's education?

————————— **Research Highlight** —————————

Continuity and Discontinuity Between Home and Early Childhood Environments

Summary of Research

Silvern (1988) argues that the home and school environments for the very young child ought to be similar. A high-quality home environment includes warmth and support, rich language interactions between adult and child, a variety of experiences and activities, nurturance and affection, opportunities to express feelings, and noninterference in learning (Carew, 1980; Holdaway, 1979; Rutter, 1985).

Children come to school with expectations about the informal use of space, time, and language. Family space is usually warm, secure, and comfortable, with clearly defined places for personal belongings. Conversely, school space is often "cool, distant, individual, insecure and supportless" (Silvern, 1988, p. 151). Family time is generally loosely organized, without time limits on activities while school time is divided into rigid blocks. Family language is based upon common experiences, meanings, and understandings, while school language is formal and often provides little basis for common or shared meanings (Silvern, 1988).

These discontinuities between school and home are often disconcerting to children. For schools and homes to achieve more continuity, they must be responsive to the basic needs of young children and provide a more home-like use of space, time, and language (Bredekamp, 1987).

Implications for Practice

Planned early childhood programs should reflect children's developing abilities and incorporate what children already know and can do. Classroom teachers must be aware of how their students use space, time, and language in order to reduce the discontinuities between home and school. Some children may need more time to finish one activity, for example, before beginning another. Teachers should alert children to transitions and help them to manage time.

Too often, parent education programs demand that parents adopt school-like methods and behaviors. Teachers give parents prepackaged lessons and materials to teach skills to their children. Such materials disregard family meanings and expect families to conform to school practices outside the school setting. Early childhood teachers at all levels must make their space, time, and language more home-like. This could mean that schools might contain smaller and more comfortable rooms, with different kinds of space (e.g., carpeted, tiled) for different activities, more flexible time periods, and more meaningful uses of language that are rooted in children's experiences. To reduce home–school discontinuity, teachers should consider sharing in intimate settings, valuing creative and unique responses of individual children, and inviting children's exploration and experimentation with ideas and materials. These strategies reduce cultural barriers to learning because children demonstrate what they *can* do rather than being forced to demonstrate what they cannot do.

Teachers must also explore new ways of communicating with parents. They need to identify what children do at home, incorporate familiar patterns into the school curriculum, and share with parents the strengths and talents of the child at school. When parents and teachers work together, they can clearly produce significant gains for children (Bronfenbrenner, 1986).

References

Asher, S. R., & Hymel, S. (1981). Children's social competence in peer relations: Sociometric and behaviorial assessment. In J. D. Wine & M. D. Smye (Eds.), *Social competence* (pp. 125–157). New York: Guilford.

Atkinson, A. H., & Green, V. P. (1990). Cooperative learning: The teacher's role. *Childhood Education, 67*(1), 8–11.

Baumrind, D. (1967). Child care practices anteceding three patterns of preschool behavior. *Genetic Psychology Monographs, 75,* 43–88.

Bredekamp, S. (Ed.). (1987). *Developmentally appropriate practice in early childhood programs serving children from birth through age 8.* Washington, DC: National Association for the Education of Young Children.

Bronfenbrenner, U. (1986). Ecology of the family as a context for human development: Research perspectives. *Developmental Psychology, 22,* 723–742.

Carew, J. V. (1980). Experience and the development of intelligence in young children at home and in day care. *Monographs of the Society for Research in Child Development, 45* 6–7. (Serial 187).

Corsaro, W. A. (1985). *Friendship and peer culture in the early years.* Norwood, NJ: Ablen.

Davies, D. (1991). Schools reaching out: Family, school, and community partnerships for student success. *Phi Delta Kappan, 72*(5), 376–382.

Deiner, P. L. (1983). *Resources for teaching young children with special needs.* New York: Harcourt Brace Jovanovich.

Eisenberg-Berg, N., Haake, R. J., & Bartlett, K. (1981). The effects of possession and ownership on the sharing and proprietary behaviors of preschool children. *Merrill-Palmer Quarterly, 27,* 61–68.

Epstein, J. L. (1986). Parents' reactions to teacher practices of parent involvement. *The Elementary School Journal, 86,* 227–293.

Epstein, J. L. (1991). Paths to partnerships: What we can learn from federal, state, district and school initiatives. *Phi Delta Kappan, 72*(5), 345–349.

Feeney, S., Christensen, D., & Moravcik, E. (1991). *Who am I in the lives of children?* (4th ed.). New York: Macmillan.

Feynman, R. (1985). *Surely you're joking, Mr. Feynman.* New York: W. W. Norton.

Freire, P. (1983). *Pedagogy of the oppressed.* New York: Continuum.

Greenberg, P. (1989). Parents as parents in young children's development and education: A new American fad? Why does it matter? *Young Children, 44*(4), 61–75.

Hay, D. F. (1984). Social conflict in early childhood. In G. J. Whitehurst (Ed.), *Annals of child development* (Vol. 1, pp. 1–44). Greenwich, CT: JAI.

Hildebrand, V. (1990). *Guiding young children* (4th ed.). New York: Macmillan.

Holdaway, D. (1979). *The foundations of literacy.* Portsmouth, NH: Heinemann.

Isenberg, J. P., & Raines, S. C. (In press). Peer conflict and conflict resolution among preschool children. In J. Gitler & L. Bowen (Eds.), *Annual review of conflict knowledge and conflict resolution: Volume 3,* New York: Garland.

Johnson, D. W., & Johnson, R. T. (1989). *Cooperation and competition: Theory and research.* Edina, MN: Interaction.

Kagan, S. L. (1989). Early care and education: Beyond the schoolhouse doors. *Phi Delta Kappan, 71*(2), 107–112.

Katz, L. G., & Chard, S. C. (1989). *Engaging children's minds: The project approach.* Norwood, NJ: Ablex.

King, M. (1971). The development of modes of some intention concepts in young children. *Child Development, 42*, 1145–1152.

Kostelnik, M. J., Stein, L. C., Whirren, A. P., & Soderman, A. K. (1988). *Guiding children's social development.* Cincinnati: South-Western Publishing Co.

Krogh, S. (1990). *The integrated early childhood curriculum.* New York: McGraw-Hill.

Kuschner, D. (1989). Put your name on your painting, but . . . the blocks go back on the shelves. *Young Children, 45*(1), 49–56.

MacDonald, R. E. (1991). *A handbook of basic skills and strategies for beginning teachers: Facing the challenges of teaching in today's schools.* New York: Longman.

Marion, M. (1991). *Guidance of young children.* Columbus, OH: Macmillan.

Miller, D. F. (1990). *Positive child guidance.* Albany, NY: Delmar.

Papalia, D. E., & Olds, S. W. (1990). *A child's world: Infancy through adolescence* (5th ed.). New York: McGraw-Hill.

Piaget, J. (1952). *The origins of intelligence in children.* New York: International Universities Press.

Rogers, C. (1961). *On becoming a person.* Boston: Houghton-Mifflin.

Rutter, M. (1985). Family and school influences on cognitive development. *Journal of Child Psychology and Psychiatry, 26*, 683–704.

Silvern, S. B. (1988). Continuity/discontinuity between home and early childhood environments. *The Elementary School Journal, 89*(2), 147–159.

Tudge, J., & Caruso, D. (1988). Cooperative problem-solving in the classroom. Enhancing young children's cognitive development. *Young Children, 44*(1), 46–57.

Wasserman, S. (1990). *Serious players in the primary classroom.* New York: Teachers College Press.

Webster, T. (1990). Projects in curriculum: Under what conditions? *Childhood Education, 67*(1), 2–3.

Assessing Creative Expression and Play

We have provided elementary education for virtually all American children for some time now, and we fret more than many societies do about meeting the diverse needs of these young people. We test them and assess them—even kindergartners are given an array of readiness measures—in order to determine what they know and don't know, can and can't do. The supreme irony, though, is that the very means we use to determine those needs—and the various remedial procedures that derive from them—can wreak profound harm on our children, usually, but by no means only, those who are already behind the economic eight ball.

Mike Rose, 1989, p. 127

After reading this chapter, you will be able to

- ☐ Define assessment and explain how it differs from testing.
- ☐ List and explain the criteria for and purposes of assessment.
- ☐ Compare and contrast developmentally appropriate and inappropriate assessment strategies.
- ☐ List and explain alternatives to standardized paper-and-pencil tests.
- ☐ Examine the early childhood teacher's roles and responsibilities in developing a comprehensive assessment program.

❏   Apply principles of developmentally appropriate assessment to the use of interviews, conferences, portfolios, checklists, and rating scales.

❏   Understand the importance of alternative assessment strategies, particularly for special populations.

❏   Describe and apply self-evaluation strategies for teachers and children.

Case Study

Picture this scenario. A group of teachers and an administrator are meeting with a group of early childhood faculty members. Next year, their district will initiate a program for 4-year-olds, and this committee is responsible for planning the curriculum. The current circumstances of their community have affected the decision to provide a prekindergarten program. The community is, by anyone's definition, in an economically depressed area, and many of the companies that were once major employers have moved on or filed for bankruptcy. Nearly 80% of the 4-year-olds qualify for free lunches, an indication that the overwhelming majority of families residing in the district are below the poverty line. These educators are determined to help the families by helping their children. They believe that starting earlier is important. Now they have questions: What should a curriculum for 4-year-olds include? How will we know if we are succeeding? How will we document the effectiveness of our program to ensure that our funding continues? The university faculty in the group talk about the need for active learning; they share videotapes and slides of high-quality programs for 4-year-olds in action; they invite discussion; and they urge the district personnel to think in terms of the 4-year-olds they know, rather than in terms of existing school practices. At the end of their day together, an administrator (whose background is in secondary education) sums it up this way: "It looks like a high-quality program for the very young has to be play-oriented rather than subject matter-oriented." It is a great moment because the group has arrived at a common philosophy, a shared vision that should enable them to provide the best possible learning experiences for young children. But the assessment question, the need to document program effectiveness, is a difficult one. If the group had decided upon an "academic" program, their task would be much easier because they could measure children's knowledge of low-level skills such as identifying colors, shapes, letters, and numbers. Designing a play-oriented curriculum is more challenging. Teachers in this program will need to

❏   Conceptualize evaluation as an ongoing process rather than an annual, group-administered, paper-and-pencil test;

❏   Rely more upon teachers' informal assessment and less upon standardized tests;

❏   Look at long-term successes, at how these children perform in kindergarten, first grade, or even high school; and

❏   Grapple with self-evaluation by teachers and children, a frequently overlooked aspect of assessment.

Theoretical Framework

Defining Assessment

As this case study suggests, assessment involves much more than testing. Assessment is the "continual process of observing and recording and otherwise documenting the work that children do and how they do it, as a basis for a variety of educational decisions that affect the child" (Bredekamp, 1991, p. 21). The outcome of assessment is to optimize children's learning and to improve classroom practice (Teale, 1988). In an authentic assessment:

- ❏ The tasks performed by children are relevant and interesting;
- ❏ Both the products and the processes used to achieve them are evaluated; and
- ❏ Attitudes as well as outcomes are considered.

Tests are only one form of assessment. Perrone (1991) says that we should ask the following questions about tests: "Are the questions clear? Do they address the particular educational concerns of teachers, of young children, of parents? Do the tests as a whole provide useful information about individual children? About a class? Do they help children in their learning? Do they support children's intentions as learners? Do they provide *essential* information to parents?" (p. 133). Figure 9.1 compares and contrasts appropriate and inappropriate assessment practices.

Purposes for Assessment of Divergent and Lateral Thinking

There are at least four reasons for assessing divergent and lateral thinking (Dacey, 1989; Jalongo, 1992):

1. *Insight.* One goal of assessing creative expression and play is to study it across the life span to understand better how these abilities develop. Biographies and case studies of exceptionally creative individuals, such as Howard Gardner's (1983) investigations into different forms of human intelligence, are good examples of assessment used to gain insights about creative potential in human beings.

2. *Program evaluation.* A second major purpose of assessment is to determine the impact of an educational program on young children's growth in creative expression and play. Consider, for instance, the teacher who creates individual folders that contain representative samples of each child's drawings and writing throughout the academic year. By combining her own insights about the child's progress with the samples, this teacher is both assessing the child's divergent thinking and making judgments about the success of the program.

3. *To identify talents, provide enrichment, and develop potential through special programs.* Consider how an observant teacher could assess children's musical talent and potential, interest and motivation. A good teacher

Authentic assessment examines development in all areas: physical, social, emotional, and cognitive.

would notice children's responses to and interests in music—such as the child who dances spontaneously to a lively tune, invents a lullaby while rocking a baby doll, or inquires about a classical piece being played at the start of the school day. Authentic assessment always expands, rather than limits, children's options. It recognizes and further develops extraordinary talents, yet gives every child opportunities to participate and succeed.

4. *Intervention.* Sometimes, assessments of children's play or creative expression suggest that the teacher ought to intervene. Studies of the play behaviors of at-risk children are a good example. Smilansky (1968) and

FIGURE 9.1   Appropriate and Inappropriate Assessment

Appropriate Assessment	Inappropriate Assessment
Recognizes the planning of instruction as the main goal	Sees accountability as the main goal
Is an ongoing process that is integrated with the curriculum	Is a scheduled event that focuses on a brief episode of behavior
Benefits the child and expands every child's potential	Is used to justify preferential treatment for a chosen few
Assesses real-world abilities in naturalistic settings (e.g., writing, problem solving)	Measures isolated skills under artificial conditions
Respects the teacher as the assessor	Trusts only outside agencies
Recognizes that children need to develop at individual rates	Emphasizes normative behavior; measures skills by age and grade
Stresses success and understanding of errors	Stresses failures, grades, scores, and mistakes
Involves a concrete, hands-on approach	Is restricted to paper-and-pencil tasks
Focuses on the whole child	Treats the child like a disembodied intellect
Supports the curriculum	Drives the curriculum
Is process-oriented and values divergent thinking	Is product-oriented and values convergent thinking

Source: Adapted from J. Isenberg & M. Farley, (1990). Readiness assessment program review committee. Richmond, VA: Virginia Department of Education.

Smilansky and Shefatya (1990) found that the play of at-risk children was less elaborate and social than that of their peers and coached the children to achieve more sophisticated levels of play.

By studying lateral and divergent behavior, we can intervene to remediate or enrich, identify strengths, recommend new and challenging activities, and learn more about developing creative potential.

Difficulties with Assessment

Whenever we speak of educational assessment, there is a tendency to value hard data and to scorn soft data. But as Wasserman (1989) points out, numbers themselves do not have meaning. It takes human intelligence to make sense out of numbers. Even when we *do* measure and interpret a number, it informs us to a limited extent. We can obtain a verbal score on an achievement test, for example, but it will not tell us if the child can create and illustrate an original story. Generally speaking, our measurement tools fall short when we try to describe complex processes. There is an old adage among psychometricians: You get what you measure. Nielsen (1990) takes the adage one step further: "Simple outcomes, simple tests, simpletons" (p. 18).

Self-expressive behaviors such as imagination, creativity, fantasy, and play are particularly difficult to measure with tests for the following reasons:

1. *These behaviors are hard to define.* Nathan is a first grader whose teacher is presenting a lesson on units of measure. He tells the children to look at several objects to be measured on a workbook page and asks, "What are some different ways that we could tell someone how long the line is without using a ruler?" Children make a variety of suggestions, such as using paper clips, erasers, or finger widths. Then the teacher calls on Nathan, who says, "You could ask an ant to walk across the line and tell you how many steps he took." One teacher might say that Nathan's response is creative; another might say that it is flippant. Because imagination, creativity, fantasy, and play are difficult to define and assess, they are often misinterpreted and discouraged.

2. *They do not lend themselves to standardized tests.* Usually assessment tools are product measures that focus on discrete academic skills. Even those tests that are designed to assess creativity sometimes rely rather heavily on a single creative behavior (such as artistic ability) or tend to assess problem solving under very restrictive conditions. Suppose that a researcher is studying block play, provides the child with a small set of blocks, and then observes the child's block play during a short time period. He may conclude that there is little originality. But the child may be accustomed to incorporating other toys in play; may work well with other children in creating large structures; or may be extraordinarily imaginative at home. Because the task was so restrictive, it could not begin to tap the full range of the child's play processes.

3. *They require real-life contexts to be valid.* A high score on a paper-and-pencil test of creativity does not provide authentic, real-world indicators of the child's creative expression, such as the ability to use modeling clay creatively, design an interesting collage, or construct an imaginative diorama based on a favorite story. Contrived situations do not supply the contexts for creative thinking.

In order to overcome these limitations in assessing creative expression and play, we must avoid the mistake of trying to understand the entire melody by studying a few individual notes (Adler, 1957). In other words, we need real-world data collected over an extended period of time in different contexts.

Criteria for Assessment

Appraisals of children's work usually rely on one or more of six criteria (Potter, 1985). The two criteria that we use most often are the ones that are the least applicable to creative expression and play: speed and correctness. *Speed* should be used only when time is essential. Usually speed is important with simple tasks and procedures, such as getting materials assembled and putting them away after drawing. *Correctness* is important when there is one right answer. Suppose that a child is painting and asks for the color green, and the teacher says, "You have red, yellow, and blue. How could you mix them to get green?" If the child says, "Mix the blue and yellow together," the response will be correct.

The four remaining criteria that are more applicable to creative expression and play are as follows:

1. *Practical workability.* A teacher who is presenting a unit on simple machines might challenge the children to use recycled materials or construction toys to demonstrate one simple machine in action. The teacher's judgment of the children's work will be based on whether or not the machine the children create really works.

2. *Aesthetic appeal.* As part of a unit on Japan, some third graders are designing dragon kites. The quality of their kite designs, to a considerable extent, will be based on their beauty, that is, their aesthetic appeal.

3. *Creativity.* In order for something to be creative, it must be both original and effective. If a teacher is observing children who are moving to music, each in a unique way, creativity is the major criterion for assessment.

4. *Model of a product or process.* Teachers sometimes evaluate children's work in terms of how well it emulates a model. A good example is the peer editing process used in writing. If the teacher sees that children are using what they have learned about editing and are providing constructive feedback to peers, then the teacher will infer that they are mastering an important aspect of the writing process.

Figure 9.2 is an overview of assessment outcomes that take these criteria into consideration.

FIGURE 9.2   Appropriate Outcomes for Assessment

Assessment should
1. Be accurate, appropriate, useful, and feasible.
2. Improve communication between families and schools by providing a better understanding of the child's progress, the school's program, the instructional activities, and teaching/learning styles (Gelfer & Perkins, 1987).
3. Involve real-world tasks that have authentic implications outside of schools or testing programs.
4. Give children the opportunity to reflect upon their own work and gain insights about their progress (Gelfer, 1991).
5. Focus on progress, products, and effort (Collins, 1991).

Assessing Creative Processes

Ms. Mastalzo, a second-grade teacher, is using a "Treasure Hunt" activity (Sigel & Cocking, 1977). She begins with groups of four to six children. The first two or three children hide an object on the playground and create a "map picture" that the other group members must interpret in order to locate the treasure. The map makers are encouraged to take the searchers' perspective into account as they create their map. Note that both the map makers and the searchers are observing, gathering, and organizing data as they scrutinize the playground.

Imagine how children are using their prior knowledge to construct and read the treasure map. Perhaps they recall that "X marks the spot," that directional arrows are used, or that symbols to represent landmarks are necessary. Maybe they have watched as their parents consult a map on a car trip or use an illuminated map in a shopping mall. Imagine the excitement of both groups as they recap where they are, decide what they need to do next, and discuss their assumptions and hypotheses. Finally, it is obvious that children must create mental images; the map makers move from reality to symbolic representations of reality, while the searchers do just the reverse—move from symbols to reality. Children would no doubt want to take turns as members of both the map maker and searcher teams, thus giving them experience in both kinds of creative thinking.

As teachers observe children during the Treasure Hunt activity, they can assess the creative thought process in action. Creative problem-solving tasks like the Treasure Hunt involve children in goal-directed, purposeful, extended lines of thought during which students

☐ Identify the task or problem type.
☐ Define and clarify essential elements and terms.
☐ Judge and connect relevant information.
☐ Evaluate the adequacy of information and procedures for drawing conclusions and/or solving problems.
☐ Develop self-monitoring problem-solving strategies.
☐ Examine assumptions, reach new conclusions, and take new action (Harste, 1989; Quellmalz, 1985).

Even though a simulation like the Treasure Hunt may seem rather humble in comparison to the results of a standardized test, it actually provides more information about how children analyze, apply, synthesize, and evaluate (Bloom, 1964). Figure 9.3 suggests 10 alternatives to standardized tests.

Assessing Creative Products

In 1988, the National Association of State Boards of Education (1988) conducted a study of early childhood education in which they concluded that the current curriculum was "shockingly understimulating" to young children. There is considerable evidence, in fact, that we have confused educational means with ed-

FIGURE 9.3   Ten Alternatives to Standardized Tests

1. Charts of behavior
2. Self-selected work samples
3. Displays of children's projects
4. Performances
5. Interviews
6. Conferences with parents
7. Audio tapes or videotapes
8. Portfolios of children's work
9. Anecdotal records
10. Developmental profiles

ucational ends. Schools that teach to the test by focusing on fragments of knowledge will produce students who are good at memorizing and poor at problem solving.

If we analyze high-quality, creative samples of children's work, we notice four essential features:

1. Children were trusted to make choices.
2. Children's feelings were accepted.
3. Children were challenged to grow.
4. Children were urged to break stereotypes (Hoffman and Lamme, 1988, pp. 22–28).

It is easy to detect these differences if we look at two primary classrooms where children are writing friendly letters. In Room 203, every child copied a letter that the teacher printed on the chalkboard. The letters are posted on the bulletin board and never mailed. In Room 204, children used whatever writing skills they had acquired—squiggles, letter-like shapes, invented spelling, or conventional spelling—to write and illustrate real cards and letters to Julie, a classmate who was injured in an auto accident and is now recuperating at home. Instead of using the letters as classroom decorations, the students have mailed them to Julie, who is enjoying the correspondence and is busily responding to each one. Contrary to popular opinion, the products of imagination are not only unusual, they are also effective (Barrow, 1988). In the first classroom, they were neither; in the second classroom, they were both.

Appropriate Assessment of Children's Creative Expression and Play

Three basic types of assessment (Goodman, 1989) are suited for the study of complex processes like creativity, imagination, play, and the arts:

1. *Observation* examines what students do as the teacher remains on the sidelines. Observation includes the informal impressions teachers form while watching children engaged in an activity like playing in the house-keeping area. Video or audio recordings of observations and subsequent analysis using a coding device might also be used.

2. *Interaction* examines the ways in which a teacher responds to and with students in order to determine the students' current level of performance and to pose new challenges at the right level of difficulty. Interaction includes the teacher's daily, face-to-face encounters with students, as well as more structured and planned types of activities, like conducting a conference or interview with the child and recording the results.

3. *Process/product analysis* refers to gathering information and gaining insights about students from that information. The teacher might collect

By listening to a child read her story aloud, this teacher is observing, interacting, and analyzing both the product and the process.

samples of students' work at various stages, arrange them to highlight growth, and analyze them to make instructional decisions. These approaches to evaluation—observation, interaction, and analysis—may be incidental or planned, use teacher-developed materials or commercially available materials, and use different methods of recording (written, oral, or mechanically recorded).

Observing Children's Creative Expression and Play

As Wasserman (1989) points out, "One of the most valuable yet rarely acknowledged assessment tools in educational practice is the sustained, thoughtful day-to-day observation of student behavior by a competent, professional teacher" (p. 368).

Appropriate observations of young children share the following characteristics:

- ❑ They use direct observational data and rely on those data for interpretations. High-inference, value-laden terminology is avoided.
- ❑ They accurately record the observable behavior of the child, both verbal and nonverbal.
- ❑ They describe the context—the time, setting, circumstances, and behaviors of other children or adults related to the episode.
- ❑ They are used by teachers to plan a developmentally appropriate program (Jalongo, 1992).

Types of Observation

Several types of observation and examples of how teachers used each type are described below.

Anecdotal Records

Anecdotes are brief episodes of student behavior selected to highlight student growth and to provide evidence of progress toward programmatic goals. Mr. Longwood, a first-grade teacher, keeps a file box of 5 × 7 inch cards on his desk. He uses this system to take brief notes on each child's progress and shares these milestones with parents during parent–teacher conferences. Figure 9.4 is an example of an anecdotal record he maintained on a child in his class.

As part of her unit on health and safety, Ms. Karyn takes her kindergarten class to visit the local hospital and creates a sociodramatic play center with a medical theme. She devotes 10 minutes each day to observing the children at play in the center, audiotapes the conversations in the center, and transcribes anecdotes or pieces of dialogue that illustrate what the children are learning. She also evaluates her own ability to extend and enrich the children's play by intro-

FIGURE 9.4 Example of an Anecdotal Record

Observation

Child's Name *Mo*   Date *10/17/93*

Activity *Grouptime*   Time *9–9:30*

Mo and his family are recent Indochinese immigrants with limited English proficiency. After several weeks of onlooker behavior, Mo participated in circletime for the 1st time. He had mastered all of the motions and lyrics to an action song and sang out enthusiastically. Mo's peers seemed to know that this was a breakthrough for him and several made encouraging remarks ("Mo knows this one now!"; "You're a good singer."). Mo beamed with pride as I invited him to lead the group in another verse of the song.

L. M. J.
Observer

---

ducing new themes, materials, and concepts. Appendix D contains some of the play texts that she collected and her interpretations of them.

Checklists or Rating Scales

Checklists may be used to identify play skills. Teachers may choose to study children's self-expression and levels of play, current play interests, patterns of play, preferred materials, or interpersonal skills (e.g., entering an ongoing play episode, negotiating for materials).

Mr. Damion works in a Head Start classroom. One of his goals is to stimulate children's imagination and to document the progress that they make in imaginative play. To do this, he used the observational scale adapted from Beaty (1986) and Garvey (1977) in Figure 9.5.

Interviews with Children

As part of her kindergarten writing program, Ms. Veder interviews children about their writing. She asks Caleb the first question on the interview, "Tell me about your writing." Figure 9.6 is Caleb's writing sample and his response to it. Figure 9.7 is a sample interview about the visual arts that can be adapted for other self-expressive activities.

FIGURE 9.5 Imaginative Play Checklist

ROLES
Pretends by replaying familiar routines
Seeks particular props to enact pretend play roles
Assigns roles or takes assigned roles
Takes on characteristics and actions related to role
Explores different roles, including:

- ❏ *Relational roles*—based on knowledge of family (e.g., parent–child)
- ❏ *Functional roles*—based on wider experience and defined by actions (e.g., "I want to be the cash register")
- ❏ *Character roles*—stereotypes or fictional roles based on TV characters and stories
- ❏ *Peripheral roles*—based on individual child's imagination (e.g., referring to an imaginary companion)

THEMES
Uses language to create and sustain event-structured play themes
Uses exciting, danger-packed themes
Uses elaborate and creative themes, subordinates own actions to the goals of the group
Experiments with fantasy themes, including:

- ❏ Averting threat and rescuing others
- ❏ Communicating (telephoning, letter writing)
- ❏ Packing/taking a trip
- ❏ Shopping
- ❏ Cooking
- ❏ Dining out/entertainment
- ❏ Treating/healing
- ❏ Building/repairing

Source: Adapted from Beaty, J. J. (1986). *Observing the development of the young child.* Columbus, OH: Merrill/Macmillan; and Garvey, K. (1977). *Play.* London: Fontana/Open Books.

FIGURE 9.6 Caleb's Writing

Caleb: This says *cat* and *dog* and that's a big *G* and one hundred and one. That's just my name and . . . yeah, my name, Caleb. And one hundred and ten and . . . uh . . . nine and six. And this is a five and a four and a fancy four and a thirteen. See? I made this pretend word and then I can find words in it. I have to underline the letters so I don't forget. . . . Watch this! D-o-d—that spells *dad!* And m-o-m spells mom. *Wait.* Oh, wait. D-*a*-d spells *dad!* Here's a *u* and an *o.* Wait, here's a fancy *u* and this is a fancy *o.* Watch! This is a little *t* and this here is a littler *t,* and now they're connected together!

(a)

(b)

FIGURE 9.7   The Visual Arts: A Process Interview

1. Why do people (paint, draw, sculpt, weave, etc.) pictures?
2. How do you get ready to make a picture?
3. How do you decide what to make?
4. Do you ever do artwork at home? (If yes) How is art at home different from the art you do at school?
5. If you had to explain to a little child how a person makes a picture, what would you tell him or her to do?
6. Show me or tell me about your best art project. Why do you think this is your best work?

Audio or Video Recordings

Mechanical means of observing become the teacher's eyes and ears while engaging in classroom activities. Ms. Maloney, a student teacher, set up a "pet store" in conjunction with a unit on economics. Through the use of videotape, she was able to analyze how divergent her questions and responses were with a second-grade girl who invited her into the play theme.

Lori: This is my pet store. May I help you today, miss? Are you looking for anything in particular?

Teacher: Yes, I would like to buy my nephew an unusual gift. He is going to be 10 years old on Monday.

Lori: Well, isn't that just special! I hope that he is a nice boy. What kinds of animals does he like?

Teacher: He likes dinosaurs and wild animals.

Lori: Well, we are out of dinosaurs. I just sold the last one yesterday, and I did not order any more. The animals are just too large for my store. We do have some parakeets, parrots, and fish.

Teacher: I'll take this parrot. He is just beautiful. Can he be taught to talk? I heard that some of them can learn to talk; is that true?

Lori: First of all, before you get too confused, this is a she. This particular type of bird can be taught to talk, but it takes a lot of time.

Teacher: What else do I need?

Lori: You'll need a cage, food, and some items for the bird to play with.

Teacher: Well, how much do I owe you for the bird, cage, food, and two toys?

Lori: The total price is $125.33.

Teacher: Do you take MasterCard?

Lori: Yes.

Individual Case Studies

Ms. Fisher is a reading specialist whose work with Jerri, a second grader, led to a case study of an individual child. By talking with the student and her family, the teacher discovered that although Jerri's parents wanted her to learn to read, they had never read to her and there were no children's books in the home. Intellectually, Jerri was capable of reading; she simply saw no reason to read, other than to please adults. Instead of focusing on the skills of reading, Ms. Fisher decided that she would give Jerri a reason to read: enjoyment. Jerri listened to and read books every day with her teacher's help, and after they discussed what they had read, the teacher kept a record of Jerri's reactions. A major breakthrough came when Ms. Fisher suggested that Jerri might like to create her own book. One of Jerri's favorites was the lift-the-flap picture book of the song *Roll Over!* by Mordecai Gerstein (1984). The edges of the pages are folded over, and by lifting them up, you can see who fell out of bed with each verse of the song. At first, Jerri used the same characters that were in the book, but as she continued to work on the project, her book became more and more original, with other animals and characters populating the pages. When Jerri had revised her book into final form, she presented it to the class, giggling throughout at her own pleasure in the book's humor. When she was finished, the children burst into spontaneous applause and rushed up to congratulate her on her achievement.

Note how this activity meets the criteria mentioned earlier for assessing creative products. Ms. Fisher *trusted* Jerri to undertake a major project and *accepted* her work. Reading together *challenged* Jerri to grow, and as she gained confidence in herself, she *broke away from stereotypic thinking* so that her work was more than a copy.

Published Scales

Play and creative expression can also be evaluated through more structured methods, such as published scales. These scales provide information on children's levels of sociodramatic play (Smilansky & Shefatya, 1990), on cognitive and social dimensions of play (Howes, 1980; Johnson, Christie, & Yawkey, 1987), on language abilities during symbolic play (Westby, 1980), or on the use of creative processes (Kulp & Tarter, 1986). Figure 9.8 lists the scales and describes their purpose and focus.

Portfolio Assessment

A technique for assembling all the different types of observations that teachers use is the portfolio. Portfolios have been used in the arts for decades. When artists apply for a job, they assemble a collection of works to demonstrate the range and depth of their expertise and submit it for review. Much the same strategy is used when compiling different types of observation of children's

FIGURE 9.8   Play Observation Scales

Scale	Focus
Parten/Piaget[*]	Examines both the cognitive and social levels of children's play and codes them into one of 12 different categories.
Howes' Peer Play Scale[†]	Uses a recording sheet to focus on two dimensions of peer play: complexity of social interaction and degree of organization and integration. Categorizes play activities into five different levels.
Smilansky's Sociodramatic Play Inventory[‡]	Analyzes group dramatic play in terms of role playing, make-believe transformations, social interaction, verbal communication, and persistence.
Westby's Symbolic Play Scale[δ]	Uses a checklist to analyze simultaneously language development and symbolic play behaviors in children aged 9 months to 3 years.

Sources: [*]Johnson et al. (1987).
[†]Howes (1980).
[‡]Smilansky (1968).
[δ]Westby (1980).

creative expression and play. Some common questions about portfolios are as follows:

1. *Why use portfolios?* Portfolios reveal and document children's learning in many different modes, on real-world tasks, over a period of time. This method of assessment gives teachers more input into assessment, is immediately understandable to parents, and encourages self-evaluation in students. The evidence collected in a portfolio also helps teachers to make instructional decisions.

2. *What is included in a portfolio?* Children's portfolios should not be cartons filled with every item ever produced by the child during the year. Rather, they should be focused and organized by learning goals. If a teacher has the language arts goal that children will read and respond to a variety of picture books, for instance, the file might contain a log of the books read by the child and stories or artwork inspired by children's books.

3. *How should it be organized?* An expandable file with accordion-folded sides makes a good portfolio. Individual folders that are keyed or color-coded to program goals can be placed inside to organize the child's

work. If exploring different art media is a program goal, for example, one of the folders might contain a sample of paintings, chalk drawings, batik, and a photograph of sculptures in clay, wood, and paper. To demonstrate the child's attainment of another art program goal, the refinement of a form, a folder might contain sketches of the work at successive stages and the finished product. Figure 9.9 presents examples of artwork from the portfolios of Shayna, Joshua, Brenda, Joey, Joanna, and Alicia.

Additionally, every portfolio should include a table of contents so that teachers, administrators, parents, and children can use it. The teacher should develop the table of contents with input from the child, then give the child responsibility for maintaining the portfolio and keeping it organized around the table of contents.

FIGURE 9.9   Format for a Portfolio of Children's Art

Table of Contents
Philosophy Statement

❏   Formulate a brief statement about the benefits of the program for the child's overall development

General Program Goals

❏   List criteria from the district's curriculum guide, professional organizations, and/or the professional literature

Child Profile
1. Include the child's photograph and/or self-portrait.
2. Include the child's dictated or written responses to items such as these:

❏   What I can do now in art that I couldn't do before
❏   What I want to learn how to do
❏   Here is my best piece of art

Specific Goals for the Visual Arts
Goal 1: Uses a variety of media
Goal 2: Refines a form
Goal 3: Uses art to respond to literature and as a stimulus for writing
Goal 4: Gains greater control over artistic media
Goal 5: Breaks stereotypes

In order to facilitate the child's participation in managing the portfolio, each goal is keyed to a color-coded folder with a label that the child can understand.

Examples of the contents of children's portfolios follow.

Folder 1 (blue): Doing New Things, Using New Materials
Shayna is a 5-year-old who is enrolled in a private school in a large suburban area. For her blue folder, she selected (1) white chalk on black paper, (2) using markers on newsprint, and (3) using crayons and glitter glue.

Folder 2 (yellow):   Trying Again
Joshua is a 5-year-old in a rural full-day kindergarten program. As evidence of his efforts to refine a form, he has included three examples of his house drawing efforts.

Folder 3 (green):   Books, Stories, and Letters
Brenda (age 6) is enrolled in first grade in a parochial
school. For her folder, she selected (1) an illustrated
reading list, (2) a drawing inspired by *There's an
Alligator Under My Bed* and (3) a letter and picture for
her sister Nicole, who is away at college.

Dear Nicole, I miss you. I like you and Holly does too.
I am learning how to read. Do you miss me?

Folder 4 (brown):   Getting Better All the Time
Joey (age 7) has been enrolled in the
same nursery school/afterschool care
program for 3 years. He has included
an example of his human figure
drawings done at the ages of 4 and 5,
as well as a current example.

Folder 5 (red):   Extra Special and Make-Believe
Joanna, age 7, is in first grade. She wanted to create
"a puppet of a beautiful princess in a dress." First,
she searched for a piece of fabric for the dress; next,
she figured out how to make a paper bag puppet
with a mouth that moved, finally, she added the
features of the princess she envisioned. Alicia, one
of her classmates, imagined "a unicorn standing on a
rainbow" and included it in her folder.

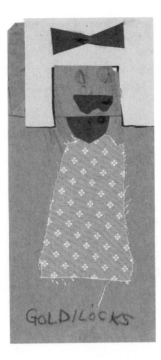

Teachers' Roles and Responsibilities

Perhaps the most important role of the teacher in child-centered assessment is to view children as informants about their own growth and as partners in the assessment process.

Matching Observation Techniques to Purposes

Teachers can nurture play from within and without (Smilansky & Sheftaya, 1990). Intervening from outside the play might include adding toy cars and people to the block area to stimulate new types of play or making comments or suggestions about a role. Intervention from inside the play means that the teacher actually gets involved in the children's play. Because entering the children's play is more intrusive, it is usually reserved for those times when children need more direct teacher intervention. Some examples of such times are when a sociodramatic play center is first introduced, when the children seem to be stalled at a particular form of play, when the children have had limited experience with group play, or when the play becomes destructive to people or property.

Providing Flexible Groups

One way of balancing individual and group experiences is to provide a mixture of spontaneous group formation (such as children deciding to play with the blocks together) and teacher-designated groups (such as playing a singing game during circle time). It is also important for children to use their creative processes both individually and in groups. A child may create a painting at the easel, but she also needs experience coordinating her efforts with those of a small group that is creating a mural, for example. A child may compose his own poem or story, but it is equally valuable for him to work with a partner or a small group to write a story or poem. A small group of primary grade children may read a story silently to themselves, but it is also appropriate for them to share that story with a child from another grade level, a parent volunteer, or a senior center volunteer. By keeping the groupings flexible, the teacher can give children experiences with a complete range of social interaction patterns as they are learning.

Noting Patterns

Notice how children approach various types of play. If a child has never ventured into the block area, invite him or her in. Perhaps a child begins the day with more boisterous forms of play and may be observed listening quietly to stories and songs later on. Dramatic changes in a child's patterns of play may be an indication that the child is dealing with a stressful situation, such as the girl who used to insist upon playing the mother's role but has begun to take on the baby's role after the birth of a new sibling.

When materials are unfamiliar to children, teachers should intervene
and demonstrate how those materials are used.

Take note, also, of children's interests and role-taking preferences. Pay attention to the roles that children select for themselves. Is a particular child regularly cast in the role of victim when monsters and superheroes are at play? Does a child always insist upon selecting the play theme? Are sex role stereotypes present?

Asking Good Questions

Opportunities for children to "live the question" are rare. "Questions can be stopped by answers" (Van Manen, 1986, pp. 40–41). How can teachers keep children's interest in the question alive? Improving the quality of learning experiences for children demands teachers who will allow children to take the lead; do less telling and more asking; and talk less and listen more.

In a hands-on science activity on sinking and floating, Ms. Zezel used the following guidelines (Raths, Wasserman, Jonas, & Rothslein, 1986) to probe her third graders' thinking:

1. *Encourage children to look carefully and use what they see to support their ideas.* After equipping the children with pans of water and various objects (e.g., a cork, paper clip, pencil, coin, popsicle stick, tennis ball, feather, piece of nylon net, bar of soap), Ms. Zezel asked: "If the goal is to find out whether objects sink or float, how will you proceed? How could we keep track of our observations?"

2. *Invite children to compare and classify.* After the children had completed their experiments and recorded them, Ms. Zezel invited them to compare and classify ("Is there anything similar about the objects that floated? The objects that sank? What differences exist between the objects that floated and sank?") and relate new information or ideas to what they already know ("Carl thinks that big objects sink; Kim says that light objects float. What other objects might you try to test this idea? Think about all of the things that you have seen floating in water. How would you explain the fact that they float?").

3. *Have children summarize and interpret.* Children recap what they know so far and explain things from their point of view ("What ideas do we now have about the properties of objects that sink? Objects that float?").

4. *Ask children to identify assumptions and suggest hypotheses.* Children are asked to articulate the assumptions they have made in a low-risk environment where they feel comfortable making educated guesses ("We now have several ideas. Some people feel that floating has something to do with air inside the object. Some people have concluded that objects float or sink, depending upon how heavy they are and the size of the body of water. We will be using the scales now to weigh each object. Refer back to your original experiment to find out if the heaviest objects always sink and the lightest objects always float").

5. *Encourage children to imagine and create.* Children use visualization to create mental images that will help them solve the problem ("If it is true that air has something to do with floating, how does a battleship float? Imagine that your house was suddenly surrounded by deep water. What materials would you use to build something that would take you across? Why?").

Developing New Teaching Strategies

Teachers must constantly strive to extend their repertoire of teaching strategies. By reading professional journals and magazines and participating in other professional development activities such as workshops and conferences, teachers can remain current and get many excellent ideas. After one teacher read an article subtitled "Do You See What I Say?" (Mundell, 1987), she incorporated the following suggestions for developing children's visual images:

1. Invite children to create images of concrete objects. Talk about each child's images and compare and contrast them, emphasizing that there are no right or wrong images.

2. Ask children to imagine familiar objects or scenes. This visualization technique is a good introduction to a story. A teacher who is sharing the wordless picture book *Junglewalk* (Tafuri, 1988), for example, might discuss the first page, where the boy has just finished reading a book and is switching off the light to go to sleep ("I wonder what he was reading. It says on the cover of his book *Jungles of the World*. Close your eyes for a minute and imagine what sorts of things he may have seen in his book"). In this way, the teacher assesses children's prior knowledge and improves their comprehension of a story told in pictures.

3. Ask children to read or tell stories with scenes that are easy to visualize. You might begin with familiar literary images, like the witch's gingerbread house in *Hansel and Gretel*. Following some discussion of the mental images children have created, you could move to an activity such as telling the story of *Tom Thumb* and then comparing the things children envisioned with the images created by artist Richard Jesse Watson (1989). Even children who are minimally proficient in English can comprehend a story that is told through vocal and facial expressions. Children who are more fluent in English can retell the story; those who are not can reenact the story in mime and words. Storytellers recognize this important advantage to listening to stories: "Somehow the very fact that they had to focus just on listening seemed to set them free." (Hinman 1987, p. 3)

Teacher and Learner Self-Evaluation

Learning to self-evaluate views an assessment of creative expression as a form of self-dialogue. Some questions Wasserman (1990) suggests are these:

Am I being fair here?

Am I overlooking aspects of performance that need attention?

Am I being overly generous or negative in my feedback?

What self-talk do I hear myself making as I respond to this child's work?

Sound decision making requires even more than interaction. It also demands that teachers deal with ethics and values. In communities of learners, we must ask these tough questions about the decisions we make:

Who benefits?

Whose interests are being served? With what effects?

What is the significance of these effects on children's lives?

To what extent do teachers' decisions have a limiting or distorting effect on the opportunities open to children? (Tennyson & Strom, 1986)

Some questions to help children grow in self-evaluation include:

- ❑ Tell me about how you worked in your group today.
- ❑ Tell me some of the things you liked about your work.
- ❑ Tell me about some of the things that did not work well for you.
- ❑ What are some things you could do for yourself? That you needed help with?
- ❑ When you had some trouble, tell me about how you solved the problem.
- ❑ What were some of the new ideas that you had?
- ❑ What did you do the best of all?
- ❑ Were there things that you didn't try? How did you feel about that?
- ❑ Which work made you feel very proud? Tell me about it.
- ❑ Tell me about how you helped with . . .
- ❑ Tell me what you did when . . . (Wasserman, 1990, pp. 223–224).

Special Populations

Assessment is being used inappropriately if the results are used to diminish children's opportunities or exclude them from special programs. In one school district with an itinerant music teacher, for example, children were routinely given a "music aptitude test" that assessed their potential for reading musical notation. On the basis of that test score alone, large numbers of children were denied the chance to learn to play a musical instrument. Important considerations, such as the child's interest and motivation, were largely ignored. From a logical standpoint, it is questionable whether *any* test can accurately predict a child's musical abilities, given the wide array of musical styles and instruments that exist. Many of the rejected children accepted the school's pronouncement that they were "unmusical," and some avoided musical activities throughout their lives. Clearly, this program had a talent-scout orientation. The assumption was that music study is for a select few rather than something to be enjoyed and experienced by all. Teachers must have the fundamental mindset that all children deserve to have their creative processes nurtured (Treffinger, 1989).

Culturally Diverse Groups

Jane Cartagena is a 3-year-old child whose parents are migrant workers. She is enrolled in a federally funded preschool program, but she has limited English proficiency and seldom interacts with the other children because they all speak English. Ms. Garner has been observing Jane each day and notes that she usually remains in the housekeeping area, performing such activities as cooking, ironing, and caring for the baby. Ms. Garner decides to try another approach. She sits outside the housekeeping corner, rings the bell on the toy telephone, and says, "Hola? Hola?" Jane pauses, then picks up the telephone and begins a conversation in Spanish with her teacher. If we consider what might have happened to Jane if her teacher had had no knowledge of Spanish or, worse yet, if the teacher had labeled her as a "problem," it is easy to see how children of different cultural backgrounds can be systematically excluded from learning experiences. Good teachers figure out what their students need in order to feel accepted, to learn, and to succeed. One of the worst disservices we can do to children is to treat them as disembodied intellects that are evaluated purely through test performance. In order to give children a chance at success, our assessment strategies must be "based on products, progress, and effort" (Collins, 1991, p. 29).

Children with Disabilities

Colin is a first grader who had a tragic accident last summer. His family was in an auto crash, and Colin's legs and spine were so damaged that the doctors wondered if he would live, much less walk again. But even worse than his physical trauma was Colin's emotional ordeal, because while he was in intensive care at the hospital, his mother died as a result of her injuries. When Colin began first grade in September, he didn't mention the accident. At Thanksgiving he wrote: "I am thankful that my dad and sister are still alive." Near Christmas time, he wrote: "I lust my mum 5 muns ago. Please . . . that I am weak." The second sentence, he explained, "Didn't come out right . . . what I want to say is that sometimes the other kids don't understand I am weak. They say 'Come on, can't you run any faster?' or 'You walk funny,' but I got hurt real bad and that's the best I can do. So I'm telling them, please don't make fun of me."

Teachers and parents sometimes limit the play of a disabled child like Colin by becoming overprotective. As a result, adults frequently lower their expectations for children's play, limit opportunities for play, and reduce the experience children have with playmates (Hughes, 1991). Sensitivity and tact are essential when breaking these barriers for children. The child who is confined to a wheelchair may find it difficult to play with unit blocks, but she can become the "city planner" or play with smaller blocks on a tray or at a table. A child like Colin who has physical limitations on speed and power can compensate for them by working to his strengths. The key to unlocking creativity is to help children "recognize and appreciate strength, beauty, and truth in their ideas and feelings" (Lansing, 1986, p. 15).

High-Achieving and Low-Achieving Children

Too often, educators have assumed that the dreary repetition of skills is appropriate for low-achieving children, while compelling, complex, and creative tasks are best suited for high-achieving children. But all children need authentic, engaging, legitimate, and memorable work, work that matters outside of school as well as in the classroom (Sheingold, 1991). As teachers, if we are serious in our desire to empower children, the evaluation practices we choose must provide feedback for the learners to grow on, rather than marks and grades that quantify children's performance, like eggs, into "jumbos, mediums, and cracks" (Wasserman, 1990, p. 212).

A recent study of portfolio assessment of children's drawings and writings concluded that while high- and average-achieving students tended to perform equally well on standardized tests and on story writing tasks, low-achieving children's performance on tests and real tasks was the most disparate. As a group, the children who scored lowest on the tests performed much better on real writing tasks than their test scores would lead one to expect (Simmons, 1991). This finding underscores the message that many of our tests, whether they are called tests of achievement, intelligence, or creativity, are actually measures of talent for paper-and-pencil types of schoolwork.

Typically, high-achieving children exhibit above-average ability, creativity, and task commitment. As a result, they need real-life experiences and activities that expose them to a wide variety of disciplines, topics, and issues; instructional methods and materials that develop both thinking and feeling processes; investigative activities and artistic productions that enable them to function as "first-hand inquirers"; and opportunities to act like practicing professionals—to become artists, scientists, writers, and so on (Hallahan & Kaufman, 1991). The teacher's role is to function as a facilitator. This involves such things as helping students translate a general concern into a clearly focused problem, providing children with the materials and methods necessary to resolve the problem, and assisting students in communicating their findings to authentic audiences (Hallahan & Kaufman, 1991).

Low-achieving children frequently have had less experience with more formal types of learning environments, but this does not mean that they should be weeded out of the educational system. Rather, the educational system must begin earlier and do a better job of preparing these children for authentic learning experiences. As Hodgkinson (1991) points out, "Every dollar spent on Head Start will save taxpayers $7 in later services that the child will not need—a superb investment" (p. 15). We must make the curriculum that inaugurates the child's experience in schools a child-centered one, one that celebrates diversity and respects children. For if we stick to the *tabula rasa* mentality, low-achieving children will be blamed and will always seem deficient, and our educational system will fail them once again. Failure in school is not the reason for exclusion from the American dream of the good life, but rather the result of that exclusion (Ogbu, 1980).

Conclusion

Creative thinking is much more than the ability to remember bits of information. It involves using that information in an imaginative, problem-solving way. In

our culture, it is common to admire the game show contestant who easily rec-
ollects fragments of knowledge or to believe that a 3-year-old who recites the
alphabet is brilliant. But, as we have seen, both of these highly touted tasks do
not even scratch the surface of human intellectual potential. Creative expression
and play must be valued in a child-centered curriculum, and in a culture that is
so enamored of assessment, this means that they must also be evaluated. By
matching our assessment tools to our program goals and materials, we can
provide more child-centered early childhood curricula.

Chapter Summary

1. Assessment is a highly controversial issue; many inappropriate practices are
   common. As a result, many major professional organizations are urging
   teachers to use a wide range of observational methods as an alternative to
   overreliance on standardized tests.
2. Assessment is an ongoing process rather than a single paper-and-pencil test.
   It should include information on the child's performance of meaningful
   tasks over an extended period of time and should look at the learner's
   attitudes, processes, and effort, as well as the products of learning.
3. In general, the purposes for the assessment of divergent thinking are to gain
   insight into creativity, evaluate progress, identify talents, provide enrichment, and optimize each child's growth in creative expression and play.
4. Child-centered alternatives to standardized tests include observations, interactions, and analysis of products or processes. The teacher's key role is in
   the day-to-day observation of children. Specific techniques include interviews, conferences, portfolios, checklists, and rating scales.

Discussion Questions

1. An administrator decides to use a test to determine which children are ready
   for kindergarten. Many of the children who are excluded each year are those
   who may be most in need of socialization experiences and an intellectually
   stimulating environment. What could be done to remedy this situation?
2. Using the observations of hospital play in Appendix D as evidence, build a
   case that children are developing physically, socially, emotionally, and intellectually through sociodramatic play.
3. A parent comments, "I expected my child to really *learn* something, but it
   looks like she's just playing. She can do *that* at home." How would you
   respond to these objections? Support your position with your readings from
   this textbook.
4. Recall some occasions when you were asked to evaluate your own performance. How did that make you feel? Was your self-assessment accurate?
   Useful?

5. Use Wasserman's (1990) self-evaluation criteria on pp. 315–316 to evaluate an episode of your behavior while trying to teach a child something. Then interview the child, using his or her ideas for enhancing learner self-assessment. Did these guidelines help you to focus on teacher and learner self-assessment? Why or why not?

6. When a large city school district announced that it would identify elementary schools for the study of music, dance, and languages, inner-city parents got in line the night before and literally camped out to get their children enrolled in a particular school. What does this behavior tell you about parental interest in traditionally nonacademic subjects? Reflect for a moment on the opening quotation by Mike Rose (1989). What can early childhood educators do to break the cycle of testing that so often excludes children, particularly those who lack all the educational advantages, from participation in the most inviting educational programs?

Writing to Learn

Using the description of the Treasure Hunt activity on page 296 as a model, design another child-centered learning activity that meets the criteria for developing higher-level thinking skills. How does your activity help children to analyze, apply, synthesize, and evaluate information? Using the questioning guidelines on pages 313–314 as a model, make a list of open-ended questions that will encourage children to observe carefully, compare and classify, summarize and interpret, identify assumptions and suggest hypotheses, and imagine and create.

Observation

Portfolio Assessment of Children's Art

A portfolio is a collection of children's work arranged to highlight progress, demonstrate processes, and share outcomes. Usually the child and teacher share responsibility for selecting what will go into the portfolio. Examine the contents of the sample art portfolios of children's paintings and drawings in Figure 9.9. Note how they are arranged, labeled, and analyzed. Figure 9.6 is a visual arts interview that can be administered to a child to encourage self-evaluation. Using these materials as examples, do the following:

1. Collect several examples of a child's *original* artwork (not dittos, worksheets, or cut-and-paste activities).
2. Match each sample to a program goal.
3. Arrange them to show the child's progress.
4. Conduct the visual arts interview with the child.
5. Be prepared to share your results with the class.

--- **Controversy** ---

How Does Testing Affect Teaching?

Many teachers respond affirmatively to the following questions:

> Do you feel any pressure to teach to the tests? If the tests were not given or used for the evaluation of individual children, teachers and schools, would you use fewer skill tests, workbooks and other simple-response pedagogical materials? Would you use a broader range of instructional materials, giving more attention to integrated learning? Would expectations for *all* children enlarge? Would you devote more attention to active inquiry-oriented programs in mathematics and science? Would you give more time to the arts? Would the curriculum be more powerful, more generative? Do you feel that you can assess children's learning in more appropriate ways than the use of standardized achievement tests? (Perrone, 1991, p. 134).

What are some of the strategies that teachers can use to make assessment more meaningful, useful, and helpful to the learner? How can these strategies be infused into the early childhood curriculum?

--- **Research Highlight** ---

Analyzing Children's Block Structures

Summary of Research

Many adults make the assumption that children are "just playing" when they create various block structures. Yet if we really begin to observe children's use of blocks, we can see a developmental progression in their representations of space. Basically, the sequence is as follows:

- ❏ *Two-year-olds* tend to place blocks by one another (in rows) or in a container, such as a box or bucket. (See Figure 9.10.)
- ❏ *Three-year-olds* tend to combine blocks by placing them on top of one another (in piles or towers). (See Figure 9.11.)
- ❏ *Four-year-olds* tend to combine rows and towers to create enclosures (walls, floors, interior spaces such as "fences"). (See Figure 9.12.)
- ❏ *Five-year-olds and primary grade children* tend to create complex configurations with inside/outside objects, some sense of scale, and landmarks or routes (e.g., buildings, cities, roads). (See Figure 9.13.)

FIGURE 9.10 Examples of Toddler Block
Structures

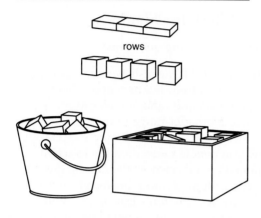

rows

placing blocks in containers

FIGURE 9.11 Examples of 3-year-olds' Block Structures

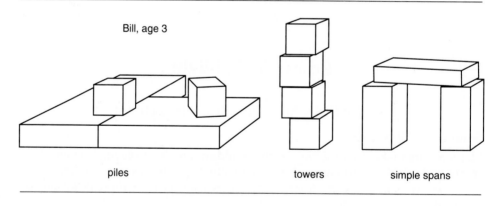

Bill, age 3

piles   towers   simple spans

Implications for Practice

Blocks are one of the most valuable and versatile materials children use. Knowledgeable teachers understand how children develop in their spatial representation with blocks. The teacher who is aware of how blocks help children develop a variety of spatial concepts also uses this knowledge to assess children's progress and supply new challenges.

Try using this knowledge of the developmental sequence in block play. Ask a child or children who have access to a large set of unit blocks to show you some

FIGURE 9.12 Examples of 4-year-olds' Block Structures

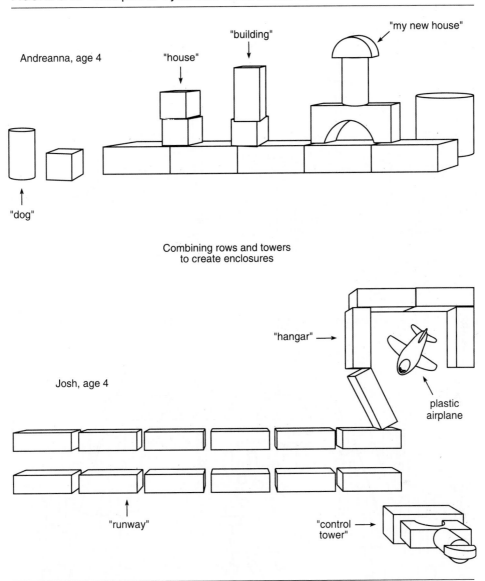

of the things they like to build. Draw a picture showing how the construction looks. Ask the child to tell you about what he or she has built. Label your drawing with any information the child gives. Write the child's age, sex, and verbal comments on a piece of paper. Then compare your observations with Reifel's (1984) research.

FIGURE 9.13   Examples of Kindergarten and Primary Grade Children's Block Structures

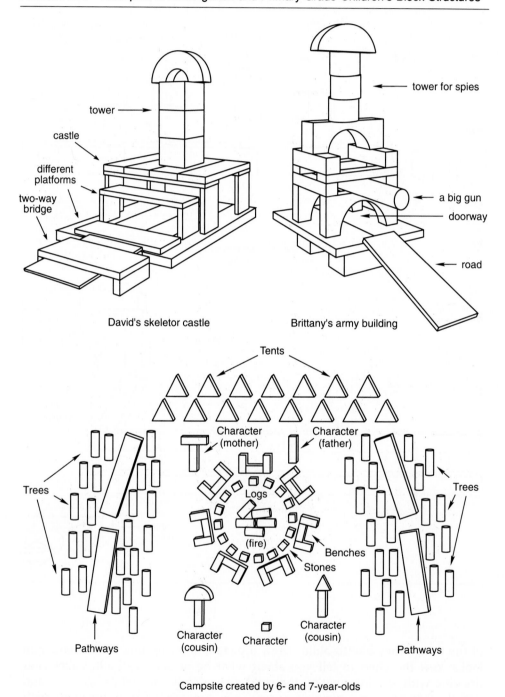

David's skeletor castle   Brittany's army building

Campsite created by 6- and 7-year-olds

References

Adler, A. (1957). *The education of children.* London: George Allen and Unwin.

Barrow, R. (1988). Some observations on the concept of imagination. In K. Egan & D. Nadaner (Eds.), *Imagination and education* (pp. 79–90). New York: Teachers College Press.

Black, J. (1979). Formal and informal means of assessing communicative competence of kindergarten children. *Research in the Teaching of English, 13,* 49–68.

Bloom, B. (1964). *Stability and change in human characteristics.* New York: Wiley.

Bredekamp, S. (Ed.). (1991). Guidelines for appropriate curriculum content and assessment in programs serving children 3 through 8. *Young Children, 46*(3), 21–38.

Bredekamp, S., & Shepard, L. (1989). How best to protect children from inappropriate school expectations, procedures and policies. *Young Children, 44*(3), 14–24.

Collins, A. (1991). The role of computer technology in restructuring schools. *Phi Delta Kappan, 73*(1), 28–36.

Dacey, J. S. (1989). *Fundamentals of creative thinking.* Lexington, MA: D. C. Heath.

Gardner, H. (1983). *Frames of mind: The theory of multiple intelligences.* New York: Basic Books.

Gelfer, J. G. (1991). Teacher–parent partnerships: Enhancing communications. *Childhood Education, 67,* 164–167.

Gelfer, J. G., & Perkins, P. G. (1987). Effective communication with parents: A process for parent/teacher conferences. *Childhood Education, 64,* 19–22.

Goodman, Y. M. (1989). Evaluation of students: Evaluation of teachers. In K. S. Goodman, Y. M. Goodman, & W. J. Hood (Eds.), *The whole language evaluation book* (pp. 3–14). Portsmouth, NH: Heinemann.

Hallahan, D. P., & Kaufman, J. M. (1991). *Exceptional children.* Englewood Cliffs, NJ: Prentice-Hall.

Harste, J. (1989). Preface to M. Siegel & R. F. Carey, *Critical thinking: A semiotic perspective* (pp. vi–viii). Bloomington, IN: ERIC/ Reading and Communication Skills.

Hinman, C. (1987). Quoted in B. Reed, Storytelling: What it can teach. *School Library Journal, 34*(2), 35–39.

Hodgkinson, H. (1991). Reform versus reality. *Phi Delta Kappan, 73*(1), 9–16.

Hoffman, S., & Lamme, L. L. (Eds.). (1988). *Learning from the inside out: The expressive arts.* Wheaton, MD: Association for Childhood Education International.

Howes, C. (1980). Peer play scale as an index of complexity of peer interaction. *Developmental Psychology, 16,* 371–372.

Hughes, F. P. (1991). *Children, play and development.* Boston: Allyn & Bacon.

Jalongo, M. R. (1992). *Early childhood language arts.* Boston: Allyn & Bacon.

Johnson, J. E., Christie, J. F., & Yawkey, T. D. (1987). *Play and early childhood development.* Glenview, IL: Scott Foresman.

Jongsma, K. S. (1989). Portfolio assessment. *The Reading Teacher, 1,* 264–265.

Kagan, S. (1989). Early care and education: Tackling the tough issues. *Phi Delta Kappan, 70*(6), 433–439.

Kulp, M., & Tarter, B. J. (1986). The creative processes rating scale. *Creative Child and Adult Quarterly, 11*(3), 166–173.

Lansing, K. M. (1986). Art and the child: Are they compatible? *Studies in Art Education, 28*(1), 1–15.

Mecca, M. E. (1989). Philosophers in the classroom. *Young Children, 65*(4), 206–208.

Meisels, S. J. (1987). Uses and abuses of developmental screening and school readiness testing. *Young Children, 42*(2), 4–6, 68–73.

Meisels, S. J. (1989). High stakes testing in kindergarten. *Educational Leadership, 46*(7), 16–22.

Mundell, D. (1987). *Mental imagery: Do you see what I say?* Oklahoma City: Oklahoma State Department of Education.

National Association for the Education of Young Children (1988). Position statement on standardized testing. *Young Children, 43,* 42–47.

National Association of State Boards of Education. (1988). *Right from the start: The report of the NASBE task force on early childhood education.* Alexandria, VA: National Association of State Boards of Education.

National Commission on Testing and Public Policy. (1990). *From gatekeeper to gateway: Transforming testing in America.* Chestnut Hill, MA: Author.

Nielsen, R. (1990). The perils of measuring "productivity." *On Campus, 9*(7), 18.

Ogbu, J. U. (1980, July). *Literacy in subordinate cultures: The case of black Americans.* Paper delivered at the Library of Congress Conference on Literacy, Washington, DC.

O'Neal, S. (1991). Leadership in the language arts: Student assessment: Present and future. *Language Arts, 68,* 67–73.

Paget, K. D. (1983). The individual examining situation. In K. D. Paget & B. A. Bracken (Eds.), *The psychoeducational assessment of preschool children* (pp. 51–61). New York: Grune & Stratton.

Perrone, V. (1991). On standardized testing. *Childhood Education 67*(3), 132–142.

Potter, F. (1985). "Good job!" How we evaluate children's work. *Childhood Education, 61,* 203–206.

Quellmalz, E. S. (1985). Needed: Better methods for testing higher-order thinking skills. *Educational Leadership, 43*(2), 29–35.

Raths, L. E., Wasserman, S., Jonas, A., & Rothstein, A. (1986). *Teaching for thinking: Theory, strategies and activities for the classroom.* New York: Teachers College Press.

Reifel, S. (1984). Block construction: Children's developmental landmarks in representation of space. *Young Children, 40*(1), 61–67.

Rose, M. (1989). *Lives on the boundary: A moving account of the struggles and achievements of America's educational underclass.* New York: Penguin.

Sheingold, K. (1991). Restructuring for learning with technology: The potential for synergy. *Phi Delta Kappan, 73*(1), 17–27.

Sigel, I. E., & Cocking, R. R. (1977). *Cognitive development from childhood to adolescence: A constructive perspective.* New York: Holt, Rinehart & Winston.

Silvern, S. (1988). Continuity/discontinuity between home and early childhood education environments. *The Elementary School Journal, 89*(2), 147–159.

Simmons, J. (1991). Quoted in K. S. Jongsma, Questions and answers: Portfolio assessment. *The Reading Teacher, 1,* 264–265.

Smilansky, S. (1968). *The effects of sociodramatic play on disadvantaged preschool children.* New York: Wiley.

Smilansky, S., & Shefatya, L. (1990). *Facilitating play: A medium for promoting cognitive, socio-emotional and academic development in young children.* Gaithersburg, MD: Psychosocial and Educational Publications.

Teale, W. H. (1988). Developmentally appropriate assessment of reading and writing in the early childhood classroom. *The Elementary School Journal, 89*(2), 173–183.

Tennyson, W., & Strom, S. (1986). Beyond professional standards: Developing responsibleness. *Journal of Counseling and Development, 64,* 298–302.

Treffinger, D. J. (1989). The potentials to productivity: Designing the journey to 2000. *Gifted Child Today, 12*(12), 17–21.

Valencia, S. V. (1990). A portfolio approach to classroom reading and assessment: The whys, whats, and hows. *The Reading Teacher, 43*(4), 338–340.

Van Manen, M. (1986). *The tone of teaching.* Portsmouth, NH: Heinemann.

Wasserman, S. (1989). Reflections on measuring thinking while listening to Mozart's *Jupiter* symphony. *Phi Delta Kappan, 70*(5), 365–370.

Wasserman, S. (1990). *Serious players in the classroom: Empowering children through active learning experiences.* New York: Teachers College Press.

Westby, C. E. (1980). Assessment of cognitive and language abilities through play. In P. A. Broen (Ed.), *Language, speech and hearing services in schools* (pp. 154–168). Minneapolis: American Language Hearing Association.

White, S. (1975). Social implications of IQ. *National Elementary Principal, 54*(4), 10.

Wortham, S. C. (1990). *Tests and measurement in early childhood education.* Columbus, OH: Merrill/Macmillan.

Children's Books

Gerstein, M. (1984). *Roll over!* New York: Crown.

Tafuri, N. (1988). *Junglewalk.* New York: Greenwillow.

Watson, R. J. (1989). *Tom Thumb.* San Diego, CA: Harcourt Brace Jovanovich.

Divergent Thinking, the Integrated Personality, and the Future

In the future, children will need to know how to learn, how to cope with change, how to build and evaluate a body of knowledge that will evolve throughout their life, and how to adapt to a changing work environment. They will need to acquire critical thinking, decision-making, and communication skills with an emphasis on the cognitive processes of inquisitiveness, sequential thinking and problem solving. To function in business and industry, they will need to learn the traits valued in the new marketplace, namely, flexibility, experimentation, autonomy, risk-taking and innovation.

Toby Jane Tetenbaum
and Thomas A. Mulkeen, 1986, p. 100

After reading this chapter, you will be able to

- ❑ Explain the historical and theoretical background of Western culture's ambivalence toward play and creative expression.
- ❑ Appreciate the many ways in which creative expression and play are curricular basics for the twenty-first century.
- ❑ Reexamine the teacher's roles and responsibilities in light of recent theory/research and social/demographic trends.
- ❑ Develop strategies for enhancing personal and professional creativity through creative teaching.

❑   Evaluate your own beliefs, practices, and biases about creative expression and play.

Case Study

Jamal is a second-grade child who has been diagnosed as having attention deficit disorder. He entered preschool as a bright, inquisitive, and animated child. In first grade, Jamal's teacher expressed concern that he "just couldn't sit still" and was disrupting the class. Now that Jamal is on medication, he is subdued and listless; in other words, he is now sufficiently passive to tolerate the tedious, inflexible curriculum of his elementary school. Jamal's parents consented to the drug therapy for their son because they became convinced that otherwise he would fail in school. Because he is an adopted child, they worried that Jamal might have some inherited learning difficulty that could only be remedied by medication to calm him down. Yet if we really listen to Jamal, we gain a different impression: "I used to think that school would be fun. Everybody kept saying, 'Oh, you're really gonna like school.' Kindergarten was fun, but it's not fun anymore. I just try real hard to be quiet, do my work, and get as many stickers as I can."

Every day across America, children are taking medication to make them sit still, be quiet, and listen. A few of them may truly need it. But many of them are misdiagnosed or simply trapped in an unyielding, uninteresting curriculum. History is replete with examples of "problem" children who became highly creative adults—Thomas Edison, Sara Bernhardt, Winston Churchill, Isadora Duncan, and Albert Einstein, to name a few. If those children were alive today, what would be their fate? Unless they were fortunate enough to be in child-centered classrooms with creative, caring teachers and privileged to be the offspring of well-informed, assertive parents, they might be on drugs designed to quell their behavior.

By the year 2000, there will be 5.4 million fewer young adults and millions of additional senior citizens, a trend that is partly due to the post–World War II "baby boom" generation's reaching old age and partly due to improved medical care (Haycock, 1991). This means that there will be many more elderly persons who need support and far fewer people to support them. Clearly, every young child needs to become a highly productive member of society, yet a larger percentage than ever before—more than one-third—will be minority and poor, "the very youngsters with whom we have been least successful in assisting to master the skills they need to become productive citizens" (Haycock, 1991, p. 277).

The one thing that can avert this loss of talent is to become talented teachers ourselves and work to develop the creative potential in every child. The final chapter of this book is about becoming teachers who foster the abilities that children will need in order to thrive in a rapidly changing society. We cannot afford to be shortsighted, to consider only the task of preparing youngsters for the next grade level (Kagan, 1989). Rather, we need to prepare children to function as adults in later life, and the one thing we can be sure of in the future is the demand for sensitive, creative, flexible problem solvers.

Theoretical Framework

Historically speaking, many deeply rooted dichotomies have dominated Western philosophy. Most people still believe, for example, that the following pairs of words are opposites: *reason/imagination, science/art, cognition/emotion,* and *facts/values.* Even contemporary thinking contributes its own potential set of dichotomies by oversimplifying the results of brain research. According to this research, the left side of the brain is analytical and practical, while the right side is intuitive and holistic. The erroneous conclusion that the left side of the brain is scientific while the right side is creative perpetuates the sort of either/or thinking that has adverse consequences for creativity and innovation (Rickards, 1985).

How Basic Is Creative Expression?

Think about the kindergarten child whose teacher held up a piece of purple construction paper and said, "What color is this?". Cris thought for a moment, then said, "graple." The teacher who is thinking literally, convergently, and vertically moved on, saying, "Can somebody help Cris?". But the teacher who really listens and respects children thinks about Cris's answer. It makes perfect sense. He has noticed—perhaps through direct experiences with popsicles or lollipops or beverages—that grape is the *flavor* associated with the color purple and has invented a word to make sense out of this observation. A good teacher might marvel out loud, saying with a tone of pleasure and surprise in his or her voice, "Grape-flavored things *are* usually purple, aren't they?" Cris's response falls somewhere between the historical dichotomies—between reason and feeling, between logic and imagination, between left brain and right brain. That largely uncharted territory between what are incorrectly regarded as bipolar opposites is where genius lies. Every child—not just the compliant, the economically advantaged, or the gifted and talented—has creative potential waiting to be set free by a great teacher.

As adults, we will systematically overlook the genius of childhood if we allow our penchant for rationality and logic to overshadow the child's natural affinity for nonliteral thinking (Egan, 1988). Rollo May (1975) poses a question that every educator should take to heart: "In our day of dedication to facts and hard-headed objectivity, we have disparaged imagination. . . . What if imagination and art are not frosting at all, but the fountainhead of human experience?" (pp. 149–150). Perhaps we *have* gotten it backward. Skills mastery is not the price of admission to creativity. Rather, it is the opportunity for joyful creative expression that inspires us to refine our skill.

Consider, for example, two children from different families who are learning to play the piano. Zhu is an 8-year-old who has been taking lessons since she was 5, and she says in all frankness to a visitor: "Just don't ask me to play the piano." Justin, the second child, first became interested in the piano as a toddler because he liked to sit on his grandfather's lap and experiment with the sounds made by the different keys. Sometimes they would sing songs together. There was a talented piano player in the ancestry of the first child, and her parents believe that early, intensive drill on the technical skills will enable Zhu to surpass even her illustrious ancestor's achievements. But which of these two children will use music to enrich their lives? And who is more likely to develop the individual, interpretive style that is the hallmark of a great pianist? Teachers and parents must remember that although skills are fundamental, they should not be developed at the expense of creativity.

Yesterday's and Tomorrow's Workers

The way we envision the future of the children in our society influences the curriculum. In the past, society's goal was to produce consensus and conformity. We had a large number of simple tasks that needed to be performed in precise ways by reliable, attentive workers in factories, mills, and mines. In other words, we needed an obedience culture.

Children today experience a world quite different from that of their parents. Global awareness, technological advances, and different family structures are just a few of the most obvious differences. Today's children form a strong peer culture because they find it increasingly difficult to relate to the experiences of their parents or other adults.

Modern schools attempt to prepare children for the technological era, one in which choices of food, clothing, media, work, and leisure predominate. In a society of "overchoice," the child's role shifts from obedience to autonomous functioning (Alwin, 1988; Toffler, 1970, 1980).

To excel in tomorrow's international workplace, we need a different type of worker, one who is capable of generating new ideas. Society needs fewer people who know how to organize for efficient production and many more people who know how to organize to make decisions (Simon, 1973). According to many experts and leaders in the field, the twenty-first century will demand the following:

❏ *Students* who possess "resilience and flexibility, a creative and integrative way of thinking, and a certain psychological sturdiness in the way they face new circumstances in the company of other people" (Minuchin, 1987, p. 254).

❏ *Schools* that encourage "experimentation, risk-taking, flexibility, autonomy" and children who have acquired "a mode of learning that places responsibility on them and that allows them the freedom to try, to test, to innovate, and to be creative" (Tetenbaum & Mulkeen, 1986, p. 99).

❏ A *work force* that is responsible and self-disciplined, can move from one challenge to another, adapt quickly to change, produce innovative solutions to problems, and acquire expertise in more than one area (Research and Policy Committee 1985; Tetenbaum & Mulkeen, 1986). Tomorrow's workers must be able to "figure out what they need to know, where to get it, and how to make meaning of it" (Task Force on Teaching as a Profession, 1986, p. 20).

❑ *Workers* who can read, write, and compute at high levels; analyze and interpret data; draw conclusions and make decisions; and function as part of a team (Haycock, 1991).

This describes the human resources we need in the future, but what can teachers expect from their teaching careers in the future? The next section describes some of the most recent projections on the characteristics of tomorrow's children and classrooms.

Teachers' Roles and Responsibilities

Imagine for a moment what your first year's class or a group of students you have not yet met will look like. Describe them as a census taker would in terms

These boys practiced cooperative, creative, and flexible problem solving skills by building this block structure.

of race, ethnic background, socioeconomic status, family structure, and home environment. Now compare your responses with these recent statistics (Hodgkinson, 1991):

❑ The racial distribution of children is projected to change dramatically from 1990 to 2010. Many states will have a *majority* of African-Americans or Hispanic youth.

❑ About one-third of preschool children are destined for school failure because of poverty, neglect, sickness, disabling conditions, and lack of adult protection and nurturance. Forty percent of the poor in the United States today are children (Reeves, 1988).

❑ The traditional family—a working father, a housewife mother, and children—constitutes less than 5% of American families (MacDonald, 1991). The number of single, female-headed households increased 35.6% from 1980 to 1990, and 4.3 million children are being reared by a mother who never married.

❑ At least 2 million school-age children have no adult supervision at all after school. Two million more are being raised by *neither* parent.

❑ Between 50,000 and 200,000 children are homeless every night in America, and 40% of shelter users are families with children.

❑ In 1987, child protection agencies received 2.2 million reports of child abuse or neglect—triple the number reported in 1976.

❑ Every day in America 27 children die because of poverty, 1,849 children are abused, and 2,987 children see their parents divorced (Children's Defense Fund, 1990).

❑ The latest Gallup poll on education indicates that 70% of 18- to 29-year-olds favor a federally supported, national, public system of preschool education.

This changing composition of students will influence how teachers teach in the future.

The Realities of Teaching

In 1970, Charles Silberman noted that it is impossible to spend a prolonged period visiting public school classrooms without being appalled by the destruction of spontaneity, of joy in learning, of pleasure in creating, and of self-esteem. What has been done to change this situation during the last two decades? Some would argue that very little progress has been made, pointing to trends in education like the back-to-basics backlash or minimum competency testing as evidence. What can be done to improve teaching, foster children's creativity, and prepare for the changes ahead? First, we as teachers must prepare ourselves for the realities of teaching.

In comparison with other professional groups, teachers tend to be altruistic, committed to serving others. At a time when 75.6% of the incoming freshmen identify ''being well off financially'' as a major life goal (Higher Education Research Institute, 1991), those who enter the teaching profession know full well that the education field does not offer the promise of wealth. In spite of their altruism and idealism, however, many preservice and new teachers are shocked by several things. Typically, beginning teachers' culture shock is a response to such factors as the stamina required by the job, the amount of paperwork, the range and intensity of students' needs, the parents who lack confidence in them, and the lack of support for their efforts within the school and district (Ryan, 1986). If the demographic trends are any indication, the pressures on today's teachers are likely to intensify rather than abate.

Some aspects of teaching that we as teachers must consider as we prepare for teaching in the twenty-first century include the following (MacDonald, 1991):

1. Recognize that you will be in a confined setting, surrounded by a culturally diverse and needy group of young children. Much of your work will be done in relative isolation from other adults.

2. Realize that managing the classroom will require the ability to concentrate on several events simultaneously, to make thousands of instant decisions each day, and to adapt quickly and flexibly to change.

3. Understand that you will have to take abstract, nonsituational knowledge and make it meaningful for young learners, many of whom have disadvantaged educational backgrounds.

4. Know that you are entering a helping profession, an occupation that draws upon and sometimes drains emotional and interpersonal resources.

5. Accept the fact that your success in the helping profession of teaching is determined by your influence on the attitudes and behaviors of other people—children, of course, but also families, colleagues, and the community at large.

6. Be aware that the best teachers are the most avid learners. Unless you become a lifelong learner, take charge of your own professional development, and become a model learner for children to emulate, your effectiveness will surely be diminished (Jalongo, 1991b).

Redefining the Teacher's Role

Most of the characteristics that will enable you to become an outstanding teacher are dependent upon your personal divergent and lateral thinking processes. Teachers for the future will need

- ❏ A repertoire of alternative teaching strategies that encourage student self-expression and intrinsic motivation.
- ❏ Well-developed powers of communication.
- ❏ A dynamic conception of human learning that uses personalized, learner-centered techniques.

❑ The adaptability to facilitate learning in a highly diverse mix of students.

❑ The personal stamina and resourcefulness to face challenging teaching responsibilities.

❑ Patterns of professional involvement that make the best use of creative energies. (MacDonald, 1991, p. 25)

Two critical methods to deal with all of these issues are (1) to redefine the teacher's role and (2) to develop your own creativity.

Teachers as Mediators of Learning

When someone says the word *teacher*, what image does your mind produce? Is it a stereotype—a faintly frumpy, middle-class, white woman? Is it another stereotype—an adult standing in front of rows of desks, putting children through their paces? These inaccurate, outmoded images of teachers must be left behind if we are to move forward:

> Today, we are asking teachers to stop teaching students isolated facts, to stop emphasizing rote learning, and to stop just covering material and preparing for multiple-choice tests. Instead, we are asking them to start teaching students how to apply skills, how to understand concepts and solve problems, how to work collaboratively and how to take responsibility for learning. In other words, we want teachers to give students the skills they will need to function in the work force and society. (David, 1991, p. 39)

One useful way of reconceptualizing the teacher's role is to think of it as that of a mediator. Mediators of children's learning use the following strategies:

1. Share their *intentions* and goals with children.
2. *Emphasize connections* between the immediate situation and other situations remote in time or space.
3. *Model the search for meaning* in all its forms—affective, motivational, and value-oriented.
4. *Build children's sense of competence and control* by helping every child to experience success and guiding the child in regulating his or her behavior (Feuerstein & Hoffman, 1982).

In order to appreciate the difference between a mediator of learning and a teacher, consider a very common lesson: teaching the difference between fantasy and reality. Ms. Clark prepares several short phrases like "A flying dog" and "A barking dog." She tells the children to listen carefully and decide whether or not what she says could really happen; then she polls the group. But if Ms. Clark were truly working to young children's strengths, she would have used a very different approach, one that capitalizes on the children's imaginations and casts her in the role of mediator.

A better and more challenging way of understanding the difference between fantasy and reality is through transitions. Children clearly make those transitions regularly while they are at play. Matthews (1977) found that children's modes of transformation fell into several categories:

- ❑ Substituting a real object for an imaginary one (using a cylindrical block for a telescope).
- ❑ Attributing a pretend function to a real object (putting on a hat and saying "This is a magical hat.").
- ❑ Ascribing animate characteristics to an object (talking to a teddy bear).
- ❑ Referring to nonexistent objects ("Okay, buddy, pull your car into my garage, and I'll see if I can fix it.").
- ❑ Referring to nonexistent situations ("We're going to a fancy restaurant.").
- ❑ Directly adopting or assigning a role ("You be the queen now and I'll be the princess.").

Notice also how this play-based way of developing the distinction between fantasy and reality allows children to retain ownership of the learning process. Ownership, as defined in problem solving, involves three things: *influence,* the opportunity for the child to take action and test hypotheses; *interest,* the personal investment in and concern about the task; and *imagination,* the drive for innovation and development of new ideas and constructive actions (Isaksen & Treffinger, 1985).

Teachers' Own Creativity

Imagine that you are assigned to write a lesson plan and are urged to "be creative." What influences might inhibit rather than facilitate your own creativity? Usually our insecurities about thinking more creatively fall into three categories (Adams, 1986):

1. *Fear of taking a risk.* Often college students do not feel sufficiently safe and secure to "break out" and take the risks associated with being different. External pressures such as grades, peer ridicule, or the censure of the instructor may make them overly fearful of making a mistake. Internal feelings, such as not wanting to appear foolish or not wanting to be noticed, also inhibit creativity.

2. *Fear of criticism.* Preservice and inservice teachers sometimes become prematurely critical of their efforts and judge ideas before they are even considered. Students who are writing a lesson plan might begin over and over, trying to make it perfect from the very start when they should be playing with ideas, allowing themselves to generate many ideas at

first and select the best ones later. It is only after many possibilities have been generated that teachers should become more judgmental.

3. *Fear of chaos.* If educators follow the safe, predictable path, they feel more in control of the situation. Writing a lesson plan that is dry and ordinary, yet meets the minimal requirements, is a way of exercising control over uncertainty. Another possible reason for teachers' confusion about producing a creative lesson plan has to do with conflicting ideas about what constitutes creative teaching.

Creative Teaching in the Future

Ask a group of teachers what it means to teach creatively, and many of them will describe clever activities or visual aids that are used in the classroom. But teaching creatively is very different. It is "where something creative happens within the student, rather than where something creative happens in front of the classroom" (Parnes, 1963, p. 236). The observation for this chapter is a self-assessment that you can use to identify strengths, uncover weaknesses, and confront your biases about creative expression and play.

The hallmark of the creative teacher is the high-quality work that her or his students produce. What makes one product more creative than another? Creative products are novel, appropriate, meaningful, satisfying, and parsimonious (Amabile, 1989). When teachers slavishly follow a prepackaged curriculum, they cannot nurture children's creativity and spontaneity. When children must rigidly follow someone else's play, creative teaching cannot occur (Torrance & Meyers, 1986).

David (1991) describes teaching creatively in the twenty-first century this way:

> curriculum and instruction must change from an emphasis on isolated facts, skills, and coverage to a focus on integrated content, on the application of skills, and on the development of conceptual understanding. Teaching must change from dispensing information and rewarding right answers to creating activities that engage students' minds and present complex problems with multiple solutions. (p. 39)

In order to teach creatively, teachers must be resourceful. A teacher in a parent cooperative nursery school who wished for a program rich in opportunities for creative expression through the visual arts decided that she would work on her dream rather than complain that the school could not supply all the materials she needed. She created easels from refrigerator boxes and paint. She sent home letters to parents asking for all sorts of "beautiful junk" to be used in collage and construction. She cut out paint smocks from heavy-gauge plastic trash bags. Instead of sending in sugary treats on their child's birthday, she asked parents to donate art materials. Notice how this teacher changed negative messages into positive ones, turned dreams into action plans, and sought gradual improvement rather than instant, dramatic change (Kriegel & Patler, 1991).

One of the best ways to teach children to be creative problem solvers is to model those behaviors ourselves as teachers.

An Agenda for the Future of Creative Expression and Play

The Association for Childhood Education International has issued position papers statements on the child's right to creative expression and play (Isenberg & Quisenberry, 1988; Jalongo, 1990). The key statements in those policy papers were as follows:

1. *Every child has a right to opportunities for imaginative expression.* Imaginative expression is not the exclusive province of special programs for the gifted and talented. It is not a curricular frill to be deleted when time is limited. Nor is imagination synonymous with enrichment, something reserved for those children who have already completed their "work." Rather, imagination is a capacity in every child that merits deliberate and intentional effort.

2. *Educating the child's imagination is a societal contribution of the first order.* One thing we can be certain about in our culture is change. The "personal inclinations required by the arts" are well suited to the demands of a rapidly changing society. These include play with images, ideas, and feelings; recognizing and constructing the multiple meanings of events; looking at things from different perspectives; and functioning as risk takers (Eisner, 1976).

3. *The educated imagination is the key to equity and intercultural understanding.* Creative productivity can be social rather than isolationist, and its outcomes need not be money-saving, labor-saving, or even artistic. Imagination dramatizes the inner workings of our minds and is the undercurrent of human interaction (Rosen, 1980). For after we gain insight into ourselves, we can use imaginative powers to identify with others, first to empathize and then to enact creative solutions to social problems (Hanson, 1986). Imagination, then, is the foundation for intercultural understanding.

4. *Children's creative productivity is qualitatively different from adults'.* We must resist *childism*, the tendency for adults to look condescendingly upon children's ideas and feelings, to regard them as less real or important than their own (Lightfoot, 1978). Children's creativity is different from adults', not inferior to it.

5. *Creative expression should permeate the entire curriculum.* When we speak of basics in education, people immediately think of reading, writing, and arithmetic. But is that what is basic? If basic means something that is fundamental to the experience of all children, then other things are surely basic. Play is certainly basic (Moyer, Egerston, & Isenberg, 1987).

What better way to learn interpersonal skills than through play!

Telling and enacting stories are basic (Nelms, 1988). Drawing, painting and sculpting are surely basic because, even before children can read, write, or calculate, they use these ways of communicating their ideas, emotions, and individuality. Music and dance are basic because even before children can speak, they can listen and move to music.

6. *Imagination is the key to artistry in teaching and excellence in our schools.* We keep searching for a panacea in education. Teachers are jaded by bandwagons, tired of legislative mandates, and weary of standardized tests that dictate the curriculum. What is worse, our schools have been sapped of the ability to surprise, so much so that the overwhelming impression after thousands of hours of observation in classrooms is that they are routinized, predictable, and "emotionally flat" (Goodlad, 1984).

   Where does the solution lie? Many prominent educators state that our schools need artistry, creativity, intuition, insight, inspiration, and reflection (Rubin, 1985; Schon, 1983; Sizer, 1984)—all intimately connected with imagination.

7. *We must refashion our schools for the twenty-first century.* School reform must, in the view of the National Educational Association, recognize that the industrial model is obsolescent in our information age (Futrell, 1989). We need to shut off the rapid assembly line of textbooks, tests, schedules, and paperwork in favor of "circles of learning" (Johnson, Johnson, Holubec, & Roy, 1984) and projects (Katz & Chard, 1989). Schools need to go beyond tolerating imagination and begin to value and educate it. Schools for the twenty-first century should encourage

FIGURE 10.1 Key Recommendations About Children's Play

Every program for young children should provide

- ☐ Appropriate play activities and equipment.
- ☐ Safe and inviting environments.
- ☐ Appropriate, planned outdoor play environments.
- ☐ Carefully planned curricula.
- ☐ Responsible parent/teacher roles.

Source: Isenberg & Quisenberry (1988).

children to select relevant topics, to reflect imaginatively, and to learn about their own creative processes as well as those of others (Hatcher, 1987; Hoffman & Lamme, 1989; Paley, 1981).

In 1970, Toffler wrote that we would live in a world of overchoice. Unless we prepare children to cope with these choices by teaching them to make decisions, they will find the number of options overwhelming. For an overview of the recommendations on children's play, see Figure 10.1.

Conclusion

A belief in the child's right to imaginative expression transforms the classroom. For too long, education has operated like a pupil postal system: we spend most of our time sorting and determining destinations. And, like the post office, we operate on the premise that environmental conditions should be ignored, that "the mail must go through." Never mind that junk mail addressed to "occupant"—the postal equivalent of a developmentally inappropriate curriculum—is what gets delivered.

In a school committed to creative expression and play, children are active participants. They learn how to bring order out of chaos, to use their frames of mind, to interpret symbols, to be open to feelings, to develop a tolerance for ambiguity, and to seek problems as well as solutions. If a school nurtures children's imagination and creativity, children will function more autonomously as they meet challenges in a supportive environment (Kamii, 1988). It means that teachers function as enablers who share their power, inviting children to manage their own learning processes and giving them time to revise their tentative notions about the world (Isaksen & Treffinger, 1985), deferring judgment until children are satisfied with their work (Klein, 1984). Education for the twenty-first century begins with the engagement of the child as a learner rather than the delivery of a curriculum.

Special Populations

As Franklin Delano Roosevelt once said, "Inequality may linger in the world of material things, but great music, great literature, great art, and the wonders of

By entering into the child's restaurant play, this teacher is validating and supporting play in her classroom.

science are, and should be, open to all." These words should guide teachers as they work with all children, particularly those in special populations.

Culturally Diverse Groups

Clearly, one of the trends in the twenty-first century will be what has been referred to as the *minority-majority,"* meaning that the groups we currently think of as minorities will increase in size and constitute a majority in many states. Understanding cultural diversity is not simply knowing about other cultures but also accepting them. In order to function in a culturally pluralistic society, adults need to have a commitment to all the cultural groups in which they participate, function in more than one culture simultaneously, and be able to examine their own culture from an outsider's perspective (Ramirez, 1983). By modeling these attitudes, we build children's self-esteem, give children a sense of their heritage, and promote intercultural understanding. Consider the following situation (Jalongo, 1992):

Ms. Ochoa teaches kindergarten in an economically depressed area where many of the children live in trailer courts. She overhears two children who are building a house with blocks as they discuss their concept of a habitat:

Bradley: No, you can't live in a trailer. You've got to live in a house.

Carol Ann: But I do live in a trailer.

Bradley: A trailer is for camping. You've gotta live in a house, or maybe an apartment.

Ms. Ochoa could ignore the children's dilemma, leaving Carol Ann with the feeling that her home is inferior and a source of shame. Instead, Ms. Ochoa initiates a "Where do they live?" bulletin board/collage. Her sources for pictures come from old magazines such as *National Geographic, Life,* and *Old House Journal.* She also finds that UNICEF has a set of notecards called "International Neighbors" and calendars that contain both photographs and children's drawings of homes from around the world. The children use these materials as resources and create their own to develop an impressive display of different habitats. As a result of Ms. Ochoa's efforts, every child's concept of what a home can be or look like is extended. Additional guidelines for building intercultural awareness, understanding, and acceptance are presented in Figure 10.2.

Children with Disabilities

"If we deny children's needs, we deny our humanity. The greatest need today is to re-establish respect for human worth. A widespread decline in the reverence for human life and loss of respect for the dignity of the individual has led to an independence toward the welfare of children. . . . In dedicating ourselves to children, perhaps we can start a general renaissance of the human spirit" (Pifer, 1982, p. 1).

In the past, there has been an emphasis on life skills for children with disabling conditions. In the future, it will become clear that our definition of life skills has been far too narrow, for although it is undeniably important for a child who cannot speak to learn to communicate, it is equally if not more important for that child to use those communication skills to create. Likewise, although it is important for children to master self-help skills like feeding or dressing or washing themselves, it is equally important for them to apply and practice these motor skills in play situations with peers.

The media routinely report about children who far exceeded routine expectations for them, who compensated for their intellectual or physical disabilities. We have just begun to get a glimpse of what, for instance, a child with Down's syndrome is capable of achieving. That knowledge has developed because someone somewhere cared enough. These adults cared so much about the child with Down's syndrome that they refused to be limited by what the child was supposedly capable of doing. The future will teach us even more about human potential and ways of enhancing that potential in children with disabling conditions.

FIGURE 10.2   Accepting Cultural Diversity: Guidelines for Teaching

1. *Be aware that multiculturalism "must begin with the adults"* (Casanova, 1987). Your attitudes and values will be communicated to students, and you will teach more by your example than by what you say. Give children a role model to emulate rather than empty words. Be aware also that multicultural understandings are pertinent in every classroom, not just in schools with many distinct cultural groups represented. If your group happens to be rather similar in background, it may need multicultural education most of all to function in the larger society.
2. *Know your students and their cultural backgrounds* (West, 1986). Too often, teachers refer to distinct groups as if they were one group—for instance, referring to Japanese, Chinese, and Vietnamese as "oriental." Each of these groups has its own identity.
3. *Expect conflict and model conflict resolution.* There will be inevitable clashes between children with different life experience—the boy who thinks that "girls can't be doctors" or the girl who thinks that "only mommies can take care of babies." Understand that children base these assumptions on what is admittedly limited personal experience. The way to resolve such conflicts is to create what Piaget called "disequilibrium" by offering compelling evidence of examples that are contrary to the child's concept.
4. *Bring the outside world into the classroom and help parents to see the value of play firsthand.* It is important to put parents back in touch with the way *they* learned as children. Parents will be more accepting of your curriculum if you show them rather than tell them how the things their children are doing are challenging and relevant. A parent may initially think that the sociodramatic play themes of camping and doctor presented in Chapters Eight and Nine are a waste of time. But if you share the rich dialogues and problem-solving behaviors that these play themes elicit, parents are more likely to recognize that authentic learning is taking place.
5. *Present modern concepts of families and occupations.* The American family has changed dramatically since the 1950s. The family composed of a father who works and a mother with two or three children who devotes full time to child care and homemaking makes up less than 10% of contemporary families. Avoid holding up one type of family structure as the standard by which others are judged. Be careful about the terminology you use to describe families too. Do not refer to children's homes as *broken* or to their remarried parents as *stepparents.* These terms are emotionally loaded and leave the impression that the family is defective or that the parents are less caring than "real" parents. Use more positive terminology such as *single-parent family* or *blended family.*
6. *Use children's literature to enrich children's play and understandings about cultural pluralism.* There are many excellent picture books that help children to sense both the rich cultural diversity and the universality of human experience. Use these books to make every child feel like a valued member of your classroom community.

Source: Jalongo (1992).

High-Achieving and Low-Achieving Children

One of the worst assumptions a teacher can make is that creativity is a form of snobbery and elitism, a way of making a few select individuals more refined, cultured, or better than the rest. Rather, we should "do what can be done to crack the old forbidding codes, to break through these artificial barriers that have so long served to exclude" (Greene, 1988, p. 53).

Giftedness is usually defined as an interaction among three clusters of traits: above-average general abilities, high levels of task commitment, and high levels of creativity (Renzulli, Reis, & Smith, 1981, p. 648). But as the demographic picture presented in this chapter suggests, many of the children in our classes will be poor and will arrive at school with limited educational backgrounds. Therefore, it is doubly important that we as teachers use that definition of giftedness not as a label but as a goal. The goal is for every child, regardless of his or her achievement record, to acquire new abilities, to learn to work diligently in completing a task, and to learn how to use creative processes. As Vivian Paley (1990) points out, "Those of us who presume to teach must not imagine that we know how each student begins to learn" (p. 78). For even though we know pedagogy and child development, each child is an individual. Good teachers watch, listen, and learn from their students; they trust children and work to the strengths of every child.

During the last decade, behaviorism has dominated educators' thinking. But research has shown that the indiscriminate use of extrinsic rewards—such as teachers' praise—or tangible reinforcers—such as stickers or stars—tends to diminish children's interest in a subject over time. Instead of enjoying a book for its own sake, they have their eyes on the prize: the hamburger or pizza. Rose (1989) contends that we have created an educational system that encourages high-achieving students to become cynical grade collectors and alienates most low-achieving children. Teachers for the twenty-first century must embrace a different philosophy. Our job is not to rank-order children's intellects and judge them like cattle in a 4-H competition. Our job is to convince children that they are capable of doing high-quality work and to give them a sense of their own power as learners. Teaching is not simply conveying information. If it were, an encyclopedia on disk could take the place of today's teachers. The real talent in teaching is bringing out the best in every child, in showing—by our own example—that being a learner is a joy in itself and offers enduring intrinsic rewards.

In Chapter One, we talked about children's natural curiosity, their vivid imaginations, and the relative ease with which they move from fantasy to reality and back again. Instead of wringing these traits out of them in the quest for logic, teachers of young children must cherish and cultivate these talents. In fact, as we have seen, creative expression and play are attributes that will be highly prized in a rapidly changing world culture.

Chapter Summary

1. Children and families in the United States have undergone rapid change. In order to meet the needs of this diverse clientele, teachers will have to redefine the teaching role.
2. The type of worker needed for an industrial society is dramatically different from the kind of worker needed in a technological society.

3. Fostering creativity in children and in ourselves as teachers is crucial as we confront the rapidly paced and challenging times ahead.
4. Teachers must function as mediators and design a curriculum that works to the child's strengths—an active imagination and natural playfulness.
5. A key challenge to teachers for the twenty-first century is to develop the creative genius in every child.

Discussion Questions

1. Compare and contrast the traditional teacher's role with the role of a teacher in the twenty-first century. What specific strategies will you use to become more future-oriented as an educator?
2. Howard Gardner (1983) says that in the future, schools and teachers will become almost like "brokers" who put families and children in contact with the necessary social services, organizations, and programs. Describe some practical ways that you could fulfill this role.
3. In reconceptualizing early childhood education for the future, how would you nourish a different view of learning and develop confident children who become lifelong learners? How would your instructional strategies and child guidance techniques help children to function more autonomously?

Writing to Learn

Using the results of your self-evaluation (see the Observation in this chapter), write a brief narrative statement about your strengths and weaknesses as a child-centered teacher. What biases do you have? How can you go about reducing your prejudices concerning children's creative expression and play?

Interview

The Ideal Educator

In Louis Rubin's (1985) research with administrators, he identified several teacher characteristics that were highly valued. While there was general agreement that knowledge, skills, and overall competence were basic requirements, administrators identified four teacher attributes that differentiated superlative teachers, that is, master teachers, from ordinary classroom teachers: spontaneity, perceptivity, originality, and insight. Interestingly, these four attributes all have a clear connection to creative expression and playfulness. Conduct your own interview with a teacher or administrator, using the scale provided. Compile the results of the class. How did your findings compare with those obtained by Rubin?

Teacher Attributes

Consider two categories of teachers, those who are average and those who are outstanding. Prioritize the following attributes in terms of their importance for teachers on a scale of 1 to 10, where 10 is most important and 1 is least important.

Attributes	Importance for Average Teacher (1–10)	Importance for Outstanding Teacher (1–10)
Dependability/reliability		
Knowledge of subject-specific content		
Understanding of children's growth and development		
Interpersonal effectiveness		
Organizational abilities		
Ability to plan for effective instruction		
Spontaneity		
Flexibility/adaptability		
Perceptivity and insight		
Creativity and originality		
Understanding of educational settings (educational philosophy, organizational mission, institutional policies)		

Observation

Do You Support Creative Expression and Play?

Using the self-evaluation below, assess your own knowledge, beliefs, values, and biases where children's creativity and play are concerned.

Self-Assessment: Beliefs and Practices About Creative Expression and Play

Instructions: Rate each item on a scale from Strongly Agree to Strongly Disagree.
(SA = Strongly Agree; A = Agree; U = Undecided; D = Disagree; SD = Strongly
Disagree)

Beliefs About Creativity and Play

Creative expression and play provide opportunities for:

emotional release	SA	A	U	D	SD
enjoyment	SA	A	U	D	SD
physical development	SA	A	U	D	SD
intellectual development	SA	A	U	D	SD
social development	SA	A	U	D	SD
problem solving	SA	A	U	D	SD
gender/sex role development	SA	A	U	D	SD
communicative abilities	SA	A	U	D	SD
decision-making skills	SA	A	U	D	SD
literacy development	SA	A	U	D	SD
investigation	SA	A	U	D	SD
other					

Curricular Issues

Creative expression and play:

provide choices	SA	A	U	D	SD
foster a feeling of competence	SA	A	U	D	SD
expand learning goals	SA	A	U	D	SD
integrate subject areas	SA	A	U	D	SD
foster language growth	SA	A	U	D	SD
other					

Assessment Issues

Creative expression and play can be used to:

encourage divergent thinking	SA	A	U	D	SD
document children's work	SA	A	U	D	SD
gain insight about creative processes	SA	A	U	D	SD
evaluate the program	SA	A	U	D	SD
identify talents	SA	A	U	D	SD
guide social development	SA	A	U	D	SD
guide intellectual development	SA	A	U	D	SD
other					

Problems with Creative Expression and Play

The things that are most troublesome about creative expression and play are:

conflict between children over play (toys, roles, use of space)	SA	A	U	D	SD
potential for chaos	SA	A	U	D	SD
lack of materials	SA	A	U	D	SD
my difficulty in generating new ideas for play themes	SA	A	U	D	SD
the influence of television	SA	A	U	D	SD
transitions into and out of play	SA	A	U	D	SD

Barriers to Creative Expression and Play

Major impediments to more child-centered teaching are:

lack of administrative support	SA	A	U	D	SD
physical environment	SA	A	U	D	SD
scheduling constraints	SA	A	U	D	SD
state regulations and policies	SA	A	U	D	SD
limited budget	SA	A	U	D	SD
standardized tests	SA	A	U	D	SD
lack of parental support	SA	A	U	D	SD

Evidence of Creative Expression and Play

In my classroom, I encourage:

freedom to create	SA	A	U	D	SD
child-initiated activities	SA	A	U	D	SD
large blocks of time	SA	A	U	D	SD
a wide array of materials	SA	A	U	D	SD
a low-risk, nurturing environment	SA	A	U	D	SD
opportunities for make-believe	SA	A	U	D	SD
a challenging outdoor environment	SA	A	U	D	SD
mutual respect between and among teachers and children	SA	A	U	D	SD
less teacher talk and more child talk	SA	A	U	D	SD

Evidence of Appropriate Assessment

In my classroom, I:

focus on the whole child	SA	A	U	D	SD
strive to communicate effectively with parents	SA	A	U	D	SD

value divergent/lateral thinking	SA	A	U	D	SD
use developmentally appropriate practices	SA	A	U	D	SD
use observational skills	SA	A	U	D	SD
compile children's work into portfolios	SA	A	U	D	SD
guide children in self-evaluation	SA	A	U	D	SD

Roles and Responsibilities

I see my most important roles in children's creative expression and play as:

facilitating children's growth	SA	A	U	D	SD
observing children's processes	SA	A	U	D	SD
preparing the physical environment	SA	A	U	D	SD
providing appropriate materials	SA	A	U	D	SD
educating parents about creative expression and play	SA	A	U	D	SD
defending the value of play to others in the field of education	SA	A	U	D	SD
evaluating the outcomes of children's creative expression and play	SA	A	U	D	SD
other					

Controversy

Are Our Lesson Planning Methods Outmoded?

Most educators are well acquainted with a lesson plan format like the following:

Purpose or goal

Behavioral objective(s)

Materials

Motivation

Procedure

Evaluation

Clearly, this sort of plan comes from the performance goals orientation. Although this approach has dominated lesson planning for the last 30 years in one form or another, it does not always lend itself to early childhood child-initiated activities. Katz (1988) compares and contrasts a performance goals orientation to a learning goals orientation as follows:

	Performance Goals	Learning Goals
View of the Child	competitive and conforming	cooperative yet individual
Focus on	project completion	ability level of child
Demands from Child	complete task at a particular level or fail	discover something and succeed
Typical Questions	I want to see how many of you can get _____right. I want to find out how good you are at _____.	I want you to learn as much as you can about _____. See how much you and your partner can find out about _____.
Child's Questions to Self	Will I measure up?	What do I need to do ?? How can I find about _____?

Kieran Egan (1989) suggests that teachers should stop thinking of lessons and units as sets of objectives to be mastered and begin to think of them as good stories to be told. The common feature of great literature is mediation between nature and culture, between binary opposites. Some examples of binary opposites are as follows:

humans	robots, androids	nonhumans
beauty	beauty disguised as ugliness	ugliness
intelligence	weak character outsmarts a much stronger character	physical strength
past	time travel from the present to past and future	future

What children's stories do you know that illustrate this fascinating middle ground between binary opposites? By using the same dynamic found in stories, Egan believes that lessons can become more exciting.

The *story framework* is an approach to teaching that uses the best features of narratives (stories) to teach a lesson. Egan's approach to planning a lesson follows this sequence:

1. *Identifying importance.* As a first step, teachers need to determine what is really important about a topic, what will evoke an emotional response from the children.
2. *Finding binary opposites.* The idea here is to find a dramatic example to illustrate why the topic matters. Some examples of binary opposites are water as a helper/water as a destroyer and fantasy/reality.

3. *Organizing content in story form.* Now the teacher finds content that dramatizes the opposites and gives the topic a story form.
4. *Conclusion.* During the conclusion, the dramatic conflict between the binary opposites is resolved.
5. *Evaluation.* Finally, teachers devise a method for determining whether children have understood the topic, grasped its importance, and learned.

Research Highlight

Expert and Novice Practice

Summary of Research

What is the difference between expert and novice practice? One thing that differentiates them is the number, richness, and flexibility of the "scripts" teachers bring to the classroom setting. Research suggests that the scripts of experts from all walks of life contain highly specialized knowledge and skills that are efficiently organized by episodes, events, or cases (Carter & Doyle, 1989). In other words, we use story structures to capture the essence of what we have come to know. Through those narratives, experts are able to

> use richly elaborated conditional knowledge to interpret situations, bring a variety of information and procedures to bear on the case, and reflect constructively on their experience. . . .Although experts' procedures and patterns of thinking are often routinized or even automatic, their methods are not formulaic. Rather, they can adapt flexibly to a wide variety of standard and novel circumstances in their domain of expertise. (Carter & Doyle, 1989, p. 61)

Implications for Practice

Preservice teachers usually feel that their classroom experiences with children are the most valuable preparation for teaching. As a result, the vast majority of teacher preparation programs have instituted field experiences for teacher certification students that begin before student teaching. What is most essential about these early field experiences, however, is the way beginning early childhood educators use them to reflect upon and enrich their professional lives. What teaching scripts have you formulated, rehearsed, and analyzed? How have you used these scripts to build your competence and confidence?

References

Adams, J. (1986). *Conceptual blockbusting* (3rd ed.). Reading, MA: Addison-Wesley.

Alwin, D. (1988). From obedience to autonomy: Changes in traits desired in children. *Public Opinion Quarterly, 52* (1), 33–52.

Amabile, T. M. (1989). *Growing up creative.* New York: Crown.

Barrow, R. (1988). Some observations on the concept of imagination. In K. Egan and D. Nadaner (Eds.), *Imagination and education* (pp. 79–90). New York: Teachers College Press.

Carter, K., & Doyle, W. (1989). Classroom research as a resource for the graduate preparation of teachers. In A. E. Woolfolk (Ed.), *Research perspectives on the graduate preparation of teachers* (pp. 51–68). Englewood Cliffs, NJ: Prentice-Hall.

Casanova, U. (1987). Ethnic and cultural differences. In V. Richardson-Koehler (Ed.), *Educator's handbook; A research perspective* (pp. 379–392). New York: Longman.

Children's Defense Fund. (1990). *Children 1990: A report card.* Washington, DC: Author.

David, J. L. (1991). Restructuring and technology: Partners in change. *Phi Delta Kappan, 73*(1), 37–40, 78.

Degenhardt, M., & McKay, E. (1988). Imagination and education for cultural understanding. In K. Egan & D. Nadaner (Eds.), *Imagination and education* (pp. 237–255). New York: Teachers College Press.

Dewey, J. (1934). *Art as experience.* New York: Minton Balch.

Egan, K. (1988). The origins of imagination. In K. Egan & D. Nadaner (Eds.), *Imagination and education* (pp. 91–127). New York: Teachers College Press.

Egan, K. (1989). *Teaching as storytelling.* New York: Teachers College Press.

Eisner, E. (1976). *The arts, human development and education.* Berkeley, CA: Mc-Cuthen.

Engell, J. (1981). *The creative imagination: Enlightenment to romanticism.* Cambridge, MA: Harvard University Press.

Feuerstein, R., & Hoffman, B. (1982). Intergenerational conflict of rights: Cultural imposition and self-realization. *Journal of the School of Education, Indiana University 58,* 44–63.

Futrell, M. H. (1989). Mission not accomplished: Education reform in retrospect. *Phi Delta Kappan, 71*(1), 8–14.

Gardner, H. (1983). *Frames of mind: The theory of multiple intelligences.* New York: Basic Books.

Goodlad, J. (1984). *A place called school: Prospects for the future.* New York: McGraw-Hill.

Greene, M. (1988). What happened to imagination? In K. Egan & D. Nadaner (Eds.), *Imagination and education* (pp. 45–56). New York: Teachers College Press.

Grilli, S. (1987). *Preschool in the Suzuki spirit.* San Diego, CA: Harcourt Brace Jovanovich.

Hanson, K. (1986). *The self imagined.* London: Routledge & Kegan Paul.

Hatcher, B. (Ed.). (1987). *Learning opportunities beyond the school.* Wheaton, MD: Association for Childhood Education International.

Haycock, K. (1991). Reaching for the year 2000. *Childhood Education, 67*(5), 276–279.

Higher Education Research Institute. (1991). The American freshman and follow-up survey: 1990 freshman survey results. Los Angeles: University of California at Los Angeles.

Hodgkinson, H. (1991). Reform versus reality. *Phi Delta Kappan, 73*(1), 9–16.

Hoffman, S., & Lamme, L. L. (Eds.). (1989).*Learning from the inside out: The expressive arts.* Wheaton, MD: Association for Childhood Education International.

Isaksen, S. G., & Treffinger, D. J. (1985). *Creative problem solving: The basic course.* Buffalo, NY: Bearly, Ltd.

Isenberg, J. P., & Quisenberry, N. L. (1988). Play: A necessity for all children. *Childhood Education, 64*(3), 138–145.

Jalongo, M. R. (1992). Children's play: A resource for multicultural education. In E. B. Vold (Ed.), *Multicultural education in the early childhood classroom* (pp. 52–66). Washington, DC: National Education Association.

Jalongo, M. R. (1991b). *The role of the teacher in the 21st century: An insider's view.* Bloomington, IN: National Educational Service.

Johnson, D. W., Johnson, R. T., Holubec, E. J., & Roy, P. (1984). *Circles of Learning: Cooperation in the classroom.* Alexandria, VA: Association for Supervision and Curriculum Development.

Kagan, S. L. (1989). Early care and education: Tackling the tough issues. *Phi Delta Kappan, 70*(6), 433–439.

Kamii, C. (1988). Autonomy or heteronomy: Our choices of goals. In G. F. Roberson & M. A. Johnson (Eds.), *Leaders in education: Their views on controversial issues* (pp. 97–108). Lanham, MD: University Press of America.

Karlstad, M. S. (1986). Art in a first grade classroom. *Insights, 19*(2), 1–10. (ERIC Document Reproduction Service No. ED 276 664.)

Katz, L. (1988). *Early childhood education: What research tells us.* Bloomington, IN: Phi Delta Kappa.

Klein, B. (1984). Power and control, praise and deferred judgment. *Journal of Creative Behavior, 17,* 9–17.

Kriegel, R. J., & Patler, L. (1991). *If it ain't broke . . . break it!"* New York: Warner.

Lightfoot, S. L. (1978). *Worlds apart: Relationships between families and schools.* New York: Basic Books.

MacDonald, R. E. (1991). *A handbook of basic skills and strategies for beginning teachers: Facing the challenge of teaching in today's schools.* New York: Longman.

Matthews, W. S. (1977). Modes of transformation in the initiation of fantasy play. *Developmental Psychology. 13,* 212–216.

May, R. (1975). *The courage to create.* New York: W. W. Norton.

McCallum, R. S., & Glynn, S. M. (1977). Hemispheric specialization and creative behavior. *Journal of Creative Behavior, 13,* 263–273.

Minuchin, P. (1987). Schools, families and the development of young children. *Early Childhood Research Quarterly, 2,* 245–254.

Mock, R. (1970). *The inner world of childhood.* New York: Appleton-Century-Crofts.

Moyer, J., Egerston, H., & Isenberg, J. (1987). The child-centered kindergarten. *Childhood Education, 63*(3), 235–242.

Nelms, B. (1988). *Literature in the classroom: Readers, texts and contexts.* Urbana, IL: National Council of Teachers of English.

Paley, V. G. (1981). *Wally's stories.* Cambridge, MA: Harvard University Press.

Paley, V. G. (1990). *The boy who would be a helicopter: The uses of storytelling in the classroom.* Cambridge, MA: Harvard University Press.

Parnes, S. J. (1963). In C. W. Taylor & F. Barron (Eds.), *The identification of creativity and scientific talent* (pp. 225–255). New York: Wiley.

Piaget, J. (1951). *Play, dreams, and imitation in childhood.* New York: W. W. Norton.

Pifer, A. (1982, October). Children—a national resource. *High/Scope Research,* 2(2), 1.

Quellmalz, E. S. (1985). Needed: Better methods for testing higher-order thinking skills. *Educational Leadership, 43*(2), 29–35.

Ramirez, M. (1983). *Psychology of the Americas: Mestizo perspectives on personality and mental health.* New York: Academic Press.

Reeves, M. S. (1988, April). Self-interest and the common weal: Focusing on the bottom half. *Education Week,* 17.

Renzulli, J. S., Reis, S. M., & Smith, L. H. (1981). The revolving door model: A new way of identifying the gifted. *Phi Delta Kappan, 62*(9), 648–649.

Research and Policy Committee. (1985). *Investing in children.* Washington, DC:

Committee for Economic Development.

Rickards, T. (1985). *Stimulating innovation.* London: Frances Pinter.

Rose, M. (1989). *Lives on the boundary.* New York: Penguin.

Rosen, H. (1980). The dramatic mode. In P. Salmon (Ed.), *Coming to know* (pp. 152–169). London: Routledge & Kegan Paul.

Rubin, L. (1985). *Artistry in teaching.* New York: Random House.

Ryan, K. (1986). *The induction of new teachers.* Bloomington, IN: Phi Delta Kappa (Fastback No. 237).

Schon, D. A. (1983). *The reflective practitioner.* New York: Basic Books.

Shulman, L. S. (1986). Those who understand: Knowledge growth in teaching. *Education Researcher, 19*(2), 4–14.

Siegel, M., & Carey, R. F. (1989). *Critical thinking: A Semiotic perspective.* Bloomington, IN: ERIC Clearinghouse on Reading and Communication Skills and Urbana, IL: National Council of Teachers of English.

Silberman, C. E. (1970). *Crisis in the classroom: The remaking of American education.* New York: Random House.

Simon, H. (1973). Applying information technology to organizational design. *Public Administration Review, 33*(3), 268–278.

Sizer, T. (1984). *Horace's compromise.* Boston: Houghton Mifflin.

Sutton-Smith, B. (1988a). Children's play. In G. Roberson & M. Johnson (Eds.), *Leaders in education: Their views on contemporary issues* (pp. 165–167). Lanham, MA: University Press of America.

Sutton-Smith, B. (1988b). In search of the imagination. In K. Egan & D. Nadaner (Eds.), *Imagination and education* (pp. 3–29). New York: Teachers College Press.

Task Force on Teaching as a Profession (1986). *A nation prepared: Teachers for the 21st century.* Washington, DC: Carnegie Forum on Education and the Economy.

Tetenbaum, T. J., & Mulkeen, T. A. (1986). Computers as an agent for educational change. *Computers in the Schools, 2*(4), 91–103.

Toffler, A. (1970). *Future shock.* New York: Random House.

Toffler, A. (1980). *The third wave.* New York: Morrow.

Torrance, E. P., & Meyers, R. (1986). *For those who wonder.* Albany, OR: Perceptive Publishing.

West, B. (1986). Culture before ethnicity. *Childhood Education, 62*(3), 175–181.

Whitehead, A. N. (1929). *The aims of education and other essays.* New York: Macmillan.

APPENDIX

A

Dance Prop Box

GOALS

☐ To provide opportunities to move from thinking and feeling to the physical expression of thought and emotion.

☐ To provide opportunities for role-playing experiences such as aerobics instructor, ballet dancer, or square dancer.

☐ To encourage oral language expression in describing different kinds of dances and feelings about dancing.

☐ To provide opportunities for talking about health, fitness, and relaxation.

MATERIALS IN PROP BOX

mats	hats	mats
feathers	headdress	assorted dance shoes
tiaras	gloves	leotards
boas	balloons	tights
bandanas	tutus	dance recital costumes
ribbons	pompoms	tambourines
long skirts	baton	masks
balls	vests	

SUGGESTED SUPPLEMENTS AND MATERIALS

book or story about dance	hand mirror	record player
records or tapes for dance	full length mirror	cubes
posters of dancers	tape player	ballet bar

VOCABULARY

aerobics	circle right	modern dance
arabesque	folk dancing	plié
ballerina	jazz	positions of the feet
ballet	jumping jacks	recital
choreographer	march	rhythm
circle left	mask	square dance

CHILD-MADE MATERIALS

tambourines
signs about the dance
bring in masks or a headdress

RESOURCE PEOPLE

Fathers, mothers, and friends of students who are dancers could come to class and tell what they do during a day of work.

INTRODUCTION OF CENTER

"Welcome to the Dance Center"

Discuss what they know about dance and about why people dance.

Explain different types of dance (e.g., ballet, folk, modern, jazz, and square dancing).

Ask the students how many have seen or participated in a dance.

Discuss the different roles they can play at the dance center: ballerina, modern dancer, tap dancer, ballroom dancer, aerobics teacher, or choreographer.

Set limits for four children in the center. As space becomes available, children may choose to join the dancers.

Model different dance forms to introduce some of the vocabulary, if appropriate.

ACTIVITIES

Inform the parents of the new center and invite them to share dance experiences with their children.

Encourage children to try out all roles in the dance center.

Use photographs of children dancing to add to the dance book.

EXTENSION

Visit a dance studio, children's dance theater, or aerobics studio.

Imagine themselves as dancers, draw pictures, or write a story about themselves as dancers.

Choreograph their own dance.

ADDITIONAL IDEAS FOR PROP BOXES

Doctor's Office	Space	Birthday Party
telephone, appointment book, tongue depressors, prescription pads and empty bottles, cotton balls, stethoscope, pencils, examination mat, dolls, doll bed, bandages	sleeping bag, Ziploc bags for food, telescope, steering wheel, control panel, space suit, helmet	candles, streamers, markers, paper, cake pans, wrapping paper, boxes, invitations
Library	**Restaurant**	**Gas Station**
children's books with pockets made from cut envelopes, videotapes, library cards, pencils, signs for story hours, cards for pocket of book, date stamp and ink pad, cash register, money, book-return box	aprons, chef's hat, menus, tray, pitcher, silverware, dishes, stove top (bottom of box) play money, cash register, pencils and order pads	spray bottles and paper towels, used and cleaned motor parts, hammer, oil funnel, flashlight, old rags, keys, automobile supply catalogues, hoses

PROP BOXES FOR FAIRY TALES

Little Red Riding Hood

tape recording and book of the story, red sweater or cape, basket for red apron, bowl, spoon for mother, ball cap with ears for wolf, axe and hat for woodcutter, bonnet for grandmother

Cinderella

tape recording and book of story, apron for Cinderella, high-heeled shoe for slipper, hats for stepaunts, crown for prince

The Three Bears

tape recording and book of the story, three different-sized bowls, spoons, blankets, three different hats for bears, hat or collar for Goldilocks, three stuffed bears

Hansel and Gretel

tape recording and book of the story, hat and axe for father, scarf for stepmother, bonnet for Gretel, hat for Hansel, witch hat for the witch, dog bone (block)

The Elves and the Shoemaker

tape recording and book of the story, a few pairs of old shoes, shawl for old woman, apron for old man, doll clothes for elves, piece of brown or black felt representing leather

Snow White and Rose Red

tape recording and book of the story, apron for mother, white and red plastic flowers, scissors from classroom, bags or boxes of beads for jewels, pixie hat for gnome, brown pixie garbage bag for bear, crown for prince, red and white collars

Source: Courtesy of Dorothy Nadeau.

APPENDIX

B

Published Rating Scales to Evaluate Preschool Settings

Frost, J. L. (1986). Playground rating system. Ages 3–8. In J. S. McKee (Ed.), *Play: Working partner of growth* (pp. 66–67). Wheaton, MD: Association for Childhood Education International.

This rating system contains 39 items to evaluate three different areas of playground quality. It evaluates what the playground should contain, the condition and safety of the equipment, and the degree and quality of challenge and learning opportunities for children. Each item is rated on a scale from 0 ("Does Not Exist") to 5 ("Excellent; All Elements"). A score may be obtained for each individual area, as well as a total playground rating score.

Harms, T., & Clifford, R. M. (1980). *Early childhood environment rating scale*. New York: Teachers College Press. 44 pages.

This rating scale provides guidelines for assessing the quality of the physical and social environments for young children in seven areas. Detailed guidelines are provided for room arrangement, furnishings, and displays, as well as for creative activities.

Harms, T., Cryer, D., & Clifford, R. M. (1990). *Infant/toddler environment rating scale*. New York: Teachers College Press. 48 pages.

This rating scale contains assessment criteria for children in group care up to 30 months of age. Criteria for furnishings and displays for children, space, learning activities, and program structure are among the seven categories rated from "Inadequate" (not meeting custodial care needs) to "Excellent" (describing high-quality care).

Harms, T., & Clifford, R. M. (1989). *Family day care rating scale*. New York: Teachers College Press. 39 pages.

This scale defines family day care comprehensively and can be used for evaluating family day care settings. It provides ratings for space, materials, and learning activities among the six categories addressed to ensure that the environment is developmentally appropriate for young children. Each item is described in four levels of quality ranging from "Inadequate" (does not meet custodial needs) to "Excellent" (high-quality care).

National Association for the Education of Young Children (1984). *Accreditation criteria and procedures of the National Academy of Early Childhood Programs*. Washington, DC: NAEYC.

A portion of these criteria describes nine aspects of the physical environment. It focuses on the arrangement of the environment, selection of materials, and interactions between adults and children.

Jones, E. (1977). *Dimensions of teaching-learning environments*. Pasadena, CA: Pacific Oaks.

This rating scale describes the physical setting and the teacher's behavior along four dimensions: soft/hard, simple/complex, intrusion/seclusion, and high mobility/low mobility. It views these dimensions along a continuum and explores the possibilities of arranging environments within them.

APPENDIX

C

Noncompetitive Games
for Children

Ballgames

Preschoolers/Kindergartners

Call Ball

Form a circle with one child in the center who tosses the ball while calling another child's name. This child tries to catch the ball after the first bounce. The child continues with other children.

Basket Ball

Children stand before a plastic basket and toss the ball into the basket. The game may be played individually, in pairs, or in groups. Emphasis is on trying to hit the mark rather than keeping score, so move the basket closer or farther away to adjust the challenge level.

School-Age Children

Letter or Number Ball

As players pass a small ball around a circle, have them say a letter or a number. Players may count or say the alphabet in unison if they go in order.

Tennis

Make "rackets" out of a nylon stocking stretched over a coat hanger. Children can bat a pingpong ball back and forth using the racket.

Lap Ball

Players form a circle and sit close to each other, with shoulders touching. They try to pass a ball around the circle from lap to lap without using their hands.

Quiet Games

Preschoolers/Kindergartners

Nursery Rhymes

Say the rhyme and follow up with action. For example: "Jack and Jill went *up* (children reach up high) the hill. Jack falls *down* (children touch the ground). Other favorite nursery rhymes include "Humpty Dumpty," "Mary Had a Little Lamb," and "Baa Baa Black Sheep."

Toyshop

Have children pretend they are a toy. When called on, each one imitates the sound and action of the toy and continues until someone guesses the name of the toy.

Clap and Tap Names

In this game, say a child's name and have the group repeat it several times, establishing a rhythm for the name. Then have the children clap the rhythm of the name while they say it. Ask them to use their feet while saying the name and, last, to move forward on that rhythm.

School-Age Children

On My Way to School . . .

Form a circle with one child in the center who says, "On my way to school this morning, I saw . . ." and then imitates what he or she saw. Others guess the imitation. The one guessing correctly goes into the center, and the game begins again.

Buzz

Players take turns counting one number at a time. Whenever they have to say a number with seven in it, they say *buzz* instead. If a player accidentally says *seven* (or *seventeen*, or *twenty-seven*), then the game begins again at number one.

Singing Games

Preschoolers/Kindergartners

Charlie Over The Water

Players join hands in a circle. One player, Charlie, is in the center. The circle moves to the left while chanting:

> Charlie over the water,
> Charlie over the sea,
> Charlie caught a blackbird
> but he can't catch me.

On the word *me* the players quickly squat. Charlie tries to tag a player before he or she gets into the squat position. The tagged child then becomes "Charlie."

Round and Round Went The Gallant Ship

In this game, children dance around in a circle with clasped hands, reciting the following verse and "bobbing" down quickly as the ship goes to the bottom of the sea:

> Three times round went our gallant ship,
> And three times round went she;
> Three times round went our gallant ship
> Then she sank to the bottom of the sea.

A tumble as the ship goes down adds much to the spirit of the play.

Did You Ever See a Lassie?

One child is in the middle of a circle. Other children grasp hands and circle around the child in the center while singing the first two lines. During lines three and four, the children drop hands and imitate the child in the middle, who thinks up some special way to hop.

Did you ever see a lassie (laddie), a lassie, a lassie,
Did you ever see a lassie, do this way and that?
Do this way and that way, and this way and that way,
Did you ever see a lassie do this way and that?

School-Age Children

Riggety Jig

The children form a standing circle. One child begins to skip inside the circle to the following tune:

As I was going down the street
Down the street, down the street
As I was going down the street
Hi Ho, Hi Ho, Hi Ho

A handsome fellow (pretty girl) I chanced to meet
Chanced to meet, chanced to meet.
A handsome fellow (pretty girl) I chanced to meet
Hi Ho, Hi Ho, Hi Ho

With the chosen partner, both children skip around the circle to the following tune:

Riggety jig, jig, and away we go
Away we go, away we go
Riggety jig, jig, and away we go
Hi Ho, Hi Ho, Hi Ho

Others clap the tune.

Singing Syllables

After one player leaves the room, the rest of the group decides on a word to sing. If the word is *November*, for example, some players will sing "No No No," some will sing "vem vem vem," and the rest will sing "ber-ber-ber," all at the same time.

Now the player who left the room returns and tries to figure out what the word is. Everyone gets a turn to be the guesser, with, of course, a new word sung each time.

Running Games

Preschooler/Kindergartners

Squirrel and Nut

The children sit in a circle with heads down and hands open. One child, the squirrel, drops the "nut" (a piece of chalk or crayon) into the hands of any other child. That child immediately gets up and tries to catch the squirrel, who is safe by reaching the place of the second child. If not caught, the other child becomes the squirrel.

Cat and Mice

The "cat" hides behind something. Four or five "mice" creep up to the cat's hiding place and start scratching on the floor. Their scratching is the signal for the cat to start chasing them, and they are safe only on reaching their holes (places). Any mouse who is tapped becomes the cat. Other mice are then chosen, and the game begins again.

Drop The Handkerchief

One child runs around the circle and drops a handkerchief behind another player. That player picks up the handkerchief and runs around the circle in the direction opposite to that of the first player. The one who reaches the vacant place left in the circle becomes IT. Then the game is repeated.

Musical Chairs

One version of musical chairs is to play music and have children find a chair *or* a lap when the music stops. A chair is removed each time, but everyone finds a seat (by sitting on a lap).

School-Age Children

Numbers Change

Players stand in a large circle and are numbered consecutively. One player, in the center, calls two numbers (not his or her own). The center player tries to secure one of their places. The one who is left without a place now becomes the center player.

In the classroom, the number caller (who also has a number) stands in front of the room and calls two numbers. While players change places, the caller tries to take a seat vacated by one of the runners whose number was called.

Kitty in The Corner

The children form a circle on the floor. Four chairs are placed in four corners of a square. A fifth child is in the middle. When the teacher calls "Kitty in the a corner," the children in the chairs change places while the child in the center seeks to get into one of the chairs. The displaced child then chooses someone to take his or her place until all have had a turn.

Squirrels in Trees

The group is divided and numbered in threes. Numbers 1 and 2 join hands to represent the tree. Number 3 is the squirrel and stands in the circle formed by the other two. There should be one or more odd squirrels without trees. The groups of threes are scattered over the play space. At a signal from a leader or the teacher, the squirrels attempt to get into trees. Only one squirrel is allowed in one tree at the same time. Someone is always left without a tree. As soon as all trees are full, the game is repeated.

Partner Games

Preschoolers/Kindergartners

Repeat

One player says a word that the other player repeats. Continue repeating the same word until one player wants to stop, which is the tricky part.

Finish My Action

One player begins an imaginary action, such as brushing teeth or raking leaves. When that player stops, the partner finishes the action. Then the partners switch roles.

School-Age Children

Copy Cat

With a partner, decide who will be the mirror and who will be the copy cat. Players must face one another as they stay together mirroring actions.

Puppeteers

One player is the puppet on the ground, unable to move. Along comes the puppeteer, who brings the puppet to life with pretend strings. The puppeteer pulls the strings, and the puppet responds to every tug. Allow everyone a chance to be the puppeteer as well as to be the puppet.

Ali Baba and The Forty Thieves

Two players stand facing each other a few feet apart. One of the players sings the words "Ali Baba and the forty thieves" to any made-up tune, at the same time doing a hand movement, such as clapping. When the singer is finished, the second player repeats the song and the motions exactly; at the same time, the first player sings the phrase again and does something different with his or her hands—hitting one arm with the opposite hand, for example.

For the next round, the second player must copy this second set of movements, along with continuing to sing, and so on, with both players singing "Ali Baba and the forty thieves" over and over, each doing a different hand movement. The activity continues until one of the players forgets the line.

References

Kamil, C., & DeVries, R. (1980). *Group games in early education. Implications of Piaget's theory.* Washington, DC: National Association for the Education of Young Children.

Sobel, J. (1983). *Everybody wins. Non-competitive games for young children.* New York: Walker.

APPENDIX

D

Observations of Medical Play

April 8: Getting started

Nick (doctor):   Come in, come in! (puts stethoscope around neck) Where's your heart?

Allen: Right here.

Nick: Nurse, get me the blood pressure kit.

Amanda: Where's my hat? A nurse can wear a hat, but I don't have one. Well, I'll put this nice new pretend hat on. There! How do I look?

Teacher: Amanda, you look just like the nurse at my doctor's office.

April 15: Drawing on prior experience

Teacher (mother):   It won't hurt my baby? Are you sure?

Markus (doctor):   Hold on to him, Mommy. Where do you think he should get his shot at?

Teacher: How about his arm?

Markus: How about his foot? I got a shot in my foot one time for stepping on a nail. A tennis shot.

Teacher: Do you mean a tetanus shot?

Markus: Yeah, that's it.

April 22: Building vocabulary

Mallory: What's that? I can't remember, and I need to use it.

Teacher: That's a thermometer. It tells you the temperature of your body.

Mallory: Oh, yeah, I remember.

Jeremy: Where's that heart thing? I want to listen to someone's heart.

Teacher: Here's the stethoscope.

April 27: Reality testing

Allen: My leg hurts, Doc.

Nick: I'll put this on. (Puts an ace bandage on for a few seconds.) Now it's time to take it off and see if your leg is better. (Allen begins removing the bandage.)

Teacher: Allen, would the patient take off his own bandage?

Allen: Whoops. Hey, Doc, take off my bandage!

Nick: Your leg's all better, but I have to give you a shot. Now lay down. Now I'm gonna give you a shot, but I'm gonna put these cotton balls in your mouth first. (Giggles and starts to move toward Allen's mouth.)

Teacher: Nick, when you go to the doctor, how does he really use the cotton ball?

Nick: (Begins to rub Allen's arm with the cotton ball.)

April 29: Introducing new materials and concepts

Teacher: I am a blood pressure kit salesperson. I would like to demonstrate how to use our new and improved blood pressure kit. First, you have the patient hold out her arm. Then you carefully put the arm cuff on like this. Next, you put the end of the stethoscope right under the cuff and hold it. Then you pump it up only three times and watch the needle. That's how you use this new kit. If you have any questions, just call me.

May 4: The high price of medical care

Today the theme of medical costs was introduced by Markus, who was playing the doctor and charged exorbitant rates. When the patient paid him, he said, "I'm rich! I'm rich!".

Teacher: How much do I owe for today's visit?

Kara: You owe me $235. Pay me now. (Holds out hand.)

Teacher: Here you go.

May 6: Negotiation

Kara and Michelle started to argue about who will play the doctor and who will be the nurse.

Michelle: Okay, you can look at his throat and ears, and I'll do the eye chart and see how tall he is.

Kara: And you can do the blood pressure, and I'll give him a shot and listen to his body.

Michelle: Allen, stand against the wall here. (She puts her hand just above his head and looks at the chart.) Allen, move away. You are four feet one inch.

Later, Kara was the patient.

Allen: Okay, Kara, cover your eye and say those letters.

Kara: Those are small letters. Ready? (Reads all the letters.) There, I did it! (Big smile.) And I didn't even miss one. (Checks the chart with both eyes uncovered.)

May 9: Incorporating new vocabulary

Greg was the nurse. He said that he had a telephone call and needed to go to the scene of an accident. I asked him if nurses usually did that. He wasn't sure. I explained that the people who go to accidents in an ambulance are called *para-medics*. Later, Greg got another accident call and said, "I'm sorry, I can't come.

You need the paramedics. I'll call 911 and get you a ambulance with paramedics on it. They'll save 'em."

Note pads, an appointment book, and a ballpoint pen were added to the center.

Michelle is playing the role of doctor and asks, "Why do I have paper?"

The teacher answered: "Did you ever see doctors write a prescription? The doctor writes down what kind of medicine you should take."

(Later) Michelle: I got my paper to write stuff out. Who needs a prescription? Who needs a bill?

     Melanie: What do you do with a prescription?

    Michelle: You take it to a drug store and they give you the medicine you need from what's written on the paper.

May 13: Connecting with life

Letha has been in and out of the hospital because she was diagnosed as having cancer (now in remission). When she returned to school, I changed the center to a veterinarian's office during our pets theme. Throughout the children's play, I heard her refer to her hospital experiences. Some examples of statements she made were "Is this like a people hospital? I was in a people hospital a long time."

When Brandon tried to give her a shot, she said, "Not me! I had enough shots already in the hospital. I got blood taken lots of times. The thing they used looked just like this, except longer." Their conversation continued:

Brandon: I never had that done. I'll take some blood from the dog to examine.

   Letha: I'll show you how, okay? You need to put on your mask like real doctors do.

Brandon: What is the mask for?

    Kurt: My bear broke his head. He was standing on his chair and fell off.

Brandon: I'll x-ray his head. But I gotta put my mask on first.

    Kurt: Why?

Brandon: So I don't spit my gum on him. No. To keep out the germs.

Maryjane: Germs? Did I hear someone say germs? This is a hospital. There should not be germs. Get out, get out.

  Markus: Guys, I got a . . . I got a . . . I need something. I got a sick fox here.

Brandon: Wait, I'm taking care of this one.

Amanda: I had a pet rabbit one time, I mean, a long time ago at home. His name was Henny. He was really sick, and he died a long time ago. My mom thought he would die, and he did.

 Melanie: I had a gerbil, and my mom thought he was gonna die because we forgot to feed him.

May 16: Symbolic play

Shawn:	I'm the doctor today.
Scott:	No, I am.
Shawn:	We both are. It's a big petpital.
Scott:	What's a petpital?
Shawn:	It's a hospital for pets.
Allen:	When my brother went to the doctor's, they found out how much he weighed and how tall he got.
Teacher:	Maybe we could do that for one of our animals.
Jeremy:	Yeah. Let's see. I'll use this block for the uh, what's that thing called?
Letha:	A scale.
Jeremy:	(Brings over a toy duck.) We need to weight him.
Shayna:	I'm the nurse. Put your duck on the scale, and I'll measure him.
Letha:	My duck is a girl.
Shayna:	Sorry. She weights, uumm . . .
Jeremy:	Twenty-five million pounds!
Letha:	She does not. Your scale must be broke.
Jeremy:	Okay, 13 pounds.
Shayna:	She's 1 foot tall, too.

May 18: Sex role stereotypes

Dee:	Can I play?
Scott:	No, we have two doctors and a nurse. That's enough.
Teacher:	I think we can find something for Dee to do.
Dee:	I could be the ambulance driver.
Scott:	No, you cannot.
Dee:	Why?
Scott:	Because! You're a girl, and girls can't be ambulance drivers.
Amanda:	They can too!
Shawn:	Can not.
Teacher:	Scott and Shawn, why do you think that girls can't be ambulance drivers?
Scott:	Because men drive better.
Shawn:	Yeah.
Amanda:	No, they do not.
Maryjane:	Men drive lousy.

Teacher: Girls can be ambulance drivers just like boys. Girls can be doctors and boys can be nurses. My doctor is a woman.

Dee: I'm gonna find something to use for my—*my* ambulance. Whoo, whoo, ambulance comin' through. Hey, there's a sick fox over here. What kind of hospital is this anyway? I said I got a sick fox over here!

Maryjane: Oh! Hey, we need a doctor over here. We have a patient.

Shawn: I'm coming. Hold your pants on. (Children from the camping play center come over.) I wish these guys would stop coming and bugging me and my patient. This is a hospital, not a picnic. Geez.

Active nature of play, 31
Activity, complete absorption of
    children in, 7
Adams, J., 337
Adler, Alfred, 294
    creativity theory of, 12
Adult/child interactions in guiding
    creative growth, 259–260
Aesthetic appeal as assessment criteria,
    295
Aesthetic skills, music in developing,
    106
Affective skills, music in developing,
    105
Alger, H. A., 188, 190–191
Almy, M., 51
Alwin, D., 331
Amabile, T. M., 6–16, 338
Apelman, M., 216, 230
Appropriateness of creative behavior, 5
Art, 60–96
    case study on, 62–63
    center for, in creative environment,
        184
    children retaining ownership in, 64
    children's art, understanding, 64–75
    children's developmental sequence in,
        65, 68–72
    cognitive aspect of, 64–65
    criteria for, 63–64
    for culturally diverse groups, 90–91
    developmental aspect of, 65
    discussion about, 76
    for disabled child, 91–92
    graphic aspect of, 65
    for high-achieving children, 91–92
    integrated into subject areas, 88–90
    learning about, 75–76
    learning through, 70, 72–75

    for low-achieving children, 91–92
    originality over conformity in, 63–64
    perceptual aspect of, 64
    process over product in, 63
    for special populations, 90–92
    vocabulary of, 75–76
Art education. *See also* Teaching art
    aesthetic goal of, 67
    art criticism goal of, 67
    art history goal of, 66–67
    art production goal of, 66
    principles of, 65–70
Art experiences, child-centered, 86–88
Ashcroft, S. C., 204
Asher, S. R., 268
Assessment
    of creative expression and play
        appropriate, 297–311
        case study on, 290
        criteria for, 294–297
        difficulties with, 293–294
        by observation. *See* Observation
        portfolios in, 304–311
        purposes for, 291–293
        for special populations, 316–318
        teachers' roles and responsibilities
            in, 312–316
        theoretical framework for, 291–294
    defining, 291
Athey, I., 36
Atkinson, A. H., 270
Attention span, time and, 177
Auerbach, S., 214, 243
Autocratic adult-child interactions in
    guiding creative growth, 259

Ball games, 364
Barbour, N., 37, 44, 182, 184, 226, 227
Barrow, R., 297

Bartlett, K., 267
Baumrind, D., 259
Bayes, L., 122
Bayless, K. M., 113
Beaty, K., 301
Behavior, prosocial, 263–266
Behavioral approach in guiding creative
 growth, 256–258
Benson, A., 113, 119
Bergen, D., 41, 47, 49
Berger, 273, 275, 276
Berk, L., 184, 189
Berns, R. M., 237
Bernstein, P., 102
Block center in creative environment,
 184
Blocks
 as divergent play materials, 229–232
 structures of, research on, 321–324
Bloom, B., 34, 296
Bodyplays in mathematics/science
 curriculum, 157–158
Bolton, Gavin, 138, 142, 157, 166
Bowker, J. E., 75
Boyd, A. E., 102–106
Brainstorming, 11
Brand, M., 118
Bredekamp, S., 35, 182, 188, 220, 235,
 255, 266, 291
Bretherton, I., 31
Brewster, A., 49
Brittain, W. L., 65
Bromley, K. D., 157
Bronfenbrenner, U., 284
Bruner, Jerome S., 34, 46, 47, 103, 104
Brutger, J. H., 66
Bruya, L. D., 196
Burns, D. E., 205
Burton, E. C., 108
Burton, T., 15
Busching, B. A., 157

Carew, J. V., 284
Carle, Eric, 162
Carlsson-Paige, N., 54, 245
Carter, K., 352
Caruso, D., 183, 269, 270, 271
Casanova, U., 344
Casey, M. B., 182, 200
Castle, Kathryn, 238, 240
Cazden, C., 36

Centers in creative environment,
 181–188
 by age group, 182–184
 art, 184
 block, 184
 classroom based on, 186–188
 discovery, 184–185
 dramatic play, 185
 library, 185–186
 literacy, 185–186
 manipulative, 186
 math, 186
 media, 186
 music, 186
 science, 184–185
 types and uses of, 184–186
 writing, 186
Chalmers, F. G., 75, 76
Characterization in language/literature/
 literacy curriculum, 160
Chard, S.C., 269, 272, 273, 340
Child(ren)
 creative abilities of, 12
 thought of, unique features of, 6–7
Children's Defense Fund, 334
Christensen, D., 268
Christie, J. F., 38, 142, 143, 217, 304
Christopherson, H., 216
Clark, J. S., 20
Clark, J. W., 20
Classical theories of play, 44–46
Classroom
 center-based, as creative environment,
  186–188
 clay in, research on, 246–247
 superhero play in, 53–54
Classroom environment, preparation of,
 to promote literacy during play,
 208–209
Clay
 child-centered art experiences using,
  87
 in classroom, research on, 246–247
 as divergent play material, 232, 233
Cleary, Beverly, 155
Clemens, S. G., 76, 79, 84
Climate of creative environment,
 174–176
Cocking, R. R., 296
Cognitive aspect of art, 64–65
Cognitive development, play in, 35–36

Cognitive-developmental theory of play, 46
Cognitive play, development of, 38–43
Cognitive skills, music in developing, 105–106
Cohen, L. M., 163
Collins, A., 295, 317
Collins, M., 120
Communication
  in creative process, 11
  in developing language/literacy skills, 36
  with families in guiding creative behavior, 273–276
  nonverbal, in social studies/health/ nutrition curriculum, 161
Competence in creative teacher, 262
Conflicts of children understanding, 266–267
Construction materials, 218, 219
  for infants, 221
  for preschoolers/kindergartners, 225
  for school-age children, 228
  for toddlers, 222
Constructive play in cognitive development, 41–43
Constructivism in guiding creative growth, 255–256
Constructivist perspective on creativity, 11
Convergent play materials, 215
Convergent thinking, 10
Cooperative problem solving in guiding creative behavior, 269–271
Corsaro, W. A., 268
Creative abilities, children's, 12
Creative activities, in fostering creative process, 18
Creative drama. *See under* Drama, creative
Creative environment, 15, 172–209
  case study on, 174
  climate of, 174–176
  indoor
    arranging, 179–189
    centers in, 181–188
    room arrangement for, 179–181, 182
    routines in, 188–189, 190–191
    transitions in, 188–189, 190–191
  outdoor. *See* Playgrounds
  space in, 176

  for special populations, 204–205
  teacher and, 199–203
  theoretical framework for, 174–178
  time and, 176–177
Creative expression
  as basic, 331–332
  play and
    assessing. *See* Assessment
    future of, agenda for, 339–341
    materials for. *See* Materials
  promoting
    in culturally diverse groups, 18–19
    in disabled children, 19
    in high-achieving children, 19
    in low-achieving children, 19–20
    teacher in, 17–18
Creative growth
  guidelines for, 266–267
  guiding, 252–284
    behavioral/social learning and, 256–258
    case study on, 254–255
    children's conflicts in, 267–269
    communicating with families in, 273–276
    construction in, 255–256
    cooperative problem solving in, 269–271
    for culturally diverse groups, 277–278
    developmentally appropriate methods for, 263–267
    for disabled children, 277–278
    for high-achieving children, 278–279
    humanism and, 256
    investigative play in, 271–272
    for low-achieving children, 278–279
    project work in, 272–273
    for special populations, 276–279
    strategies for, 269–273
    teachers' roles and responsibilities in, 258–262
    theoretical framework for, 255–258
Creative potential, unlocking, 13–14
Creative process
  assessing, 296
  stages, 11
Creative products, assessing, 296–297
Creative teacher, 260–262, 337–339

Creativity
  as assessment criteria, 295
  criteria for, 5–6
  defining, 4–11
  education and, 14–18
  levels of, 12–13
  play in developing, 38
  preschoolers', teachers' judgment of,
      23–25
  schools nurturing, 15–17
  young child and, 2–25
Culturally diverse groups
  art in, 90–91
  assessing creative expression and play
      in, 316–317
  creative drama for, 161–162
  creative expression in, 18–19
  future of creative expression/play for,
      342–343, 344
  guiding creative growth for, 277–278
  materials for creative expression and
      play for, 241
  music and movement for, 124
  play in, 49
Cultural skills, music in developing, 106
Cunningham, P., 155
Curriculum, early childhood, 28–55

Dacey, J. S., 10, 14–15, 199, 291
Dales, R., 105
Dance, prop box for, 357–360
D'Angelo, K., 123
Dank, H. L., 241
Dansky, J. L., 38
Darrow, A. A., 124, 125
Daubman, K. A., 15
D'Aulaire, E. P., 162
D'Aulaire, I., 162
David, J. L., 336, 338
Davidson, L., 111
Davies, D., 274
Day, B., 110
Day, M., 62
De Bono, E., 10
Deiner, P. L., 50, 277
Delibes, Leo, 117
De Mille, Richard, 3, 21
Democratic adult-child interactions in
      guiding creative growth, 260
Design, activities for extending
      experiences with, 82–83

Desire in creative teacher, 261–262
Developmental aspect of art, 65
DeVries, R., 216, 235, 236, 237
Dewey, John, 34
Dillon, D., 137
Disabled children
  art for, 91
  assessing creative expression and play
      in, 317
  creative drama for, 162
  creative environment for, 204–205
  creative expression in, 19
  future of creative expression/play for,
      343
  guiding creative growth for, 277–278
  materials for creative expression and
      play for, 241
  music and movement for, 124–125
  play in, 49–50
Discovery center in creative
      environment, 184–185
Divergent play materials, 215–216,
      232–234
Divergent thinking, 10
  assessing, purposes for, 291–293
  integrated personality and, 328–339
    case study on, 330–331
    in special populations, 341–345
    teachers' roles and responsibilities
        for, 333–339
    theoretical framework for, 331–333
    workplace of future and, 332–333
Divito, N., 161
Dixon, G., 75, 76
Dixon, S., 128
Donoghue, M., 146, 153, 155, 156, 166
Dough as divergent play material, 232,
      233
Doyle, W., 352
Drama
  appreciation of, 142
  child-centered art experiences using,
      144–145
  creative, 134–168
    activities/experiences for, 145–147
    case study on, 136
    for culturally diverse groups,
        161–162
    for disabled children, 162
    forms of enactment and, 138–140
    for high-achieving children, 163

Drama, *continued*
  creative, *continued*
    importance for curriculum, 140–142
    integrated into subject areas,
      157–161
    integrating into curriculum,
      142–145
    for low-achieving children, 163
    meaning of enactment and, 137
    selecting and presenting
      experiences and materials for,
      143–144
    for special populations, 161–163
    theoretical framework for, 136–140
  developmental appropriateness of,
    166–167
  formal, 138
  informal, 138, 139
  interpretive, 138, 139
  scripted, 138, 139
  story, 138, 139
    reasons to use, 155
    suggestions for classroom, 155–156
Dramatic play, 138, 139
  center for, in creative environment,
    185
  characteristics of, 43
  in cognitive development, 40–41
  in language/literature/literacy
    curriculum, 160
  suggestions for classroom, 146–149
  uses of, 145–146
Drosdeck, S., 227
DuCharme, E., 89
Dyeing, child-centered art experiences
  using, 88

Education. *See also* Art education; music
  education
  creativity and, 14–18
  play in, 34
Edwards, L. C., 142
Egan, Kieran, 14, 331, 351–352
Egerston, H., 180, 339
Eheart, B. K., 183
Ehlert, L., 67
Eisenberg-Berg, N., 267
Eisner, E., 92, 339
Eliason, C., 119
Elkind, David, 33, 43, 103, 244
Ellis, M. J., 33

Emotional development, play in, 37
Enactive stage of musical development,
  103
Enactment
  forms of, 138–140
  meaning of, 137
Engel, M., 93
Environment(s). *See also* Creative
  environment
  classroom, preparation of, to promote
    literacy during play, 208–209
  supportive musical growth and, 106
  teaching/learning, dimensions of,
    178
Epstein, J. L., 282
Erickson, K. L., 137, 140
Erikson, E. H., 27, 32, 46, 103, 104
Esbensen, S., 194
Exercise play in cognitive development,
  40
Expert and novice practice, difference
  between, 352
Exploratory responses to materials, 216
Expression, creative. *See* Creative
  expression

Fabric, child-centered art experiences
  using, 88
Fairweather, P. D., 128
Family, communication with
  obstacles to, 273–276
  one-way, 275
  strategies for, 275–276
  two-way, 275–276
Fantasy, 7–9
Fantasy play in cognitive development,
  40–41
Farley, M., 293
Feelings
  coping with, 38–39
  expressing
    in mathematics/science curriculum,
      158
    play in, 37
  identifying, in mathematics/science
    curriculum, 158
Feeney, Stephanie, 213, 218, 221, 222,
  225, 228, 268
Fein, G. G., 37, 41
Fernie, D., 118
Feuerstein, R., 336

Fingerplays in mathematics/science curriculum, 157–158
Flack, Marjorie, 36
Flexibility of creative behavior, 6
Flournoy, V., 74
Floyd, S., 150
Fluency of creative behavior, 5–6
Fox, D. B., 103, 128, 129
Fox, M., 137, 152
Freedom, psychological, in unlocking creative potential, 14
Freire, P., 262
Freud, S., 32
Fromberg, D. P., 31, 32, 33, 48
Frost, J., 191, 192, 194, 196, 197
Frost, J. L., 191, 196, 198, 208
Functional play in cognitive development, 40
Furell, M. H., 340
Future
  of creative expression and play, agenda for, 339–341
  creative teaching in, 338–339

Gackenbach, D., 62
Gag, Wanda, 162
Gaitskell, C. D., 62
Galda, Lee, 36, 167–168
Galdone, Paul, 155
Games
  child-constructed, 237–240
  competitive versus cooperative, 235–236
  definition of, 235
  invented, 238–240
  making, with children, 240
  noncompetitive
    ball, 364
    partner, 368
    quiet, 364–365
    running, 366–367
    singing, 365–366
  organized, 234–237
  with rules in cognitive development, 43
  teachers' roles and responsibilities for, 236–237
  value of, 236
Gardner, Howard, 8–9, 65, 101, 128, 291, 346
Gardner, M., 105

Garreau, M., 174, 177, 189, 200
Garvey, C., 32, 36, 37, 41
Garvey, K., 301
Gelfer, J. G., 295
Getty Center for Education in the Arts, 66
Glazer, T., 122
Glosenger, F. L., 241
Golomb, C., 96
Goodlad, J., 340
Goodman, Y. M., 297
Gottfried, A. W., 221, 223
Graphic aspect of art, 65
Green, V. P., 270
Greenberg, M., 105, 106, 108, 112
Greenberg, Polly, 253, 273, 274
Greene, M., 345
Griego, M., 124
Gross motor materials, 217–218, 219
  for infants, 221
  for preschoolers/kindergartners, 224
  for school-age children, 228
  for toddlers, 222
Growth, creative. *See* Creative growth
Guidance, developmentally appropriate, 263–276
Guilford, J. P., 5, 215

Haake, R. J., 267
Hagan, J., 246
Hall, M. A., 109
Hallahan, D. P., 204, 205, 318
Halliday, M. A. K., 36
Hanson, H., 339
Harrison, A., 4
Harste, J., 296
Hatcher, B., 341
Hay, D. F., 267
Haycock, K., 330, 333
Health
  art integrated into, 89–90
  creative drama integrated into, 160–161
  music and movement integrated into, 123–124
Hearing-impaired children, creative environment for, 204
Hendrick, J., 16, 216, 233, 236
Henkes, K., 143
Henkes, R., 90
Hennings, D. G., 137, 151

Herberholz, B., 77
Hewitt, K., 214
High-achieving children
  art for, 91–92
  assessing creative expression and play
    in, 317–318
  creative drama for, 163
  creative environment for, 205
  creative expression in, 19
  future of creative expression/play for,
    344–345
  guiding creative growth for, 278–279
  materials for creative expression and
    play for, 241–242
  music and movement for, 126
  play in, 50–51
Higher Education Research Institute,
  334–335
Highwater, J., 124
Hildebrand, V., 189, 236, 255, 260, 262,
  263, 267
Hill, Patty Smith, 34
Hinman, C., 315
Hoban, T., 67
Hodges, D. A., 128
Hodgkinson, H., 318, 334
Hoffman, B., 336
Hoffman, S., 297, 341
Hohman, C., 186
Holdaway, D., 284
Holden, C., 6
Holubec, E. J., 340
Hoskisson, K., 138, 145, 146, 155, 166
Howe, N., 38
Howes, C., 304, 305
Hughes, F., 126
Hughes, F. P., 10, 184, 220, 223, 227,
  235, 236, 317
Humanism in guiding creative growth,
  256
Humanistic perspective on creativity, 11
Hunt, J. M., 34
Hunt, T., 152, 153
Hurwitz, A., 62
Hutchins, P., 62
Hutt, C., 216
Hutt, S. J., 216
Hymel, S., 268

Iconic stage of musical development, 104
Iden, A. M., 15

Illumination in creative process, 11
Imagination, 7–9
  play in developing, 38
Imaginative thinking, creative drama
    developing, 141
Incubation in creative process, 11
Infants
  creative outdoor environments for,
    197–198
  developmentally appropriate materials
    for, 220–221, 223
Inhelder, B., 35
Inhibition, lack of, in children, 7
Instinct theory of play, 46
Integrated personality, divergent
    thinking and, 328–339
Interpretive drama, 138, 139
Investigative play in guiding creative
    behavior, 271–272
Isaacs, Susan, 34
Isaksen, S. G., 337
Isbell, R., 150
Isenberg, J. P., 34, 35, 38, 40, 52, 180,
    194, 214, 216, 221, 222, 225, 228,
    244, 268, 293, 339, 341

Jackson, P. W., 5
Jacob, B., 40
Jacobs, J. E., 214, 221, 222, 225, 228
Jacobs, L. B., 142, 155, 156
Jalongo, M. R., 49, 120, 122, 123, 177,
    241, 291, 299, 335, 339, 342, 344
Jefferson, B., 64
Jenkins, L., 119
Johnson, D. W., 270, 340
Johnson, E. P., 142, 143
Johnson, Harriet, 230
Johnson, J. E., 38, 44, 48, 217, 218, 221,
    222, 225, 228, 304, 305
Johnson, R. T., 270, 340
Johnston, T., 74
Joint Committee on the Role of Informal
    Drama in the Classroom, 145
Jonas, A., 74, 123, 314
Jones, Elizabeth, 17, 174, 176, 177, 178
Judgment, deferring, in fostering
    creative process, 18
Jung, Carl, creativity theory of, 12

Kagan, S. L., 273, 282, 331
Kamii, C., 216, 235, 236, 237, 341

Kaplan-Sanoff, M., 49
Kates, D., 113, 119
Katz, A., 16
Katz, L., 340, 350
Katz, L. G., 269, 272, 273
Kaufman, J. M., 204, 205, 318
Keats, E. J., 122
Kelley, L., 108
Kellogg, R., 65–80
Kellogg, Steven, 198
Kendall, F. E., 49
Kennedy, C., 174, 177, 189, 200
Kiefer, B. Z., 156
Kindergartners
    creative classroom environment for,
        183–184
    creative outdoor environments for,
        198
    developmentally appropriate materials
        for, 223–226
Kinsman, C., 184
Kitano, M., 16
Klein, B., 18, 194, 341
Kodaly, Zoltan, 104, 105
Kohlberg, L., 235, 236
Kohn, A., 6
Kostelnik, M. J., 53, 263, 268, 269
Kriegel, R. J., 338
Kritchevsky, S., 176, 179, 180, 191, 194
Krogh, S., 262
Kukla, K., 155
Kulp, M., 304
Kuschner, D., 274

Lamme, L. L., 297, 341
Language
    art integrated into, 89
    creative drama integrated into,
        159–160
    development of, play in, 36
    music and movement integrated into,
        122–123
Lansing, K. M., 317
Lateral thinking, 10
    assessment of, 291–293
Learning
    art and, 70, 72–76
    teachers as mediators of, 336–337
Leavitt, R. L., 183
Leeper, S. H., 104
Leonhard, C., 105

Lester, J., 156
Levin, D., 245
Levin, D. E., 54
Levine, E., 241
Levstik, L. S., 156
Lewis, H., 246
Library center in creative environment,
    185–186
Lightfoot, S. L., 339
Lippman, M., 182, 200
Literacy
    art integrated into, 89
    center for, in creative environment,
        185–186
    creative drama integrated into,
        159–160
    development of, play in, 36
    promotion of, classroom preparation
        for, 208–209
    skills in, creative drama and, 142
Literature
    creative drama integrated into,
        159–160
    music and movement integrated into,
        122–123
Littleton, Danette, 21, 199
Lobel, A., 156
Lopez, S., 128
Loughlin, C., 174, 179, 180, 186, 188
Low-achieving children
    art for, 91–92
    assessing creative expression and play
        in, 317–318
    creative drama for, 163
    creative environment for, 205
    creative expression in, 19–20
    future of creative expression/play for,
        344–345
    guiding creative growth for, 278–279
    materials for creative expression and
        play for, 241–242
    music and movement for, 126
    play in, 50–51
Lowenfield, Viktor, 61, 65

MacDonald, R. E., 256, 259, 260, 274,
    334, 335, 336
Magarick, Marion, 213, 218, 221, 222,
    225, 228
Make-believe play in cognitive
    development, 40–41

Manipulation in response to materials, 216

Manipulative center in creative environment, 186

Manipulative materials, 218, 219
  for infants, 221
  for preschoolers/kindergartners, 224
  for school-age children, 228
  for toddlers, 222

Marion, M., 256, 263

Martin, M. D., 180, 186

Maslow, Abraham, 256
  creativity theory of, 12

Materials
  for creative expression and play, 212–247
    blocks as, 229–232
    case study on, 214
    children's response to, 216–217
    construction, 218, 219
    convergent and divergent, 215–216
    developmentally appropriate, 220–229
    divergent, 229–232
    everyday, 218–220
    gross motor, 217–218, 219
    history of, 214–215
    for infants, 220–221, 223
    for kindergartners, 223–226
    manipulative, 218, 219
    modeling materials as, 232, 233
    natural, 218–220
    organized games as, 234–237
    for preschoolers, 223–226
    sand and water as, 232, 233
    for school-age children, 226–227, 228
    self-expressive, 218, 219
    skill/concept, 217, 219
    for special populations, 240–242
    teachers and, 227, 229
    theoretical framework for, 214–217
    for toddlers, 220–223
  effect on children's representations of human form, 96

Math center in creative environment, 186

Mathematics
  art integrated into, 89
  creative drama integrated into, 157–159
  music and movement integrated into, 121–122

Matthews, W. S., 337

May, Rollo, 331
  creativity theory of, 12

Mayer, M., 62

Mayesky, M., 146

McAllester, D., 106

McCaslin, Nellie, 135, 137, 138, 140, 141, 142, 143, 151, 153, 157, 161, 162, 163, 165, 166, 167

McDonald, D. T., 106, 109, 112, 124

McKee, J. S., 221, 222, 225, 228

McLaughlin, J., 124

Meaningfulness of play, 31

Media, art integrated into, 88–90

Media center in creative environment, 186

Medical play, observations of, 369–374

Meek, L. H., 8

Mergen, B., 243

Messick, S., 5

Metacognition, 9–10

Metz, E., 103–108

Meyers, R., 338

Miller, K., 198, 199

Minority-majority in future, 342

Minuchin, P., 331

Modeling materials, 232, 233

Model of product/process as assessment criteria, 295

Modern theories of play, 46–47

Monighan-Nourot, P., 43, 215

Montessori, Maria, 104

Moran, J. D., 23–24, 216

Moravcik, E., 268

Morgan, J., 143, 144

Morrison, G., 241

Morrow, Lesley Mandel, 173, 208, 209

Motivation, intrinsic, of play, 31

Movement
  in mathematics/science curriculum, 158–159
  and music. *See under* Music, movement and
  in social studies/health/nutrition curriculum, 161

Moyer, J., 180, 339

Muldaur, M., 122

Mulkeen, Thomas A., 329, 332, 333

Mundell, D., 315

Music
  in aesthetic skill development, 106
  in affective skill development, 105

Music, *continued*
  in cognitive skill development,
    105–106
  in cultural skill development, 106
  movement and, 100–129
    case study on, 102
    in child development, 105–109
    connection between, 108–109
    for culturally diverse groups, 124
    for disabled children, 124–125
    development of, 109, 110–111
    for high-achieving children, 126
    integrated into subject areas,
      121–124
    for low-achieving children, 126
    for special populations, 124–126
    theoretical framework for, 102–105
  in perceptual skill development, 105
  in psychomotor skill development,
    105
  in social skill development, 106
  types of, 116–117
Musical development, theories of,
  103–104
Musical experience, children and, 103
Musical growth of young children,
  106–108
Musicality, naturalness of, 128–129
Music education, 104–105. *See also*
    Teaching music and movement
Music laboratory, research on, 129

Nadaner, D., 14
Nash, C., 182
National Academy of Early Childhood
  Programs, 176
National Art Education Association, 70
National Association for the Education
  of Young Children, 17
National Association of State Boards of
  Education, 296
Natural/everyday materials, 218–220
  for infants, 221
  for preschoolers/kindergartners, 225
  for school-age children, 228
  for toddlers, 222
Neisworth, J. T., 177
Nelms, B., 340
Nelson, K., 142
Neumann, E., 32
Nicolson, M. W., 23–24

Nielsen, R., 294
Nonrepresentational use of materials,
  216
Novice and expert practice, difference
  between, 352
Nowicki, G. P., 15
Nutrition
  art integrated into, 89–90
  creative drama integrated into,
    160–161
  music and movement integrated into,
    123–124

O'Brien, R., 162
Observation(s)
  in assessing creative expression and
    play, 299–304, 305
    anecdotal records in, 299–300
    audio recordings in, 303
    checklist in, 300–301
    individual case studies in, 304
    interviews with children in,
      301–303
    published scales in, 304
    rating scales in, 301
    video recording in, 303
  of medical play, 369–374
Ogbu, J. U., 318
Olds, S. W., 255, 256, 257
Orff, Carl, 104
Originality
  and conformity in art, 63–64
  of creative behavior, 5
Ownership in art, children's retention
  of, 64

Paley, Vivian G., 33, 54–55, 167, 341
Pantomime, 149, 151–152
  in language/literature/literacy
    curriculum, 159–160
  in mathematics/science curriculum,
    158
Papalia, D. E., 255, 256, 257
Paper, child-centered art experiences
  using, 86–87
Pappas, C. C., 156
Parnes, S., 4–5
Parnes, S. J., 338
Parten, Mildred, 43–44
Patler, L., 338
Pellegrini, A. D., 36

Pepler, D., 38
Perceptual aspect of art, 64
Perceptual skills, music in developing, 105
Perkins, P. G., 295
Perlmutter, J., 177
Permissive adult-child interactions in guiding creative growth, 259–260
Perrone, V., 291, 321
Perspective-taking ability, creative drama developing, 142
Peters, D. L., 177
Peters, V., 150
Peterson, M., 115
Phelps, C., 188
Phyfe-Perkins, E., 174
Physical development, play in, 38
Physically disabled children
    creative environment for, 204–205
    guiding creative growth for, 277–278
Piaget, Jean, 32, 34, 35, 37, 39, 40, 46, 47, 103, 104, 237, 255
    creativity theory of, 12
Picasso, Pablo, 61
Pifer, A., 343
Play. *See also* Dramatic play
    centers for, dramatic play and, 149
    characteristics of, 31–32
    classical theories of, 44–46
    cognitive, development of, 38–43
    in cognitive development, 35–38
    controversies surrounding, 32–34
    creative, 339–341. *See also*
        Assessment; materials
    creativity and, 38
    in culturally diverse groups, 49
    defining, 31–34
    development of, 38–44
    in disabled children, 49–50
    in early childhood curriculum, 28–55
    educational role of, 34
    in emotional development, 37
    in high-achieving children, 50–51
    imagination and, 38
    investigative, in guiding creative behavior, 271–272
    in language development, 36
    with language in developing language/literacy skills, 36
    in literacy development, 36

    in low-achieving children, 50–51
    medical, observations of, 369–374
    modern theories of, 44–46
    and nonplay, differentiating, 33
    in physical development, 38
    reasons for, 44–47
    role, in language/literature/literacy curriculum, 160, 161
    social, development of, 43–44
    in social development, 37
    sociodramatic
        suggestions for classroom, 146–149
        uses of, 145–146
    for special populations, 48–51
    superhero, in classroom, 53–55
    teachers' roles and responsibilities in, 47–48
    war toys, controversies over, 245–246
Playgrounds in creative environment
    adventure or "junk," 192–193
    by age group, 197–199
    characteristics of, 194–197
    creative, 193–194
    equipment/materials for, 194
    safety/supervision of, 196–197
    storage on, 196–197
    traditional, 192
Playthings, history of, 214–215
Pleasurable nature of play, 32
Populations, special
    art for, 90–92
    assessing creative expression and play in, 316–317
    creative drama for, 161–163
    creative environment for, 204–205
    fostering creative process in, 18–20
    future of creative expression/play for, 341–345
    guiding creative growth for, 276–279
    materials for creative expression and play for, 240–242
    music and movement for, 124–126
    play for, 48–51
Portfolio assessment, 304–311
Postman, N., 14
Potter, F., 294
Pottery, child-centered art experiences using, 87
Power sharing, in fostering creative process, 17

Practice play in cognitive development, 40
Praise, in fostering creative process, 18
Preexercise theory of play, 46
Preschoolers
 creative classroom environment for, 183–184
 creative outdoor environments for, 198
 developmentally appropriate materials for, 223–226
Prescott, E., 176
Pretend play in cognitive development, 40
Problem solving
 cooperative, in guiding creative behavior, 269–271
 creative drama developing, 141
Process(es)
 creative, assessing, 296
 over product in art, 63
Products, creative, assessing, 296–297
Project work in guiding creative behavior, 272–273
Prop box(es)
 for dance, 357–360
 for dramatic play, 146–148
 in social studies/health/nutrition curriculum, 160–161
Psychoanalytic perspective on creativity, 11
Psychoanalytic theory of play, 46
Psychological freedom in unlocking creative potential, 14
Psychological safety in unlocking creative potential, 14
Psychomotor skills, music in developing, 105
Puppetry in social studies/health/nutrition curriculum, 161
Puppets, creating and storing, 154–155

Quellmalz, E. S., 296
Quisenberry, N. L., 34, 35, 38, 52, 194, 216, 339, 341

Raines, R. C., 268
Raines, S., 150
Ramirez, M., 341
Ramsey, M. E., 113

Rand, Otto, creativity theory of, 12
Raths, L. E., 314
Rating scales to evaluate preschool settings, published, 361–362
Readers theater
 in creative drama, 156–157
 in mathematics/science curriculum, 158
Reading, experiment with, in developing language/literacy skills, 36
Recapitulation theory of play, 46
Recreation/relaxation theory of play, 45
Reeves, M. S., 334
Reifel, S., 323
Reis, M., 345
Reis, S. M., 23
Relevance of creative behavior, 5
Renck, M. A., 122
Renfro, N., 152, 153
Renzulli, J. S., 23, 345
Representational use of materials, 217
Research and Policy Committee, 333
Rickards, T., 331
Ririe, S. R., 108
Risk taking, encouragement, 17–18
Roberts, 235
Roe, B. D., 155
Roehmann, F., 107
Roeper, A., 242
Rogers, Carl, 13, 255, 256
 creativity theory of, 12
Rogers, F., 246
Role models, musical growth and, 107–108
Role play
 in language/literature/literacy curriculum, 160
 in social studies/health/nutrition curriculum, 160, 161
Room arrangement for creative environment, 179–181, 182
Roomet, L., 214
Roosevelt, Franklin Delano, 341–342
Rose, Mike, 289–320
Rosen, H., 339
Roskos, K., 36
Ross, E. P., 155
Ross, H. S., 38
Rothslein, A., 314